No Professor's Lectures Can Save Us

No Professor's Lectures Can Save Us

Can Save Us

William James's Pragmatism, Radical Empiricism, and Pluralism

JOHN J. STUHR

OXFORD
UNIVERSITY PRESS

OXFORD
UNIVERSITY PRESS

Oxford University Press is a department of the University of Oxford. It furthers
the University's objective of excellence in research, scholarship, and education
by publishing worldwide. Oxford is a registered trade mark of Oxford University
Press in the UK and certain other countries.

Published in the United States of America by Oxford University Press
198 Madison Avenue, New York, NY 10016, United States of America.

Library of Congress Cataloging-in-Publication Data
Names: Stuhr, John J., author.
Title: No professor's lectures can save us : William James's pragmatism, radical empiricism,
and pluralism / John J. Stuhr.
Description: New York, NY, United States of America : Oxford University Press, [2023] |
Includes bibliographical references and index.
Identifiers: LCCN 2022027428 (print) | LCCN 2022027429 (ebook) |
ISBN 9780197664636 (pb) | ISBN 9780197664629 (hb) | ISBN 9780197664650 (epub)
Subjects: LCSH: James, William, 1842-1910.
Classification: LCC B945 .J24 S745 2023 (print) | LCC B945 .J24 (ebook) |
DDC 191—dc23/eng/20220815
LC record available at https://lccn.loc.gov/2022027428
LC ebook record available at https://lccn.loc.gov/2022027429

DOI: 10.1093/oso/9780197664629.001.0001

1 3 5 7 9 8 6 4 2

Paperback printed by Marquis, Canada
Hardback printed by Bridgeport National Bindery, Inc., United States of America

For
Samuel Stuhr Berliner
and
Arthur Stuhr Berliner

Throw away the lights, the definitions,
And say of what you see in the dark
That it is this or that it is that,
But do not use the rotted names.
          —Wallace Stevens, "The Man with the Blue Guitar" (1937)

Contents

Acknowledgments

My intellectual and personal debts here are infinite. My awareness of them is finite—like me. My space to express these debts is more finite still. This is a recipe for unintended incompleteness.

I was privileged to be able to study philosophy and to be shown why philosophy matters by gifted and committed teachers: Roy O. Elveton, Gary Iseminger, Maury Landsman, Perry C. Mason, and, in classics, David Porter at Carleton College; John J. Compton, Michael Hodges, John Lachs, Charles E. Scott, and Donald Sherburne at Vanderbilt University; and John J. McDermott, Sandra Rosenthal, Charles Sherover, and Bruce Wilshire from other institutions and across many years.

I have been fortunate to have been able to teach the work and spirit of William James, pragmatic philosophy more broadly, and philosophy still more widely to amazingly bright, challenging and receptive, and hard-working undergraduate and graduate students at Emory University, Vanderbilt University, Penn State University, the University of Oregon, and Whitman College. As their teacher, I have gained much from them, and they have fed what James called "a temperament of life" rather than one of abstraction.

Both I and this book have benefited immensely—including what James called "knowledge by acquaintance"—from faculty colleagues and friends at these same institutions: Joseph J. Maier at Whitman; Cheyney Ryan and Maxine Sheets-Johnstone at Oregon; Vincent Colapietro, Richard A. Lee, John Russon, Charles Scott (again!), Shannon Sullivan, and Nancy Tuana at Penn State; Michael Hodges and John Lachs (both again!), José Medina, Kelly Oliver, Lucius Outlaw Jr., and Charles E. Scott (for a third time!) at Vanderbilt; and John Lysaker, Melvin Rogers, Michael Sullivan, Jessica Wahman, and George Yancy at Emory.

Repeatedly and over many years, I have learned philosophy, multiple modes of its expression, and what it can be—what it could be made to be, what we might make it—from "regulars" at the annual American Philosophies Forum conferences: Steven Brence, Vincent Colapietro, Megan Craig, Mark Fagiano, Jennifer Hansen, Robert Innis, Céline Leboeuf, John Lysaker, Mary

Magada-Ward, José Medina, Eduardo Mendieta, Carlos Pereda, Melvin Rogers, Scott Stroud, Nancy Tuana, Jessica Wahman, Cory Wimberly, Emily Zakin, and Charles E. Scott (surprise!). This group has provided immeasurable personal, not just professional, space, resources, and meanings.

I also want to thank renowned James scholars Nancy Frankenberry and Megan Craig. They provided deeply engaged, nuanced, and substantive praise, criticism, further ideas, and specific suggestions that made this book stronger. Thanks too to Lucy Randall at Oxford University Press for her straightforward, organized, and supportive attention and assistance. She has been the embodiment of the Platonic Form of a great editor. Lauralee Yeary and Brent Matheny at Oxford and Ganga Balaji at Newgen Knowledge Works helped make the transition from completed manuscript to published book remarkably efficient and effective.

There are two people whose impact is even larger, too large to come close to fully acknowledging. I can only point. At the graduate school of the University of Chicago and under the co-direction of philosophy professors Charles Hartshorne and Richard McKeon, Ruth Stuhr, my mother, wrote her thesis on the philosophy of William James. It then informed her teaching, and when she switched from academia to the world of politics, educational administration, and public service it informed her work in those areas too. If there were not genetic links from her philosophical interests and orientation to mine, then at least I am sure there was a kind of unconscious intellectual osmosis over the years. Finally, for more than a decade now, as a result of her own specialization in American pragmatism, the naturalistic and Santayana-like bent of her own vision, her original and sharp-minded thinking and eagle-eyed editing, and much more, Jessica Wahman has made all my thinking stronger and all my writing better. And much more.

Rock Stream, New York
November 2021

* * *

Grateful acknowledgment is made to the following publishers for permission to revise parts of the following copyrighted publications.

An earlier, briefer version of parts of chapter 1 appeared under the title "Redeeming the Wild Universe: William James's *Will to Believe*" in *Understanding James, Understanding Modernism*, ed. David H. Evans (New York: Bloomsbury, 2017).

An earlier, significantly briefer version of parts of chapter 4 appeared under the title "Looking Toward Last Things: James's Pragmatism Beyond Its First Century" in *100 Years of Pragmatism: William James's Revolutionary Philosophy*, ed. John J. Stuhr (Bloomington: Indiana University Press, 2010).

An earlier, briefer version of two sections of chapter 7 appeared under the title "Radical Empiricism: William James and Gilles Deleuze" in *Contemporary Pragmatism* 18, no. 4 (2021).

Abbreviations of the Works
of William James

My references to the writings of William James appear in my text in standard, abbreviated form. They are references to *The Works of William James*, the critical edition published by Harvard University Press (Cambridge, MA, 1975–1988). The abbreviations are to titles, followed by page number(s):

APU   *A Pluralistic Universe* (1979 [1909])
ECR   *Essays, Comments, and Reviews* (1987 [1865–1909])
EP   *Essays in Philosophy* (1978 [1876–1910])
EPSY *Essays in Psychology* (1983 [1878–1890])
EPR   *Essays in Psychical Research* (1986 [1869–1909])
ERE   *Essays in Radical Empiricism* (1976 [1912])
ERM   *Essays in Religion and Morality* (1982 [1884–1910])
MT   *The Meaning of Truth* (1975 [1909])
MEN   *Manuscript Essays and Notes* (1988 [mostly undated])
ML   *Manuscripts and Lectures* (1988 [1872–1907)
P   *Pragmatism: A New Name for Some Old Ways of Thinking* (1975 [1907])
PBC   *Psychology: Briefer Course* (1985 [1892])
PP   *The Principles of Psychology*, 2 vols. (1981 [1890])
SPP   *Some Problems of Philosophy* (1979 [1910])
TT   *Talks to Teachers and to Students on Some of Life's Ideals* (1983 [1899])
VRE   *The Varieties of Religious Belief* (1978 [1902])
WB   *The Will to Believe and Other Essays in Popular Philosophy* (1979 [1897])

Additionally, references to James's letters also appear in my text. They are references to the 12 volumes of *The Correspondence of William James*, edited by Ignas K. Skrupskelis and Elizabeth M. Bishop, published by the University of Virginia Press (Charlottesville, VA, 1992–2004). The abbreviation is CJR, followed by volume number and page number(s).

Introduction

Seven Introductions

No Professor's Lectures Can Save Us: William James's Pragmatism, Radical Empiricism, and Pluralism? That's a mouthful. What's going on here? How is it going?

"Our universe is to a large extent chaotic," William James wrote. "No single type of connexion runs through all the experiences that compose it." *What's* going on? Several things, plural things, diverse things, much all at once, a cosmos.

"Philosophy," James asserted, "has always turned on grammatical particles" of different "orders of inclusiveness and intimacy"—for example, "with, near, next, like, from, towards, against, because, for, through, my" (ERE, 24). *How* is it going? In many ways all at once, small and large, near and distant, familiar and foreign, with and without, aware and unnoticed.

1. ON: Most immediately, this book is *on* or about the philosophy of William James (1842–1910), the influential American psychologist and philosopher. I have sought to explicate clearly and accurately James's writings. I hope this book helps its readers grasp and make use of James's concerns and worldview as well as the interests and temperament that pervade and enliven them.

2. ACROSS: This book ranges *across* or spans James's work—his psychology, pragmatism, radical empiricism, pluralism, and writings on religion, ethics, and politics and society. Each chapter has a principal focus:

   - Chapter 1—*The Will to Believe and Other Essays in Popular Philosophy*
   - Chapter 2—*The Principles of Psychology* and *The Varieties of Religious Experience*
   - Chapter 3—James's ethics, particularly "The Moral Philosopher and the Moral Life" and "On a Certain Blindness in Human Beings"
   - Chapter 4—James's writings on social and political matters

No Professor's Lectures Can Save Us. John J. Stuhr, Oxford University Press. © Oxford University Press 2023. DOI: 10.1093/oso/9780197664629.003.0001

This neat and tidy list notwithstanding, topics, themes, and claims from virtually all of James's books surface, interweave, reappear, intersect and take leave from, sample, resample, and flow alongside almost all the rest of his work. Scholars with particular interests can chop up and treat James's books and his views in isolation from each other—for example, conceptually partitioning his pragmatism from his radical empiricism or his psychology from his pluralism—but in reality, they are all mixed up and much-at-once with each other, both in terms of their development by James and in terms of their philosophical content and force for others. Both the organization and the style of this book are intended to capture and resonate with this central fact of James's philosophy.

3. WITH: Throughout this book, I write largely *with* or mainly in agreement with James. This is not because James has produced logical arguments so rationally compelling that I have been forced to agree with him (and think that everyone else must also agree with him—and thus with me). Rather, it is because I have found that in my everyday experience I largely share James's temperament, that James expansively and illuminatingly expresses the feel and flow of this experience, and that James's writings give articulate voice to my temperament. I agree with James that one's philosophy is an *expression* of one's worldview and one's preferred or best working *attitude*; a mode of *feeling* the push and pull of life; and an attunement to which one is led or forced by the totality of one's experience. I agree with James that different philosophies express different propensities to attend and emphasize differently. I agree with James that a philosophy is description and expression, suggestion and hypothesis.

4. WITHOUT: My large agreements with James acknowledged, there are also important points of difference, points at which my worldview is *without* or outside of James's philosophy. Here I realize that many philosophers, particularly those eager to score conceptual knockouts, take these kinds of *differences* to be *disagreements* or oppositions. I do not.[1] This view, I think, mistakenly treats the reality of plural worldviews

---

[1] See my "Introduction: Expressivism and Pragmatism" and the chapter "Philosophies as Fashions" in *Pragmatic Fashions: Pluralism, Democracy, Relativism, and the Absurd* (Bloomington: Indiana

and their uses as *logical contradictions* (such that at best only one can be true) rather than *ontological or existential differences*. This meta-philosophical point aside, in this book I express reservations about—and alternatives to—the ways in which James sometimes seemed to:

- Sharply separate the intellect and the passions as bases for warranted belief
- Argue from the logical possibility of an unseen world to the reasonableness of belief in it
- Diagnose our blindness to the experience and lives of others without equal analysis of our blindness to our own experience, lives, and selves
- Assert that some experiences (like mystical experiences) are absolutely noetic or immediate-knowledge affairs rather than experiences that give rise to fallible beliefs that have to be tested, like all beliefs, by consequences and results in a social world
- Understand innovation, creativity, and genius in terms of unhabitual perception largely in isolation from the perseverance and work needed to develop them and the action needed to manifest and test them
- Characterize "pure experience" in terms of its immediacy and unity without equal emphasis on the ways in which immediacy itself is mediated

Of course, I expand and explain these points—I take them to be suggestions—in the chapters that follow.

5. THROUGH: While this indeed is a book on or about the philosophy of William James, it is mostly and ultimately a book *through* James or by means of James. I am concerned to *use* James's philosophy to address and illuminate central issues about the nature of the self, freedom, morality, community, truth, reality, and possibility. I take this point to be a pragmatic one: I am concerned to put James to use, to treat his thought as an instrument. I take the right response to a claim that a thinker is worth my time and effort to be: Show me, show me the practical difference it makes.

University Press, 2016).

6. FROM: James wrote that we all are prone to claim that our views and conclusions are the only logical, correct ones when they actually are "all the while, at bottom, accidents more or less of personal vision which had better far better be avowed as such" (APU, 10). I intend to avow that fact and have sought to do so throughout these pages—they are *from* or by me. This means that no reader of this book should take it to be—or take it as pretending to be—"the finally correct" or "finally complete" or just plain "final" book on James (as if any undertaking could be complete except in relation to some particular person's particular purposes). My central philosophical purposes here are these:

- To exhibit and explicate the philosophical scope, strengths, coherence, and continuity of James's philosophy
- To extend the Jamesian insight, missed by vicious intellectualism, that experience outstrips language, which constantly remakes, adds to, and permeates it
- To highlight the practical implications for philosophy itself of James's fashion of connecting in practice experiences, reflection, transitions, temperaments, powers, and the possibilities for more meaningful and fulfilling experiences
- To focus on James's vision of philosophy and, more important, life as an irreducibly moral endeavor—arenas of values of finite human beings in a dynamic, diverse, changing world in which they do not live forever
- To set forth an ethics and a politics that are pluralistic, perspectival, and fallible, this-worldly, evidence-based on matters of belief, and richly imagination-based in commitment to the invention of future possibilities and the action needed to realize them

In avowing my own individual vision and purposes, I do not mean to suggest that any individual's vision and purposes are merely private and untouched by, or unconnected to, the views and interests of others. My outlook and goals have been constructed and reconstructed over and over through the work of many others; the separation between self and others is blurry, porous, unstable. As the many notes and "Works Cited" pages make clear, I have referred to more than a hundred other thinkers whose work I find important and perceptive (whether in a manner habitual or unhabitual to me), work that has entered into my own in all kinds of ways. From my perspective, in all honesty, intellectual engagements that fail to do this strike me as suffering from a "Columbus discovered America" syndrome: They announce a happy enough fact about themselves and their own learning as though it were a fact about the world and as if it were news to everyone else who long has lived in that world. I understand "the anxiety of influence," but there are also responsibilities and generosities of influence—not to mention the deep irony of setting forth a supposedly relation-free study of James, philosopher of relations par excellence.

7. FOR: Authors do not have the power, thankfully, to choose or even foresee their readers. Furthermore, no book is for everyone. Within those limits, I aim here in part to address James, pragmatism, American thought and culture, and professional philosophers. More broadly and probably more importantly, this book is especially *for* all persons who:
   • Value open-mindedness and feeling and thinking in new, unorthodox, unhabitual ways
   • Demand that this feeling and thinking be connected concretely in action (rather than speculation or conceptual gymnastics alone)
   • Strive to make this action serve dynamic selves and diverse but inclusive lives and possibilities
   • Recognize that such lives are never fully imagined from any limited perspective (and its particular blindness) and are always under way and in the making—if, each of them, only for a short time

Tell me what's going on: Near the very end of "The Moral Philosopher and the Moral Life," James wrote that every day we each face choices between good and evil, between life and death. In a tone I take to be both egalitarian and humble, he added: "From this unsparing practical ordeal *no professor's lectures* and no array of books *can save us*" (WB, 162; italics added).

James was right: By themselves, lectures and books and their authors will not save your life. They won't win you friends. Reading a book—even this one!—will not get you a promotion or make you wealthy. They won't make someone else love you, understand you, or even treat you kindly—or ensure that you treat others with love, understanding, and kindness. They will not take away all your fears or longings. They won't bring you recognition, physical health, or personal well-being. No one has flourished *merely* by reading a book or *simply* by taking in a lecture. Realization of purposes requires living, not just a theory of life. It requires living reflectively and not just a life of reflection. Above all, it requires action—and the hope, faith, or melioristic temperament to take up action in the face of possibilities without guarantees. And this requires the attention and hard work of staying at it, keeping up the action.

I hope that this book *on*, *across*, *with*, and *through* James, at times *without* (and even *against*) James, and always *from* my own fallible angle of vision and selective purposes, can contribute *for* its readers—for you—to this larger pragmatic, radically empirical, and pluralistic endeavor. James's writings, when taken both in full and critically, constitute an invaluable resource for the future and its new problems, new possibilities, and new forms of personal and social life. In this sense, all persons who enter into and take up James's vision and worldview share a journey with no end other than itself, a pluralistic admission—ever not quite!—and a pluralistic direction: TOWARD.

1

Possibilities, Faith, and Action

Redeeming the Wild Universe Through
The Will to Believe

In 1897, William James published his first book of philosophy, *The Will to Believe and Other Essays in Popular Philosophy*. This collection of ten essays written between 1879 and 1896 followed two earlier volumes in psychology, *The Principles of Psychology* in 1890 and *Psychology (Briefer Course)* in 1892. In his preface, James expressed a theme and mood, a passion and attunement, that run through all of his writings in philosophy. He asserted that all philosophies express a particular personal point of view, and that no one point of view can fully illuminate or rationally explain our existence or render it a single fact:

> After all that reason can do has been done, there still remains the opacity of the finite facts as merely given, with most of their peculiarities mutually unmediated and unexplained. To the very last, there are the various "points of view" which the philosopher must distinguish in discussing the world; and what is inwardly clear from one point remains a bare externality and datum to the other. The negative, the alogical, is never wholly banished. Something—call it "fate, chance, freedom, spontaneity, the devil, what you will"—is still wrong and other and outside and unincluded in *your* point of view, even though you be the greatest of philosophers. Something is always mere fact and *givenness*; and there may be in the whole universe no one point of view extant from which this would not be found to be the case. (WB, 6)

For those who recognize this multiplicity of points of view (James called this "pluralism") and those who take for their hypothesis that this multiplicity and partiality constitute "the permanent form of the world" (James called this "radical empiricism"), then, James continued:

No Professor's Lectures Can Save Us. John J. Stuhr, Oxford University Press. © Oxford University Press 2023.
DOI: 10.1093/oso/9780197664629.003.0002

There is no possible point of view from which the world can appear an absolutely single fact. Real possibilities, real indeterminations, real beginnings,
real ends, real evil, real crises, catastrophes, and escapes, a real God, and a
real moral life, just as common-sense conceives these things, may remain
in empiricism as conceptions which that philosophy gives up the attempt
either to "overcome" or to reinterpret in monistic form. (WB, 6–7)

Unfortunately, it frequently has proven tempting to attempt to understand James's philosophy in a profoundly abstract, intellectualist, and anti-
Jamesian manner—namely, to understand James's work from a supposedly
single point of view for which James's philosophy is rendered a single fact.
This approach has been especially tempting for professors of philosophy and
their students, many of whom are gripped by what James in 1903 critically
called "the Ph.D. octopus" and about which he asked Americans: "And is individuality with us also going to count for nothing unless stamped and licensed and authenticated by some title-giving machine?" (ECR, 74).[1] It has
proven tempting, that is, to try to understand James's philosophy in terms of
intellectual doctrines and shorthand labels for them.

On the one hand, James may seem to have invited exactly this sort of project.
He frequently developed his own philosophy in relation to his classification
or typology of philosophies according to their claims—often contrasting the
doctrines within pairs of philosophies like the pair of empiricism and rationalism and the pair of "tender-minded" versus "tough-minded" thought
in *Pragmatism* or the pair of dualistic theism and pantheism and the pair of
monism and pluralism in *A Pluralistic Universe*. On the other hand, James
may appear to have frustrated this kind of effort to understand his philosophy by applying (in a manner more "popular" than rigorous or technical)
so many different labels to it. He variously called his philosophy "pragmatism," "humanism," "radical empiricism," "neutral monism," "pluralism,"
"common sense," "pantheism," and "supernaturalism."

Faced with all this, intellectualist friends of James have attempted to
understand his philosophy by arguing that all the various doctrines are
sound and either cohere or amount to the same thing. Meanwhile, intellectualist enemies have attempted to demonstrate that James's many

---

[1] In the context of title-giving institutions—a topic taken up more fully in chapters 3 and 4—
consider also James's self-description: "I am against bigness & greatness in all their forms" (CWJ 8,
546). In this context, see also Lisi Schoenbach, *Pragmatic Modernism* (New York: Oxford University
Press, 2011), chaps. 3 and 5.

supposed doctrines and isms are not sound or that they do not cohere and that, for example, to maintain James's pragmatism (and his admiration for Charles Peirce and John Dewey) one must abandon radical empiricism or that to hold on to humanism one must reject faith in an unseen world (and James's admiration of Benjamin Blood and his criticism of Walt Whitman).

So, how are we to understand James's philosophy? We should begin by understanding, as James put it, that even if we do insist on classifying every thinker and labeling every worldview, still "individuality outruns all classification" (APU, 7) and so all intellectualist efforts at capturing a philosopher's vision are bound to fail. This insight in mind, my thesis is simple: To understand James's philosophy, it is crucial to understand James's general account of philosophies as personal points of view. And it is crucial to understand James's own personal point of view and vision—a vision presented nowhere more vividly, fully, and effectively than in *The Will to Believe*.

For James, a philosophy is not the result of supposedly pure reason directed at supposedly absolute, universal, and experience-independent facts. Instead, philosophies are reflections of irreducibly and vitally personal characters and personal decisions—local here-and-now, there-and-then decisions in which reasoning is irreducibly volitional and passional and gives rise to worldviews that are constituted and permeated by preference and desires, feelings and moods, affinities and attunements. For James, to view a philosophy as the product of a reason separated from will and emotion is to take leave of our actual lives and world. It is make-believe.

This view of the nature of philosophy is manifest throughout all of James's writings.[2] In *Pragmatism*, for example, he described philosophy in terms of "attitudes," "temperament," and a personal "feeling" of the universe and a "total push and pressure of the cosmos," and as "our more or less dumb sense of what life honestly and deeply means" (P, 31, 11–15, 24, 9). And he claimed that philosophers frequently try to hide from others and from themselves the fact that this is so:

---

[2] Chapter 5 takes up more fully James's notion of temperament in the context of his pragmatism. See also my discussion of philosophy and temperament in *Pragmatic Fashions: Pluralism, Democracy, Relativism and the Absurd* (Bloomington: Indiana University Press, 2015), 30–59. James claimed that philosophies *express* personal character, values, and worldview; a given philosophy *appeals to and is chosen by* persons on the basis of their own character, values, and worldview; and philosophies in turn *exhibit* the characters, values, and worldviews of those who formulate, articulate, and hold them. Philosophies, for James, all at once express, appeal to, and exhibit temperaments.

Of whatever temperament a professional philosopher is, he tries when philosophizing to sink the fact of his temperament. Temperament is no conventionally recognized reason, so he urges impersonal reasons only for his conclusions. Yet his temperament really gives him a stronger bias than any of his more strictly objective premises. . . . There arises thus a certain insincerity in our philosophic discussions: the potentest of all our premises is never mentioned. . . . What the system pretends to be is a picture of the great universe of God. What it is—and oh so flagrantly—is the revelation of how intensely odd the personal flavor of some fellow creature is. (P, 11, 24)

Instead, James observed, philosophies irreducibly have intensely "personal flavor," and "temperaments with their cravings and refusals do determine men in their philosophies and always will" (P, 24).

Similarly, in *A Pluralistic Universe*, James described a philosophy as a "vision" and "expression" of one's "intimate character," as an individual "loyalty" to one's own world, and as a personal mode "of feeling the whole push, and seeing the whole drift of life, forced on one by one's total character and experience, and on the whole *preferred*—there is no other truthful word—as one's best working attitude" (APU, 14, 10, 14–15). Calling different philosophies "accidents of personal vision," James asked each philosopher to avow this fact and to stop claiming that his or her "conclusions are the only logical ones, that they are necessities of universal reason" (APU, 10). And he stressed what he took to be a shared striving and a hope: "We crave alike to feel more truly at home with it [the universe], and to contribute our mite to its amelioration. It would be pitiful if small aesthetic discords were to keep honest men asunder" (APU, 11).

James movingly set forth this view of philosophy throughout *The Will to Believe*. In the first essay, "The Will to Believe," James considered "the actual psychology of human opinion" and the bases of belief. He observed that "when we look at certain facts it seems as if our passional and volitional nature lay at the root of all our convictions," while "when we look at others, it seems as if they could do nothing when the intellect had once said its say"— and so from this perspective it may "seem preposterous on the very face of it to talk of our opinions being modifiable at will" (WB, 15). From this perspective it will seem "wrong always, everywhere, and for anyone, to believe anything upon insufficient evidence" no matter what one may desire or feel (WB, 18). I cannot justifiably believe, for example, that the world is just the way I want it to be or that a belief is true just because I think it is true or want it to be true. In such cases, as James acknowledged, our desires and our passions do not constitute sufficient rational basis for beliefs we may will or want to believe. We have to determine the evidence, we have to determine if the practical consequences that a belief leads us to expect are the ones that actually occur, we have to verify our belief. That point made and stressed, James argued that verification is never entirely independent of will and sentiment. What we count as evidence and justification, what right we have to believe when we lack sufficient evidence for justification of belief, and what makes hypotheses living or dead for each of us, James continued, is our individual "willing nature." Our willing nature, for James, meant "all such factors of belief as fear and hope, prejudice and passion, imitation and partisanship, the circumpressure of our caste and set" (WB, 18). We believe, James wrote, on the basis of some "authority" and the "prestige" of opinions that flow from it, on the basis of "faith in someone else's faith":

> Our belief in truth itself, for instance, that there is a truth, and that our minds and it are made for each other—what is it but a passionate affirmation of desire, in which our social system backs us up? We want to have a truth; we want to believe that our experiments and studies and discussions must put us in a continually better and better position towards it; and on this line we agree to fight out our thinking lives. But if a pyrrhonistic sceptic asks us *how we know* all this, can our logic find a reply? No! Certainly it cannot. It is just one volition against another. (WB, 19)

As a result, James concluded, "pure insight and logic are not the only things that produce our beliefs" and that "our non-intellectual nature does influence our convictions. There are passional tendencies, embodied affects, and volitions that run before and others which come after belief, and it is only the latter that are too late for the fair; and they are not too late when the previous passional work has been already in their own direction" (WB, 19–20).

James's point here was not that our desires and our feelings simply *trump* our reason. It was not that volitions and passions produce beliefs and theories but that reason does *not*. It was not that we should accept some sharp dualism between reason and the passions and then come down wholly on the side of the passions against a philosophical tradition that largely has sided with reason. James's point here was not irrationalist or dualist. It was not an attack on reason and a defense of cravings and sentiments. Instead of any and all of this, it was a denial of all reason/passion dualisms and a rejection of the understanding of reason—pure reason, reason independent of experience, reason universal and complete rather than perspectival—that results from this dualism. It was the assertion that rationality itself is a sentiment.

In "The Sentiment of Rationality," James claimed that rationality is recognized by its "subjective marks":

> A strong feeling of ease, peace, rest . . . lively relief and pleasure . . . This feeling of the sufficiency of the present moment, of its absoluteness—this absence of all need to explain it, account for it, or justify it—is what I call the Sentiment of Rationality.

Modes of reasoning and "conceiving the cosmos" that are marked by this fluency and sufficiency "produce the sentiment of rationality" (WB, 57–58).

How is this sentiment of rationality produced? James distinguished two ways in which the sentiment of rationality is produced: theoretically and practically. Theoretically, the sentiment of rationality is produced in large part by simplification and generalization—the reduction of manifoldness to simplicity and the grouping of diversity into "monotony." James called this a passion for parsimony, a labor-saving economy of means in thought, named it "the philosophic passion *par excellence*," and gave many everyday examples of it at work (WB, 58–59). But, James continued, the sentiment of rationality is also produced theoretically by a "sister passion" for distinguishing and differentiating—a passion "to be acquainted with the parts rather than to comprehend the whole." This passion for particularity and difference, James continued, constitutes a preference for "any amount of incoherence, abruptness, and fragmentariness (so long as the literal details of the separate facts are saved) to an abstract way of conceiving things" that dissolves, obscures, or overlooks full concreteness (WB, 59).

James recognized that these two theoretical passions—clearness and simplicity, particularity and generalization—set up rival claims on all thinkers, with the philosophic attitude of each thinker determined by the relative balance of these two passions. All philosophies, James claimed, are compromises of one sort or another between these two passions. And each of these compromises proceeds by classifying diverse items under a single heading or label in virtue of some supposed common essence. All these compromises, however, are marked by two failings. First, they are always incomplete. James wrote:

When, for example, we think that we have rationally explained the connection of the facts *A* and *B* by classing both under their common attribute *x*, it is obvious that we have really explained only so much of these items as is *x*. . . . [S]o far as *A* and *B* contain *l*, *m*, *n*, and *o*, *p*, *q*, respectively, in addition to *x*, they are not explained by *x*. . . . All those data [*l*, *m*, *n and o*, *p*, *q*] that cannot be analytically identified with the attribute invoked as universal principle [*x*], remain as independent kinds or natures, associated with the said attribute but devoid of rational kinship with it. (WB, 60–61)

"Hence," James concluded, "the unsatisfactoriness of all our speculations." Not only are they always incomplete but, second, they are "a most miserable and inadequate substitute for the fullness of the truth," a "monstrous abridgment of life," an "absolute loss and casting out of the real." And this is why, James proclaimed, "so few human beings truly care for philosophy" (WB, 61). Nothing is the equivalent of life but full, lived life—life as actually lived and not merely thought.

If philosophers honestly recognized this point, James suggested, they would understand that "the bottom of being is left logically opaque to us"—whether we be "boors" who immediately admit this fact or philosophers who construct systems of classification and unification that, nevertheless, are not "secure from the blighting breath of the ultimate Why?" (WB, 64). Philosophers would also come to understand, James believed, that their theories are not universal, timeless, or placeless claims to grasp reality as a single fact (devoid of otherness) but, instead, particular ways of classifying things for particular purposes. In short, they would become instrumentalists or pragmatists filled with "ontologic wonder":

Every way of classifying a thing is but a way of handling it for some particular purpose. Conceptions, "kinds," are teleological instruments. No abstract concept can be a valid substitute for a concrete reality except with reference to a particular interest in the conceiver. The interest of theoretic rationality, the relief of identification, is but one of a thousand human purposes. (WB, 62)

The sentiment of rationality can also be produced in a second way—a practical rather than theoretical way. To produce in practice the fluency and sufficiency of the sentiment of rationality, James asserted, a philosophy first and foremost must *"banish uncertainty from the future"* (WB, 67). If it is to produce strong feelings of ease, peace, relief, and being accounted for, a phi-losophy cannot leave us with a "haunting sense of futurity" that makes us uneasy in the present. But this is the nature of our practical lives: We do not know what will come next, but we know it will be novel and we also know that we have not classified the novel, the strange, circumstances fraught with peril or advantage. Novelty, James observed, becomes an irritant, and custom functions as a sedative.

And this holds for philosophy too: "An ultimate datum, even though it be logically unrationalized, will, if its quality is such as to define expectancy, be peacefully accepted by the mind; whist if it leave the least opportunity for ambiguity in the future, it will to that extent cause mental uneasiness if not distress" and fail to produce the sentiment of rationality (WB, 68). James cited many, many examples of just this phenomenon:

> Take again the notion of immortality, which for common people seems to be the touchstone of every philosophic or religious creed: what is this but a way of saying that the determination of expectancy is the essential factor in rationality? The wrath of science against miracles, of certain philosophers against the doctrine of free-will, has precisely the same root—dislike to admit any ultimate factor in things which may rout our prevision or upset the stability of our outlook. . . . In spite of the acutest nihilistic criticism, men will therefore always have a liking for any philosophy which explains things *per substantiam*. (WB, 69)

No philosophy, James concluded, can triumph—can be viewed as rational—if it emphatically denies the possibility of gratifying the desire of having expectancy defined (WB, 70).

If defining expectancy is a necessary condition for a philosophy's ration-ality in practice, it is not a sufficient condition of that rationality. To produce in practice the sentiment of rationality, a philosophy must not simply pro-vide an account of the real future but must also define that future in a manner congenial to and congruous with our powers and aims. In a passage that may be considered a kind of key to his entire philosophy, James wrote that "the intellect is built up of practical interests" and that cognition "is incomplete until discharged in act" (WB, 72):

> For a philosophy to succeed on a universal scale it must define the fu-ture *congruously with our spontaneous powers*. A philosophy may be

unimpeachable in other respects, but either of two defects will be fatal to its universal acceptance. First, its ultimate principle must not be one that essentially baffles and disappoints our dearest desires and most cherished powers. . . . Incompatibility of the future with their desires and active tendencies is, in fact, to most men a source of more fixed disquietude than uncertainty itself. . . . But a second and worse defect in a philosophy than that of contradicting our active propensities is to give them no object whatever to press against. A philosophy whose principle is so incommensurate with our most intimate powers as to deny them all relevancy in universal affairs, as to annihilate their motives, at one blow, will be even more unpopular than pessimism. . . . This is the opposite condition from that of nightmare, but when acutely brought home to consciousness, it produces a kindred horror. In nightmare we have motives to act but no power; here we have powers, but no motives. A nameless *unheimlichkeit* comes over us at the thought of there being nothing eternal in our final purposes, in the objects of those loves and aspirations which are our deepest energies. The monstrously lopsided equation of the universe and its knower, which we postulate as the ideal of cognition, is perfectly paralleled by the no less lopsided equation of the universe and the *doer*. We demand in it a character for which our emotions and active propensities shall be a match. (WB, 70–71)

All great periods of expansion and revival, James summarized, have said to us: "The inmost nature of reality is congenial to *powers* which you possess" (WB, 73).

As soon as we recognize that a philosophy that produces in practice the sentiment of rationality must be one that defines reality as congenial to our powers—one's own powers—we realize that we cannot dictate or even specify in advance for all persons just what constitutes this congeniality. As soon as we recognize that a philosophy, if it is to be rational in practice, must define reality as congenial to our powers, we then recognize that "we" may, and frequently do, differ from one another in our hopes, powers, undertakings, and views about what kind of reality sustains and is congenial to them. As soon as we make clear the nature of the sentiment of rationality in practice, then personal temperament—the multiple, different personal temperaments of different persons—takes center stage. As James observed, although all people "will insist on being spoken to by the universe in some way, few will insist on being spoken to in just the same way" (WB, 75). This means in practice that rather than insisting that there is simply one rational, correct philosophy, we should insist that in practice there legitimately might be as many different rational philosophies as there are different personal temperaments. The result is "eternal variation"—philosophical pluralism.

Because in practice—and despite the "pretension" of philosophers to have developed "systems of absolute certainty" (WB, 76)—no single philosophy can fully and finally and for all establish itself, it remains theoretically possible to doubt any one of them. This means, James crucially realized, that no one holds a philosophy on the basis that it alone has been proven theoretically possible. Instead, everyone holds a philosophy on the basis of faith. What did James mean by "faith"? James put it this way: "Faith means belief in something concerning which doubt is still theoretically possible; and as the test of belief is willingness to act, one may say that faith is the readiness to act in a cause the prosperous issue of which is not certified to us in advance" (WB, 76). As William Gavin has noted, for James, faith "involves risk; it is akin to moral courage."[3] And as Ralph Barton Perry explained, belief is confidence in practice—and confidence in advance of fuller verification.[4] Against critics who view faith as unscientific or "illogical" or "shameful," James argued that in practice it is not only legitimate but also wholly unavoidable. It is unavoidable because we must act prior to and without full knowledge of the consequences of that action. It is unavoidable because we live forward and know only backward. "The only escape from faith," James wrote with some exasperation, "is mental nullity. . . . We cannot live or think at all without some degree of faith. Faith is synonymous with working hypotheses." He added: "The only difference is that while some hypothesis can be refuted in five minutes, others may defy ages. . . . The longer disappointment is delayed, the stronger grows" our faith in that hypothesis (WB, 78, 79). James held this view whether the hypothesis in question concerned engineering, chemistry, biology, and physics or God, immortality, morality, and freedom. Even though doubt is theoretically possible, we believe; we put our working hypotheses to work; we act on, and in, faith.

This, then, is James's general account of philosophies: a philosophy is an expression of some personal temperament and it constitutes some particular working hypothesis or particular worldview. To the extent that this philosophy is marked by feelings of ease and peace and fluency and sufficiency,

[3] William J. Gavin, *William James in Focus: Willing to Believe* (Bloomington: Indiana University Press, 2013), 11.
[4] Ralph Barton Perry, *The Thought and Character of William James*, vol. 1 (Westport, CT: Greenwood Press, 1974 [1935]), 210.

then it produces the sentiment of rationality. These feelings and this rationality exist not so much in, and for, theory (life is irreducibly opaque to our thought and logic) as in, and for, practice (when expectancy is congruous with, and congenial to, our powers is defined and provided). Different philosophies will seem congenial and succeed in this for different persons—philosophy is forever a site of variation and pluralism. In practice, however, all successful philosophies are irreducibly matters of faith and values—matters of actions undertaken and lives lived without advance guarantee or advance confirmation.

In this light, what is James's own philosophy? What philosophy did he believe defined expectancy in a manner congruous with his powers and congenial to his aims and demands? In the face of theoretically possible doubt, in what did he have faith? *The Will to Believe* makes evident four central articles of faith or commitments, commitments that appear again and again in James's later philosophical writings.

1. First, for James, something really must be at stake in this struggle—and life must really be a struggle (rather than, say, Walt Whitman's loafing in the grass or Chautauqua's middle-class comfortable existence). There must be real goods and real bads, there must be real ideals and real butchering of ideals, there must be real triumphs and real tragedies, and there must be moments temporarily seized and opportunities permanently lost.[5] There must be real possibilities, including possibilities for amelioration and possibilities for loss. There can be neither impossibility nor inevitability.[6] This must be an open, in-the-making

---

[5] In "'Damned for God's Glory': William James and the Scientific Vindication of Protestant Culture," David Hollinger wrote: "James compares the idealists to the prodigal son who doesn't really risk anything because he knows he can count on his father to make it all right in the end. 'We want a universe,' he mocks the absolutists, 'where we can just give up, fall on our father's neck, and be absorbed into the absolute life as a drop of water melts into the river or sea.' This is not a realistic view of our human situation, says James. Life as lived, as available to an empiricism, suggests that we reside in an uncertain universe with real conflicts and real victories and real defeats." See Wayne Proudfoot, ed., *William James and a Science of Religious Experience* (New York: Columbia University Press, 2004), 25. In this same context, Robert J. Richardson captured central features of James's vision this way: "William James defended 'incompleteness, "more," uncertainty, possibility, fact, novelty, compromise, remedy and success' as being authentic realities." *The Heart of William James* (Cambridge, MA: Harvard University Press, 2010), xvi.

[6] James often labeled this position "humanism"—a term that obviously has many meanings in different contexts and in the hands of different writers. Patrick Dooley has viewed this label as useful for describing all of James's philosophy: "Humanism is the driving force and unifying issue in James's thought. His thought begins and ends with man, and humanism functions efficiently and teleologically to unify and integrate his philosophy." *Pragmatism as Humanism: The Philosophy of William James* (Chicago: Nelson-Hall, 1974), 179.

universe, and we must have a future not yet determined or complete. We must be free—freedom being the most basic precondition for the real possibility of our exercise of genuine powers, the very condition of our really having powers at all.[7]

2. Second, for James, life is a genuine struggle and strenuous engagement that demands our creative and transformative energies and powers for its improvement and redemption. He asked rhetorically: "Does our act then create the world's salvation so far as it makes room for itself, so far as it leaps into the gap? Does it create, not the whole world's salvation of course, but just so much of this as itself covers of the world's extent" (P, 137–138)? The world by itself is without moral value, without goods and bads and obligations. The exercise of our powers brings into being new and real values, new and real truths, and new and real worlds; the good, the true, and the real are not ready-made, awaiting our discovery and gaze, but instead are matters of our ongoing creation and recreation if only we take up this challenge. "Thus do philosophy and reality, theory and action, work in the same circle indefinitely," James concluded (APU, 49).[8] As John E. Smith put it, for James, efficacy is embedded in experience and, as Charlene Haddock Seigfried added, James thought "it is the philosopher's task to demonstrate the legitimacy of this postulate."[9] As John J. McDermott has explained: "If James is correct, as I think he is, that reality is evolutionary, developmental,

[7] In *The Metaphysical Club*, Louis Menand wrote: "Everything James and Dewey wrote as pragmatists boils down to a single claim: people are the agents of their own destinies." While this assertion surely captures the central place in James's thought of real possibilities and real freedoms to actualize some of them, from the standpoint of politics and culture it simply is not the case that James (and Dewey) thought that all people always are the *sole* agents of their destinies. Indeed, providing people with greater freedom and agency is a head agenda item for the pluralistic democracy that they both championed. Similarly, for James (and Dewey), from the standpoint of biology and nature, it is not the case that the *only* forces, powers, and conditions that impact the individual human organism are somehow "in" the organism alone. *The Metaphysical Club: A Story of Ideas in America* (New York: Farrar, Straus and Giroux, 2001), 371.

[8] This point runs through David C. Lamberth's "A Pluralistic Universe a Century Later: Rationality, Pluralism, and Religion" in *William James and the Transatlantic Conversation: Pragmatism, Pluralism, and the Philosophy of Religion*, edited by Martin Halliwell and Joel D. S. Rasmussen, 133–149 (New York: Oxford University Press, 2014).

[9] John E. Smith, *The Spirit of American Philosophy*, rev. ed. (Albany: State University of New York Press, 1983), 67. Similarly, Richard P. Mullin noted that James's "meliorism leads its adherents to believe that the individual can be effective and to act on that belief." *The Soul of American Philosophy: The Ethical and Spiritual Insights of William James, Josiah Royce, and Charles Sanders Peirce* (Albany: State University of New York Press, 2007), 37. Charlene Haddock Seigfried, "Devising Ends Worth Striving For: William James and the Reconstruction of Philosophy," in *Recovering Pragmatism's Voice: The Classical Tradition, Rorty, and the Philosophy of Communication*, edited by Lenore Langsdorf and Andrew R. Smith (Albany: State University of New York Press, 1995), 118.

and processive rather than static or complete in any way, then it is imperative to realize that positions taken by human diagnosis and human intervention are significantly, although partially, constitutive of the future course of events."[10]

3. Third, the universe must support the free exercise of our powers in our life struggles. For James, this support is supplied sufficiently fully in experience only in a universe with a divine thinker, only in a universe with a God, only in a universe that includes an unseen spiritual world, a supernatural order, a world with infinite perspective. Faith in the existence of this universe is, for those who have this faith, wholly rational and fully justified in practice (and the pretend logic of atheistic, agnostic, and positivistic philosophers never proves otherwise).

4. Fourth, finally, so that this faith in an unseen, supernatural, spiritual, infinite order of the universe does not stand at odds with faith in the creative efficacy of our individual powers, James believed that in some cases our faith brings this universe into being, that there are truths and facts made true and factual only by, and after, our faith.

These four themes run through and crisscross each other throughout all the essays in *The Will to Believe*. "The Dilemma of Determinism" makes strikingly evident the first theme. "The Moral Philosopher and the Moral Life" richly illustrates the second theme. "Is Life Worth Living?" clearly develops the third theme. And both "The Sentiment of Rationality" and "The Will to Believe" centrally express the fourth theme.

James began "The Dilemma of Determinism" by disclaiming "all pretension to prove to you that the freedom of the will is true," and instead announcing that he hopes to lead others "to follow my own example in assuming it true and acting as if it were true" (WB, 115). In the context of this aim, James characterized determinism as the view that "those parts of the universe already laid down absolutely appoint and decree what other parts shall be" (WB, 117) and, thus, the rejection of the reality of possibilities. By contrast, indeterminism "denies the world to be one unbending fact" and admits possibilities in excess of actualities (WB, 118). Because the supposed debate between determinists and indeterminists is thus a debate about the reality of

[10] John J. McDermott, "A Relational World: The Significance of the Thought of William James and John Dewey for Global Culture," in *The Drama of Possibility: Experience as Philosophy of Culture* (New York: Fordham University Press, 2007), 151.

possibilities rather than the reality of actual facts—and, indeed, the determinist and indeterminist do not disagree about actual facts—and because James held that science deals only with actual facts and draws conclusions based only on facts, he concluded that no amount of factual knowledge that something actually happened gives "us the least grain of information as to whether another thing might or might not have happened in its place or facts": "If we have no other evidence than the evidence of existing facts, the possibility-question must remain a mystery never to be cleared up" (WB, 119).

In this light, James recast the issue as a practical one and, thus, as a difference in temperament and faith, a difference in experienced realities. In doing so, he created "a way in which the general outline of the Darwinian position might be held without denying existence to self-conscious purposive thinking" and "human self control."[11] Determinists (that is, those with deterministic sentiments), he suggested, feel antipathetic toward the notion of chance—crazy unreason, the rejection of intelligible laws, something that is not the unconditional property of the whole, and ambiguity and uncertainty rather than expectancy about the future. Indeterminists (i.e., those with indeterminist sentiments) feel antipathetic toward the notion of a universe in which some part "can claim to control absolutely the destinies of the whole" (WB, 124).

And the indeterminists feel no intimacy with both of the possible consequences or implications of determinism. Pessimism is the first possible consequence of determinism in practice. In the face of problems, loss, suffering, abuse, deprivation, intolerance, injustice, violence, murder, war, and horrific and frightful atrocities, determinists must conclude that these things could not have been different but that it would have been better if they had been different. James explained: "Determinism, in denying that anything else can be in its stead, virtually defines the universe as a place in which what ought to be is impossible—in other words, as an organism whose constitution is afflicted with an incurable taint, an irremediable flaw." Referring to a murder, James put this point more specifically:

> Regret for the murder must transform itself, if we are determinists and wise, into a larger regret. It is absurd to regret the murder alone. Other things

[11] Joseph Blau, *Men and Movements in American Philosophy* (Englewood Cliffs, NJ: Prentice-Hall, 1952), 233.

being what they are, *it* could not be different. What we should regret is the whole frame of things of which the murder is one member. I see no escape whatever from this pessimistic conclusion, if, being determinists, our judgment of regret is to be allowed to stand at all. (WB, 126)

This suggests a second possible practical consequence of determinism: an escape from pessimism by giving up judgments of regret and all other moral judgments. For a determinist who takes this path, the universe is not good or bad or some mixture of both, either now or at any time past or future. Instead, the universe, indifferent in itself, simply is; it is not good or bad or less good than it should be or a site of moral progress or regress; it just is. Of this view, James wrote:

The world must not be regarded as a machine whose final purpose is the making real of any outward good, but rather as a contrivance for deepening the theoretic consciousness of what goodness and evil in their intrinsic natures are. Not the doing either of good or of evil is what nature cares for, but the knowing of them. . . . For, after all, is there not something rather absurd in our ordinary notion of external things being good or bad in themselves? Can murders and treacheries, considered as mere outward happenings, or motions of matter, be bad without anyone to feel their badness? And could paradise properly be good in the absence of a sentient principle by which goodness was perceived? Outward goods and evils seem practically indistinguishable except in so far as they result in getting moral judgments made about them. (WB, 129–130)

This subjectivism in theory, James claimed, fosters fatalism in practice. Persons who lack energy and the disposition to strive become wholly passive—there is no reason to strive when there is no possibility of doing or making better. And persons with energies and the will to act become wholly reckless—there is no reason to refrain from doing anything when there is no possibility that doing something else is better. For subjectivism in practice, nothing can be bettered and so everything is permitted.

As James noted, none of this disproves determinism at the theoretical or logical level—and, equally, none of it proves determinism at the theoretical level. James's point is that because it is not possible to theoretically prove either position, because there is no theoretical proof for or against determinism, we must recognize limits "foreign and opaque to our understanding" and thus recognize that "the only escape is by the practical way" (WB, 134). For persons with pluralistic temperaments and radically empirical worldviews, James stressed, indeterminism stands as the only rational way of representing them:

> For in the view of that philosophy the universe belongs to a plurality of semi-independent forces, each one of which may help or hinder, and be helped or hindered by, the operations of the rest. . . . What interest, zest, or excitement can there be in achieving the right way, unless we are enabled to feel that the wrong way is also a possible and a natural way—nay, more, a menacing and an imminent way? And what sense can there be in condemning ourselves for taking the wrong way, unless we need have done nothing of the sort, unless the right way was open to us as well? I cannot understand the willingness to act, no matter how we feel, without the belief that acts are really good and bad. I cannot understand the belief than an act is bad, without regret at its happening. I cannot understand regret without the admission of real, genuine possibilities in the world. Only *then* is it other than a mockery to feel, after we have failed to do our best, that an irreparable opportunity is gone from the universe, the loss of which it must forever after mourn. (WB, 135)

Indeterminism and a "pluralistic, restless universe" will not be acceptable, James realized, "to a mind possessed of the love of unity at any cost," to an absolutist mind, to persons who are at home only after the "tragic reality" of the world is transformed into "an insincere melodramatic exhibition" (WB, 136). For a pluralist, on the other hand, it is indeterminism that in practice is marked by the sentiment of rationality—and there is no theory or fact that compels pluralists to deny indeterminism and its world of real possibilities, real values, and real desires and strivings. As James put it in his 1882 "On Some Hegelianisms": "In short, the notion that real contingency and ambiguity may be features of the real world is a perfectly unimpeachable hypothesis"—"Hegel's own logic, with all the senseless hocus-pocus of its triads," notwithstanding (WB, 216).

In "The Moral Philosopher and the Moral Life," James set forth (seven years after "The Dilemma of Determinism") a radically empirical, radically relational account of these values, desires, and strivings. After claiming that our values originate in many sources, both our nurture and our nature, both our environment and inward forces, James asserted that the terms central to morality—terms such as "good," "bad, and "obligation"—"mean no abso-lute natures, independent of personal support." Rather, "they are objects of feeling and desire which have no foothold or anchorage in Being apart from the existence of actually living minds" (WB, 150). This means that values—goods and bads—are not properties of things that exist independently of us. Rather, goods and bads are relations between things and the interests or demands of sentient beings. Values are made, not simply found. There was, for James, no need for Ezra Pound's 1934 modernist advice, "make it new"; there is no other alternative to remaking and making anew, and the only question is *which* new to make, which new to forsake. To say, for example, that a sailboat is good is not to assert that the sailboat in itself possesses some property. Instead, it is to say that the sailboat satisfies someone's interest. For one concerned with purchase price, to say that the sailboat is good is to say that it is not too expensive. For one concerned with professional competi-tion, to say that the sailboat is good is to say that it is very fast on open water. And for one concerned with environmental sustainability, to say that the sail-boat is good is to say, for example, that it was manufactured in non-polluting ways using renewable materials. There is, James wrote, "no single point of view . . . from which the values of things can be unequivocally judged" (WB, 146). In addition, it is important to understand (as developed in chapter 3) that James viewed truth as just *"one species of good"* and so his pragmatic theory of truth is simply one species or application of his more general ac-count of values: *"The true is the name for whatever proves itself to be good in the way of belief"* and it is *"only the expedient in the way of our thinking, just as 'the right' is only the expedient in the way of our behaving"* (P, 42, 106).

Just as these interests may conflict for, or within, a given individual (the very same person might want a sailboat that is both inexpensive and fast, even though fast sailboats are expensive), so too interests may conflict among different individuals (one person may want to build a marina, while another person may want to ban waterfront development and a third person may approve of a new marina but only if it is open to a certain class of people). In the face of competing claims and obligations, plural and often opposed demands, and the necessity of "butchering" "some part of the ideal" (WB, 154), James observed:

> Various essences of good have thus been found and proposed as bases of the ethical system. . . . No one of the measures . . . has, however, given general satisfaction . . . so that after all, in seeking for a universal principle

we inevitably are carried onward to the most universal principle—that *the essence of good is simply to satisfy demand.* The demand may be for anything under the sun. There is really no more ground for supposing that all our demands can be accounted for by one universal underlying kind of motive than there is ground for supposing that all physical phenomena are cases of a single law. The elementary forces in ethics are probably as plural as those of physics are.... Since everything which is demanded is by that fact a good, must not the guiding principle for ethical philosophy (since all demands conjointly cannot be satisfied in this poor world) be simply to satisfy at all times *as many demands as we can*? (WB, 152–153, 155)

And he added:

The course of history is nothing but the story of men's struggles from generation to generation to find the more and more inclusive order. *Invent some manner* of realizing your own ideals which will also satisfy the alien demands—that and that only is the path of peace! . . . [And yet] there is nothing final in any actually given equilibrium of human ideals, but that, as our present laws and customs have fought and conquered other past ones, so they will in their turn be overthrown by any newly discovered order which will hush up the complaints that they still give rise to, without producing others louder still. . . . On the whole, then, we must conclude then that no philosophy of ethics is possible in the old-fashioned absolute sense of the term. Everywhere the ethical philosopher must wait on facts. (WB, 155, 156, 157)

If the moral philosopher, the theorist, must wait, one who would live a moral life, practitioners, living sentient beings, cannot wait. They must act (and, as James often pointed out, not to act is also to act). From this practical standpoint, James characteristically focused on temperament and mood rather than doctrine.[12] Calling the difference between them the "deepest difference practically, in the moral life of man," James described and

---

[12] Sarin Marchetti has referred to this as the "modality" of James's philosophy. When this means that James is committed above all to a particular worldview, I think this is correct. When it means that "James philosophized without theories," as Marchetti claimed, then I think James's pragmatism, radical empiricism, and pluralism show this is mistaken—assuming the term "theory" is not taken to mean only views that are supposedly universal, final and closed to future experience, or merely intellectualism run amok. "A Philosopher Without Theories," in *The Jamesian Mind*, edited by Sarin Marchetti (New York: Routledge, 2021), 1.

differentiated the "easy-going" mood (a "shrinking from present ill") and the "strenuous" mood (an indifference to present ill in order to pursue a greater, more distant ideal) (WB, 159–160). Precisely because satisfying as many demands as possible and inventing some manner to realize a more and more inclusive order are hard work with no guarantee of success in one's lifetime—because this hard work will be undertaken only by persons in the strenuous mood rather than the easy-going mood—James realized that the moral life demands a philosophy that effectively calls forth and enacts the strenuous mood.[13]

How is it possible in practice to look past present ills and to call forth or energize the strenuous mood? For James, this was the fundamental, most pressing practical moral question. In answering this question, James passed from what I have identified as his second major article of faith, that our lives create values and that these values have no independent or advance existence, to his third, that there is an unseen and infinite perspective, a God. James replied that the strenuous mood "needs the wilder passions to arouse it, the big fears, loves, and indignations; or else the deeply penetrating appeal of some one of the higher fidelities like justice, truth, or freedom" (WB, 160). And he added:

> This too is why, in a merely human world without a God, the appeal to our moral energy falls short of its maximal stimulating power. Life, to be sure, is even in such a world a genuinely ethical symphony; but it is played in the compass of a couple of poor octaves, and the infinite scale of values fails to open up. Many of us . . . would openly laugh at the very idea of the strenuous mood being awakened in us by those claims of remote posterity which constitute the last appeal of the religion of humanity. . . . This is all too finite, we say; we see too well the vacuum beyond. . . . When, however, we believe that a God is there, and that he is one of the claimants the infinite perspective opens up. The scale of the symphony is incalculably prolonged. The more imperative ideals now begin to speak with an altogether new objectivity and significance . . . Every sort of energy and endurance, of courage and capacity for handling life's evils, is set free in those who have religious faith. For this reason the strenuous type of character will on the battlefield

---

[13] David Rondel noted succinctly that "strenuousness is thus indissolubly connected to action." "Strenuous Citizenship," in *The Jamesian Mind*, edited by Sarin Marchetti (New York: Routledge, 2021), 216.

of human history always outwear the easy-going type, and religion will drive irreligion to the wall. (WB, 160, 161)

For James, this is the pragmatic, practical meaning of belief in God: the fullest arousal of the strenuous mood. As he put it in his 1881 "Reflex Action and Theism": "Infra-theistic conceptions, materialisms and agnosticisms, are irrational because they are inadequate stimuli to man's practical action" (WB, 106). And when each of us is challenged in and by life to take up the strenuous mood, "it is simply our total character and personal genius that are on trial; and if we invoke any so-called philosophy, our choice and use of that also are but revelations of our personal aptitude or incapacity for moral life." As noted in the introduction, James concluded that "from this unsparing practical ordeal no professor's lectures and no array of books can save us" (WB, 162).

In "Is Life Worth Living," James placed related but different emphasis on this practical reasonableness of belief in the reality of infinite perspective and God. Rather than arguing that belief in God supports directly the strenuous mood necessary for moral life, he argued that this belief constitutes a remedy to pessimism, melancholy, and contemplation of suicide—and in this way sustains a strenuous mood in life.[14] After noting that some full-fledged temperamental optimists—James thought Walt Whitman was one—simply never feel this pessimism and never seriously consider that life is not worth living, James sought to sweep away "certain views that often keep the springs of religious faith compressed" in the lives of many people "pent in to the hard facts, especially as science now reveals them" (WB, 40). This pessimism, or religious pessimism—James called it "the nightmare view of life" (WB, 41)— has its reflective source in "the contradiction between the phenomena of nature and the craving of the heart to believe that behind nature there is a spirit whose expression nature is" (WB, 40–41). A mind pent in by the hard facts of science but at the same time "craving for communion" while nonetheless realizing "how desperately difficult it is to construe the scientific order of nature either theologically or poetically"—this is a mind marked by "inner discord and contradiction" (WB, 41). It may be possible to resolve this inner discord by holding on to the hard fact of science and giving up the desire to read nature religiously. But is it possible, James asked, to discover and believe

---

[14] See my *Pragmatic Fashions*, 206–221.

in "supplementary facts" about nature "which permit the religious reading to go on" (WB, 41)?

James thought there were two ways to do this: a naturalistic way and a supernatural way. James judged the first, naturalistic way only partly successful at best. He thought it might seem "a poor half-way stage," if one marked by "instinctive curiosity, pugnacity, and honor" (WB, 48):

> Where the loving and admiring impulses are dead, the hating and fighting impulses still respond to fit appeals. . . . It is, indeed, a remarkable fact that sufferings and hardships do not, as a rule, abate the love of life; they seem, on the contrary, to give it a keener zest. The sovereign source of melancholy is repletion. Need and struggle are what excite and inspire us. (WB, 45)

To the suicidal person, James advised, a naturalist can appeal not in the name of the universe's general and abstract evil, but in the name of the particular, individual, local evils that are one's own business. To the suicidal, pessimistic, melancholic person, "you can appeal—and appeal in the name of the very evils that make his heart sick there—to wait and see *his* part of the battle out." If one has "a normally constituted heart," you can appeal, James wrote in overtly sexist language, to "manliness and pride" (WB, 48, 47).

For James, there is a second, fuller, more successful way to resolve the contradiction between the human demand for meaning and value and the seemingly value-free scientific account of nature devoid of "harmonious spiritual intent" and "mere *weather*" (WB, 49). At its core, this way is religious belief in "supplementary facts" about the universe—facts that supplement our scientific account of nature. At its core, it is belief in the supernatural, belief that "the so-called order of nature, which constitutes this world's experience, is only one portion of the total universe, and that there stretches beyond this visible world an unseen world of which we now know nothing positive, but in its relation to which the true significance of our present mundane life consists." James called this belief "religious faith" and added that "one must in some fashion die to the natural life before one can enter into life eternal" (WB, 48).

Is belief in the supernatural rational? Does it produce the sentiment of rationality? Do we—do persons temperamentally so inclined—have a right to believe that there is a supernatural order of this sort? James answered:

I wish to make you feel . . . that we have a right to believe the physical order to be only a partial order; that we have a right to supplement it by an unseen spiritual order which we assume on trust, if only thereby life may seem to us better worth living again. (WB, 49)

On what basis did James think we have a right to believe in this super-natural order? How would belief in this order be any more justified than a child's belief in the existence of unicorns, Santa Claus, or the tooth fairy—or, in less happy moments, orcs, dementors, or monsters under the bed or in the closet? Belief in the supernatural just will not seem rational, James realized, to persons who idolize science, equate rationality as such with science, affirm not simply scientific method but full-blown scientism, and fail to re-alize that "our science is a drop, our ignorance a sea" (WB, 50). Such persons, James thought, will advise that we hold no beliefs and take no action unless and until we have sensible, scientific evidence. This may sound fine in theory, James argued, but it is not even possible in practice in all cases that demand our action. James wrote that neutrality—withholding belief—is "outwardly unrealizable, where our relations to an alternative are practical and vital":

Our only way, for example, of doubting, or refusing to believe, that a certain thing *is*, is continuing to act as if,it were *not*. . . . And so if I must not believe that the world is divine, I can only express that refusal by declining ever to act distinctively as if it were so, which can only mean acting on certain critical occasions as if it were *not* so, or in an irreligious way. There are, you see, inevitable occasions in life when inaction is a kind of action, and must count as action, and when not to be for is to be practically against; and in all such cases strict and consistent neutrality is an unattainable thing. (WB, 50, 51)

And so James called the scientistic duty to remain neutral when neutrality is not possible in practice "the most ridiculous of commands" and one that scientific practice itself constantly violates (WB, 51). Scientific practice is also a kind of faith; it is not the triumph of the intellect over the passions, but merely the triumph of one sort of passion over other sorts of passions (WB, 30). James stressed:

But the inner need of believing that this world of nature is a sign of some-thing more spiritual and eternal than itself is just as strong and authoritative in those who feel it, as the inner need of uniform laws of causation ever can be in a professionally scientific head. The toil of many generations has proved the latter need prophetic. Why *may* not the former one be prophetic too? And if needs of ours outrun the visible universe, why *may* not that be a sign that an invisible universe is there? What, in short, has authority to debar us from trusting our religious demands? Science as such assuredly has no authority, for she can only say what is, not what is not; and the agnostic "thou shalt not believe without coercive sensible evidence" is simply an expression (free to anyone to make) of private personal appetite for evidence of a certain peculiar kind. (WB, 51)

This passage and line of thought immediately raise three questions. First, if one accepts James's argument, how is belief in a supernatural order different from a child's belief in unicorns or an adult's felt license to conceive self, others, and the world in whatever way produces happiness?

Second, granting as a psychological fact that some people do have a need to believe in a reality beyond the visible, natural world, how is it possible that this need is a sign that there is an invisible universe?

Third, given James's rejection of all sharp separations of perception and conception, sentiment and reason, and purpose and thought, how can he claim that there are some questions (say, scientific ones) that should be answered on the basis of reason and others (say, religious ones) that should be answered on the basis of passion? Indeed, if rationality is a sentiment, when do we ever face an issue that is not directed to our "passional nature"?

James directly addressed these first two questions both in the final pages of "Is Life Worth Living?" and a year later, in 1896, in his well-known "The Will to Believe." I do not believe he ever did respond, at least in any sufficiently consistent and full way, to the third question. In response to the first question, James limited "the right to believe" in two ways. First, he confined it to particular practical situations in which we are confronted with a "genuine" option (an option that has two "live" hypotheses), a "forced" character (because one or the other of its alternatives is not avoidable), and a "momentous quality" (an irreversibility, uniqueness, and large significance) (WB, 14–15). Second, he restricted his thesis to cases in which the issue cannot be resolved on intellectual grounds—that is, "passional tendencies and volitions which run before" belief, rationality itself being a sentiment (WB, 19–20):

> *Our passional nature not only lawfully may, but must, decide an option be-*
> *tween propositions, whenever it is a genuine option that cannot by its nature*
> *be decided on intellectual grounds; for to say under such circumstances, "Do*
> *not decide, but leave the question open," is itself a passional decision—just*
> *like deciding yes or no—and is attended with the same risk of losing the truth.*
> (WB, 20)

Just as James claimed that our different values are linked to our different feelings and strivings, so too he asserted that our different accounts of reality—for example, a radically empirical account or a naturalistic account or a supernatural account—are linked to our passions and wills such that "no concrete test of what is really true has ever been agreed upon" (WB, 22). Each person's conviction that his or her evidence is really objective "is only one more subjective opinion added to the lot":

> There is this—there is that; there is indeed nothing which someone has
> not thought absolutely true whilst his neighbor deemed it absolutely false;
> and not an absolutist among them seems ever to have considered that the
> trouble may all the time be essential, and that the intellect, even with truth
> directly in its grasp, may have no infallible signal for knowing whether it be
> truth or no. (WB, 23)

And as a result, James argued, we must judge truth claims not on the basis of their origins but on the basis of their results, on the basis of where belief in them leads, on the basis of the extent to which they issue in experiences that continue to confirm them—or falsify them (and thus estrange us to that degree from our former, believing selves). The right to believe must be paired with an equal obligation to question and reject one's former habits of belief, including desires for belief.[15] In a spirit sometimes thought to be characteristically American, when asked to determine the truth or falsity of beliefs, James asked not "Where are you from?" but rather "What can you do?"

Accordingly, James argued that his thesis about "the right to believe" extends to all moral questions. In all such cases, he contended, we must act on the basis of faith in what might happen with our action or could happen

---

[15] Both these sides of epistemic responsibility are discussed by José Medina in "The Will Not to Believe: Pragmatism, Oppression, and Standpoint Theory," in *Feminist Interpretations of William James*, edited by Erin C. Tarver and Shannon Sullivan, 235–260 (University Park: Penn State University Press, 2015).

with our action. And although we have no advance guarantee or the sort of certainty that some skeptics demand, it is only the faith that leads to our action that makes success possible. So too James argued that his "right to believe" thesis extends to religious questions. When religious issues present themselves as genuine options, James argues, we have no advance knowledge of truth and certainty, and so must decide on the basis of our passions and wills. If these decisions are confirmed in an individual's experience, they are in consequence true. And James added that we thus must reject as irrational any "rule of thinking" that prevents us "from acknowledging certain kinds of truth if those kinds of truth were really there" (WB, 31–32). James did not argue that religious belief—belief in the supernatural—is theoretically true; rather, he argued that there can be no theoretical objection to those who adopt in practice religious beliefs that continue to be confirmed in their experience and that continue to produce feelings of fluency and sufficiency— the sentiment of rationality. This, of course, is the response that James, in his pragmatic moments, makes to all issues of confirmation, validation, verification, satisfactory leading, and epistemic justification. (And so it is unclear how this point even begins to address my third question.)[16]

This at last brings into sharp relief the fourth major theme that runs through James's philosophy: the view, beyond the claim of a "right to believe," that sometimes faith in a fact helps create that fact, that belief plays a part in bringing into being its own object, and that in practice our faith, like any other action, is an efficacious force in this in-the-making universe (a universe that, if anything at all really is at stake in our believings and doings, cannot have an infinite, omniscient, omnipotent, predetermining God). James gave everyday examples of this phenomenon in our personal actions: the mountain climber who successfully crosses a crevasse in part because he believes he can do so, the friend whose belief that another person will be his friend helps bring about a deep friendship, the man who has faith that he will receive a promotion at work and thus strenuously and at some risk sacrifices in ways that verify his faith and produce his promotion. (Yes, in James's examples, the striving, strenuous agents are always men.) James summarized: "The desire

---

[16] In "Pragmatism as Romantic Polytheism," Richard Rorty asserted, "James should not have made a distinction between issues to be decided by intellect and issues to be decided by emotion.... What he should have done instead was to distinguish issues that you must resolve cooperatively with others and issues you are entitled to resolve on your own"—which of course (surprise!) is just the sharp separation Rorty drew in *Contingency, Irony, and Solidarity*. Rorty's essay is included in *The Revival of Pragmatism: New Essays on Social Thought, Law, and Culture*, edited by Morris Dickstein (Durham, NC: Duke University Press, 1998), 31.

for a certain kind of truth here brings about that special truth's existence" (WB, 28); "our faith beforehand in an uncertified result *is the only thing that makes the result come true*" (WB, 53). Joan Richardson has called this James's "conversion, his exchange, of religious for secular terms":

> His first experiment was to act *as if*, his first act of free will to act *as if* there were free will: "We can act *as if* there were a God; feel *as if* we were free; consider Nature *as if* she were full of special designs; lay plans *as if* we were to be immortal; and we find these words to make a genuine difference in our moral life." The first proof was, of course, the success of this deliberate verbal act. Subsequent tests and proofs became the content of his life's work.[17]

Moreover, James argued that this same thing—faith in a fact helping to create the fact—takes place "in great cosmical matters, like the question of religious faith" (WB, 29). He began with what he called a "trivial example":

> Just as a man who in a company of gentlemen made no advances, asked a warrant for every concession, and believed no one's word without proof, would cut himself off by such churlishness from all the social rewards that a more trusting spirit would earn—so, here, one who should shut himself up in snarling logicality and try to make the gods extort his recognition willy-nilly, or not get it at all, might cut himself off forever from his only opportunity of making the gods' acquaintance. (WB, 31)

Trust and action, like distrust and inaction (which are simply trust in other things and action in other ways), turn one possible universe—one of multiple "maybes"—into an actual universe (WB, 54). From the moral point of view, James wrote, life is what we make of it: "Please remember that optimism and pessimism are definitions of the world and that our own reactions on the world, small as they are in bulk, are integral parts of the whole thing, and necessarily help to determine the definition" (WB, 54).

Will a faith in an unseen, supernatural world verify itself? James's answer was straightforward: Maybe. Who knows? Our lives through and through are maybes, and his point was not that there is or is not an unseen world but,

---

[17] Joan Richardson, "William James's Feeling of If," in *A Natural History of Pragmatism* (New York: Cambridge University Press, 2007), 119.

rather, that there is no theoretical, abstract, or non-passional basis for any such belief. Even if that belief "disguises" itself "in scientific plumes," as James observed in "Great Men and Their Environment" (WB, 189), still it provides no basis for concluding that all supernatural belief is irrational or unjustified for those persons for whom this belief works, for whom it issues in the sentiment of rationality. James sometimes declared himself one of those persons:

> For my own part, I do not know what the sweat and blood and tragedy of this life mean, if they mean anything short of this. If this life be not a real fight, in which something is eternally gained for the universe by success, it is no better than a game of private theatricals from which one may withdraw at will. But it feels like a real fight—as if there were something really wild in the universe which we, with all our idealities and faithfulness, are needed to redeem. (WB, 55)

This faithfulness, as James pointed out in his preface to *The Will to Believe*, is anything but reckless. It is the open-eyed, self-aware right of individuals to employ personal faiths at personal risks, risks that no one fully escapes (WB, 8).

This, then, is James's universe and his philosophy:

1. Life with real possibilities, an open universe, a site for melioristic action for those who have faith and exercise their powers in action
2. A radically empirical moral universe with relational goods and bads and obligations, goods created rather than ready-made in our lives, and creation that is strenuous and demands a universe congenial to our strivings
3. Faith in a universe with infinite perspective and a spiritual, supernatural dimension, a faith that is not irrational in theory, a faith that works in practice
4. Faith that is itself creative, transformative, and productive in part of its own facts, a faith that is a co-creator of the universe

At infrequent times James may seem to have laid down the law for others. He claimed, for example, that a universe without God is only a symphony played on a few poor octaves and one that cannot sufficiently motivate the strenuous mood. This can sound too sweeping and not sufficiently attuned to the different temperaments of more secular folks, those whom he labels instinctive optimists or this-worldly naturalists. But, unlike most philosophers, James did not claim that his philosophy was the one right philosophy or one true philosophy. And he did not claim that philosophical theorizing proves anything by itself. Instead, he claimed his philosophy was his personal philosophy—an invitation to his readers to find resonance with their own lives and worldviews. Seen from one perspective, this is a thoroughgoing pluralism that invites all persons to develop their own, always-personal philosophies. Seen from a different perspective, this is an empiricism and individualism that denies that one's experience can be trumped or dismissed by other people's theories. This is a message that very much needs to be heard and acted on today, and, in the spirit of this message, it is appropriate to put it in James's words:

> We *act*, taking our life in our hands. No one of us ought to issue vetoes to the other, nor should we bandy words of abuse. We ought, on the contrary, delicately and profoundly to respect one another's mental freedom—then only shall we bring about the intellectual republic; then only shall we have that spirit of inner tolerance without which all our outer tolerance is soulless, and which is empiricism's glory; then only shall we live and let live, in speculative as well as in practical things. (WB, 33)

2

Avoiding Old-Fogeyism

Plasticity, Habits of Genius, and Acts of Greatness

Human beings are creatures of habit. Whether explicitly articulated or implicitly embodied and unconsciously performed, any philosophy is an expression of some actual individual's habits of thought and reason, habits of attitude and temperament, habits of vision and worldview, and whole habitual way of undergoing and acting in the world. What are the consequences of this for understanding and leading flourishing lives?

1. Habit

Following chapters on the scope of psychology and the functions and conditions of brain activity, the first topic James addressed in *The Principles of Psychology* was habit. He began: "When we look at living creatures from an outward point of view, one of the first things that strike us is that they are bundles of habits." And when we look at human beings, he added, those bundles of habits seem somewhat variable and, "to a great extent, to be the result of education" rather than instinctual "necessity implanted at birth" (PP, 109).[1] Similarly, in *Talks to Teachers*, he claimed that "all our life, so far as it has definite form, is but a mass of habits—practical, emotional, and intellectual—systematically organized for our weal or woe, and bearing us irresistibly towards our destiny, whatever the latter may be" (TT, 47).

James's claim is not original, even if made in a particularly forceful manner and supported by scientific evidence. Aristotle and other ancient Greek thinkers stressed this same point and drew from it consequences for ethics and politics. Since James's day, many scholars have hammered home the

---

[1] Gerald Myers has captured well the pragmatism of James's *Principles of Psychology*—the strategy of tracing the practical differences between different psychological hypotheses about, for example, the nature of habit, attention, consciousness, conception, perception, reasoning, and the emotions. "Introduction: The Intellectual Context" (PP, xx–xxii).

No Professor's Lectures Can Save Us. John J. Stuhr, Oxford University Press. © Oxford University Press 2023.
DOI: 10.1093/oso/9780197664629.003.0003

centrality of habit in human life—often making a habit of reinforcing James's words, as if to provide performative evidence that we all really are creatures of habit. Following James, John Dewey, for example, famously noted that by the word "habit" he meant "to express that kind of human activity which is influenced by prior activity and in that sense acquired; which contains within itself a certain ordering or systematization of minor elements of action; which is projective, dynamic in quality, ready for overt manifestation; and which is operative in some subdued subordinate form even when not obviously dominating activity." In Jamesian fashion, he added: "All habits are demands for certain kinds of activity; and they constitute the self. In any intelligible sense of the word will, they *are* will."[2] In a similar vein, James Clear has noted that habits are not about having something but about becoming someone: "Quite literally, you become your habits."[3]

The formation of habits, James argued, is evidence of the *plasticity* of human nature and especially human nervous tissue. James characterized this plasticity as the possession of an inner structure and outer form "weak enough to yield to an influence, but strong enough not to yield all at once," and he called this his "first proposition": "*The phenomena of habit in living beings are due to the plasticity of the organic materials of which their bodies are composed*" (PP, 110). James labeled this proposition a "chapter in physics rather than physiology or psychology." He explained the physical process of habit formation:

The only impressions that can be made upon [the brain and spinal cord] are through the blood, on the one hand, and through the sensory nerve-roots, on the other; and it is to the infinitely attenuated currents that pour in through these latter channels that the hemispherical cortex shows itself to be so peculiarly susceptible. The currents, once in, must find a way out. In getting out, they leave their traces in the paths which they take. The only thing they *can* do, in short, is to deepen old paths or to make new ones; and the whole plasticity of the brain sums itself up in two words when we call it an organ in which currents pouring in from sense-organs make with extreme facility paths which do not easily disappear. . . . The most complex habits . . . are, from the same point of view, nothing but concatenated

[2] John Dewey, *Human Nature and Conduct*, vol. 14 of *John Dewey: The Middle Works, 1899–1924* (Carbondale: Southern Illinois University Press, 1983 [1922]), 31, 21.
[3] James Clear, *Atomic Habits: An Easy and Proven Way to Build Good Habits and Break Bad Ones* (New York: Avery/Penguin, 2018), 41.

discharges in nerve-centres, due to the presence there of systems of reflex paths, so organized to wake each other up successively. . . . For the entire nervous system is nothing but a system of paths . . . Whatever obstructions may have kept it at first from being a path should then, little by little, and more and more, be swept out of the way. (PP, 112–113)

By observing that instincts facilitate the establishment of habits and that habits can transform instincts "beyond their original automatic stage,"[4] James purposely blurred the boundaries between instincts—pre-established elec-trophysiological current paths—and habits—reinforced and new paths. This account of habits and their physical origins, James concluded (by quoting a colleague), holds that the "*human nervous system grows to the modes in which it has been exercised*" (PP, 117). And, just as the line between instinct and habit is blurry, so too the line between habitual action and conscious, direc-tive action is blurry and permeable. Multiple neural pathways are at work as we engage in many actions; those actions are rarely, if ever, either 100 percent or 0 percent habitual, or 100 percent or percent consciously directed.

This means, as Wendy Wood (who called James's thought "extraordi-nary" and "well ahead of his time with regard to insight into the nature of habits") noted in *Good Habits, Bad Habits: The Sciences of Making Positive Changes That Stick*, that habit "refers to *how* you perform an action, not *what* the action is."[5] What are the practical consequences of all this? James explained: "*Habit simplifies the movements required to achieve a given result, makes them more accurate, and diminishes fatigue*," and "*habit diminishes the conscious attention with which our acts are performed*" (PP, 117, 119). In short, what we do habitually we do more efficiently, more effectively, and in a manner that requires less energy and less attention. Habit streamlines an individual's action and frees consciousness to focus on other things. And it allows us to persist; conscious attention and reflective drive more quickly wander and wane and quit. Viewed from the perspective of these results, habits are immensely valuable and seem to have only an upside. So too habit streamlines our social interactions and social relations, enabling us to take up each new social interaction with precedent, custom, and institutionally established pathways. James captured this in his famous observation that it is

---

[4] David E. Leary, *The Routledge Guidebook to James's Principles of Psychology* (New York: Routledge, 2018), 52.
[5] Wendy Wood, *Good Habits, Bad Habits: The Science of Making Positive Changes That Stick* (New York: Picador, 2019), 25. The remarks about James are on 37.

not reflection or introspection that drives our lives: "Habit is thus the enormous fly-wheel of society, its most precious conservative agent" (PP, 125). This led James to formulate the first of four ethical maxims that he took to be implications of the nature and reach of habit:

> The great thing, then, in all education, is to *make our nervous system our ally instead of our enemy*. It is to fund and capitalize our acquisitions, and live at ease upon the interest of the fund. *For this we must make automatic and habitual, as early as possible, as many useful actions as we can,* and guard against the growing into ways that are likely to be disadvantageous to us, as we should guard against the plague. (PP, 126)

By making useful actions habitual, we avoid having to fight constant, forever battles for self-control. Self-control is a function of the development of useful habits that in turn largely replace the need for self-control in each situation. As John Dewey observed in his 1922 *Human Nature and Conduct,* "It [habit] has a hold upon us because we are the habit."[6] Now, James's first maxim, to make habitual useful action, has practical application only if it is possible to identify which actions are "useful actions" and "our ally." For pluralists about human natures and their fulfillments, this will not be a one-size-fits-all list, but a question about method nonetheless looms large: How—by what criteria, by what method, on the basis of what evidence—can we identify useful and beneficial actions and distinguish them from our actions that are our own enemies?

James's second ethical maxim flows from his account of brain activity: "Never suffer an exception to occur till the new habit is securely rooted in your life" (PP, 127). "Continuity of training," often difficult training, is necessary, especially at the outset; it is the only way to overcome obstructions and establish new pathways. The issue here is an instrumental one: Expert opinion agrees, James counseled, that the task of acquiring a new habit and replacing an old one should be as abrupt, sustained, and complete as is possible. He added:

> We must be careful not to give the will so stiff a task as to insure its defeat at the outset; but, *provided one can stand it,* a sharp period of suffering, and then a free time, is the best thing to aim at, whether in giving up a habit like

---

[6] Dewey, *Human Nature and Conduct,* 21.

that of opium, or in simply changing one's hours of rising or of work. It is surprising how soon a desire will die of inanition if it be *never* fed. (PP, 128)

James here recognized the myth that changing habits requires only intention and the willpower to carry it out. James recognized the force and pull of older, existing habits—and thus the ease with which we fall back into them despite our new intentions. James recognized that moving from an old habit to a new one is a matter of action, of repeated behavior, of attentively acting over and over again in the new way until that way becomes habitual, automatic, speedily and effortlessly cued, and unconscious procedural memory.

James's third ethical maxim is closely related to this and has strong pragmatic, action-oriented focus: "*Seize the very first possible opportunity to act on every resolution you make, and on every emotional prompting you may experience in the direction of the habits you aspire to gain*" (PP, 128). Why is this? Again, James drew on his account of the nature of the brain and its activity: "It is not in the moment of their forming, but in the moment of their producing *motor effects*, that resolves and aspirations communicate the new 'set' to the brain" (PP, 128). The brain science may have been new when James wrote these words, but the underlying ethical idea is old: In *Nicomachean Ethics*, Aristotle advised that to become a virtuous person—a person virtuous in habit, in second nature, in character—one should act virtuously and that over time virtuous actions could forge virtuous character. Merely resolving on New Year's Day to lose weight or contribute more to one's community does not, by itself, make one thinner or a more constructive force in the lives of others. Agreeing with the proverb that hell is paved with good intentions (that are only intentions), James advised that no matter how good someone's maxims and sentiments may be, if that person does not take advantage of "every concrete opportunity to *act*," everything may remain unchanged (PP, 129).

James's final ethical maxim thus is a strategy for action: "*Keep the faculty of effort alive in you by a little gratuitous exercise every day.*" James called this being "systematically ascetic" and "heroic in little unnecessary points," and he urged that we do every day or two something we would rather not do (PP, 130). This amounts to a kind of meta-habit—it is the acquisition of the habit of being able to give up other habits that are not, or are no longer, useful. In a gripping mixed metaphor, James viewed this as a kind of self-issued insurance policy on oneself: Those who little by little and day by day have acquired "the habits of concentrated attention, energetic volition, and self-denial in unnecessary things" "will stand like a tower when everything rocks" all around them and "softer fellow-mortals are winnowed like chaff in the blast" (PP, 130).

This account of habit is, in the end, a cautionary tale or warning at both the personal and political levels—a humanistic sermon, even:

> The hell to be endured hereafter, of which theology tells, is no worse than the hell we make for ourselves in this world by habitually fashioning our characters in the wrong way. Could the young but realize how soon they will become mere walking bundles of habits, they would give more heed to their conduct while in the plastic state. We are spinning our own fates, good or evil, and never to be undone. Every smallest stroke of virtue or of vice leaves its never so little scar. (PP, 130–131)

Avoiding behavior at odds with new habits still in the making, seizing opportunities and emotional promptings to act, engaging regularly in a little gratuitous exercise to nourish one's capacity for exertion—it is action that creates habits. Now, it is important to keep in mind here that habits created *by* action are not only habits *of* action. In other words, we are not just creatures of habit in our actions; we are creatures of habit throughout and across our whole lives. Yes, we act in habitual ways, but we are also creatures of habit in matters of attention, sensation and sensitiveness, bodily processes, perception, desire, temperament and intimacies, conception, reason and reflection, language and communication, and relationships and associations—and more. We have habitual interests and thus selectively attend to (and miss) experience in habitual ways. We carve up and conceptualize our experience in habitual ways, habitually employing some conceptual schemes rather than others and habitually speaking some languages rather than others. In this light, for example, empiricism is simply the *habit* of explaining things in terms of parts, and rationalism is simply the different *habit* of explaining things in terms of wholes. Our sensations and perceptions are habitually intermingled with these habitual concepts, and thus they too are matters of habit. We habitually perceive in some ways rather than others, habitually manifest certain blindnesses rather than others, habitually are conscious of some things and not conscious of others. As James put it, our conceptions function habitually as preperceptions, ensuring that we normally see what we've habitually conceived as something to be seen. Our emotions and desires run along established, socially educated, habitual paths—from preferences for certain kinds of food to particular sorts of neighbors and friends to personal voting and political choices.

And so too our truths and our philosophies. James's view of the nature and importance of habit is clearly on display in his pragmatism and pragmatic theory of truth:

> Our nouns and adjectives are all humanized heirlooms, and in the theories we build them into, the inner order and arrangement is wholly dictated by human considerations, intellectual consistency being one of them. . . . We plunge forward into the field of fresh experience with the beliefs our ancestors and we have made already; these determine what we notice; what we notice determines what we do; what we do again determines what we experience; so from one thing to another, altho the stubborn fact remains that there is a sensible flux, what is *true of it* seems from the first to last to be largely a matter of our own creation. (P, 122)

We *habitually* feel the push and pull of the world in particular ways; we *habitually* philosophize one way rather than another. Our temperaments, attitudes, emotions, memories, imaginations, and worldviews are matters of habit. Again in this light, pluralism—living pluralism and not simply abstract doctrine—is simply an expression of experience of irreducible multiplicity, and living monism is expression of confirmation of ultimate unity. Whether characteristically upbeat and happy, pessimistic and despairing, strenuous or quietist, confident and peaceful, or fearful and agitated, our feelings, moods, and affect are matters of habit. Because our feelings and emotions are matters of habit and character, they too are the results of habituation and the embodied exercise of those habits. Megan Craig has captured James's vision here:

> James offers an experiential, fluid description of emotion in which feeling, infinitely fringed, seeps through a porous body that remains enigmatically susceptible and precariously sensitive—at the mercy of the world. . . . The sense that emotional engagement is fundamental to ethical attentiveness, to an expanding field of values and significance, goes together with James's conviction that emotion must be exercised rather than exorcised, for only in expanding the heart and honing a whole-bodied capacity for feeling does one stand any chance of expanding one's mind.[7]

---

[7] Megan Craig, *Levinas and James: Toward a Pragmatic Phenomenology* (Bloomington: Indiana University Press, 2010), 108–109. In a related context, Craig wrote: "The possibility of personal

To propose an addition to James's list of habit maxims: Keep the faculty of emotional connection, the ability to emotionally engage in previously unhabitual ways, alive in you every day.

Because human habits are largely the result of education and environment rather than instinct, these habits, though they be habits *of* individuals, are fully social—habits *of* and *by* society. Habitual action, thought, and feeling may be located *in* an individual, but they are the localized *results* of larger social and environmental processes that include but are not limited to individual choices. The notion of a *wholly* or purely self-made habit is a complete fiction. No creature of habit is *only* self-educated or self-made. Moreover, these social forces are at work early in life and, indeed, complete most of their work early:

> [Habit] dooms us all to fight out the battle of life upon the lines of our early nurture . . . It is well for the world that in most of us, by the age of thirty, the character has set like plaster, and will never soften again. If the period between twenty and thirty is the critical one in the formation of intellectual and professional habits, the period below twenty is more important still for the fixing of personal habits. (PP, 126)

By taking seriously the role and range of habit, it becomes evident that everyone is an empiricist—in the non-technical sense that all people hold a worldview that resonates with, is informed by, and illuminates their lives and worlds as they habitually experience them to be. Pragmatists recognize this point when, with James, they describe philosophies as suggestions that cannot be finally proved by any lecture or a book but only by the actual experience of each person. "My only hope," James wrote at the end of *A Pluralistic Universe*, "is that [my lectures] possibly have proved suggestive." "I must leave the issue in your hands. Whatever I may say, each of you will be sure to take pluralism or leave it, just as your own sense of rationality moves and inclines" (APU, 149, 147).

---

transformation is one of James's central obsessions," but "just because there are opportunities to begin again, it does not mean that one can begin from the beginning": "In the moment when one finds oneself most bereft or without ballast, the sheer existence of anything can appear a miracle" (166, 176). "James and the Ethical Importance of Grace," in *The Jamesian Mind*, edited by Sarin Marchetti (New York: Routledge, 2021).

2. Habitual Dangers

James called habit society's "most precious conservative agent." It is important to understand that habits are *conservative in two very different senses*.
First, as "the enormous fly-wheel of society," habits store and save energy;
they literally *conserve energy*. They allow us to act proficiently without
expending much perceptual, conceptual, emotional, or behavioral attention.[8] Habits thus are instrumental; they are efficient instruments for result-
producing action—what James termed "useful actions," as distinct from
"disadvantageous" ones.

Habits are conservative in a second sense: They tend to sustain the status
quo; they *conserve society as it is and has been*. This means they conserve both
social goods and social ills—including ills to which a society, or large parts of
it, may be blind or not conscious. James's extended illustrations of the conservative agency of habit make this clear—in part in ways that do not seem to
be what he intended. He wrote:

> [Habit] alone is what keeps us all within the bounds of ordinance, and saves
> the children of fortune from the envious uprisings of the poor. It alone
> prevents the hardest and most repulsive walks of life from being deserted by
> those brought up to treat therein. It keeps the fisherman and the deck-hand
> at sea through the winter; it holds the miner in his darkness, and nails the
> countryman to his log-cabin and his lonely farm through all the months
> of snow; it protects us from invasion by the natives of the desert and the
> frozen zone. It dooms us all . . . [to a pursuit] for which we are fitted, and it is
> too late to begin again. It keeps different social strata from mixing. Already
> at age twenty-five you see the professional mannerism settling down on the
> young. . . . You see the little lines of cleavage running through the character,
> the tricks of thought, the prejudices, the ways of the "shop," in a word, from

---

[8] If, with James, we think of emotions as bodily habits and also think, with James, that habits often
are unconscious, then it may seem that James was wrong to conclude that all emotions are consciously
felt. Reading James insightfully and charitably, Shannon Sullivan reached this conclusion: "James
is wrong to equate emotion with conscious feeling." The Jamesian response, I think, is that an unconscious emotion is consciously felt in some way. In Sullivan's example from Freud, a woman is
not conscious of her erotic feelings for her brother-in-law, but these feelings manifest themselves
in physical pain in her thigh—and she is "consciously aware of her painful thigh." It is this pain, this
felt awareness, that James had in mind when he claimed emotions are always felt in some way. That
said, I think Sullivan is surely right to claim that, "whether consciously felt or not," all bodily states
"say something about a person's relationship to and engagement with the world" and "all emotions
are bodily." Shannon Sullivan, *The Physiology of Sexist and Racist Oppression* (New York: Oxford
University Press, 2018), 47.

which a man can by-and-by no more escape than his coat-sleeve can suddenly fall into a new set of folds. . . . An invisible law, as strong as gravita-
tion, keeps him within his orbit . . . till his dying day. (PP, 125–126)

Both the content and the assumptions of the above passage invite, at the
very least, a lot of critical questions. When James advises us to *"make automatic and habitual, as early as possible, as many useful actions as we can,"* is
it "useful" to keep the poor from rising up against the "children of fortune"?
Is it even "useful" that there be envious poor people and high levels of social and economic inequality? Is that something that should be conserved?
What would be involved in being protected "from invasion by the natives of
the desert and the frozen zone"? Is this a claim that it is "useful" to avoid war
and armed conflict? Or that it is "useful" to avoid immigration, or maybe just
the immigration of certain people to certain places? Or something else? Is
it "useful" for different social strata not to mix? Or different racial or ethnic
groups? Or people of different religions or nations? Is it "useful" that rich and
poor, young and old, not mix? Are "tricks of thought" and "prejudices" really "useful" to conserve? And in these examples, why are all those who fish,
mine, and wear coat-sleeves male? And if they are, is that also something
"useful" to conserve? Is one's first "orbit" therefore a good orbit, one that is
"useful" and worth maintaining, simply because it is initial?

Presumably all responses to these questions are themselves bound up
with habitual attitudes, emotions, conceptions, and worldviews. Responses
to these kinds of questions are products of habits as well—so that, for example, a racist, sexist, authoritarian, or democratic society is likely to instill
racist, sexist, authoritarian, or democratic habits in its members, who in turn
are likely to be only partially conscious of this habituation and likely to find
racist, sexist, authoritarian, or democratic actions to be thoroughly advanta-
geous and, yes, "useful."

If a short course of experience makes clear the utility of habits, it also
makes evident that habits are useful in the service of bad ends as well as good
ones. And this is precisely why James worried about the lasting and terrible
effects of bad habits: Through them we produce and sustain a hell on this
earth for ourselves and our society. *Habits, when they are bad habits, are a hell
of a danger. And when they are unconscious bad habits, they are even worse.*

This is true of societal habits as well as individual ones. As an example, this
means that racist practices function in and through habits. This is the idea,
as Helen Ngo explained, that racism finds expression not simply in overt

discrimination or violence but also "perhaps more potently in the subtle bodily gestures, reactions and behaviors—not always explicitly intended— that are routinely enacted" and that routinely inform perception, gesture, and memory that are, thus, habitually racialized.[9]

Habits are dangerous in a second way. If we take seriously the reality of time and change, then what once may have been "useful actions" that James advised us to make habitual can become "disadvantageous" actions at a later time. *If we embrace a radically empirical view of the world as a dynamic, changing, in-process world, then a good habit can become a bad habit as conditions change.* Good nutritional habits for a twenty-year-old are unlikely to be good nutritional habits for that person fifty years later. Last century's standard building practices may be very bad building practices in the face of far-reaching climate and weather change. And effective face-to-face classroom teaching habits simply may not work for remote online teaching during a pandemic. If the world did not change—perhaps from generation to generation or at least across an average life span—then once a habit of useful action had taken root, it would thereafter remain a useful habit. If, on the other hand, the world really does change, then habits that were useful in earlier conditions can become thoroughly hellish when later conditions are different but the earlier habit remains. In these cases, we become fanatics—repeating over and over what no longer works. We become robots—programmed by our earlier habits of perception, conception, and feeling to be affected and to respond in the same old ways. We become closed-minded—failing even to see the existence of new conditions as we simply continue our old prejudices, our habitual judgments, and live in our habitual world.

In this context, James insightfully observed that most all of us (okay, maybe not you, but people you know) end up stuck with old beliefs, old attitudes, and an inability to experience genuine novelty and change. He observed:

---

[9] Helen Ngo, *The Habits of Racism: A Phenomenology of Racism and Racialized Embodiment* (Lanham, MD: Lexington Books, 2017), 13. See also Alia Al-Saji, "The Racialization of Muslim Veils: A Philosophical Analysis," *Philosophy and Social Criticism* 36, no. 8 (2010): 875–902. And see Linda Alcoff, *Visible Identities: Race, Gender, and the Self* (New York: Oxford University Press, 2006). Gail Weiss has noted problems that occur "when vision is depicted as the primary or even the only way of constructing a perspective" or discerning influences on it. *Refiguring the Ordinary* (Bloomington: Indiana University Press, 2008), 14. Weiss added: "If James is correct that an individual's character becomes 'set' like plaster by the time she is thirty, this is not the fault of the habits she has acquired, but rather is due to a failure to seize upon the possibilities those habits offer for transforming the givens of one's world" (91). If James is right, I think, two points follow here: (a) seizing or not seizing possibilities for transformation, being able or unable to seize them, is also a matter of habit; and (b) some conscious and unconscious habits expand or greatly limit possibilities for transforming individual and social life.

Most of us grow more and more enslaved to the stock conceptions with which we have once become familiar, and less and less capable of assimilating impressions in any but the old ways. Old-fogeyism, in short, is the inevitable terminus to which life sweeps us on. (PP, 754)

What is the main danger for a human creature or a human society of habit? It is the likelihood of becoming an old fogey, a person stuck in (and embodied by) past routines formed under past conditions that no longer exist.[10]

Given that fact, what is the practical challenge for a human creature of habit? It is to avoid becoming an old fogey. Because it is not possible for humans to avoid acquiring habits, the challenge is how to become a creature of flexible habits—a creature whose habits remain sufficiently plastic, immature, and open to taking useful new pathways as the world itself changes.[11] The practical challenge is how to acquire and sustain a habit of having flexible, open habits that are useful even if they concern action not yet secured or mastered.

3. Finitude and the Habit of Happiness

As noted, James's response to this practical challenge is this: Make habitual as soon as possible as many useful actions as possible, and equally make habitual as soon as possible avoidance of as many disadvantageous actions as possible. This is surely good advice, I think, but stated this way it is too general to provide direct practical help. The reason for this should be immediately clear to anyone familiar with James's radically empirical and relational world of pure experience or his radically empirical account of the moral life: Being useful or being disadvantageous is a relation; nothing just is simply by itself useful or harmful; to be useful or harmful is always to be useful or harmful *for* a particular person (or "sentient being") *with respect to* a particular purpose. An ibuprofen tablet may be useful to a sick person aiming to reduce pain, but it is

---

[10] It is important to note that routines frequently are marked by routine enjoyment and satisfaction, and this fact is usually a key factor in habit formation. Of course, the mere fact that someone experiences pleasure in doing something repeatedly does not establish that this action contributes to, or is part of, a flourishing life. See, for example, Leah Fessler, "The Unexpected Pleasure of Doing Something Over and Over Again," *New York Times*, November 11, 2019.

[11] Megan Craig noted this line of thought in James's writings and connected it to issues of gender and sexism as well as larger political realities of habit. Megan Craig, "Habits, Relaxation, and the Open Mind," in *Feminist Interpretations of William James*, edited by Erin C. Tarver and Shannon Sullivan (University Park: Penn State University Press, 2015), 178–179.

not useful for an office worker whose goal is a paperweight heavy enough to hold a stack of reports on a table near a ventilation duct. A Russian grammar tutorial may be useful for a person eager to learn a new language, but it is probably not useful to an adult native of Russia. A chainsaw can be useful to a property owner who want to clear some ground for a new house, but it is not useful for a philosophy professor out for a recreational hike in the mountains. So if we are to make useful actions habitual, we need to specify the purposes with respect to which those actions are useful. We need to ask: Useful for what? Useful for whom? Who—which creature(s) of habit—is empowered to determine the answers to these questions?

The kinds or varieties of useful actions are nearly endless—because the varieties of human desires and purposes that issue in these actions are nearly endless. There are actions useful in fishing and mining, useful in teaching kindergarten and administering a retirement center, useful in a competitive basketball game and in a solo vocal performance, useful in undercover espionage and in global diplomacy, and useful in writing a philosophy book and in reading one too.

So a sharper focus and smaller topic is needed: *What actions are useful for human happiness and flourishing?*[12] How can they be made habitual as much and as soon as possible? How can habits of flourishing be created?

Immediately this question calls for pluralism: Different people experience happiness and flourishing in all kinds of different activities, relationships, and lives. The diversity of human lives and their fulfillments must be embraced rather than narrowed or reduced.[13] We must resist what John Lachs has termed "the allure of the 'all.'"[14]

James tried to capture some of this diversity in his chapters "The Religion of Healthy-Mindedness" and "The Sick Soul" in his *Varieties of Religious Experience*. He there defined religion simply as "*the feelings, acts, and experiences of individual men in their solitude, so far as they apprehend themselves to*

---

[12] This is the focus of essays by Rebecca Newberger Goldstein, Mark Johnson, Jessica Wahman, Dan Haybron, Valerie Tiberius, John Lachs, John Stuhr, Lori Gallegos, José Medina, John Sadler, Jennifer Hansen, James Pawelski, and Michele Moody-Adams in *Philosophy and Human Flourishing*, edited by John J. Stuhr (New York: Oxford University Press, 2022). In addition, this issue is explicitly addressed in the context of William James's philosophy by Phil Oliver in "Pursuing Happiness" in his *William James's "Springs of Delight": The Return to Life* (Nashville, TN: Vanderbilt University Press, 2001), 101–153.

[13] See my "Flourishing: Toward Clearer Ideas and Habits of Genius," in *Philosophy and Human Flourishing*, edited by John J. Stuhr (New York: Oxford University Press, 2022).

[14] John Lachs, "The Allure of the All," in *Philosophy and Human Flourishing*, edited by John J. Stuhr (New York: Oxford University Press, 2022).

stand in relation to whatever they may consider the divine" (VRE, 34). From a scientific perspective only (and saying nothing about "religion as metaphysical revelation"), he added:

> For when all is said and done, we are in the end absolutely dependent on the universe; and into sacrifices and surrenders of some sort, deliberately looked at and accepted, we are drawn and pressed into our only permanent positions of repose. Now in those states of mind which fall short of religion, the surrender is submitted to as an imposition of necessity, and the sacrifice is undergone at the very best without complaint. In the religious life, on the contrary, surrender and sacrifice are positively espoused: even unnecessary givings-up are added in order that the happiness may increase. *Religion thus makes easy and felicitous what in any case is necessary*; and if it be the only agency that can accomplish this result, its vital importance as a human faculty stands vindicated beyond dispute. It becomes an essential organ of our life, performing a function which no other portion of our nature can so successfully fulfill. From the merely biological point of view, so to call it, this is a conclusion to which, so far as I can now see, we shall inevitably be led. (VRE, 49)

The upshot, for James, is this: Because a flourishing life is not merely a life without complaint, a life merely putting up with life, so actions that are useful for human happiness and flourishing—and thus which should be made habitual as fully and quickly as possible—*must enable and constitute religion.* A fully flourishing life, again for James, is a life marked by religious feelings, acts, and experiences.[15]

How is this possible? How is it possible to make "easy and felicitous what in any case is necessary"? How can individuals live against a background of intimacy in a universe so foreign that it sacrifices all of them? How can anyone be happy when "the first gift of natural existence is unhappy" (VRE, 71)? How can finite individuals lead flourishing yet finite lives? How can any worldview successfully "define the future *congruously with our spontaneous powers*," as James demanded in "The Sentiment of Rationality," if those

---

[15] Ellen Kappy Suckiel noted that James's aim in his discussions of religion "was to show, piece by piece and one by one, from an epistemic point of view, how the field is open to the genuine possibility of God's existence, and how one may justifiably believe in God if one so chooses. James thought it sufficient to show how, by retaining a probabilistic, hypothetical, and open-minded stance, we may make intelligent judgments in favor of religious claims." *Heaven's Champion: William James's Philosophy of Religion* (Notre Dame, IN: University of Notre Dame Press, 1996), 15.

powers are entirely extinguished in the future? How can the message of any era be that "the inmost nature of reality is congenial to *powers* which you possess" (WB, 73) when it is a biological fact that all those powers are finite and will be completely crushed by the time a next era arrives?

James labeled one way of answering these questions as "healthy-mindedness" and called it a "whole optimistic way of thinking" (VRE, 70). This sounds promising. James, writing as a psychologist rather than a metaphysician, described healthy-mindedness, "a soul of sky-blue tint" (VRE, 73) and a "'once-born' type of consciousness" (VRE, 74), this way:

> In many persons, happiness is congenital and irreclaimable. "Cosmic emotion" inevitably takes in them the form of enthusiasm and freedom. I speak not only of those who are animally happy. I mean those who, when unhappiness is offered or proposed to them, positively refuse to feel it, as if it were something mean and wrong. We find such persons in every age, passionately flinging themselves upon their sense of the goodness of life, in spite of the hardships of their condition, and in spite of the sinister theologies in which they may be born. From the outset their religion is one of union with the divine. (VRE, 72)

In its involuntary form, healthy-mindedness is "a way of feeling happy about things immediately." In its voluntary form, "systematic healthy-mindedness" takes goodness as the essential and universal character of reality and, as a matter of "religious policy," "deliberately excludes evil from its field of vision" (VRE, 78). The exemplar of healthy-mindedness, James contended, is Walt Whitman, for whom "all things are divinely good," sin is a matter of indifference, and evil a disease (VRE, 76–77, 109).

Should we then make habitual as much and as soon as possible those actions that produce either an immediate or a reflective *healthy-minded* life? Should we strive to make our characters once-born?

Before addressing this pressing question, James described a second, "more morbid" type of feeling, attitudes, and actions. For the "sick soul," "the evil aspects of our life are of its very essence" and "the world's meaning comes home to us most when we lay them most to heart" (VRE, 112). The sick soul is "congenitally fated to suffer from its [evil's] presence"—not just a curable maladjustment of one's life to one's environment "but something more radical and general, a wrongness or vice in [one's] essential nature, which no alteration of the environment, or any superficial rearrangement of the inner self can cure, and which requires a supernatural remedy" (VRE, 114). These persons, James asserted, have a low threshold for helplessness, fear, discord, anguish, pain, and misery (VRE, 115):

> Failure, then, failure! So the world stamps us at every turn. We strew it with our blunders, our misdeeds, our lost opportunities, with all the memorials of our inadequacy to our vocation. And with what a damning emphasis does it then blot us out! No easy fine, no mere apology or formal expiation, will satisfy the world's demands, but every pound of flesh exacted is soaked with all its blood. The subtlest forms of suffering known to man are connected with the poisonous humiliations incidental to these results. (VRE, 117)

"Back of everything" for the melancholic "twice-born" sick soul, James added, is "the great spectre of universal death, the all-encompassing blackness" (VRE, 118).

James asked: "Does it not appear as if one who lived more habitually on one side of the pain-threshold might need a different sort of religion from one who habitually lived on the other" (VRE, 115)? A pluralistic response to this question would seem to have to be an unqualified yes. However, James responded in a different way from a perspective that he claimed to be that of an "impartial onlooker"—a perspective that was James's own.[16] Here is the crucial passage:

> It seems to me that we are bound to say that morbid-mindedness ranges over the wider scale of experience, and that its survey is the one that overlaps. The method of averting one's attention from evil, and living simply in the light of good is splendid as long as it will work. It will work with many persons; it will work far more generally than most of us are ready to suppose; and within the sphere of its successful operation, there is nothing to be said against it as a religious solution. But it breaks down impotently as soon as melancholy comes; and even though one be quite free from melancholy one's self, there is no doubt that healthy-mindedness is inadequate as a philosophical doctrine, because the evil facts which it refuses positively to account for are a genuine portion of reality; and they may after all be the

---

[16] See Paul J. Croce's account of how James framed "his own introspective account, edited for public display." *Young William James Thinking* (Baltimore: Johns Hopkins University Press, 2018), 252.

best key to life's significance, and possibly the only openers of our eyes to the deepest levels of truth. (VRE, 136)

This telling passage calls, I think, for a three-part response. First, it is not particularly surprising that James made this judgment in 1902—regardless of whether it is right or wrong—because it parallels the judgments he made in many other slightly earlier essays on issues of morality and religion. It is similar to his concluding claim in his 1891 "The Moral Philosopher and the Moral Life" that life in "a merely human world without God" "falls short" and encompasses only part of the full range of human experience: "Life, to be sure, is even in such a world a genuinely ethical symphony; but it is played in the compass of a couple of poor octaves" (WB, 160). It is similar to his 1896 assertion in "The Will to Believe" that religion "says that the best things are the more eternal things, the overlapping things, the things in the universe that throw the last stone, so to speak, and say the final word," and "we are better off now if we believe" this to be so (WB, 29–30). And it repeats his strong criticisms in his 1895 "Is Life Worth Living?" of the temperamental optimism of healthy-minded Walt Whitman and his "naturalistic honesty" that restricts life to "natural experience" and confronts only particular evils, paying no attention to "evil at large" (WB, 35–36).

Second, even so, James's judgment here is entirely at odds, in my view, with virtually all of his pragmatism, his radical empiricism, and his pluralism:

- For pragmatism, there is no "deepest level of truth." There are only truths more or less fully verified, corroborated, evidenced by experience—that is, by experiences. The truths about the total cost of all the books on my desk, the number of elementary physical forces in the universe, the extent to which my daughter enjoyed a particular film, the history of racism in the United States and around the world, and the degree to which James reports his life as relatively morbid rather than relatively happy are all—equally—truths. If there is cosmic evil and experience of this evil verifies belief about its existence, this truth is no deeper and no more ontologically or epistemologically fundamental than any truths verified by happy or non-melancholic experience. Truths do not have different "depths" (though they do have different degrees of verification). James or I or you or someone else may well be more interested in one than another or may experience some as having more far-reaching personal consequences than others, but for a pragmatist who views truth as a property of some beliefs, there are no deeper and no shallower truths; there is not a hierarchy but a republic of truths.

- For a radical empiricist, James's "evil facts" are relations. They are facts within particular, concrete experience, facts in relation to the experience of a particular, concrete experiencer. When James asserts that a portion of reality simply does consist of "evil facts," by definition this is what the healthy-minded person—if described free of caricature—denies precisely because this is not how that person experiences things. Facts, for a radical empiricist, are not facts for experience in the abstract; if they are facts at all, they are facts for experience in the concrete—and thus for some *one's* experience (and possibly not for some *one* else's). When experiences differ, whether on small or large matters, it is not that one is fuller or more overlapping or more expansive than the other; it is only that they are different. For a radical empiricist, the mosaic of experience has no backing; there is no basis other than past, present, and future experiences by which to judge what does or does not count as "a genuine portion of reality."

- James's judgment about the philosophical superiority of the morbid and melancholy temperament of sick souls is at odds not only with his pragmatism and radical empiricism but also with his pluralism. In "The Absolute and the Strenuous Life," published four years after *The Varieties of Religious Experience*, James noted that pluralism "has no saving message for incurably sick souls" and so it is "bound to disappoint them" (MT, 124). Presumably so too pluralism has a saving message for the healthy-minded and it is likely to satisfy them. But the relevant point here is methodological rather than psychological. James claimed that he was an "impartial onlooker" to the varieties of religious experience, a reporter engaged in mere description rather than judgment. But for a pluralist—and for James himself—there is no such thing as an *impartial* onlooker. James surely was not impartial here: In "The Sentiment of Rationality" he had declared that a fatal flaw in any worldview is to provide our energies "no object whatever to press against" and thus to render our powers irrelevant. In this light, James himself found the world something "to press against" at every turn and anything but an abiding source of happiness, and he thus supposed that healthy-minded folks really must experience the same thing, even if they loaf in the grass and celebrate the natural world and their finite lives. A philosophy, James the pluralist later argued, reflects irreducibly personal experience, intimate character, feelings, preferences, "accidents of personal vision"—by irreducibly personal experience and personal sense of the universe (APU, 10, 14–15). It is just this fact that James claimed philosophers often try to hide from others—and that James himself here seems to be hiding when he declared his own perspective "impartial." A passage quoted in chapter 1 thus bears partial repetition in this context:

Of whatever temperament a professional philosopher is, he tries when philosophizing to sink the fact of his temperament. . . . There arises thus a certain insincerity in our philosophic discussions: the potentest of all our premises is never mentioned. . . . What the system pretends to be is a picture of the great universe of God. What it is—and oh so flagrantly—is the revelation of how intensely odd the personal flavor of some fellow creature is. (P, 11, 24)

There is a third and final point that is warranted in response to James's endorsement of morbid-mindedness over healthy-mindedness. James simply turned reflective healthy-mindedness into a silly caricature. The reason the healthy-minded "positively refuse" to feel unhappiness is not because they first feel cosmic unhappiness but then deny it is so. Rather, they "refuse" to report feeling this kind of unhappiness because they do not feel it. It is not that they experience "the darker aspects of the universe" and then, in an effort to deceive themselves, simply pretend to others that they had no such experience. It is that they do not experience their finite lives in the universe as dark in the way that the morbid-minded sick souls do. It is not that they feel the need for divine deliverance and then attempt to deny this feeling. It is that they do not experience anything from which to be divinely delivered (VRE, 385). Here and elsewhere—particularly in "Is Life Worth Living," an 1895 address to Harvard's Young Men's Christian Association later published in *The Will to Believe and Other Essays in Popular Philosophy*—James's descriptions of Walt Whitman, "the supreme contemporary example" of healthy-mindedness, constitute caricature if not complete error.[17] James himself quoted at length an account of Whitman by a "disciple" and close associate. The passage does

---

[17] For an extended discussion of this point and an expression of a fully "healthy-minded" philosophy, see my "Absurd Pragmatism" in my *Pragmatic Fashions: Pluralism, Democracy, Relativism, and the Absurd* (Bloomington: Indiana University Press, 2016), 206–221.

not in any way support the conclusions James draws from it. It reads, in part, as follows: "When I first knew [him], I used to think that he watched himself, and would not allow his tongue to give expression to fretfulness, antipathy, complaint, and remonstrance. It did not occur to me as possible that these mental states could be absent in him. After long observation, however, I satisfied myself that such absence or unconsciousness was entirely real" (VRE, 76). James misread and manipulated this passage so that its meaning became, for James, this: "The only sentiments he allowed himself to express were of the expansive order" (VRE, 76). James added that Whitman is "more than your mere animal man" because he is "aware enough of sin for a swagger to be present in his indifference toward it" (VRE, 77). But Whitman's swagger is not a response to the cosmic sin of the morbid-minded; it is a response to what the melancholy, death-dreading, and morbid-minded believe to be cosmic sin—which for Whitman is not cosmic sin at all but rather a "well-join'd scheme." Thus Whitman wrote, for example, in "Crossing Brooklyn Ferry":

> The simple, compact, well-join'd scheme, myself disintegrated,
> every one disintegrated yet part of the scheme . . .
> We understand then do we not?
> What I promis'd without mentioning it, have you not accepted?
> What the study could not teach—what the preaching could not
> Accomplish is accomplish'd, is it not? . . .
> Flow on, river! Flow with the flood-tide and with the ebb-tide!

As Whitman made clear in his writing, his view is that "life and death, and all things are divinely good" (VRE, 76) and that "what will be, will be well—for what is, is well," including one's own disintegration. James wrote that a nameless eeriness, weirdness, uncanniness, and sinisterness "comes over us at the thought of there being nothing eternal in our final purposes, in the objects of those loves and aspirations which are our deepest energies" (WB, 71). A more fully pluralistic view, a view more attuned to differences in experiences and lives, would be that this eeriness comes over *some* of us. Morbid-mindedness simply does not range over a "wider scale of experience." It is not more inclusive, even if it appears more inclusive to morbid-minded persons who take their own personal experience as the measure of what is to count as inclusive. Morbid-mindedness does not range over healthy-minded experience. Moreover, healthy-minded persons, if equally unattuned to pluralism, could just as well respond that it is their outlook that ranges over the wider scale of experience because it includes and then transforms what is morbid. The healthy-minded are not advancing a childish strategy of closing one's eyes to something bad so that it will go away or not exist as long as they are not looking at it. Healthy-mindedness is not less wide or inclusive than morbid-mindedness, because it too recognizes the wrongs, losses, and tragedies of life. It simply responds in a different way. And the healthy-minded are not mounting a disinformation campaign or promulgating fake news or even just spreading a garden-variety lie. Healthy-mindedness is an honest expression of Whitman's experience and vision: "What is called good is perfect and what is called bad is just as perfect." In fact, this is a once-born version of what James identified as twice-born religious rebirth: the sense that ultimately all is well, harmony, and the willingness to be.[18]

These three large critical points and my whole line of thought here are not intended as an *argument for* healthy-mindedness—or as an *argument against* it. Instead, they are a pluralistic and anti-abstractionist insistence that no one conclude that somebody's else's different experience either (a) *must* be or *really* is or at bottom *turns out to be* just like one's own—and then plead for confession of this supposed fact—or (b) must be *lesser*, more *superficial, less inclusive*, and *less fully meaningful and attentive* if it really does differ from one's own. Pluralism requires nothing less.

Accordingly, to make habitual as much and as soon as possible actions that are useful for human flourishing is to make habitual experiences of background intimacy rather than foreignness, experiences in which we feel the universe congenial to our powers—whether one takes joy and health or evil and sickness as the essence of the universe and ourselves in it. Pluralism about universes of intimacy would allow us to remark, upon contrasting the habitually healthy-minded and the habitually sick soul, "how different!" or even "how intensely odd" (P, 24) but not "how great an antagonism" (VRE, 136–137). James re-found firmer ground, I think, in parts of his "Conclusions" to *The Varieties of Religious Experience*:

> No two of us have identical difficulties, nor should we be expected to work out identical solutions. . . . Each attitude being a syllable in human nature's total message, it takes the whole of us to spell the meaning out completely. . . . We must frankly recognize the fact that we live in partial systems, and that

---

[18] This aspect of James's view of a reborn religious life is noted in a different context by Russell Goodman in *Wittgenstein and James* (New York: Cambridge University Press, 2002), 47.

parts are not interchangeable in the spiritual life.... From this point of view, the contrasts between the healthy and the morbid mind, and between the once-born and the twice-bon types ... cease to be the radical antagonisms which many think them. ... [T]he final consciousness which each type reaches of union with the divine has the same practical significance for the individual; and individuals may well be allowed to get to it by the channels which lie most open to their several temperaments. (VRE, 384–385)

The universe habitually speaks in different ways to different people, who, in turn, respond in ways that are differently useful, successful, and flourishing. Put in other words: Different people habitually selectively attend, habitually hear different parts of the universe's message, and so they habitually flourish or fail to flourish in astonishingly plural ways. Each of us thinks "me" and "not me" differently (and, James stressed, we do this because of habits that have physical bases and practical effects). James wrote, "Each of us dichotomizes the Kosmos in a different place" (WB, 74). Each of us, Walt Whitman wrote earlier, *is* a kosmos.

4. Genius in Action

Even a thoroughgoing pluralism and a radical empiricism do not, by themselves, protect human creatures of habit from the second way in which habits are dangerous. *By definition*, habits are conservative and relatively static, stable, and self-reinforcing. *By experience*, the world, in contrast, is dynamic and changing. The collision course is clear: Even habits that were highly useful—plural and different habits useful for plural and different people—in an earlier time may readily become highly disadvantageous and even counterproductive in a later, different time.

To respond in ways useful for flourishing, a creature of habit must have changing habits in changing times. In other words, a flourishing creature of habit must have the habit of acquiring useful habits that also are flexible—habits as flexible as the world's own frequent and dynamic flexes. This is the habit of acquiring new useful habits that previously were not habits and of dropping no longer useful habits that previously worked.[19] James sometimes labeled this kind of flexibility (or at least part of this flexibility) as "genius,"

---

[19] Jessica Wahman provided an extended development of this point in her "Pragmatic Stories of Selves and Their Flourishing," in *Philosophy and Human Flourishing*, edited by John J. Stuhr (New York: Oxford University Press, 2022).

and he characterized genius as *"the faculty of perceiving in an unhabitual way"* (PP, 754; PBC, 286; italics added).[20] Or, as Craig Wright put it some 130 years later in *The Hidden Habits of Genius: Beyond Talent, IQ, and Grit*, when it comes to genius, "originality matters"—at least since Immanuel Kant claimed in 1780 that genius is "the very opposite of the spirit of imitation" and repetition.[21] James's stress on genius as a kind of original perception is echoed by a later observation Wright made:

> Mary Shelley, Joanne Rowling, and Pablo Picasso were all visionaries who hit hidden targets. Embedded in the words "visionary" and "imagination" are "vision" and "image." Picasso saw in images; Rowling saw a narrative attended by images; Shelley had a vision she expressed through words. Albert Einstein also saw things.... "I rarely think in words at all," he said.[22]

This is an account of genius as functional. It is genius understood in terms of flexibility, inventive imagination, social action, and the capacity to experience in ways that have not been habitual in the past and do not simply imitate and reproduce the way things are or the way things have been or the way things previously were taken always to be. Just as James's pragmatism reconstructs the notion of truth, and just as his radical empiricism reconstructs the notion of experience, so too his account of habit makes possible a new understanding of genius that is not elitist, exclusionary, tied to some atomistic individualism, or bound up with entrenched social privilege and oppression. As such, it is a capacity for both individual and societal change. In short, James used "genius" in an unhabitual way.

---

[20] James used "genius" dozens and dozens of time across his published work (particularly those works dealing with psychology, teaching, and ethics), his unpublished manuscripts, and his lectures.

[21] Craig Wright, *The Hidden Habits of Genius: Beyond Talent, IQ, and Grit—Unlocking the Secrets of Greatness* (New York: Dey Street, 2020), 5. Wright quoted Kant's *Critique of Pure Reason*. It is worth noting that Wright adds on to a Jamesian account of genius by requiring genius not only to produce "original works or insights" but also to change the world across cultures and time. Wright summarized: "In brief, the greatest genius produces the greatest impact on the greatest number of people over the longest period of time" (6). I find this problematic for several reasons that include: (a) Given this definition, people who lived a very long time ago, other things equal, are much more likely to meet this definition's criteria for genius status—but it seems counterintuitive, at least to me, to conclude that there must have been many more geniuses long ago than there have been since; (b) Nazi leaders who created the "Final Solution" to the "Jewish Question" no doubt had and still have a massive impact on huge numbers of people in huge numbers of ways—but, again, it seems counterintuitive to conclude that the extent of their impact is one key measure of their genius; and (c) while it sounds wholly quantitative to talk about "greatest impact" and "greatest number" of people and "longest" period of time, there is no way to quantify adequately any of these changing metrics, particularly if one considers indirect as well as direct impacts.

[22] Wright, *The Hidden Habits of Genius*, 69.

What is the work of this "faculty of perceiving in unhabitual ways," of seeing what previously was missed? (It is interesting here to compare James's characterization of genius as seeing in unhabitual ways with both his claim that philosophy is "the habit of always seeing an alternative" (EP, 4) and his championing of conceptual flexibility.)[23] James described it as the power of highly sustained, highly focused and concentrated *attention*, active *imagination*, and novel *association*. The link between will and attention is especially crucial here: *"The essential achievement of the will, in short, when it is most 'voluntary' is to ATTEND to a difficult object and hold it fast before the mind. The so-doing is the fiat,"* a resolve with contemplated motor consequences (PP, 1166; PBC, 386). He also discussed correlations and possible links between genius and assorted psychological problems and pathologies, as well as various social conditions.

In this context, Eduardo Mendieta has helpfully called attention to the ways in which James viewed war as a failure of imagination and also viewed the human inability to liberate itself from war as a failure of both imagination and will. James wrote: "If we speak of *the fear of emancipation from the fear regime*, we put the militarist attitude into a single phrase: fear regarding ourselves now taking the place of the ancient fear of the enemy" (ERM, 168). And Mendieta commented: "Those who worship the gods of war preserved a religion that is the continuation of human immaturity, subordination, and moral tutelage. The unwillingness to face this fear of ourselves free from the disciplining and commanding fear of the enemy is in fact an unwillingness to engage our moral and aesthetic imaginations."[24] It is a failure to perceive and to act in unhabitual ways.

It is worth pointing out here that although we may say that someone— Hypatia, Aristotle, Leonardo, Mozart, Marie Curie, Einstein, Picasso, Miles Davis, Fei-Fei Li—*is a genius*, to be a genius is to be a genius *in some particular area or activity rather than others*, because of the need for attention and

---

[23] Peter Hare, "Deep Conceptual Play in William James," in *Pragmatism with Purpose: Selected Writings*, edited by Joseph Palencik, Douglas R. Anderson, and Steven A. Miller (New York: Fordham University Press, 2015), 236.

[24] Eduardo Mendieta, "Transcending the 'Gory Cradle of Humanity': War, Loyalty, and Civic Action in Royce and James," in *Pragmatism, Nation, and Race: Community in the Age of Empire*, edited by Chad Kautzer and Eduardo Mendieta (Bloomington: Indiana University Press, 2009), 235. Giles Gunn has stressed that, as James was one of the first modern intellectuals to recognize, there is space for this imagination because "even where ideology is omnipresent, it need not be construed as necessarily omnipotent." Giles Gunn, "Beyond Transcendence or Beyond Ideology? American Cultural Criticism and William James," in *Thinking Across the American Grain: Ideology, Intellect, and the New Pragmatism* (Chicago: University of Chicago Press, 1992), 35.

focus. A genius painter is not typically also a genius mathematician. A genius scientist is not usually also a genius soccer goalie. And a genius musician is not typically a genius brain surgeon or even a genius at every commonplace daily task.

If genius is the faculty of perceiving in an unhabitual way, then two additional points must be stressed or added to thicken this idea. First, as James made clear from the *Principles of Psychology* to *Some Problems of Philosophy*, perception and conception are intermixed, made of the same sort of stuff, irreducibly intermingled. There are no bare sensations, no bare perceptions, no bare conceptions—these notions are all abstractions. And so this means that if genius is the faculty of perceiving in an unhabitual way, then wrapped up and immersed in this is the faculty of conceiving in an unhabitual way. Genius is the habit of *experiencing* in an unhabitual way—a way different from our old-fogey responses and a way different from the certain blindness that human beings habitually have to their own habits of perception and conception and affect.

Second, even if sensation, perception, conception, imagination, desire and satisfaction, memory, and temperament are all rolled up together in unhabitual experience, genius requires something more. It requires action— and James did believe in a close connection between attention and will.[25] Consider a scientist who *only imagines* a whole new process for drugs to deliver protection against pandemic viruses, musicians who *merely hear in their heads* new atonal or polytonal pieces, or a high jumper who *idly conceives* of a new way to leap over the bar. In all these kinds of cases, genius involves something more: creating and testing the new drug or at least communicating the idea to others who can follow up; writing a score or performing or recording or, again, communicating the new music to others who may do these things; and actually trying the new jumping technique or coaching others or providing instruction in how to do it. A genius minus some form of action and world change is simply a dreamer. James described life as a "bundle of habits" and, in this context, genius is the habit of partial unbundling and rebundling sometimes. Genius is a faculty of transforming the world in an unhabitual way.

---

[25] In addition to the chapters on attention and will in *The Principles of Psychology*, see, for example, Gerald E. Myers. *William James: His Life and Thought* (New Haven, CT: Yale University Press, 1986), 198–209.

This action requires energy. Referring to the "amount of energy available for running one's mental and moral operations," James claimed that raising one's level of energy is "the most important thing that can happen" to a person (ERM, 130). He observed: "Compared with what we ought to be, we are only half-awake. Our fires are damped, our drafts are checked. We are making use of only a small part of our possible mental and physical resources" (ERM, 131). But sometimes "excitements, ideas, and efforts" (ERM, 132) stimulate us to tap into the fuller and deeper reserves of our energies. The practical demand, then, is to make habitual our greater energetic responses, to make our "normal tasks and stimulations"—our interests, ideas, and actions—capable of habitually calling forth our highest levels of energy and our greatest plastic powers. Here genius is not simply the ability to perceive in unhabitual ways. It is also the ability to unlock one's greatest energies in the active and embodied service and advance of unhabitual perception.

Here a long-standing practical question emerges: If genius is an act or a habit of transforming the world in an unhabitual way, is it inborn, an innate or natural ability, or is it made, a product of education and effort? Is it possible to produce a society with lots of members who perceive and think and act in unhabitual ways—a flexible and genius society—or is genius restricted to rare individuals who appear as mysteries and surprises? The outlines of a pragmatic response to this either/or question are likely clear in advance: Genius is the result of both inward and outward factors, both those causes that James called, respectively, "brain-born" and those he characterized as environmental in "The Moral Philosopher and the Moral Life." Genius is the result of both nature and nurture.

The important point here is not simply that there are two separate kinds of causes of genius—two instead of one or the other. Rather, the crucial point is that the very presupposition that there is a sharp separation between, say, our genes and our brains, or our pineal glands and our environmental influences, is itself mistaken. So too is the separation of an individual organism from its environment, both natural and cultural, and the assignment of habit's location to the organism alone. A habit belongs no more to an individual organism than it does to an environment. As John Dewey put it, all habits require "the cooperation of organism and environment"; habits "are things done by the environment by means of organic structures or acquired dispositions."[26] Technological developments have allowed scientists

---

[26] Dewey, *Human Nature and Conduct,* 15.

to confirm this view. Fueled by fMRI brain scan technology, this has produced what Wendy Wood has called a "habits renaissance." She explained:

> [Neuroscientists] started to notice that activity in brain regions shifted as people repeatedly performed a task and started responding more automatically.
>
> Technically speaking, when people initially learned a task, their brains showed marked activity in areas involved in decision-making and executive control (prefrontal and hippocampal regions). With repetition, brain activity increased in other neural areas (the putamen and basal ganglia), as if new areas of the new brain got involved with repeated actions. . . . Our minds do not just consciously make initial decisions; they also respond repeatedly through habit.

"Your actions, Wood explained, "have rewired your brain."[27] This rewiring by means of habituation may save energy and be highly efficient. As such, it may contribute to individual and societal flourishing. But it may have the opposite effect. Bessel Van Der Kolk pointed this out in his aptly titled *The Body Keeps the Score*. Discussing "facing trauma" and feelings of fear and damage "beyond redemption," he wrote:

> While we all want to move beyond trauma, the part of our brain that is devoted to ensuring our survival (deep below our rational brain) is not very good at denial. Long after a traumatic experience is over, it may be reactivated at the slightest hint of danger and mobilize disturbed brain circuits and secrete massive amounts of stress hormones. This precipitates unpleasant emotions, intense physical sensations, and impulsive and aggressive action. These posttraumatic reactions feel incomprehensible and overwhelming.

He added that when people are compulsively pulled back into the past, "they suffer from a failure of imagination, a loss of mental flexibility."[28]

---

[27] Wood, *Good Habits, Bad Habits*, 38–39, 59.

[28] Bessel Van Der Kolk, *The Body Keeps the Score* (New York: Penguin Books, 2014), 2, 17. Following James, he states: "The mind is a mosaic" (282). Moreover, in a chapter titled "Language: Miracle and Tyranny," the author stresses another Jamesian theme: "We can get past the slipperiness of words by engaging the self-observing body-based self system, which speaks through sensations, tone of voice, and body tensions" (240).

More generally, habitual actions "rewire" and create changes in one's whole body and not simply the brain. There are multiple and reciprocally constitutive relations among habits, thoughts, emotions, actions and experiences of actions, and the acting body's physiology (including but not limited to neurophysiology). Selves, their actions, and their bodies and minds in/through/with their natural and cultural environments are habits, processes and sites of habituation. James thus asserted that mental states, for example, lead to deliberate actions but "also changes in the caliber of blood-vessels, or alteration in the heart-beats, or processes more subtle still, in glands and viscera . . . no mental modification ever occurs which is not accompanied by a bodily change" (PP, 18). He repeated this view in *Talks to Teachers*:

> The fact is that there is no sort of consciousness whatever, be it sensation, feeling, or idea, which does not directly and of itself tend to discharge into some motor effect. The motor effect need not always be an outward stroke of behavior. It may be only an alteration of the heart-beats or breathing, or a modification in the distribution of blood, such as blushing or turning pale; or else a secretion of tears, or what not. But in any case, it is there in some shape when any consciousness is there. (TT, 102)

Noting that other philosophers often downplay or omit physiology in their accounts of habit "even when habit is appreciated as a bodily phenomenon," Shannon Sullivan has explained this Jamesian point in detail and with clarity:

> The relationship between habit and physiology is much more than metaphorical, however. On my view, physiological functions are habits, not just similar to them, and a person can have a distinctive character based on the kinds of physiological habits that help compose her. The central point of comparison is that both habit and physiology are transactional; they are constituted in and through a dynamic relationship with their environment. . . . The cyclical relationship between physiological function and habit and their environments demonstrates their plasticity, which means that function and habit are simultaneously durable and corrigible. . . . A live organism only stays alive by means of an active relationship with its environment: when environments change or conflict with each other, then the

habits—the selves—built in transaction with them are disrupted and must change too.[29]

The workings of our genes themselves, contemporary science has found, are impacted by our environments, and they have varying effects depending on those environments. This means genes and environments work irreducibly in interacting, integrated ways. Both are malleable in part and to a degree; both matter and work only with each other. The Dalai Lama summarized this succinctly in his foreword to *Train Your Mind, Change Your Brain: How a New Science Reveals Our Extraordinary Potential to Transform Ourselves.* Counter to the dogmatic doctrine of the unchanging human brain, he wrote:

> Buddhist practitioners familiar with the workings of the mind have long been aware that it can be transformed through training. What is exciting and new is that scientists have now shown that such mental training can also change the *brain*. Related to this is evidence that the brain adapts or expands in response to repeated patterns of activity, so that in a real sense the brain we develop reflects the life we lead. This has far-reaching implications for the effects of habitual behavior in our lives, especially the positive potential of discipline and spiritual practice. Evidence that powerful sections of the brain, such as the visual cortex, can adapt their function in response to circumstances reveals an astonishing malleability unforeseen by earlier, more mechanistic interpretations of the brain's workings.[30]

This book's author, Sharon Begley, both stressed the fact *that* the brain is malleable and focused on *how* this change occurs. She explained:

> The revolution in our understanding of the brain's capacity to change well into adulthood does not end with the fact that the brain can and does change.
>   Equally revolutionary is the discovery of how the brain changes. The actions we take can literally expand or contract different regions of the brain, pour more juice into quiet circuits and damp down activity in

---

[29] Sullivan, *The Physiology of Sexist and Racist Oppression*, 11, 12, 13. Sullivan's chapters "The Hips," "The Gut," "The Epigenome," and "The Stomach and the Heart" detail ways in which habits "rewire" that extend far beyond the neurological.

[30] The Dalai Lama, "Foreword," in Sharon Begley, *Train Your Mind, Change Your Brain: How a New Science Reveals Our Extraordinary Potential to Transform Ourselves* (New York: Ballantine Books, 2007), viii.

buzzing ones. The brain devotes more cortical real estate to functions its owner uses more frequently and shrinks the space devoted to actions rarely performed. . . . Most of this happens because of what we do and what we experience in the outside world. . . . But there are also hints that mind-sculpting can occur with

no input from the outside world. That is, the brain can change as a result of the thoughts we have thought.

Echoing James in many ways—though she spoke of "older adults" rather than "old fogeys" and of "new challenges" rather than "keep[ing] the faculty of effort alive in you by a little gratuitous exercise every day"—she concluded:

Older adults are frequently told that, to keep their minds sharp, they need to stimulate it with activities such as crossword puzzles and reading. But activities done repeatedly become second nature, demanding less attention than new skills do. The result is a brain that gets fewer and fewer chances to keep its acetylcholine system tuned up. The result of an inability to pay attention which is not uncommon in many older adults, is trouble remembering new information and experiences. And because of the centrality of attention to neuroplasticity, a brain that cannot pay attention is a brain that cannot tap into the power of neuroplasticity. Given this, rather than engaging in activities you are already good at in order to keep an aging brain in shape, it makes much more sense scientifically to take up new challenges.[31]

In his *Keep Sharp: Build a Better Brain at Any Age*, Sanjay Gupta stressed this point about our brains and neurogenesis and, like Begley, referred to James:

We used to believe that we were born with a finite number of neurons for life. . . . Now we know differently. The brain remains plastic throughout life and can rewrite itself in response to your experiences. It can also generate new brain cells under the right circumstances. . . . This has led to the burgeoning new field of neuroplasticity—the ability of the brain to form and reorganize synaptic connections. The brain's plasticity was first documented more than 100 years ago in William James's 1890 book *The Principles of Psychology*. . . . The brain constantly and dynamically shapes

---

[31] Begley, *Train Your Mind, Change Your Brain*, 8–9, 249.

and reshapes itself in response to experiences, learning, or even an injury. What's more, what you choose to focus your attention on rewires the brain from a structural and functional perspective.[32]

As James earlier put it, even more succinctly, "everything here is plastic." This does not mean that every individual has the capacity at birth to be or to do literally anything or everything. Neuroplasticity or physiological flexibility more generally is not infinite. However, it does mean that our capacities are not fixed and that they simply are what they are at birth independent of the resources available (or unavailable) for their development and the substantial amounts of time, attention, and effort that this development requires.

This reinforces James's initial claims that habits result from action and education rather than instinct or innate nature. Accordingly, an individual's habits and character—the interpenetration of habits—are expressions of a society's educational practices, including (but far more than) formal schooling.[33] As creatures of habit, individuals are sites of societal habit-building processes, whether the aims and values embedded in these processes are explicit and consciously endorsed or implicit and unconsciously enacted.

To note this is to recognize not simply that individuals and their habits are plastic but also to realize that social associations and cultures also are plastic and that they are forces of both habituation and its results. From a theoretical perspective, this is important because it necessitates revision of one strand of James's initial main theses about habit—his claim that habit is society's "most precious conservative agent." James, remember, held that habits are conservative in two senses: they conserve energy, and they sustain the societal status quo. But the second strand of this claim, that habits conserve a culture's features and its status quo, simply is not a necessary, fixed truth about habits and societies, all habits and all societies. At best, James's claim is an overgeneralization—a description true in some cases but overextended in application to all cases—and a sober recognition of the entrenched powers of the status quo. As John Lachs has recognized, "the guardians of the status quo do not welcome the consideration of possibilities because they make their living from existing arrangements":

---

[32] Sanjay Gupta, *Keep Sharp: Build a Better Brain at Any Age* (New York: Simon and Schuster, 2021), 86–87.
[33] Dewey, *Human Nature and Conduct*, 29.

Institutions resist change even more mightily: they are conservative systems interested in safeguarding the actual, of which they are salient parts.

Everything in the world seems to want to hold on to existence, which can be accomplished only by rejecting all other possibilities. Change is death to what exists now.[34]

And thus in some societies—perhaps even most societies—habit has been or continues to be a conservative agent. But whether this is the case in a particular society depends on different, dynamic particulars. It is a matter of histories of habit formation; it is not a feature of a supposed essence of all habit. If one treats societies with the same pluralism that James recognized so fully among individuals, then it has to be allowed that habit can play a liberal, liberating, dynamic role rather than simply a conservative one. It can be a force of growth and liberation and not only a force of stagnation and oppression.

As a result, to successfully provide individuals (creatures of habit) with flexible, flourishing, useful habits that support and sustain their genius in changing conditions, societies (also creatures of habit) must themselves be flexible in their associations, practices, institutions, and meanings. If human creatures of habit are to manifest genius—flexibility and the capacity for living in previously unhabitual ways—then the social institutions and conditions that educate them also must prize genius and sustain the conditions needed for its presence. I take John Dewey to have made this point forcefully:

Even liberal thinkers have treated habit as essentially, not because of the character of existing customs, conservative. In fact, only in a society dominated by modes of belief and admiration fixed by past custom is habit any more conservative than it is progressive. It all depends on its quality. Habit is an ability, an art, formed through past experience. But whether an ability is limited to repetition of past acts adapted to past conditions or is available for new emergencies depends wholly upon what kind of habit exists. . . . We are confronted with two kinds of habit, intelligent and routine. All life has its élan, but only the prevalence of dead habits deflects life into mere élan. . . . A spiritual life which is nothing but a blind urge separated from

[34] John Lachs, "Learning About Possibility," in *Freedom and Limits*, edited by Patrick Shade (New York: Fordham University Press, 2014), 427.

thought . . . is likely to have the attributes of the Devil in spite of its being ennobled by the name of God.[35]

To the extent that habit is a central fact about individuals, the production or education of habits is a central fact about societies. An individual's acquisition of habits is not a merely individual activity.[36] Individual habits of genius and the great actions that issue from them are made possible when, and only to the extent that, societies take flexible, intelligent habits (rather than thoughtless routine) as ideals and then create and recreate the means necessary for the progressive realization of these ideals. Genius in the educated requires genius in the educators. It is not a matter of solely individual self-help or self-betterment or making positive changes in oneself. It is a matter of social action and reconstruction as social conditions change—action that will be opposed by many who are empowered and profit from the status quo and its ways of excluding others from needed resources, and routine habits. (There are powerful cultural forces that explain why traditional lists of geniuses have been overwhelmingly populated by unimpoverished white males.) The pragmatic or practical consequence of James's psychology and his pluralism is a progressive, intelligent social agenda—an agenda that so far, and still, is very distant and anything but a cultural habit.

To understand habit, including the habits of healthy-mindedness, morbid-mindedness, and genius, in this way is to understand the notion of the compounding or compenetration of consciousness less (or at least potentially less) in terms of unseen realities and more in terms of customs—customs as societal habits both compounded and, in turn, compounding. It is to understand any compounding of consciousness not as an *ontological* possibility but, instead, as an *experiential and social* fact—whenever and wherever it is a fact. Moreover, it is to recognize that the whole complex of issues here is not simply one of "great men and their environments." It is, at least as much, one of great environments and their people—but also far-from-great sexist, racist, class-divided, and unjust environments.[37] The fact that people's habits

---

[35] Dewey, *Human Nature and Conduct*, 48, 51, 53. In addition, this passage makes clear that Dewey did not share the same enthusiasm that James, particularly in *A Pluralistic Universe*, had for the philosophy of Henri Bergson.

[36] "Though education and habituation may have individuals as their focus, they do not occur in private isolation," Patrick Shade observed in *Habits of Hope: A Pragmatic Theory* (Nashville, TN: Vanderbilt University Press, 2001), 108.

[37] Erin Tarver partly focused on this point in the context of gender and subjectivity in her "Lady Pragmatism and the Great Man," in *Feminist Interpretations of William James*, edited by Erin C. Tarver and Shannon Sullivan (University Park: Penn State University Press, 2015), 98–117.

arise from education rather than instinct (as James realized) and the fact that this education is a social affair (again, as James realized) stand against James's judgment in his 1880 "Great Men and Their Environment" that "the causes of production of great men lie in a sphere wholly inaccessible to the social philosopher. He must simply accept geniuses as data, just as Darwin accepts his spontaneous variations" (WB, 170)

James was right that social evolution results from the interactions of individuals and social environments: "Both factors are essential to change. The community stagnates without the impulse of the individual. The impulse dies away without the sympathy of the community" (WB, 174). However, precisely because habits of genius are the work of a social environment's educational forces, genius is not simply data to accept and dumbly admire. Rather, it is a reality with causes that can be investigated and subsequently more fully controlled. The issue is not *whether* "great men" or individuals more generally have the "power of initiative" but *how*—by what means—it is that they come to have this power and live in conditions in which it can be developed and exercised.

James claimed that "if anything is humanly certain it is that the great man's society, properly so called, does *not* make him before he can remake it" (WB, 176). But this cannot be true—much less certain—unless one believes that human greatness is *wholly* a result of instinct rather than education or unless one holds that *only* forces inside the individual are operative. Here as in all his writings, James wanted possibilities, indeterminism, unfinishedness but with intimacy, initiatives, novelties, activities, and "spontaneous upsettings" (with a rather patrician tone). He wanted the "Importance of Individuals" (WB, 190–195):

> It is one of the tritest truisms that human intelligences of a simple order are very literal. They are slaves of habit, doing what they have been taught without variation; dry, prosaic, and matter-of-fact in their remarks; devoid of humor, except of the coarse physical kind which rejoices in a practical joke; taking the world for granted; and possessing in their faithfulness and honesty the single gift by which they are sometimes able to warm us into admiration. . . . But turn to the highest order of minds, and what a change! Instead of thoughts of concrete things patiently following one another in a beaten track of habitual suggestion, we have the most abrupt cross-cuts and transitions from one idea to another, the most rarefied abstractions and discriminations, the most unheard-of combinations of elements, the

subtlest associations of analogy; in a word, we seem suddenly introduced into a seething caldron of ideas, where everything is fizzling and bobbing about in a state of bewildering activity, where partnerships can be joined or loosened in an instant, treadmill routine is unknown, and the unexpected seems the only law. (WB, 184–185)

Now, the fact that fizzling idiosyncrasy, bobbing spontaneity, bewildering creativity, and genius-level unhabitual perception exist is not in question. Nor is the fact that they are the results of education rather than instinct alone. Acceptance of these facts does not entail some form of evolutionary, social, or cultural determinism, any more than their denial entails some type of genetic or biological determinism (or, for that matter, belief in some sort of magical, mysterious realm of individual existence entirely independent and untouched by all other forces and conditions).

The causes of human genius and human flourishing are not wholly inaccessible. As Wood pointed out, these causes depend on three general factors: surroundings and context, repetition, and reward—bigger and better rewards than we otherwise would experience.[38] In a complementary analysis, before concluding that small changes compound in big ways, Clear argued that in order to create a new habit, four imperatives must be observed: make it obvious, make it attractive, make it easy, and, make it satisfying.[39] The causes of genius can be subjected to intelligent inquiry. We can investigate whether geniuses are stifled by play-free rote learning and teaching driven by standardized tests. We can figure out the impact of repetitive and exhausting work routines on creativity. We can study the ways communication technologies and social pressures impact the capacity for sustained attention. It is possible to gather evidence on the consequences of crushing forms of dehumanization, immiseration, insecurity, war, and environmental destruction on commitment to ideals, perseverance, and self-trust. We can examine whether learning more than one language, reading across times and places, experiencing cultures other than one's own, and engagement with the arts and sciences expands imagination and attunement to the novel and unhabitual.

The annual *World Happiness Report* is an example of in-depth, data-driven, and intelligent inquiry directed at just these kinds of issues—at the

---

[38] Wood, *Good Habits, Bad Habits*, 83–158.
[39] Clear, *Atomic Habits*, chaps. 4–17.

extent to, and ways in which, human genius, health, and flourishing depend on social environments marked by dependability and security, freedom, generosity, social and institutional trust, meaningful social connections, relative equality of life quality, and sustainable and sustaining natural environments.[40] The upshot is clear: Habits of genius depend upon cultural and natural conditions that enable their development and expression. The ability to perceive in unhabitual ways results in very large part from habitual, customary, institutionalized societal practices of education driven by commitment to genius and the resources it requires.

William James wrote that we should make our useful actions matters of habit as much and as soon as possible. Anything less, he warned, consigns us to a hell to be endured in this life and in this world. For individuals to accomplish this in any widespread way, social groups in turn must ensure that useful ideals, actions, and organizations are matters of social habit and social reality as much and as soon as possible.

Societies, at least as much as individuals, cannot afford to become old fogeys. Indeed, without ongoing hard work, even a pluralistic universe readily becomes a static, stuck, old-fogey universe. From a structural and functional perspective, this is how societies can rewire themselves and their pathways. This possibility is the basis for social meliorism. For individual genius to flourish in an ever-changing world, social groups—from families to neighborhoods to companies to nations—must perceive, educate, and act in part in *radically unhabitual* ways. Societies must, as James put it, seize the very first possible opportunity to act on this resolution and every day keep alive the capacity for this effort.

Anything less would not be pragmatic.

---

[40] The 2020 World Happiness Report: https://worldhappiness.report/ed/2020/. The COVID-focused 2021 report: https://worldhappiness.report/ed/2021/. The 2022 report: https://worldhappiness.report/ed/2022/. The World Happiness Report is a publication of the United Nations' Sustainable Development Solutions Network and is written by a group of independent experts.

3

More Inclusive Ideals

Ethical Lives After Old-Fashioned Moral Philosophy

On the whole, then, we must conclude that no philosophy of ethics
is possible in the old-fashioned absolute sense of the term. . . . [A
philosopher's] books upon ethics, therefore, so far as they truly
touch the moral life, must more and more ally themselves with a
literature which is confessedly tentative and suggestive rather than
dogmatic. . . . Treated in this way ethical treatises may be voluminous and luminous as well; but they never can be *final*, except in
their abstractest and vaguest features; and they must more and more
abandon the old-fashioned, clear-cut and would-be "scientific"
form. (WB, 158)[1]

1. James as Ethical Philosopher

What would it mean to flat-out abandon old-fashioned ethics? What would
this mean for moral philosophy? More important, what would it mean for
moral life?

My response to these questions employs a two-part strategy. First, I seek to
show that the core of the philosophy of William James is his ethics—his vision
of the moral life (or, better, multiple moral lives and moral societies). On my
account, James's far more familiar epistemology (his pragmatic method and
pragmatic theory of truth) and his well-known ontological commitments
(his radical empiricism, his "stream of experience" psychology, his view of
the many-and-the-one, and his embrace of a pluralistic universe) are irreducibly normative endeavors that both support this ethics and constitute

---

[1] Jessica Wahman provided insightful comments on an earlier draft of this chapter.

No Professor's Lectures Can Save Us. John J. Stuhr, Oxford University Press. © Oxford University Press 2023.
DOI: 10.1093/oso/9780197664629.003.0004

crucial parts and consequences of it.[2] Regardless of any of the very many (and brilliantly shifting) names he applied to his own thought—pragmatism, humanism, radical empiricism, neutral monism, pantheistic spiritualism, noetic pluralism—this thought is first and last an ethics. James himself is first and last an ethical thinker.

Persons primarily interested in epistemological and metaphysical issues— what is sometimes thought of as "first" philosophy—do not generally or commonly interpret James's philosophy in this way, if they engage James's thought at all. This is unfortunate, both because there is great value in crit- ically viewing James's philosophy as irreducibly an ethical philosophy and because there are many resources in his particular ethics for individual and social life in a changing world of diverse people. In order to make use of these resources, it is crucial to contrast James's understanding of philosophy with contemporary professional philosophy and, even more, it is vital to contrast James's ethical vision with traditional moral philosophy and the aims and methods of traditional moral philosophers. The second part of my strategy in this chapter is to draw out these contrasts and to develop their practical import.

Although this vision of James's philosophy differs from that of many scholars, it assuredly is not without precedent. Indeed, I believe that many of James's own contemporaries—including thinkers as different as George Santayana, Josiah Royce, and John Dewey—viewed James's philosophy as centrally and consistently focused on ethical issues.[3] Indeed, Dewey called James "everywhere and always the moralist." Years later, John J. McDermott, the leading James scholar of the second half of the 20th century, insight- fully and movingly captured this aspect of James's thought, temperament,

---

[2] For example, a current count of scholarly articles included in major humanities databases reveals roughly five times more publications about James's pragmatic theory of truth than his ethics; roughly four times more about his psychology than his ethics; and slightly more than four times more con- cerning his account of religious experience and faith than his ethics. Here, and throughout this chapter, I follow James in using "ethics" and "morals" interchangeably.

[3] As examples, see the following: George Santayana, "William James," in *Character and Opinion in the United States* (New York: W. W. Norton, 1921); George Santayana, "The Genteel Tradition in American Philosophy," in *The Genteel Tradition: Nine Essays by George Santayana*, edited by D. L. Wilson (Cambridge, MA: Harvard University Press, 1967 [1921]); Josiah Royce, "William James and the Philosophy of Life," in *William James and Other Essays on the Philosophy of Life*, ed- ited by J. J. McDermott (New York: Literary Licensing, 2014 [1911]); Josiah Royce, *The Sources of Religious Insight* (Washington, DC: Catholic University of America Press, 2001 [1912]); Josiah Royce, *The Problem of Christianity* (Washington, DC: Catholic University of America Press, 2001 [1913]); John Dewey, "William James," *Journal of Philosophy, Psychology and Scientific Methods* 7, no. 19 (1910): 505–508; John Dewey, "The Development of American Philosophy," in *Philosophy and Civilization* (New York: Capricorn Books, 1963 [1931]).

and vision across many of his essays and books.[4] Two more recent authors also have taken up this perspective on James's ethics in sustained ways that partly overlap (and partly don't)—Sarin Marchetti's *Ethics and Philosophical Critique in William James*[5] and Trygve Throntveit's *William James and the Quest for an Ethical Republic*.[6] I hope to engage many of their ideas as I proceed.[7]

2. Professional Philosophy vs. Philosophy as Personal Vision

I recognize that my claim that ethics is the center or core of James's philosophy, or any philosophy, could seem absurd at the outset to many readers—especially readers who view philosophy as an academic field of study (with many subfields that often have little connection to ethics understood as just one more subfield) populated by professional researchers, teachers, and their students. On this view, philosophy, like art history, chemistry, classics, comparative literature, mathematics, psychology, and so many other long-established, newer, and just emerging fields, is a body of knowledge with familiar if not fully fixed subdivisions: multiple problem areas that include,

---

[4] Many of the James-focused and James-inspired essays in John J. McDermott's *The Culture of Experience* (1976) and *Streams of Experience* (1986) have been collected in *The Drama of Possibility: Experience as Philosophy of Culture*, edited by D. Anderson (New York: Fordham University Press, 2007).

[5] Sarin Marchetti, *Ethics and Philosophical Critique in William James* (New York: Palgrave Macmillan, 2015). Subsequent references to this book appear in this chapter's text and are abbreviated EPC followed by the relevant page number.

[6] Trygve Throntveit, *William James and the Quest for an Ethical Republic* (New York: Palgrave Macmillan, 2014). Subsequent references to this book appear in this chapter's text and are abbreviated QER followed by the relevant page number. While the title of this book may suggest that it concerns only or primarily James's ethical theory, it ranges across almost all of James's work. Indeed, perhaps Throntveit's greatest strength is his careful, informed, and well-written historical and philosophical interweaving of James's pragmatism, radical empiricism, psychology, and politics with his ethics.

[7] In doing so, in addition to the first two chapters of this book, my own prior work on James and ethics provides background context. For example, see the following: "Socrates and Radical Empiricism" and "Persons, Pluralism, and Death," in *Genealogical Pragmatism: Philosophy, Experience and Community* (Albany: State University of New York Press, 1997); "Pragmatism, Pluralism, and the Future of Philosophy: Farewell to an Idea," in *Pragmatism, Postmodernism, and the Future of Philosophy* (New York: Routledge, 2003); "Looking Toward Last Things: James's Pragmatism Beyond Its First Century," in *100 Years of Pragmatism: William James's Revolutionary Philosophy*, edited by John J. Stuhr (Bloomington: Indiana University Press, 2010); "Chance Vistas and Sincerity in the Cosmic Labyrinth," "Philosophies as Fashions," and "Absurd Pragmatism," in *Philosophical Fashions: Pluralism, Democracy, Relativism, and the Absurd* (Bloomington: Indiana University Press, 2016); and "Redeeming the Wild Universe: William James's Will to Believe," in *Understanding James, Understanding Modernism*, edited by David Evans (London: Bloomsbury, 2017).

for example, metaphysics, epistemology, logic, ethics and politics, and aes-
thetics; many historical divisions that include, for example, ancient Greek
philosophy, medieval Arabic philosophy, early modern European thought,
and twentieth-century Anglo-American philosophy; and many different lin-
eages and methodological commitments including, for example once again,
dialectical materialism, critical race theory, phenomenology, pragmatism,
feminist philosophies, and analytical philosophy. This body of knowledge or
discipline is part of a social practice or disciplining activity or profession of
philosophy. Like all professions, it is marked by distinctive knowledge and
expertise, educational preparation, and institutions that deliver, judge, cer-
tify, and limit possession of this knowledge and, thus, grant and maintain
membership in this profession. Understood this way, a person who has received a Ph.D. in philosophy from an accredited institution of higher education, published articles in specific journals and books with specific presses,
and held membership in particular scholarly societies is, for better or worse,
a *professional* philosopher. In contrast, the following are not philosophers
in this philosophy-as-profession sense: an inebriated dive bar patron who
holds forth about "my life's philosophy"; a political leader who proclaims an
America First "philosophy"; a Wall Street MBA who spends their spare time
reading Ayn Rand books; a dedicated vegan who devours Peter Singer's work
during lunch breaks in the park; or a dedicated hermit with a mail-order
diploma in universal metaphysics and an attic with fourteen handwritten
volumes (unread by anyone else) of a planned fifty-volume work on life and
the afterlife in the cosmos. Of course, there are gray areas between these sorts
of more clear-cut cases.

Now, among other things, I am a philosopher in this professional sense.
So too are some of the people who reviewed this book and guided it to publication. So too, it seems likely (if sadly), are most of its readers. Moreover,
William James also was a professional philosopher. James did not have a
Ph.D. in philosophy (or any other discipline)—his only educational degree
was an M.D. from Harvard—but his professional philosophy credentials
were extensive: He was, finally, a professor of philosophy at Harvard; he
supervised undergraduate and graduate students there; he published articles
and books in professional philosophy outlets; and he even was, if reluctantly,
an early president of the American Philosophical Association. Nonetheless,
James greatly deplored philosophy as a profession—something no doubt
easier for him to do from *within* the comforts and prestige of his professional position. This is *not* how he understood philosophy—philosophy that

matters. It is not how he *wanted* to understand philosophy. Moreover, this view of philosophy as a profession of experts in a particular body of knowledge runs against the whole spirit and temperament of James's philosophy.

Indeed, this fact pervades James's writings as a whole. It is part of the color, tone, and feel of his writing. It is perhaps most explicit in his 1903 *Harvard Monthly* essay "The Ph.D. Octopus." This essay, one part criticism and one part proposal for change, was outwardly motivated by the opening observation and charge that "the love of truth" possessed by college and university faculty "can be made still greater by adventitious rewards":

> America is thus as a nation rapidly drifting towards a state of things in which no man of science or letters will be accounted respectable unless some kind of badge or diploma is stamped upon him, and in which bare personality will be a mark of outcast estate. It seems to me high time to rouse ourselves to consciousness, and to cast a critical eye upon this decidedly grotesque tendency. Other nations suffer from the Mandarin disease. Are we doomed to suffer like the rest? (ECR, 74)

Is individuality in America, he added, "going to count for nothing unless stamped and licensed and authenticated by some title-giving machine?" This "Mandarin disease" or "Doctor Monopoly," James (again, without a Ph.D.) maintained, creates many unintended "evils." He claimed that it interferes "with the free development of talent," obstructs supply and demand in the teaching profession, fosters "academic snobbery by the prestige of certain privileged institutions," transfers "accredited value" from ability and achievement to "an outward badge," diverts student attention from truth to exams, and blights hopes and promotes invidious sentiments (ECR, 75–76, 344). To guard against promoting "officialism and snobbery and insincerity," James argued (in a way that may sound paradoxical today) that universities should lower their (professional) standards for both students and faculty and pay more attention to personal recommendations and evidence of genuine individuality than to "extraneous tests" and "bread-winning degrees."

More than a century later, it is clear that this is a war that James completely lost, to the extent that he did more than protest in writing against it. His complaint and criticism largely did not register. They were not considered seriously. They surely were not embedded in the institutional structures of higher education. In short, his proposals were not enacted (and if they had been enacted it is far from clear they would have proven the least bit effective). Today the American university is not merely in the grip of the Ph.D. octopus. The American university now *is* the Ph.D. octopus. And its departments of philosophy would not hire, much less tenure, a Socrates, an Emerson, a Whitman, or a James.[8]

The point here is not merely historical. It is principally methodological. To the extent that professional philosophers seek to understand James's philosophy, they must begin by recognizing that his view of philosophy—including his view of his own work—stands outside of, and in opposition to, much of their professional theories and practices. James's philosophy cannot be well grasped in the terms and categories of a profession it did not want to enter, the profession's badges that it did not seek to earn or want to wear, or the problems and puzzles it did not take up, much less care to solve. James simply did not think of philosophy as a whole in professional terms—except to criticize what the Ph.D. octopus profession counted narrowly as professional. And so he also did not think of ethics in professional terms—did not think of "theoretical ethics" or "meta-ethics" or "applied ethics" as simply some of many professional subfields of some professional philosophy.

3. Ethics as Personal

Instead, James showed us how to think of philosophy, including his own writings, in terms that are irreducibly *ethical*—terms that are irreducibly *personal* and *practical.*

What does this mean?

First, for James, to view *ethics as personal* is to view values as *relational*, to understand them as *personal relations*. It is to believe that values only exist *in relation to* the demands, desires, interests, and needs of some actual person or persons.[9] James put this clearly in "The Moral Philosopher and the Moral Life," claiming that goods and evils and other values simply do not exist independent of, or unrelated to, sentient beings. Rather, for James values have

---

[8] See, for example, Bruce Wilshire, "William James's Prophetic Grasp of the Failures of Academic Philosophy," in *William James and Education*, edited by Jim Garrison, Ron Podeski, and Eric Bredo (New York: Teachers College Press, 2002), 42–57.

[9] This is a point I have stressed in "Socrates and Radical Empiricism," in which I highlight the far-reaching differences between James's relational ethics and traditional—Socratic—ethics by means in part of a brief imagined dialogue between Socrates and James (rather than Euthyphro). *Genealogical Pragmatism: Philosophy, Experience, and Community* (Albany: State University of New York Press, 1997), 147–155, 161–163.

their status and existence only in relation to, by, and for some particular person:

> Goodness, badness, and obligation must be *realized* somewhere in order to really exist; and the first step in ethical philosophy is to see that no merely inorganic "nature of things" can realize them. Neither moral relations nor the moral law can swing *in vacuo*. Their only habitat can be a mind which feels them; and no world composed of merely physical facts can possibly be a world to which ethical propositions apply. (WB, 145)

This means, for James, that the only backing or basis that any and all values have is ultimately and wholly personal and experiential. As Ellen Kappy Suckiel put it: "James's position is a thoroughgoing naturalism: moral value is fully constituted by the satisfaction of demand."[10] This is one of the reasons that James endorsed a philosophy more allied with literature and with modes of expression that situate values in specific persons, real or fictional, rather than some abstract order or universal law. Sarin Marchetti helpfully has noted that this endorsement runs throughout James's philosophy (and not just his ethics). Indeed, James enacted this endorsement by quoting as philosophically illuminating long passages from writers such as Stevenson, Tolstoy, Whitman, Wordsworth, and others (EPC, 54). When confronted with ethical disagreement, James claimed that "there is no single point of view . . . from which the values of things can be unequivocally judged" and held that no "particular consciousness [divine as well as human] in the universe can enjoy this prerogative of obliging others to conform to a rule which it lays down" (WB, 146, 147). There are, James claimed explicitly, no absolute or impersonal goods and no absolute or impersonal evils, just as there are no non-moral goods or evils (WB, 158).

Second, for James to view *ethics as personal* is thus to view values as *pluralistic* and *perspectival*. Multiple persons and multiple demands create multiple values and plural points of view from which to propose, take up, and judge them.

Now, James repeatedly noted that philosophers, so long as they are philosophers, "will not put up" with this situation or kind of world, one of personal and irreducibly plural values (WB, 147). However, he showed

---

[10] Ellen Kappy Suckiel, *The Pragmatic Philosophy of William James* (Notre Dame, IN: University of Notre Dame Press, 1982), 50.

equally repeatedly that there is no way—no way at all—for philosophers (or anyone else) to escape from or set aside the irreducibly personal basis of ethics. Thus he observed that if a philosopher is poised to declare some ethical views superior to others, this supposed superiority "cannot be explained by any abstract moral 'nature of things' existing antecedently to the concrete thinkers themselves with their ideals" (WB, 147)—because there simply is no such abstract, antecedent moral nature, order, or calculus.

We must avoid assuming, James declared bluntly, "an abstract moral order in which the objective truth resides," and so we must avoid trying to prove that this abstract moral order is more accurately captured by one's own values than by those of one's adversary. There simply is no such overarching abstract moral order: "Our ordinary attitude of regarding ourselves as subject to an overarching system of moral relations, true 'in themselves,' is therefore either an out-and-out superstition, or else it must be treated as a merely provisional abstraction" from a deity who commands that we hold particular values and whose command alone we should treat as obliging us to do so (WB, 148).[11] James added:

> Do we, perhaps, think that we cover God and protect him and make his impotence over us less ultimate, when we back him up with this *à priori* blanket from which he may draw some warmth of further appeal? But the only force of appeal to *us*, which either a living God or an abstract ideal order can wield, is found in the "everlasting ruby vaults" of our own human hearts, as they happen to beat responsive and not responsive to the claim. (WB, 149)

All of our values, James held, "even the largest obligations," are "personal demands" (WB, 149).

James explained that he realized how hard it is to give up this "superstitious view" of some abstract moral order—but James held that this, hard or

---

[11] James is so clear here, I think, in his rejection of a fixed moral order and his refusal to offer traditional moral imperatives and calculations that it seems almost impossible either to disagree with Marchetti's statement of his book's central aim or often to find it other than a re-statement of James's own words. Marchetti writes, "The chief idea animating the [Marchetti's] book is that James advanced no substantive moral position" and "as a corollary point, I claim that James aimed at silencing the distinctively philosophical temptation of thinking and portraying our human possibilities as inscribed in some fixed picture of the human being" (EPC 21, 22). Reading James, this seems to me just what James wrote, and so right on target.

not, is what the realities of our lives demand. Traditional moral philosophers, James alleged, simply have not met this demand. Experience and the history of moral philosophy have shown that this demand has proven too much for them—or at least most of them. Instead of giving up the superstition of an abstract and already finished moral order, moral philosophers ("just because" they are philosophers) add their "own peculiar confusion" and insist "that over all these individual opinions there is a *system of truth*" waiting to be discovered (WB, 158, 151).

How did moral philosophy come to this? Moreover, if (*contra* James) there really is an antecedent moral order and some universal system of truth about it, why have previous philosophers not already discovered them? James briefly outlined his response to these questions, and his remarks could serve as a very short and wholly disillusioned introduction to most of the history of Western moral philosophy:

> Shall we [philosophers] then simply proclaim our own ideals as the lawgiving ones? No; for if we are true philosophers we must throw our own spontaneous ideals, even the dearest, impartially in with that total mass of ideals which are fairly to be judged. But how then can we as philosophers ever find a test; how avoid complete moral skepticism on the one hand, and on the other escape bringing a wayward personal standard of our own along with us, on which we simply pin our faith? . . . One method presents itself, and has as a matter of history been taken by the more serious ethical schools. . . . If it were found that all goods *quâ* goods contained a common essence, then the amount of this essence involved in any one good would show its rank in the scale of goodness. . . . Various essences of good have thus been found and proposed as bases of the ethical system. . . . No one of the measures that have been proposed has, however, given general satisfaction . . . so that, after all, in seeking for a universal principle we inevitably are carried onward to the most universal principle,—that *the essence of good is simply to satisfy demand.* The demand may be for anything under the sun. (WB, 151–152)

At this point, the failure of the old-fashioned moral philosopher has been made clear, and James merely stressed once again that there is no reason to suppose the existence of some universal ethical ideal or standard waiting to be discovered by more able thinkers or more chosen or more fortunate people:

There is really no more ground for supposing that all our demands can be accounted for by one universal underlying kind of motive than there is ground for supposing that all physical phenomena are cases of a single law. The elementary forces in ethics are probably as plural as those of physics are. The various ideals have no common character apart from the fact that they are ideals. No single abstract principle can be so used as to yield to the philosopher anything like a scientifically accurate and genuinely useful casuistic scale. (WB, 153)

James's point here was not that some *particular* philosopher or school of thinkers has failed. He was not recommending that Aristotelians convert to Christianity, that Christians adopt a religion of reason and become Kantians, or that Kantians refocus on consequences and proclaim utilitarianism. Rather, he was demonstrating that any and all moral philosophy, understood as an abstract search for an impersonal basis or impersonal principles or impersonal criteria for ethics, is a long-running show that always has failed and only can fail. There can be no ethical theory independent of values embodied in the life of some particular person or persons. *In short, the ethics of persons cannot be impersonal.*

Of course, for James this point held more broadly and across his philosophy: Like ethics, whole philosophies of persons cannot be impersonal. This ethical commitment informs James's pragmatism, his radical empiricism, and his pluralism. For James, philosophies ultimately are reflections and expressions of personal characters, lives, and decisions, as noted in chapter 1. And because the lives of persons are irreducibly passional, the philosophies or persons are irreducibly marked by personal preferences and desires, feelings and moods, affinities and attunements, and selective attention and demands.

As previously noted, this is why, in *Pragmatism*, James characterized philosophy in terms of temperaments—different philosophies in terms of different temperaments. Our ways of feeling our whole lives and whole world are *always* at work, even when they are unrecognized or covered up, submerged beneath supposedly impersonal reasoning and professional demands for supposedly impersonal systems (P, 11, 24). In like manner, in *A Pluralistic Universe*, James described philosophy not in terms of universally binding conclusions resulting from universally necessary inferences rooted in thoroughly objective premises but, instead, as expressions of vision, attitude, and preference (APU, 10). In viewing philosophies as expressions of personal visions, James presented a view of philosophy as a creative art: Philosophers and "philosophies paint pictures"—the phrase he used to title the introduction to his *The Many and the One* (MEN, 3; see also MEN, ix, 326, 364 and P, 279). It is precisely because James took this methodological point to be so decisive that he always especially bristled at critics who pronounced that his views simply abstractly, rationally, logically *could not* be true—as if their conceptualizing could establish once and for all anything about the way the world actually is. For James, reason and thought and affect and feeling are all bound up with one another; we can distinguish and name them separately, of course, but this does not mean that they exist or function separately. No matter how meticulously reasoned it may be, for James a passion-free philosophy does not exist. In essays such as "The Will to Believe," "The Moral Philosopher and the Moral Life," "On a Certain Blindness in Human Beings," and "What Makes a Life Significant," he set forth this view as it impacts ethics.

In this light, suppose moral philosophers, reflecting on the absence of any useful casuistic scale, nonetheless go on to theorize abstractly and quasi-formulaically. Suppose they just keep on doing what they have been doing. For example, suppose, in James's words, that they assert that we all should "*satisfy as many demands as we can,*" that we should awaken "the least sum of dissatisfactions," and that we should "*invent some manner* of realizing your own ideals which will also satisfy the alien demands" (WB, 155). Are these kinds of imperatives and claims sufficiently broad and sweeping so as to be impersonal? Do they provide an effective and impersonal casuistic scale? No. No, despite the seemingly abstract, impersonal form of these imperatives. James insisted that *in practice* these sorts of moral formulas or slogans about which course of action really satisfies the most demands or really creates some new, even greater satisfaction are *at base irreducibly personal decisions* (and not a "path of escape" for the moral philosopher to reach some impersonal, universal realm). This calculation, this decision, this judgment, *in practice* always reflects its time and place and always is stamped by some person's particular interests and particular way of calculating, conscious or not. In practice, both the *what* and the *how* of our moral calculations are personal.

As a result, James held that "the true philosopher" must see "there is nothing final in any actually given equilibrium of human ideals, but that as our present laws and customs have fought and conquered other past ones, so they will in their turn be overthrown by any newly discovered order which will hush up the complaints that they still give rise to, without producing others louder still" (WB, 156).

Third, this leads to the realization that to view *ethics as personal* is to view values as *partial, limited, temporal,* and *fallible.* Our values are formed not on the basis of omniscience but always on a mix of knowledge and ignorance. They express not a God's-eye view or a fantasy view from nowhere but, instead, a view based on only some experience, some partial vantage point at some particular time, and on what George Santayana referred to as some "chance vista in the cosmic labyrinth."[12] James called this a "blindness" in all human beings concerning the "feelings of creatures and people different from ourselves." He stated:

> Our judgments concerning the worth of things, big or little, depend on the *feelings* the things arouse in us. . . . But this feeling is in each of us a vital secret, for sympathy with which we vainly look to others. The others are too much absorbed in their own vital secrets to take an interest in ours. Hence the stupidity and injustice of our opinions, so far as they presume to decide in an absolute way on the value of other persons' conditions or ideals. . . . The subject judged knows a part of the world of reality which the judging spectator fails to see, knows more while the spectator knows less . . . (TT, 149–151)

And to the extent that the self is a changing multiplicity, as James held, presumably we are each at all times blind to some dimensions of ourselves and not just others. Further (although this is not a point James developed), to the extent that the self is an irreducibly social being, presumably in being blind to others we thereby are blind to yet other important aspects of ourselves in this way too.

Now, James recognized that it is possible to address and lessen our blindness in concrete cases through communication with others (who are different) and by making changes in our own institutions, practices, places, and perspectives. It is possible, if difficult to change our perspective. We may attain a greater vision and come to see "an inner significance in what, until then, we had realized only in a dead, external way" (TT, 138). This important point noted, for James some amount of blindness is an intrinsic, permanent

---

[12] George Santayana, "Philosophical Heresy," in *Obiter Scripta* (New York: Charles Scribner's Sons, 1936 [1915]), 100.

part of the human condition. *This means that even the vision that identifies a particular blindness is itself bound up with an a manifestation of another partial blindness.* And it means that the judgment that some one limited perspective is the wider, fuller, more accurate or more moral one is a judgment made from within the limits of that perspective itself and its own blindness to other conditions, feelings, and ideals. James concluded with a warning: "Hands off: neither the whole of truth nor the whole of good is revealed to any single observer, although each observer gains a partial superiority of insight from the peculiar position" in which each stands (TT, 149). Our values are partial and fallible, plural and perspectival, and relational and created.

4. Ethics as Practical

What does it mean to understand ethics not only in irreducibly personal terms but also in practical ones? What does it mean to view ethics practically and concretely rather than only theoretically and abstractly?

First, for James, to view *ethics as practical* is to view values *contextually*, to view them as products of historical, cultural arrangements, institutions, customs, associations, relationships, and social conditions rather than something antecedent to, and independent of, the demands of embodied persons in particular times, places, and cultures.[13] One immediate consequence of this, James observed, is that in practice "the pinch is always here" for all ethical judgments. All ethical judgments, James held, are judgments to satisfy some demands and disappoint others. Accordingly, he claimed that "pent in under every system of moral rules are innumerable persons whom it weighs upon, and good which it represses; and these are always rumbling and grumbling in the background, and ready for any issue by which they may get free" (WB, 156). To make perhaps painfully evident to his 1891 Yale Philosophical Club audience for "The Moral Philosopher and the Moral Life," James stressed that this pinch is always concrete rather than abstract and that it is frequently unknown, rather than recognized, by those who hold (and benefit from) the conquering values of some time and place. We must be open to the "voice of complaint," James advised, and he thus provided many examples of pinch and struggle created (rather than resolved)

---

[13] Throntveit provided an extremely illuminating historical account of the personal development of James's own "ethical origins" in his first chapter (QER, 9–38).

by what might have been regarded by many as the correct or best morality of the day and its laws and customs: abuses built into the institutions of private property, industrialism and wage labor, and marriage laws; exclusions and violence central to ideologies of capitalism and merely formal egalitarianism; the destructiveness of social Darwinism, imperialism, and nationalism (WB, 156–157). Today the examples likely would be different—if, sadly, only in part—, but James's point remains: There is no final and impersonal measure for comparing competing values and there is no impersonal or non-exclusionary finality to ideals themselves. Our examples and our proposed measures for their competing values will be different still tomorrow.

Second, to understand *ethics as practical* is to view values as inhabiting a world of real *possibilities* rather than a closed, determined and deterministic, already-made world. For James, values are not merely discovered; they are made and re-made and continuously made over yet again. Their existence, their actually being made, presupposes the reality of the possibility of their creation, their being made. As Marchetti put it, ethics expresses a human possibility (ECP, 129). As Throntveit put it in reference to James's essay, "The Dilemma of Determinism," "the logical conclusion is that the world needs in it nothing essentially different from us to be a moral one" (QER, 51). Throntveit here fittingly quoted from James's own conclusion to this essay: "The great point is that the possibilities are really here"—to which James noted, I add, that it is the demand on us to decide from among these possibilities "here and now" that "gives the palpitating reality to our moral life" (WB, 140).

Now, there is nothing utopian about this Jamesian world of possibilities and possible actions on their behalf. For James, while there are real moral possibilities, their realizations can never be complete or fully ideal. As a result, James termed human values and human life "tragically practical." While in some cases it may be possible to invent some manner of effectively harmonizing or unifying or satisfying some competing demands, still in all cases moral ideals always outstrip moral realities. When we fail to satisfy a demand, obviously there is real loss, but also when we successfully do satisfy one demand, there is a different but equally real loss as other demands pass unmet. In a well-known passage, James explained:

> The actually possible in this world is vastly narrower than all that is demanded; and there is always a pinch between the ideal and the actual

which can only be got through by leaving part of the ideal behind. There is hardly a good which we can imagine except as competing for the possession of the same bit of space and time with some other imagined good. Every end of desire that presents itself appears exclusive of some other end of desire. (WB, 153–154)

The realization of any future is the permanent exclusion of every other possible future and its values and meanings.

The sacrifice of some part of our moral ideals is constant and unavoidable. But this does not mean that some partial success is guaranteed. In some situations, desperate situations, almost all or perhaps even all of the ideals of some persons may be butchered. As demands, our values are marks of possibility. As possibilities, many of our values are marks of loss. For James, life's losses are as real and deep as its gains and the energies required to attain them.

At this point, James recognized, the practical question remains: If we must "butcher" some part of the ideal, which part should we butcher? How do we determine which course of action satisfies the most demand? If there is no "self-proclaiming set of laws" or any "abstract moral reason" (WB, 151) on which we could rely, then what should we do? If "every one of hundreds of ideals has its special champion already provided in the shape of some genius expressly born to feel it, and to fight to death in its behalf" (WB, 157) then which of these ideals should one embrace? If moral philosophers must not "substitute the content of their clean-shaven systems for that exuberant mass of good with which all human nature is in travail" (WB, 155), how then should they theorize the moral life?

Third, when we are faced with the question of how to theorize the moral life, to take *ethics as practical* is to view values as always *unsettled, under way, and unfinished* and thus to view moral philosophy itself as always and equally unsettled, under way, and unfinished. Of course, it is fine to say, as James did claim, that any answer to these questions must be viewed as experiments and judged "by actually finding, after the fact of their making, how much more outcry or how much appeasement comes about" and that ethics, like the sciences, must wait on the facts and "instead of being deducible all at once from abstract principles, must simply bide its time, and be ready to revise its conclusions from day to day" (WB, 157). But this does not address the practical issue: Judgment may wait on the results of action, but action itself always must precede those results. What is the moral life according to the moral philosopher? For the moral philosopher, what is one to do? And what is the moral philosopher to do?

James's answer to this question is clear: The moral life is life in which we satisfy the most demands we can at present and create some new way and some new conditions to satisfy an even larger, more inclusive set of demands in the future—something that may well require a more inclusive process for determining just what constitutes satisfying a more inclusive set of demands. Along the way, we can draw on all the insights, norms, standards, regulations, practices, and lessons that past experience provides us. The important question, however, is not simply how to theorize the moral life but, rather, how to *live* it. The important question ultimately is about the moral life and not merely the moral philosopher. Here James stressed two points. First, assessments of morality must wait on its consequences. There can be no moral theory proven in advance of, or in abstraction from, these facts. The truth of moral judgments, like the truth of all beliefs, must be cashed out satisfactorily in practice, demonstrated by their consequences, found to work in life. Second, there will be multiple, contested, conflicting views about what counts as "the most demand," what counts as "awakening the least sum of dissatisfaction," and what counts as satisfying more, previously "alien demand." There will be no neutral starting point, no god's-eye view, and no self-evident first principle from which to make this assessment or adjudicate these conflicts. Any critical moral assessment of the moral life is always rooted in some presupposed values; any inference requires an assumption. Because of this, the moral philosopher begins with working assumptions rather than a final foundation. Moral prescriptions are hypotheses.

Sarin Marchetti has interpreted James as claiming that moral philosophers should stop being prescriptive and instead become hortatory or exhortative or instructive. Stressing that for James ethics is an "instructive rather than prescriptive" practice, Marchetti wrote:

> Borrowing James's term of art, I read in his work a defense and articulation of an *exhortative* or *hortatory ethics*: according to James, philosophical ethics should drop its foundational pretenses and rather acquire an exhortative tone—that is, it should help us deal with the difficulties of the moral life often caused by our own attitudes toward our ordinary practices and their reflective counterparts and desiderata. Ethics practiced in a Jamesian way should thus be instructive rather than prescriptive. (EPC, 18)

Now, any hortatory ethics, unless it is to be wholly abstract or entirely without focus, exhorts not in the abstract or in theory but, rather, in concrete practice. It exhorts a particular someone (some concrete person or persons) to do a particular something (some concrete act or series of acts) in a particular context (at a particular time and place).

What is it that James exhorted us to do? Marchetti answered this way: James invited us to "look at the moral life in a novel and reflective way so as to open new fields of experimentation and problematization, challenging our most rooted intellectual and ordinary assumptions and often deflecting our practices" (EPC, 23). And this way: James was interested in "unfolding a certain way of thinking our moral life as a field for self-fashioning free from the burdens of some prescriptions which dictate its possibilities" (EPC, 23). Calling James's philosophy "therapeutic and transformative," Marchetti added that James's ethics exhorts in a "quietist" manner: He provides "not *arguments* trying to *convince* us about the validity of some views" that he himself held; instead, his exhortations "are *invitations* to *operate* and *perform ourselves* some change in the way we look and react to the concepts and experiences that hold a grip on us and inform our ordinary practices" (EPC, 24, 25). To do this, Marchetti observed, is to "abandon *explanatory* ambitions" and stick to or return to the "needed *clarificatory* role that characterized its noble Greek origins and that flower in the writings of Emerson" (EPC, 26). Finally, for Marchetti, to do this is to view James's thought, including but not only his pragmatism, as method rather than substantive doctrine (EPC, 29). Marchetti claimed that this method is "an instrument through which one might gain a privileged position from which to resolve the difficulties pervading one's moral life" (EPC, 58).

Marchetti surely was correct that there are many careless and superficial interpretations of James's "The Moral Philosopher and the Moral Life" that portray James as some sort of utility-maximizing consequentialist or efficiency expert for the industrial age.[14] And he surely was correct in his oft-repeated desire to rescue James from the restrictions of "foundational slumbers" (EPC, 48–49; see also 65ff.). Here my sense of James scholarship may differ from Marchetti's: I don't find that most or even many James scholars do view James as a foundationalist—in ethics or in philosophy more generally. Ethics and philosophy may need to be rescued (still, again,

---

[14] Throntveit noted that James himself undermined "quantitative readings" of his ethics (see QER, 97).

seemingly always yet again) from foundationalism (EPC, 52), but James's ethics and philosophy do not.

This small scholarly matter aside, Marchetti was above all concerned to motivate a central dualism—ethics is *either* prescriptive *or* hortatory—and then to argue that James's writings on ethics are hortatory and, thus, anti-prescriptive. I suspect that this dualism and the many, many related dualisms Marchetti employed—for example, arguments/invitations, explanation/clarification, and substance/method—do not strongly mesh with or greatly illuminate James's ethical vision or his vision of the task of ethics. Ditto for the idea of a "privileged position" for resolving ethical difficulties—for James there are no "privileged" moral or epistemic positions. Why is this? A hortatory ethics is an ethics that aims to exhort someone to do something, to strongly urge or encourage or request or recommend or commend or direct life in some ways rather than others, or to call on us to make some choices rather than others or to act to satisfy some demands and disappoint others. So, isn't exhortation, understood this way, a form or kind of prescription? Well, pragmatism tells us that the answer to this question depends on what we mean by "prescription." To prescribe is often defined as to advise, recommend, advocate, suggest, endorse, promote, or champion. In these ordinary senses, to exhort and to prescribe seem very similar, even practically equivalent. To prescribe can also be understood as to authorize or stipulate or fix or delimit. Clearly these undertakings have connotations that are more at odds with a Jamesian temperament.

Marchetti portrayed James as anti-prescriptive (as well as anti-foundational). In contrast, I think that instead of asking *whether* James avoids all prescription, we should ask *what kind* of prescription he offers. This strikes me as more consistent with James's own ethical vision and his anti-dualistic philosophy. It also seems to me more useful in practice. Although our values are unsettled and unfinished (such that there never can be any final moral prescription, calculation, or imperative), they also are very much under way and in use (such that all exhortation is exhortation to do some things and to forgo others, to satisfy some demands and to disappoint others).[15] That our

---

[15] Because, in my view, there is no other option, Marchetti himself ends up employing prescriptive ethical language in discussions of hortatory ethics. For example, he writes that for James "ethics should be hortatory rather than prescriptive" (ECP, 22). It does not get any more prescriptive than that. Again: "James gives us some hints about the *form* moral thought should take" (ECP, 51). Here the force of "should" is thoroughly prescriptive. And once more: "According to James the moral philosopher should not be biased by such [theological] hypotheses" (ECP, 116). Here again James prescribes a way of thinking that "should" be adopted by the moral philosopher.

practices of prescriptions do not issue from, and cannot be evaluated by, criteria that are independent of our practices themselves does not render those practices any less prescriptive. It means, rather, that no prescription is first or foundational and no prescription is final and settled no matter what future experience may be.

For James, ethics is prescriptive not in the sense that a fixed universe mandates obedience to a particular rule or requires action on behalf of some ends rather than others but in the sense in which ethics articulates an *ideal*. As Throntveit put it, for James ethics constitutes "a *method* rather than a *code of conduct*" (QER, 86–87), a method for resolving plural, competing, and contested demands, a method for our "ethical republic here below" (WB, 150). James strongly recommends and takes up—prescribes—this method. Throntveit captured well James's embrace of an unsettled, under-way, unfinished universe and its unsettled, under-way, and unfinished values—what Throntveit described as "ethics in its most fundamental sense of the term: a practical guide to conduct proceeding from an apprehension of the good" (QER, 85). He wrote:

> The eternally unfinished nature of the universe is rather the condition of its ever-present potential for integration—a potential that we must help to actualize if we seek a hospitable space for our personal faiths. . . . His [James's] ethics is not a fixed program, but an ideal of private and public interests converging—an ideal derived from experience, yet suggesting at every moment the terms and consequences of its own realization. . . . By its very nature then, James's empiricist deliberative ethics resists codification. Clearly, however, to strenuously embrace the uncertainty affording both freedom and unity was, if not an iron rule, a cardinal virtue in James's eyes. Moreover, James emphasized three other virtues that empowered strenuous ethical republicanism: experimentalism, historical wisdom and empathy. . . . To free his readers for this task, James urged them to adopt a radically empiricist approach to moral life: to reflect critically on the "abstract conceptions" defining their habitual values, and to "tolerate, respect, and indulge" other people "harmlessly interested and happy in their own ways."[16] (QER, 85–86, 102, 105)

---

[16] Throntveit correctly added James's important qualification here: Persons who pursue ways that are not harmless and whose wills go against the good of the whole "must be sacrificed" (QER 105). The Jamesian moral universe really is a universe of losses as well as gains.

5. The Moral Life—Without Old-Fashioned, Absolute Moral Philosophy

The moral life, of course, requires more than adoption of a particular attitude. What is the task—the Jamesian reconstructed task of the moral philosopher who philosophizes without a practice-free, universal moral order and without a set of abstract, impersonal moral rules? The answer that James provided to this question ultimately is deflationary (for moral philosophy, not for the moral life): It strips the moral philosopher and moral philosophies of universality, finality, certainty, infallibility, abstract moral orders, and the capacity to defend any set of values without employing those values in their very defense.[17] Grasping this point in its five aspects is crucial for any understanding of James's ethics.

First, the moral philosopher's efforts to characterize, identify, or theorize the moral life and its ideals issue always from *substantial ignorance of past and future experience*. This is cause for humility, even substantial humility. James wrote that the thinkers who have created our moral ideals are largely unknown, that the evolution of the sensibilities that nurture and grow from these ideals is also largely unknown, and that the key question as to which of many conflicting ideals "will give the best universe there and then" can be answered "only through the aid of the experience" of others (WB, 158).

Second, the moral philosopher's account of the moral life is directed always to a *substantially unique situation* to which this sort of past and future knowledge, even if we had it, would have only limited application. As a result, all ideals and rules have only limited relevance, "for every real dilemma is in literal strictness a unique situation; and the exact combination of ideals realized and ideals disappointed which each decision creates is always a universe without precedent, and for which no adequate previous rule exists." Accordingly, James concluded, that compared to other people, "the philosopher *quâ* philosopher, is no better able to determine the best universe in the concrete emergency" (WB, 158).

This leads directly to a third point: *The moral philosopher has no special knowledge of, insight on, or perspective on the moral life.* With respect to the moral life, the moral philosopher has no epistemic privilege. In the phrase of Philip Kitcher, for James the moral philosopher is not and cannot be "a

---

[17] See my "It's All Relative: Beyond Absolutism and Nihilism," in *Philosophical Fashions: Pluralism, Democracy, Relativism, and the Absurd* (Bloomington: Indiana University Press, 2016), 98–115.

prescriptive outsider."[18] The moral philosopher, thus, must not be considered a professional expert about moral ideals and the calculations required by ethical decisions. This is because the moral philosopher has no specialized or professional body of knowledge of moral ideals and calculations. In making this point, James here explicitly distanced himself from moral philosophers and rejected identification with them. Faced with practical decisions about which demands to satisfy and which to disappoint and with questions about which of many possible universes is the better or "more inclusive whole," James asserted: "In all this the philosopher is just like the rest of us non-philosophers, so far as we are just and sympathetic instinctively, and so far as we are open to the voice of complaint. [The philosopher's] function is in fact indistinguishable from that of the best kind of statesman at the present day" (WB, 159). And for good measure he stressed this same point at the close of "The Moral Philosopher and the Moral Life": "The ethical philosopher, therefore, whenever he ventures to say which course of action is the best, is on no essentially different level from the common man" (WB, 162).

Fourth, James stressed that in practice it is reasonable to adopt a *presumptively conservative orientation or temperament* toward one's values. James's point here was epistemic; he was not endorsing a right-wing, rear-guard, or nostalgic politics. He was recognizing that we must use our values in the very act of assessing our values, that we must rely on some of our habits in order to reconstruct other of our habits. He was recognizing that we are creatures of habit—personal and social habit—and that habits, if they have not been abandoned in favor of newer habits, often have proven themselves in practice. He asserted that in both ethics and physical science "the presumption . . . always is that the vulgarly accepted opinions are true, and the right casuistic order that which public opinion believes in" (WB, 157). He put it this way:

The course of history is nothing but the story of men's struggles to find the more and more inclusive order. . . . So far then, and up to date, the casuistic scale is made for the philosopher already far better than he can ever make it for himself. An experiment of the most searching kind has proved that the laws and usages of the land are what yield the maximum of satisfaction to the thinkers taken all together. The presumption in cases of conflict must

[18] Philip Kitcher, *Preludes to Pragmatism: Toward a Reconstruction of Philosophy* (New York: Oxford University Press, 2012), 332.

always be in favor of the conventionally recognized good. The philosopher must be a conservative, and in the construction of his casuistic scale must put the things most in accordance with the customs of the community on top. (WB, 155–156)

For James, the force of moral convention and custom is real; it embodies the results of much past experience. But it is only *presumptive and partial*, and does not reflect everyone's past experiences. These experiences are often contested and silenced experiences, experiences of some excluded others, or the new and unique realities that now loom large. This is why, immediately following the above passage, James added that "there is nothing final in any actually given equilibrium of human ideals" and that "it is at all times open to any one to make the experiment" to break with an older order on behalf of a new one (WB, 156). Endorsing this openness, Marchetti observed that "moral principles, when portrayed as the outcome of a society whose values are already established and not negotiated any more, lead to moralism and conservatism" (ECP, 107). However, values that are initially established and values that are not open to further negotiation are two very different things. Just as Peirce argued that we must begin to philosophize not with universal doubt but with the beliefs we have at that time, so too James thought that we must begin to think ethically by means of values established in our society, and that it is from this starting point—the values with which we begin—that subsequent experience leads us to, and forces on us, further negotiations of these values. For James, this kind of beginning (but not necessarily ending) conservatism is unavoidable: Single individuals, even relatively creative ones, do not invent from scratch their own personal values, any more than they invent from scratch their own language. We all begin with values and ways of life made by others in the past. Any reconstruction of these values is precisely that—a *re*-construction and not a magical something-from-nothing first creation. For James, of course, big and small reconstructions of values are always possibilities. Indeed, he noted that the "highest ethical life—however few may be called to bear its burdens—consists at all times in the breaking of rules which have grown too narrow for the actual case" (WB, 158). Moreover, for James, this initial conservatism goes hand in hand with a progressivism—a progress judged not abstractly but by its own standards.[19] Thus James

---

[19] Erin Tarver provided a critical perspective on this issue and its assumptions and implications for matters of gender in her "Lady Pragmatism and the Great Man," in *Feminist Interpretations of William*

observed that the course of history is the story of human exclusions and struggles for a more and more inclusive moral order (WB, 155).

This fourth point will be familiar to readers of James's *Pragmatism* and his theory of truth. Or, I think, in a pluralistic spirit, to most readers. I note here, for example, that Marchetti observed that "detecting the presence of moral considerations in James's writings on pragmatism is not an easy task" (ECP, 159). In contrast, Throntveit claimed "James's defense of the moral life resulted in a radical-empiricist metaphysics entailing a pragmatic doctrine of truth" (QER, 83), and he later observed that "the true and the good are indistinguishable in James's writings" (QER, 106). As I suggested in section 3 and like Throntveit, I find the task of linking James's ethics to his pragmatism and pluralism to be quite easy—and very much necessary to catch James's vision. For example, in "What Pragmatism Means" James made this same point about conservatism in the context of beliefs and truths (rather than actions and goods):

> The individual has a stock of old opinions already, but he meets a new experience that puts them to a strain. . . . The result is an inward trouble to which his mind till then had been a stranger, and from which he seeks to escape by modifying his previous mass of opinions. He saves as much of it as he can, for in this matter of belief we are all extreme conservatives. So he tries to change first this opinion, and then that (for they resist change very variously), until at last some new idea comes up which he can graft upon the ancient stock with a minimum of disturbance of the latter, some idea that mediates between the stock and the new experience. . . . This new idea is then adopted as the true one. It preserves the older stock of truths with a minimum of modification. . . . The most violent revolutions in an individual's beliefs leave most of the old order standing. . . . New truth is always a go-between, a smoother-over of transitions. It marries old opinion to new fact so as ever to show a minimum of jolt, a maximum of continuity. . . . The point I now urge you to observe particularly is the part played by older truths. . . . Their influence is absolutely controlling. (P, 34–35)

This parallel between James's language about truths and his language about goods is a consequence of his commitment, explored in detail in chapter 5, to

James, edited by Erin C. Tarver and Shannon Sullivan (University Park: Penn State University Press, 2015), esp. 109–116.

the view that "truth is *one species of good*." Truth is a subset of the good, a category "coordinate with it" rather than "distinct" from it. Just as James believed that there is no antecedent moral order or universal moral rule, so too he believed there is no purely objective truth; just as he believed that values are made rather than merely discovered, so too he believed that truths are made and that verities are products of verification processes. James put this succinctly: "*The true is the name for whatever proves itself to be good in the way of belief*" (P, 42). It is "*only the expedient in the way of our thinking, just as the 'right' is only the expedient in our way of behaving*" (P, 106). In this same way, then, for James epistemology is simply a subset of ethics. Accordingly, if we were to have no concern for clunky titles or scholarly marketing, *Pragmatism* might be retitled *The Moral Philosopher and the Epistemic Life*.

Fifth, for James the moral life is a life of ongoing self-interrogation, self-response, and self-reconstruction. Marchetti called this a life of "self-constitution" and "self-fashioning" (ECP, 119ff., 157ff.), but in my view, this easily can be a misleading notion in the context of James's philosophy. In *The Principles of Psychology*, for example, James describes human consciousness as the consciousness of an organism in, of, by, and through an environment (biological, psychological, environmental, historical, cultural). As a result, environmental constitution of the self is a force at least as powerful as self-constitution. Furthermore, James described the many ways in which an individual is only partly and selectively attentive in and to the world. As a result, even when self-constitution is at work, much of that work occurs outside an individual's attention and purposes. James's account of habit and habit formation, as discussed in chapter 2, hammers home this point: We often acquire habits unknowingly, unintentionally, and thus are often largely unaware of the constitution of ourselves—the constitution of the self that becomes hell to change.

For James, we must and do engage in many moral calculations, trade-offs, and decisions—we determine to satisfy some demands and to disappoint others. These calculations are important, even unavoidable, parts of any ethics. However, for James an ethical life includes more. It includes our calling into question our own moral calculations, considering alternatives, exploring the extent to which we are open (or closed) to "complaint" from others, trying to identify ways in which our own calculations and the moral ideals on which they are based are blind, fixed, narrow, unsympathetic, and exclusionary and ways in which they cause both complaints by others and our silencings of those complaints. With respect to our moral ideals and calculations at any time and point, James directed us to ask: What other persons do my ideals, decisions, and actions "weigh upon," restrict, and repress? What abuses, including abuses to which I have been blind, do I commit in their names? What sorrows do I produce and what opportunities do I destroy? What outcasts do I create and what causes do I crush? How can I create in myself more sympathy and more openness "to the voice of complaint" (WB, 159)? How can I cultivate a habit of openness, interrupt myself, uncomfortably dislocate myself—cultivate habits that are flexible rather than merely fixed?

For a pragmatist, of course, it is not enough to ask these questions. One must act on one's answers. It is not enough merely to reflect on and be open to revising those answers. Ethics ins not merely the theory of ethical practice. But James here stressed that there are no final answers to these questions, and so there is no point at which we finally can be done with them. For James, as for Socrates, the moral life is a self-examined life, and this self-examination is a lifelong undertaking. For James, as for Socrates, the moral life is an unfinished self-examining life. Moreover, this fact about ethical life is not a schoolbook problem that awaits solution or an illness that requires therapy. It is a constitutive condition and dimension of human life.

So, James recognized that what counts to someone as "satisfying the most demand" or as the more inclusive moral order depends not on some supposed freestanding moral realities but rather on which particular persons and their particular ways of calculating the "most" demand are authorized and empowered to imagine, identify, measure, and compare alternatives. Given that there is always a plurality of perspectives from which "most" demand might be determined—given that the ethical universe is pluralistic rather than monistic—James suggested that we might see this fact less as a failure of moral philosophy in theory and more as a fortunate work-to-do outcome in practice for a world in which persons often treat their own oddly personal demands as though they were universal goods. James wrote:

> Think, furthermore, of such individual moralists, no longer as mere schoolmasters but as pontiffs armed with the temporal power, and having authority in every concrete case of conflict to order which good shall be butchered and which shall be suffered to survive, —and the notion really turns one pale. All one's slumbering revolutionary instincts awaken at the thought of any single moralist wielding such powers of life and death. Better chaos forever than an order based on any closet-philosopher's rule,

even though he were the most enlightened possible member of his tribe. No! (WB, 155)

This passage points the way from James's account of the moral life to a Jamesian politics consistent with, and both in service of and a partial outcome of, such a life.[20] It points from James as moral philosopher to what Throntveit called "Citizen James" (QER, 109ff.).[21]

The above passage also illuminates James's description of his own philosophical temperament:

> As for me, my bed is made. I am against bigness & greatness in all their forms; and with the invisible molecular moral forces that work from individual to individual, stealing in through the crannies of the world like so many soft rootlets, or like the capillary oozing of water, and yet rending the hardest monuments of man's pride, if you give them time. The bigger the unit you deal with, the hollower, the more brutal, the more mendacious is the life displayed. So I am against all big organizations as such, national ones first and foremost; against all big successes and big results; and in favor of the eternal forces of truth which always work in the individual and immediately unsuccessful ways, under-dogs always, till history comes, after they are long dead, and puts them on top. (CWJ, 8:546)

This was James's vision: He stood against the big, the absolute, the eternal, the universal, the final, the complete, the certain, the self-same, the sure and self-sure, the necessary, and all sweeping and tidy theories. In ethics and across his philosophy, he stood in favor of the personal and the practical: the relational and dynamically experiential that outstrips classification; the plural and perspectival; the partial and fallible and ever-not-quite; the contextual, real places and times, the concrete; an open world with genuine

---

[20] For an original, historically informed account of James's politics, see Alexander Livingston, *Damn Great Empires: William James and the Politics of Pragmatism* (New York: Oxford University Press, 2016). In addition, in his fourth chapter, Throntveit provided a remarkably historically and philosophically nuanced account of a Jamesian view of individual and community, democratic habits, and pragmatic polity (QER, 109–138). And in the first two parts of his fifth chapter, Throntveit illuminated connections between James's ethical philosophy and American "progressives" on both domestic and international matters (including Jane Addams, W. E. B. Du Bois, Louis Brandeis, Herbert Croly, and Walter Lippmann) (QER, 139–160).

[21] In "James's Political Consciousness," Throntveit referred to James's account of consciousness as "inherently political" and noted that "individualism" is "far too thin a term" for James's politics. *The Jamesian Mind*, edited by Sarin Marchetti (New York: Routledge, 2021), 222, 225.

possibilities, only some of which may be realized; and the unsettled, unfinished, always under way, and always unconcluded (about which, therefore, there is nothing to conclude). If and whenever philosophy and life parted ways, James stood always against the moral philosopher and he stood always with the moral life.[22]

6. Strenuous Ethics

I have claimed that for anyone who endorses a Jamesian view of ethics, *the deepest difference, theoretically*, in moral philosophies is the difference between an ethics that is avowedly personal and practical and an ethics that is abstract.

This is the difference between moral philosophies that answer no and those that answer yes to the following questions that James put to them in "The Moral Philosopher and the Moral Life" and his pragmatism, radical empiricism, and pluralism as well:

Are there values independent of the demands of sentient beings? Antecedent to and independent of human demands and reflection, is there a moral order or moral nature of things?

Is there a universal moral standard or objective moral truth? Is there a single impartial and complete point of view from which to judge conflicts and disagreements about values?

Is there any single principle that yields an accurate and useful casuistic scale?

Are there values independent of particular contexts? Is the moral universe complete and fully actual?

Can the moral philosopher settle finally or fully finish with moral problems?

For James, old-fashioned absolutist and abstract moral philosophy answers yes to all these questions. By contrast, James answered no to all these questions. In so doing, he set forth an ethics that is irreducibly personal (relational, pluralistic and perspectival, and partial) and irreducibly practical

---

[22] In a similar vein, in a letter (CWJ, 9:186) aptly quoted by Marchetti (ECP, 79), James explained his goal as defending experience against philosophy.

(contextual, marked by genuine possibilities, and always unsettled and unfinished). He set forth an ethical vision after—or beyond or other than—
traditional moral philosophy and moral philosophers.

At this point, thinkers whom James disparagingly called old-fashioned
absolutists and abstract "closet-philosophers," their patience tried, will want
to know what proof James provided for his claims. Here these thinkers have
been, are, and always will be disappointed and irritated, perhaps smugly
irritated. Just as James provided no abstract ethical theory, he provided—
consistently—no abstract proof for his ethical vision. In saying that James
provided no "abstract" proof (of the sort commonplace in professional philosophy), I mean two things. First, James recognized that his ethical vision
rested on his personal temperament rather than supposedly impersonal
reason and formal logic—reasoning abstracted from the natures of particular persons and practices. Accordingly, anyone who feels the whole push
and pressure of the cosmos like James; anyone who has a Jamesian dumb
sense of what life deeply means and what is at stake in it; anyone who has
a similarly odd Jamesian personal flavor and intimate character; anyone
who has Jamesian best working attitudes and preferences ("there is no other
truthful word")—these persons will resonate with James's ethical vision. They
will find it intimate, rational, and illuminating. Other folks who feel none
of this, who take and feel life dramatically differently, who live with other
crucial commitments, simply will not find that James's vision captures their
experiences or produces the sentiment of rationality in their lives. This does
not mean that James is abstractly correct or abstractly incorrect about ethics.
It means that in a pluralistic universe of persons, there is no abstract ethics.

Second, James recognized fully and honestly that this rejection of all impersonal ethics has methodological consequences for ethical practice and
its disagreements and conflicts. It is not possible to rationally justify particular values without appealing to, and making use of, those very same
values (often in generalized form) in the very effort to justify them. Deep
differences in conclusions in ethics reflect deep differences in starting points
in ethics. These starting points, for James, are not premises of neat moral
syllogisms. Rather, they are matters of feeling, mood, temperament, habit,
and experience.

In a much-cited passage, James thus held that the "deepest difference,
practically, in the moral life" is the difference between the "shrinking from
present ills" that is the "easy-going mood" and, in contrast, the "strenuous mood" that is "indifferent to present ills if only the greater ideal be

obtained" (WB, 159–160). This latter mood, a willingness to confront and endure present difficulties in order to realize in the future larger, more inclusive goals, is "strenuous" precisely because it involves attitudes and actions that are difficult to engage. As detailed in the previous section: to recognize and ameliorate one's own ignorance and blindness is nothing short of hard work, endlessly if finitely hard work; to confront new and unique situations without wholly falling back on old habits forged in, and for, other conditions is very demanding—James termed it the mark of genius; to do this with the awareness that one brings no special, expert, or privileged knowledge to the task creates self-doubt, produces pause, and often is paralyzing; to rely not too much on the conventional and established, recognize at times its shortcomings, and then act to break its rules and forge a new and conflict-reconciling moral order is more than daunting; and to lead a self-interrogating, examined life significantly open to, and in dialogue with, those who are silenced, excluded, or denied amounts to a lifetime of striving.

Because the strenuous mood is oriented to the greater ideal, the more demand-harmonizing and demand-satisfying life, fidelity to the more inclusive order, it is in practice *the medium of the moral life* in James's ethical vision.

The practically pressing question, then, is this: How is, or can, the strenuous mood be created, cultivated, and sustained? It might seem—incorrectly, I think—that James's answer was this: only in a world with God. James wrote:

[The strenuous mood] needs the wilder passions to arouse it, the big fears, loves, and indignations; or else the deeply penetrating appeal of some one of the higher fidelities, like justice, truth, or freedom. . . . This too is why, in a merely human world without a God, the appeal to our moral energy falls short of its maximally stimulating power. . . . When, however, we believe that a God is there, and that he is one of the claimants, the infinite perspective opens out. . . . The more imperative ideals now begin to speak with an altogether new objectivity and significance. . . . Our attitude towards concrete evils is entirely different in a world where we believe there are none but finite demanders, from what it is in one where we joyously face tragedy for an infinite demander's sake. Every sort of energy and endurance, of courage and capacity for handling life's evils is set free in those who have religious faith. For this reason, the strenuous type of character will on the battle-field of human history always outwear the easy-going type, and religion will drive irreligion to the wall. (WB, 160–161)

He added:

> It would seem, too,—and this is my final conclusion,—that the stable and
> systematic moral universe for which the ethical philosopher asks is fully
> possible only in a world where there is a divine thinker with all-enveloping
> demands. (WB, 161)

Many readers of this last section of "The Moral Philosopher and the Moral
Life" have taken it as a claim by James that God exists or as justification for
belief in God. I think this is incorrect. Instead, James here claimed that the
existence (and also the non-existence) of God cannot be disproven by any
merely abstract—logical, dialectical, formal, rational, closet-philosopher—
argument. And he here claimed that history shows that belief in God
provides a psychologically very strong basis for indifference to present ills on
behalf of greater ideals. Other readers have viewed this last section as inconsistent or mismatched with the rest of the essay—as a move from an ethics of
the demands of finite sentient beings to an ethics of the demands or perspective of an infinite being.[23] This too I think is incorrect. Instead, James claimed
that any ethical vision is the vision of a finite sentient being whose ideals,
though irreducibly personal, may be more and more inclusive (and inclu-
sively compelling) and less and less simply selfish.

Here it is helpful to recall that while James claimed that the stable and
systematic moral order desired by moral philosophers requires a divine thinker, this is a point about moral philosophy rather than about the
moral life. James already—and throughout—showed that there is no moral
order or moral nature of things, no objective moral standard, no impartial
or ready-made or complete or infinite moral point of view. Old-fashioned,
traditional moral philosophy, James thought, needed a fixed and universal
basis for its calculations, and in a world of plural finite persons and their
conflicting demands, James recognized that logically only the perspective of
an infinite being could meet that need. If we are to have an old-fashioned,
absolutist moral philosophy, as well as old-fashioned, absolutist notions of

---

[23] Wanting to "dissipate the suspicion of inconsistency" on the part of James, Marchetti
wrote: "I have tried to tell a fairly linear story about James's methodological approach to ethics in
'Moral Philosopher,' showing how from such a perspective most of the interpretative disagreements
over this text and the charges of inconsistencies it attracted might be reconsidered and explained
away. However, as in the best philosophical and literary texts, there is always one piece missing or
hardly matching. This is a troubling piece . . . in which metaphysical and religious considerations
come to the fore" (ECP, 111–112).

God, then we are going to need some old-fashioned absolute—some universality, infinity, and finality, some God. As James put it: "In the interests of our own ideal of systematically unified moral truth, therefore, we, as would-be philosophers, must postulate a divine thinker" (WB, 161).

However, this is just the kind of moral theory and moral truth that James rejected. John Lachs has illuminated this point by contrasting James's radically empirical and pluralistic ethics with James's Harvard colleague Josiah Royce's idealist and absolutist ethics:

> For James, God does not play a consolatory function, assuring us that He will supplement our imperfect efforts. Contrary to Royce's view, we are left alone to do what needs to be done; all the action comes from human beings trying to make the world a little better. We postulate God for inspirational reasons. He is indispensable for letting "loose in us the strenuous mood." So God's function in James is motivational, while in Royce it is metaphysical.[24]

In this same context, Ellen Kappy Suckiel has stressed an important aspect of the development of James's thought. She wrote:

> Given James's naturalistic ethical theory in "The Moral Philosopher and the Moral Life," it seems puzzling that he could have expressed such a profound ethico-religious sensibility in *The Varieties of Religious Experience*. While several explanations come to mind, perhaps the most plausible is that by the time he came to write *The Varieties of Religious Experience*, James no longer believed that God was transcendent and empirically inaccessible.[25]

Thus, no matter what the would-be moral philosopher thinks must be done, James immediately added this point: "Meanwhile, exactly what the thought of the infinite thinker may be is hidden from us even were we sure of

---

[24] John Lachs, "Moral Holidays," in *Freedom and Its Limits*, edited by Patrick Shade (New York: Fordham University Press, 2014), 441.

[25] Ellen Kappy Suckiel, "William James," in *A Companion to Pragmatism*, edited by John R. Shook and Joseph Margolis (Malden, MA: Blackwell, 2006), 40. In the same volume, see Nancy K. Frankenberry's very clear identification of ten principles of the naturalistic outlook in American thought and nine epistemological assumptions they make: the primacy of perception, the reality of relations, the interactive model of experience, the cognitive value of feeling, the linguistic turn (an assumption definitely not present in the writings of James, she noted), the instrumental role of conceptual reasoning, the absence of foundations, pragmatism as a mediating method, and the rejection of both realism and anti-realism (337–345).

his existence; so that our postulation of him after all serves only to let loose in us the strenuous mood" (WB, 161). When the moral life presents us, as it always does, with decisions and trials, James wrote, "it is simply our total character and personal genius that is on trial; and if we invoke any so-called philosophy, our choice and use of that also are but revelations of our personal aptitude or incapacity for moral life," expressions of "dumb willingnesses and unwillingnesses" of our "interior characters" (WB, 162), and reflections of those ruby vaults of our human hearts. If someone is drawn, habitually drawn, to a particular moral philosophy—theistic or otherwise—it is only as that moral philosophy calls forth the strenuous mood that it makes possible a moral life. And it is only as choice and action produce increasingly inclusive ideals and practices that this possibility is actualized. Whenever the strenuous mood motivates actions that crush more inclusive ideals and practices, we see the energy, confidence, epistemic arrogance, and immoral commitments of zealots, authoritarians, fanatics, sectarians, and maniacs.[26] William James's ethics is a vision of a difficult and vigorous ethical republic as well as an extended criticism of all ethical authoritarianism, tyranny, and subjugation—realities from which alone "no professor's lecture and no array of books can save us" (WB, 162). This ethical republic is an ideal—and, at present and in large part, only an ideal. For pragmatists, it is only *after* conscious and concerted personal and political action on behalf of an ideal that, by its consequences, we reasonably can assess it. *After* traditional moral philosophers and old-fashioned moral philosophy—*beyond* traditional moral philosophers and old-fashioned moral philosophy—there is no better time than the present for personal and political action on behalf of James's ethical vision.

---

[26] In his "Introduction," Throntveit recognized the depth of James's pluralism and what we might regard as epistemic totalitarianism: "Despite his faith in the pragmatist virtues of experimentalism, historical wisdom, and empathy, the crux of James's strenuous ethos was epistemic humility permitting the critical analysis and informed revision of any and all assumptions and practices" (3).

4

The Political Philosopher and
the Political Life

The nation blest above all nations is she in whom the civic genius of the people does the saving day by day, by acts without external picturesqueness; by speaking, writing, voting reasonably; by smiting corruption swiftly, by good temper between parties; by the people knowing true men when they see them, and preferring them as leaders to rabid partisans or empty quacks. . . . Democracy is still upon its trial. The civic genius of our people is its only bulwark, and neither laws nor monuments, neither battleships nor public libraries, nor great newspapers nor booming stocks, neither mechanical invention nor political adroitness, nor churches and universities nor civil-service examinations can save us from degeneration if the inner mystery be lost.

—William James, "Robert Gould Shaw Oration" (ERM, 73–74)

It grows tiresome to repeat the indictment, but "good" government in the concrete means a government that seeks to make some connection with the actual mental condition of the governed.

—William James, "Governor Roosevelt's Oration" (ECR, 164)

History shows that no force endures like hatred of the alien ruler. . . . We Americans certainly do not monopolize all the possible forms of goodness.

—William James, "Secretary Taft a Biased Judge" (ECR, 179–180)

If democracy really does depend on the civic genius of its citizens, on what cultural resources, actions, policies, associations, and institutions does "civic genius" depend? How can habits, flexible habits, of civic genius be created, nurtured, embodied, and sustained?

No Professor's Lectures Can Save Us. John J. Stuhr, Oxford University Press. © Oxford University Press 2023.
DOI: 10.1093/oso/9780197664629.003.0005

Consider this hypothesis: The principal bulwark of democratic civic virtue is an embodied temperament or habituated vision among its people that rejects absolutism, embraces facts and evidence, and embraces many different kinds of fulfilling lives among its people. Such a vision is radically empirical, pragmatic, and pluralistic.

William James painted a compelling portrait of just this vision of social life. In order to locate, understand, and make use of his valuable democratic political thought, it is crucial to attend to his psychology because his *radically empirical, pragmatic, and pluralistic* political thought flows from, and with, his *radically empirical, pragmatic, and pluralistic* philosophical psychology. Refusing to isolate James's politics from his psychology allows us to grasp James's political thought more in terms of method and temperament than in terms of doctrine. This politics is radically empirical in its understanding of political values as relational. It is pragmatic in its methodology. And it is pluralistic in its temperament. It goes hand in hand with the conclusion that for politics as for ethics "no philosophy is possible in the old-fashioned absolute sense of the term" and that no political philosophy can be final. It is thus addressed to political life—to political lives—*after* political philosophers and theorists.[1]

1. Life and Some of Its Conceptualizations, Theorizations, and Abstractions

Political theories are just that: theories, conceptualizations, abstractions. Nonetheless, our concepts often and habitually lay immediate claim to us— and we often and habitually lay passionate claim to them. William James— a theorist—understood well the attractions of theory and, just as much, its pitfalls. In part quoting from Harvard colleague Josiah Royce's 1908 *Philosophy of Loyalty*, James observed:

> Abstractions will touch us when we are callous to the concrete instances in which they lie embodied. "Loyal in our measure to particular ideals, we soon set up abstract Loyalty as something of a superior order to be infinitely

---

[1] I here parallel the language that James used in "The Moral Philosopher and the Moral Life." I view James's political writings, in addition to their specific foci, as collectively doing for political theory what "The Moral Philosopher and the Moral Life" did for ethical theory—philosophizing *after* and in light of the recognition that old-fashioned philosophical theories of ethics are no longer possible.

loyal to; and Truth at large becomes a 'momentous issue,' compared with which truths in detail are 'poor scraps, mere crumbling successes.'" . . . We thus see clearly what is gained and what is lost when percepts are translated into concepts. Perception is solely of the here and now; conception is of the like and unlike, of the future, of the past, and of the far away. But this map of what surrounds the present, like all maps, is only a surface; its features are but abstract signs and symbols of things that in themselves are concrete bits of sensible experience. We have but to weigh extent against content, thickness against spread, and we see that for some purposes the one, for other purposes the other, has the higher value. Who can decide off-hand which is absolutely better, to live or to understand life? We must do both alternately, and a man can no more limit himself to either than a pair of scissors can cut with a single one of its blades. (SPP, 42, 44)

Just as experience for James is famously "double-barreled," inclusive of both the *what* and the *how* of our lives, the subjective and the objective irreducibly all at once and together, so too experience is double-*bladed*, inclusive of both our percepts and our concepts, the concrete immediate and the abstract mediate all at once and irreducibly together (ERE, 3–19).[2]

To repeat: Theories—even political theories—are abstractions.[3] They are works and sites of concepts. Within these theories, concepts are defined and clarified (sometimes more successfully, sometimes less) and their relations to other concepts—conceptual relations—are stipulated and defined (again sometimes with much success, sometimes with little). In each particular theory, some of these concepts are proclaimed as central and others are given

---

[2] See also John Dewey's well-known citation of this idea in the first chapter of his *Experience and Nature*: "We begin by noting that 'experience' is what James called a double-barreled word. Like its congeners, life and history, it includes *what* men do and suffer, *what* they strive for, love, believe and endure, and also *how* men act and are acted upon, the ways in which they do and suffer, desire and enjoy, see, believe, imagine—in short processes of *experiencing*. 'Experience' denotes the planted field, the sowed seeds, the reaped harvests, the changes of night and day, spring and autumn, wet and dry, heat and cold, that are observed, feared, longed for; it also denotes the one who plants and reaps, who works and rejoices, hopes, fears, plans, invokes magic or chemistry to aid him, who is downcast or triumphant. It is 'double-barreled' in that it recognizes in its primary integrity no division between act and material, subject and object, but contains them both in an unanalyzed totality." John Dewey, *Experience and Nature*, vol. 1 of *John Dewey: The Later Works, 1925–1953* (Carbondale: Southern Illinois University Press, 1988 [1925]), 18.

[3] James's view is that theories and their concepts are abstractions from immediate sensible life. This point is not incompatible with a recognition that theories may enter into immediate, sensible life in myriad ways—as causal forces, responses and expressions, embodied aspects of individual and social life, and so on. There is nothing contradictory about the notion of acts or functions of mediation having their own experienced immediacy.

secondary or peripheral place. And of course concepts central in some one given political theory may be only implicit or even altogether absent, whether intentionally or unintentionally, in other theories—for just a few examples, think Plato's concept of the philosopher-king, Locke's idea of the state of nature, Marx's class of the proletariat, Du Bois's analysis of double consciousness, Addams's idea of a fully social ethics, Dewey's notions of the public and democracy as a way of life, Arendt's concept of action, Rawls's idea of justice as fairness, Fanon's understanding of decolonialization, Deleuze's and Guattari's concept of schizoanalysis, or Anzaldúa's concept of borderlands.

Different theorists, like all persons, attend differently to their different lives—to what James termed the "one great, blooming, buzzing confusion" of life, an undifferentiated continuum, a flowing stream or river (in *Principles of Psychology*); a world of pure experience and fluent immediacy (in *Essays in Radical Empiricism*); and their perceptual fluxes or immediate sensible lives (in *Some Problems of Philosophy*). James thus characterized the work or function of conception or theory as discrimination and comparison of what we attend to—a kind of carving out or cutting up, the making of the whole of life to which we attend into concepts, chopped-up parts, identifiably different things. As John Dewey later would observe in his *Experience and Nature*, language turns events into objects.

Here James highlighted two points: first, the *selectivity and interestedness* of attention; and second, the *active, additive, creative* function of discrimination and comparison. As a result, concepts are actively made or reactively "taken" rather than simply "given" or passively received.[4]

First, in *The Principles of Psychology*, for example, he presented a view of experience marked and pervaded by active selective attention and so also by active selective inattention.[5] This attention is not merely a matter of

---

[4] See David Leary's discussion of attention as active but "only in response to what is presented to it." Leary also discusses James's account of differing modalities and selectivities of attention. *The Routledge Guidebook to James's Principles of Psychology* (New York: Routledge, 2018), 151, 153–155. See also his "The Psychological Roots of William James's Thought," in *The Jamesian Mind*, edited by Sarin Marchetti (New York: Routledge, 2021), 35–48.

[5] Discussing the selectivity of attention (and making the case for Freud's notion of the unconscious), Vincent Colapietro has referred to "the acts and habits of *actively ignoring*" what is available to our awareness. "James's Rejection of the Unconscious: A Fallacious Disavowal?," in *The Jamesian Mind*, edited by Sarin Marchetti (New York: Routledge, 2021), 116. However, inattention for James is wholly distinct from active ignoring—because the latter is a matter of *intentional* disregard or conscious refusal to *acknowledge*. James believed that we are not conscious of a great deal that goes on around us—from the world to other people to ourselves. Some of this is the result of selective attention due to temporary purposes at a given moment, and some of it is the result of habits of attention that have made the conditions of their own operation opaque or even impossible to note. For James, there is much about which we are not conscious, but there is no such thing as "the unconscious," any more than consciousness exists as a thing. Rather, consciousness and unconsciousness are

reflection but instead is embodied, as John Wild observed: "The adult person carries the general pattern of his world with him in his body and nervous system, and the selective attention through which he builds it up is choosing the world that is about to be."[6] James put it this way:

> Millions of items of the outward order are present to my senses which never properly enter into my experience. Why? Because they have no interest for me. *My experience is what I agree to attend to.* Only those items which I notice shape my mind—without selective interest, experience is an utter chaos. Interest alone gives accent and emphasis, light and shade, background and foreground—intelligible perspective, in a word. It varies in every creature, but without it, the consciousness of every creature would be a gray chaotic indiscriminateness, impossible for us even to conceive. . . . [E]ach of us literally *chooses*, by his ways of attending to things, what sort of a universe he shall appear to himself to inhabit. (PP, 380, 381, 401)

> [Thought] *is always interested more in one part of its object than another, and welcomes and rejects, or chooses, all the while it thinks.* The phenomena of selective attention and of deliberative will are of course patent examples of this choosing activity. But few of us are aware how incessantly it is at work in operations not ordinarily called by these names. . . . But we do far more than emphasize things, and unite some, and keep others apart. We actually *ignore* most of the things before us. (PP, 273)

Note that this view is thoroughly pluralistic or multiplicitous along two different axes. First, many different persons have different interests and, as a result, they attend to different items; attention varies among creatures and the universes they appear to themselves to inhabit. And second, the "same" one person has different interests over different times and at different places. As a consequence of the changing selectivity of attention, the self is a multiplicity rather than a simple selfsame unity, and selves inhabit a world that is pluralistic rather than singular. "Self" and "world," though single words,

functions, not things. Here, Shannon Sullivan's observation provides a helpful way to contrast James and Freud: "A crossroads between physiology and psychology quickly emerged in Freud's thinking, and Freud chose the latter path"—while, I think, James chose the former. *The Physiology of Sexist and Racist Oppression* (New York: Oxford University Press, 2018), 60.

6 John Wild, *The Radical Empiricism of William James* (Garden City, NY: Doubleday, 1969), 122.

name (or are conceptual substitutes for) plural realities. And so, as James put it, "philosophy must thus recognize many realms of reality which mutually interpenetrate" (SPP, 56).

Second, James identified the process or function by which attention carves up, singles out, and identifies (or holds fast) distinct things as *conceiving*. This is an active, additive, productive, creative process—a process that creates things and does not merely represent or mirror supposedly antecedent or independent things. As a result, if conceived one way, the world is full of one set of things; if conceived another way, the world is populated by quite different things. James explained:

> Each act of conception results from our attention singling out some one part of the mass of matter for thought which the world presents, and holding fast to it, without confusion. . . . Each conception thus eternally remains what it is, and never can become another. . . . *This whole function of conceiving, of fixing, and holding fast to meanings, has no significance apart from the fact that the conceiver is a creature with partial purposes and private ends.* (PP, 436, 437, 456)

Conceptions are instruments to serve the interests that selves have in understanding the world. James wrote that the "conception of consciousness as a purely cognitive form of being" is "anti-psychological":

> Every actually existing consciousness seems to itself at any rate to be a *fighter for ends*, of which many, but for its presence, would not be ends at all. Its powers of cognition are mainly subservient to these ends, discerning which facts further them and which do not. (PP, 144)

"The entire sweep of James's thought," John E. Smith observed, "is intelligible only against the background of the individual seen as a being of plans, purposes, and concerns."[7] In *Some Problems of Philosophy*, James made this same point that selective and purposive attention identifies and sorts the immediacy and flux of our lives by conceiving of stable, fixed, and, as a result, highly useful concepts. He observed:

---

[7] John E. Smith, *Themes in American Philosophy: Purpose, Experience and Community* (New York: Harper and Row, 1970), 17–18. This stress on the centrality of purpose in James's thought is also set forth by M. Gail Hamner, *American Pragmatism: A Religious Genealogy* (New York: Oxford University Press, 2003), 126–138.

Out of this aboriginal sensible muchness attention carves out objects, which conception then names and identifies forever. . . . We say *what* each part of the sensible continuum is, and all these abstracted *whats* are concepts. *The intellectual life of man consists almost wholly in his substitution of a conceptual order for the perceptual order in which his experience originally comes.* (SPP, 32, 33)

This substitution takes place by discrimination and comparison, by both breaking apart and reuniting, by both analysis and synthesis—by what James called "dissociation" and "association":

Our original sensible totals are, on the one hand, subdivided by discriminative attention, and, on the other, united with other totals—either through the agency of our own movements, carrying our senses from one part of space to another, or because new objects come successively and replace those by which we were at first impressed. The "simple impression" of Hume, the "simple idea" of Locke are both abstractions, never realized in experience. Experience, from the very first, presents us with concreted objects, vaguely continuous with the rest of the world which envelops them in space and time, and potentially divisible into inward elements and parts. (PP, 461)

To further distinguish his empirical psychology and philosophy from earlier atomistic and non-radical "empiricism," James claimed that "*Association, so far as the word stands for an effect, is between THINGS THOUGHT OF— it is THINGS, not ideas, which are associated in the mind. We ought to talk of the association of objects, not of the association of ideas*" (PP, 522).

These concepts, these carved-out little parts of life, are the building blocks of big, sometimes grandiose theoretical edifices—whole theories and philosophies (including political theories). They are assembled in propositions that are claimed to be true or false. These concepts are used and reused habitually and differently by different makers of different concepts, different bands of producers of different discriminations and comparisons, different schools of thought, different tribes of philosophers. (The tribes of political philosophers include, but are not limited to, liberals, conservatives, libertarians, anarchists, authoritarians, totalitarians, fascists, theocrats, populists, oligarchs, monarchists, aristocrats, social contract theorists, socialists, communists, critical theorists, decolonialists, feminists, critical race theorists, poststructuralists, communitarians, deliberative democrats, and republicans—and this list just begins to scratch the surface of the varieties of political theories.)

And in these different uses, different concepts deployed within different theories are continuously contested and reconstructed, consciously and unconsciously, by different tribes of theorists who carve up different lives and encounter different problems and opportunities at different times and places in different ways. All concepts and theories—again, including political concepts and theories—thus are, variously, affirmed and championed; modified and transformed; faulted, consigned to earlier eras and only historical interest, recovered, rediscovered, or predicted to be ahead of their time; or taken as evidence of intellectual shortcomings, theoretical pathologies, or even moral evils. Each tribe of theorists employs its concepts as weapons against the use, if not also the users, of alternative concepts. Each cluster of concepts and theory whispers, "Think this way, not some other way." Each tribe of political theorists seeks what James strikingly called a "theoretic conquest"—"the revelation of a deeper level of reality in things." Here James added:

> Concepts not only guide us over the map of life, but we revalue life by their use. . . . The mere possession of such vast and simple pictures is an inspiring good: they arouse new feelings of sublimity, power, and admiration, new interests and motivations. . . . So strongly do objects that come as universal and eternal arouse our sensibilities, so greatly do life's values deepen when we translate percepts into ideas! The translation appears as far more than the original equivalent. (SPP, 41–42)

Now, in making this point James definitely was *not* engaged in any wholesale criticism of concepts, propositions, theories, or other intellectual abstractions. Pragmatism, ever attentive and attuned to sentiments and sensations, practice and action, and immediacy and particulars, is not for all that simply anti-concept, anti-theory, or anti-abstraction. To think otherwise is to buy into exactly the kind of either/or dualism about practice and theory that pragmatism explicitly rejects.

In this context, three points merit brief emphasis and steady attention.

First, James clearly recognized the immense value or "import" of concepts (including political concepts), thoughts, theories, and abstractions. In part this value is instrumental and mediate: By substituting concepts for imme-diate experience, it becomes possible to identify and control or "handle" and "harness" (SPP, 39) the conditions and the consequences of subsequent expe-rience. In another part, this value is enriching and immediate: Concepts map our world, but this mapping becomes itself part of our world, a renewal and expansion of our world, a new world, a back-and-forth melding or interpen-etration of concept and percept, a concept-funded world immediately expe-rienced now as meaningful in particular ways. Finally, in a third part, this value is not a function of relations between percepts and concepts, between practice and theory, but instead a function of relations among concepts them-selves: When concepts are constructed, "new relations are then found among them, connecting them in peculiarly intimate, 'rational,' and unchangeable ways" and creating fields like mathematics and logic—fields James character-ized as "vast unmoving systems of universal terms" in which "nothing *hap-pens*" and their man-made truths are eternal (SPP, 41). James numbered and summarized this three-part import or value of concepts this way:

1. They steer us practically every day, and provide an immense map of re-lations among the elements of things, which, though not now, yet on some possible future occasion, may help to steer us practically;
2. They bring new values into our perceptual life, they reanimate our wills, and make our action turn upon new points of emphasis;
3. The map which the mind frames out of them is an object which possesses, once it has been framed, an independent existence . . . The "eternal" truths it contains would have to be acknowledged even were the world of sense annihilated. (SPP, 43)

The second point worth emphasis here is that although concepts and abstractions do have value, this value is limited. Failure to recognize this limit constitutes what James called "the abuse of concepts," a practice he labeled derogatorily as "the intellectual creed" and the "Platonizing persuasion" he found commonplace (SPP, 44). In *A Pluralistic Universe*, he called it "vicious intellectualism"—treating experience as no more than what the concepts we substitute for it *explicitly* name and include within our particular vocabulary (APU, 32, 109). For James, life always outstrips concepts, experience always exceeds theory; life is never fully captured or mapped by conceptual decom-position, language, thought, theories, and intellectual abstraction—even if "the barriers to clarity can themselves be modes of communication."[8] James explained:

> Conceptual knowledge is forever inadequate to the fullness of the reality to be known. Reality consists of existential particulars as well as of essences and universals and class-names, and of existential particulars we become aware only in the perceptual flux. The flux can never be superseded. We must carry it with us to the bitter end of our cognitive business, keeping it in the midst of the translation even when the latter proves illuminating, and falling back on it alone with the translation gives out. (SPP, 45)

When concepts are substituted for percepts and the immediacy of life, James continued, we also thereby substitute conceptual relations for the relations of life. However, "since the relations of concepts are of static comparison only, it is impossible to substitute them for the dynamic relations with which the perceptual flux is filled." Moreover, because concepts are discontinuous terms, they cover the continuity of flux-filled life only incompletely, "essential features of the flux escaping whenever we put concepts in its place" (SPP, 46).

Many of the problems and "dialectic contradictions" and supposed puzzles of philosophy, James added, result from assuming that "our flowing life" can be and must be "cut into discrete bits and pinned upon a fixed relational scheme," some set of concepts, some theory (SPP, 48, 54).

The remedy for this abuse of concepts is the recognition of their limits. James thus advised: "Use concepts when they help, and drop them when they hinder understanding," remembering always that "the deeper features of reality are found only in perceptual experience" that concepts cannot represent or replace—the "whole of immediate perceptual experience" being something that finite beings (including even theorists and philosophers) are able to compass for only a few of its passing moments in their short and passing lives (SP, 53).

This leads to a third point of emphasis: While a *concept* of a concept and a *concept* of the immediate (or perceptual) flux of life can be neatly distinguished and abstracted or separated from each other—they are, after all, concepts—*in our actual lives concepts and flux (or percepts) are irreducibly intermingled and anything but pure.* Conception is not perception-free,

---

[8] Richard Poirier, *Poetry and Pragmatism* (Cambridge, MA: Harvard University Press, 1992), 148.

and perception is not conception-free. We conceive *on the basis of* what we perceive, but also (at least after the brief initial blooming, buzzing confusion is no longer total) we also perceive on the basis of *what* we conceive. Perceptions are funded with, and by, conceptions. James also made this same point in *The Principles of Psychology* by contrasting sensations, the function of "mere *acquaintance* with a fact," from perceptions, the function of knowledge *about* a fact. He explained:

> Perception always involves Sensation as a portion of itself; and Sensation in turn never takes place in adult life without Perception also being there. . . . *A pure sensation is an abstraction.* (PP, 652–654)

Asserting that percepts and concepts are "made of the same kind of stuff" and that they "melt into each other when we handle them together," James put it this simile-packed way:

> How could it be otherwise when the concepts are like evaporations out of the bosom of perception, into which they condense again whenever practical service summons them? No one can tell, of the things he now holds in his hand and reads, how much comes in through his eyes and fingers, and how much, from his apperceiving intellect, unites with that and make of it this particular "book"? The universal and the particular parts of the experience are literally immersed in each other, and both are indispensable. Conception is not like a painted hook, on which no real chain can be hung; for we hang concepts upon percepts, and percepts upon concepts interchangeably and indefinitely. . . . The world we practically live in is one in which it is impossible, except by theoretic retrospection, to disentangle the contributions of intellect from those of sense. They are wrapt and rolled together as a gunshot in the mountains is wrapt and rolled in fold on fold of echo and reverberative clamor. Even so do intellectual reverberations enlarge and prolong the perceptual experience which they envelop, associating it with remoter parts of existence. And the ideas of these in turn work like those resonators that pick out partial tones in complex sounds. They help us to decompose our percept into parts and to abstract and isolate its elements. . . . Perception prompts our thought, and thought in turn enriches our perception. The more we see, the more we think; while the more we think, the more we see in our immediate experiences, and the greater grows

the details and the more significant the articulateness of our perception. (SPP, 58, 59)

This means that we cannot decide—and do not have to decide—practically whether it is better "to live or to understand life" because it is not possible for adults to do wholly and only one of these. That is a fake choice, a false dualism. The practical issue is not *whether* to live or *whether* to understand but, rather, *how and in what specific and interwoven ways to both live and think*— to mediate immediacy and so to transform it into a new immediacy, to abstract from and theorize practice and so reconstruct that practice so as to see immediately new things.[9]

The fact that percepts and concepts are mixed together rather than "pure," melted into each other rather than separate, is not at odds with or even in tension with James's insistence that the full reality of existential particulars in perceptual flux cannot be captured by, or translated into, general and fixed conceptual schemes. The point is that perceptual flux—a flux mediated by and shot through with concepts—constitutes a particular immediacy that cannot be fully and successfully translated into concepts and language. Your experience reading this particular sentence and this particular point in this particular place in this particular history would not be what it is if, for example, you lacked the concept "book." Percepts and concepts are mixed in your experience. However, to conceptualize what you are doing as, for example again, "reading a book" is to substitute a general and static product of reflection on your experience for the particular and in-flux experience that gave rise to the reflection. It is to treat the object of reflection about experience as the object of experience itself. It is to reduce life's particular immediacy to conceptualization's mediated generalities The pragmatic point here is not that human beings have immediate, non-inferential knowledge but, rather, that human living includes more than conceptualizing and knowing. And the point is that human beings and their lives are pluralistic and overflow and outstrip the class-names of concepts and words. Last, the point is that conceptualization reworks and *transforms* experienced flux in ways that are always selective and always partial.

---

[9] Maria Bagharamian and Sarin Marchetti noted in a different context that pragmatism insists on both the central importance of language and thought (which they identify as a mark of twentieth-century analytic philosophy) and the primacy of experience (which they identify as the emphasis of twentieth-century phenomenology and continental European philosophy). Maria Baghramian and Sarin Marchetti, *Pragmatism and the European Traditions: Encounters with Analytic Philosophy and Phenomenology Before the Great Divide* (New York: Routledge, 2018), 3.

It is important, both for personal life and for politics, that this reconstructive, transformative, additive function of cognition not be understood simply as empowerment, enrichment, expansion, and boundless freedom. If initially creative in function, acts of conceiving, like other acts, also become habitual, fixed, static. Our conceptions have an "ideational preparation" function and dimension: They direct our attention in particular ways and at once lead us to be inattentive in others. As such, conceptions function as a kind of selective blindness, a habituated selective blindness: They allow someone to see some things only as they prevent that same person from seeing other things. Conception, James observed, functions often as *preperception*. This is not confirmation bias; it is what we might call "conception bias":

> It is for this reason that men have no eyes but for those aspects of things which they have already been taught to discern. Any one of us can notice a phenomenon after it has once been pointed out, which not one in ten thousand could ever have discovered for himself. . . . In short, *the only things which we commonly see are those which we preperceive* and the only things which we preperceive are those which have been labeled for us, and the labels stamped into our mind. (PP, 420, 421)

Concepts and theories, including political theories, are mind and body stamping machines, both individually and socially. They prepare us to attend and perceive in some ways and not in others. Different concepts and different theories stamp lives and societies in different ways.

As a result, someone else's ideas, beliefs, and values may seem different, odd, baseless, bad, blind, wrong, and out of whack in one's own world and to one's own get-off-my-lawn way of conceiving things. James added: "If we lost our stock of labels we should be intellectually lost in the midst of the world" (PP, 421). This is true, but even so, if we lost, discarded, or traded in some of our stock of labels on a regular basis—if we had the habit of perceiving in unhabitual ways—we might more often see different things (that we did not already preperceive) and the different worlds of different people. And we might through this different vision come to create and inhabit a different world.

This overturning of stock labels is what, in related contexts, James called "genius" and the flash of greatness.[10] He observed that here, instead of thoughts of concrete things patiently following one another in a beaten track

---

[10] See chapter 2, sections 1, 2, and 4.

of habitual suggestion, we have the most abrupt cross-cuts and transitions from one idea to another, the most rarefied abstractions and discriminations, the most unheard-of combinations of elements, the subtlest associations of analogy; in a word, we seem suddenly introduced into a seething caldron of ideas, where everything is fizzling and bobbing about in a state of bewildering activity, where partnerships can be joined or loosened in an instant, treadmill routine is unknown, and the unexpected seems the only law.[11] So, if *too little* preperception can leave us without routine, unmoored, and frantically lost in a world that is thus unstable and foreign, as James noted, then equally, I think, *too much* preperception can leave us saddled by old habits and ways of life, lost in a world that no longer is the familiar one in and for which those habits first were formed and worked. This is a pressing personal and political problem: in a changing world, how to nurture neither too little nor too much preperception, preclusion, and prejudice—plural, different, often contested preperceptions, preclusions, and prejudices?

To summarize this section: For more than twenty years—from his 1890 landmark *Principles of Psychology* and the early essays collected in his 1891 *The Will to Believe and Other Essays in Popular Philosophy* through his writings, manuscripts, and letters on pragmatism, radical empiricism, and pluralism to his posthumous 1911 *Some Problems of Philosophy: A Beginning of an Introduction to Philosophy* (in which he frequently cited his own earlier writings), William James consistently set forth a *pluralistic* and *pragmatic* psychology and philosophy of human experience. Beginning with the central and irreducible immediate and novel flux of our lives—what he called his "insuperability of sensation" thesis (SPP, 45)—James stressed both that language is not capable of grasping or expressing the temporality of experience[12] and that the selectivity of attention results in multiple, different

---

[11] In his "Great Men and Their Environment," James described great persons—he wrote "great men"—as agents of change, "ferments, initiators of movement, setters of precedent or fashion, centres of corruption, or destroyers of other persons, whose gifts, had they had free play, would have led society in another direction" (WB, 185, 170; see also PP, 400, 500, 754, 976, and 984–993).

[12] On this point, Charlene Haddock Seigfried wrote:

> James concedes that although we ought to say that we have a feeling of "by" just as we say that we have a feeling of "blue," we actually do not. He ascribes this peculiarity to the fact that language does not lend itself to such usage because it has been habitually used to express only the substantive parts as objects of feeling. Consequently, it does not lend itself to expressing the transitive aspect of experience as the object of feeling. In other words, it sounds queer to say: "I saw 'and'" but not queer to say "I saw 'blue,'" even though the sentence, "I saw a blue and a yellow ball," is perfectly normal and may express a single impression*Chaos and Context: A Study in William James* (Athens: Ohio University Press, 1978), 13.

concepts, theories, and abstractions that are simply different ways of cutting up and mapping the flux—all resulting in multiple realms of reality. This is the *pluralism* of James's philosophical psychology. Moreover, he stressed that although life-as-conceived never fully captures or translates life-as-lived, the origin of concepts is their utility, and they have immense practical value as instruments for harnessing the immediacies of life in order to drive them more fully and more regularly toward our goals and purposes (SPP, 38, 39). This is the *pragmatism* of James's philosophical psychology. It is this pluralistic and pragmatic philosophical psychology that is at work in James's political thought.

2. Naming and Harnessing James's Political Thought

In "The Types of Philosophic Thinking" in *A Pluralistic Universe*, James, an inveterate classifier, noted that although "individuality outruns all classification, yet we insist on classifying every one we meet under some general head." This recalls his claim that percepts always outstrip concepts, that any individual or particular bit of life is more than its decomposition in and by conceptualization, theory, and abstraction. He continued: "As these heads usually suggest prejudicial associations to some hearer or other, the life of philosophy largely consists of resentments at the classing, and complaints of being misunderstood" (APU, 7). (With seeming optimism that in retrospect may not have been warranted, James immediately added that the resentments and complaints rampant among philosophers who are professors show "signs of clearing up" and that there is coming to be "on the whole less acrimony in [philosophical] discussion.")

Now, individuality surely does outrun classification, but when it comes to James's political thought, classification threatens to outstrip individuality—because so very, very many different and seemingly incompatible labels have been applied to his work.

Many insightful scholars of James's work have rightly noted this fact—even as some of them have advanced brand-new labels in ways that have enlarged this very fact. For example, in his perceptive *William James on Democratic Individuality*, Stephen S. Bush observed the "striking range" of interpretations of James's political thought and claimed that "we can group them under some broad headings: quietist, anarchist, communitarian, reformer, anti-imperialist, pluralist, democrat, republican, and liberal." And in a genuinely Jamesian and, I think, refreshing, pluralistic tone, Bush recognized that these nine categories are neither mutually exclusive nor finally complete. After briefly surveying each of these labels (in an appropriately footnote-filled manner), he then proposed a tenth label: "Democratic individualist is the designation I think best fits James, but I recognize that his political commitments fit other designations as well."[13]

Of course, as he recognized, Bush's first designation or label, "quietist," is not so much a name for a particular approach to, or school of thought about, James's political writings. Instead, it designates a group of scholars who have believed that there simply is no political theory—or no sufficiently developed political theory—to be found in James's writings. It is a label for a group of scholars who have held one or more of the following three views:

1. James in fact had no political philosophy at all and his psychology, pragmatism, radical empiricism, and pluralism are basically apolitical. "If we look to James as a pragmatist concerned with American life," Bruce Kuklick judged, "our expectations go unfulfilled."[14] It is in this spirit, for example, that James T. Kloppenberg characterized James's philosophy as unconcerned with, and disconnected from, politics.[15] Similarly, Vivian J. McGill asserted that "James gave no direct attention to economics . . . and had nothing to say against the basic tyrannies in the economic world," tyrannies "surely more dangerous to the zest and rich variety of life he desire than the poor dragons of Bradley and Royce which he slew so gaily."[16] Historian Bruce Kuklick put it bluntly: James was not a social and political thinker "of any stature."[17] And Richard Hoftstadter, claiming that James had only the "remotest interest in systematic or collective social reform," concluded "he had no sustained interest in social theory as such."[18] (Here it is worth pointing out that James did not have any sustained interest in any theory as such

[13] Stephen S. Bush, *William James on Democratic Individuality* (Cambridge, UK: Cambridge University Press, 2017), 22.
[14] Bruce Kuklick, *The Rise of American Philosophy: Cambridge, Massachusetts, 1860–1930* (New Haven, CT: Yale University Press, 1977), 309.
[15] James T. Kloppenberg, *Uncertain Victory: Social Democracy and Progressivism in European and American Thought, 1870–1920* (New York: Oxford University Press, 1986), 189.
[16] Vivian J. McGill, "Pragmatism Reconsidered: An Aspect of John Dewey's Philosophy," *Science and Society* 3, no. 3 (1939): 291.
[17] Kuklick, *The Rise of American Philosophy*, 306.
[18] Richard Hofstadter, *Social Darwinism in American Thought* (Boston: Beacon Press, 1955), 134.

or theory isolated from practice and its consequences.) Political historian George Sabine put it most directly: "So far as I can see James had no political philosophy." And philosopher Peter Jones asserted, "James published almost nothing on social or political philosophy, although towards the end of his life he spent some time reflecting on the issues of war and peace, and also on the military virtues."[19]

2. James did write some scattered brief letters to newspaper editors on some of the issues of the day, touched on some social issues of his day in personal correspondence with friends and family and professional colleagues, and wrote a handful of occasional essays filled with his sentiments, observations, and, sometimes, proposals—all of which fall far short of constituting a robust political theory or comprehensive political philosophy. In this spirit, for example, Paul Conkin wrote that "except on the issue of imperialism, James remained largely aloof from national politics," preaching "his own gospel of individualism" rather than advancing any program of "political and economic reform."[20] Similarly, Edward H. Madden noted that it is a measure of James's complete lack of engagement or "involvement in the struggle against racism that he did not even mention," much less actually do anything relevant to, major post–Civil War events such as "the Civil Rights Act of 1875; the debate between emigration or assimilation of American blacks, with Frederick Douglass fighting for assimilation; the Supreme Court decision (of 1883) declaring the 1875 act unconstitutional; the *Plessy v. Ferguson* decision (1896) that established the separate-but-equal doctrine; the Niagara Movement and the subsequent emergence of the National Association for the Advancement of Colored

[19] George Sabine, letter to Harold Stoke, quoted in Alexander Livingston, *Damn Great Empires! William James and the Politics of Pragmatism* (New York: Oxford University Press, 2016), 1; Peter Jones, "William James," in *American Philosophy*, edited by Marcus G. Singer (New York: Cambridge University Press, 1985), 61.

[20] Paul Conkin, *Puritans and Pragmatists: Eight Eminent American Thinkers* (Bloomington: Indiana University Press, 1968), 275. Conkin here observed that James exhibited the "standards of a middle-class Victorian gentleman." For a different view, see both George Cotkin, *William James, Public Philosopher* (Baltimore: Johns Hopkins University Press, 1990) and Ralph Barton Perry's chapter "James the Reformer" in his very influential *The Thought and Character of William James, as Revealed in Unpublished Correspondence and Notes, Together with His Published Writings* (Boston: Little, Brown, 1935), 2:300–322. In chap. 1 of *Damn Great Empires!*, Alexander Livingston provided an extended and insightful account of the political context and political purposes of Perry's account of James as individualist and liberal. He observed: "It is a great irony that James, the pacifist anti-imperialist, would be made to symbolize the moral purpose of state power at war" and that his writings would be interpreted as "apologia for democratizing imperialism" and "American global power" (51).

People (of which a student of James's, W. E. B. Du Bois, was one of the organizers)."[21] As many scholars have noted, this same point—James's lack of engagement—applies to matters of sexism, women's suffrage, women's education, and women's roles in families and workplaces. Constantly employing the sexist language and stereotypes and thinking of his day, James championed "manliness," and wrote almost nothing about these issues.[22] What he did write—he labeled his own pragmatism as "feminine" in style,[23] and he rejected arguments for the subordination of women—is very cautious and very little. Whether with respect to matters of race, gender, class, or other social issues, John J. McDermott put the point in this succinct way: "James was genial but self-centered and abysmally ignorant of massive social inequalities."[24]

3. James's few writings on political matters were merely voluntaristic and moral exhortations to individual self-fulfillment, sometimes self-congratulatory and self-serving, that consistently lacked attention to the workings of political power and political institutions, economic structures, social organizations and technologies, international

[21] Edward H. Madden, "Introduction," in *The Correspondence of William James, 1895–1899*, edited by I. K. Skrupskelis and E. M. Berkeley (Charlottesville: University of Virginia Press, 2000), 8:xxxv. Madden went on to describe James as a "man in and very much of his time and class," a "nineteenth-century northern liberal, *ambivalent*," with "jostling and conflicting private and public views," neither "crusader nor racist" (xxxvi). Another essay by Madden and George R. Garrison paints a similar picture of James as "not much of a reformer even in the areas where he extended himself" and unexpectedly blind "on the issues of racism, women's rights, British oppression of the Irish, and British imperialism in general." They conclude that James should be viewed "as a person who, in some instances, had what looked like good ideas to us today, and who implemented them occasionally in something less than a striking fashion." George R. Garrison and Edward H. Madden, "William James—Warts and All," *American Quarterly* 29, no. 2 (1977): 207–211.

[22] See two excellent studies here: Charlene Haddock Seigfried, *Pragmatism and Feminism: Reweaving the Social Fabric* (Chicago: University of Chicago Press, 1996), 111–141; Kim Townsend, *Manhood at Harvard: William James and Others* (New York: W. W. Norton, 1996).

[23] On this point, see Deborah Whitehead's *William James, Pragmatism, and American Culture* (Bloomington: Indiana University Press, 2016), esp. 83–111. In "The Missing Perspectives: Where Are All the Pragmatist Feminists and Feminist Pragmatists," Charlene Haddock Seigfried observed: "Femininity and masculinity are social and psychological interpretations of gender that both exhibit and mask unequal power relations. Feminism exposes the negative impact of such stereotypical attributions of gender characterizations. However, some aspects of experience that have been associated with women, labeled *feminine*, and consequently devalued in patriarchal cultures have also been positively revalued by feminists. . . . That I find James's metaphorical and suggestive style more congenial to my own way of thinking than an analytic and explicit style can be understood as the expression of a feminine style without implying that all women think this way or that no men do. . . . From my point of view, he [James] is rejecting a prevalent form of masculine style for a feminine one." In *Pragmatism and Feminism*, 33.

[24] John J. McDermott, review of Jacques Barzun's *A Stroll with William James*, *The New England Quarterly* 57, no. 1 (1984): 130. Compare Eddie Glaude's judgment: "James and Dewey did in fact demonstrate in their daily lives a commitment, however limited, to antiracist politics." *In a Shade of Blue: Pragmatism and the Politics of Black America* (Chicago: University of Chicago Press, 2007), 2.

relations and global interconnections, embodied histories and conflicting cultural customs, and issues of race, gender, class, and other
realities driving most of the demands for social reform and activism
even in his own time—much less the contested demands of the present.
It is in this spirit, for example, that Cornel West found James's philosophy to be "one of political impotence" filled with "apolitical notions
of how to change the world."[25] Similarly, M. C. Otto claimed James was
"blind" to the large political role of institutions, which he took only to
endanger "the purity of individuality" and the "'sacredness of private
integrity.'"[26] Loren Goldman has similarly stressed that to the extent
James does have political concerns, their focus is ethical life rather than
government and its institutions.[27] James Campbell, echoing both Otto
and George Fredrickson's *The Inner Civil War*, claimed that James's individualism left him unable to recognize or respond "to a world that
was becoming increasingly integrated and interdependent,"[28] made
him mostly silent on "social issues that appear central at present," and
revealed him powerless and unable to recognize "that individualism itself could lead to social problems."[29] John Patrick Diggins judged that
"James's pragmatism, in contrast to Peirce's and Dewey's, is too pluralistic, if not anarchistic, to give purpose and direction to thought by

[25] Cornel West, *The American Evasion of Philosophy* (Madison: University of Wisconsin Press, 1989), 59, 60.

[26] M. C. Otto, "On a Certain Blindness in William James," *Ethics* 53, no. 3 (1943): 189–190. Otto's point that James failed to see structural problems and think in institutional terms is embraced as a limit of James's thought by Loren Goldman in "Revisiting the Social Value of College Breeding," in *Pragmatism Applied: William James and the Challenges of Contemporary Life*, edited by Clifford Stagoll and Michael P. Levine (Albany: State University of New York Press, 2019), 48–49.

[27] Loren Goldman, "Another Side of William James: On Radical Approaches to a 'Liberal' Philosopher," *William James Studies* 8 (2012): 38.

[28] George Fredrickson, *The Inner Civil War: Northern Intellectuals and the Crisis of Union* (Urbana: University of Illinois Press, 1993 [1965]); James Campbell, "DuBois and James," *Transactions of the Charles S. Peirce Society* 28, no. 3 (1992): 571. Note that this assertion is very different from another (and more justified) one that Campbell has made in the same context—namely, that "James's evaluation of institutions was mostly negative." It is surely correct that James held a mostly nega-
tive evaluation of cultural institutions—James wrote, "*Every* great institution is perforce a means of corruption—whatever good it may also do." But this evaluation *presupposes* that James actually did recognize and respond to a world of increasingly integrated and interdependent institutions, organ-
izations, and practices. Of course, whether this evaluation of institutions strengthens or weakens (as Campbell claimed) James's political philosophy is a different question—a question about the value of this philosophy and not one about its existence or non-existence. James Campbell, *Experiencing William James: Belief in a Pluralistic World* (Charlottesville: University of Virginia Press, 2017), 215, 239. For an interpretation very different from Campbell's on this point, see, for example, Deborah Coon, "'One Moment in the World's Salvation': Anarchism and the Radicalization of William James," *Journal of American History* 83, no. 1 (1996): 70–99.

[29] Campbell, *Experiencing William James*, 215, 227.

advocating organized inquiry and cooperative intelligence as a means of addressing social problems.[30] And, as a final example, Barbara Thayer-Bacon, praising James for his undercutting of the relativism/absolutism dualism, concludes that "one weakness James has is his clinging to an individual model" and his failure to "consistently address pluralism in terms of the diversity of human beings."[31]

In the face of these and even more seeming disagreements about whether or not James even had any political philosophy and, if he did, what that political philosophy actually is and how it should be classified, it may be tempting to ask: *Which interpreter's argument or case is most justified and, so, which interpretation of James is the right one, the true one, the full and final and correct one?* (When it is put this way, it should be easy to see how this kind of question often produces feelings of resentment and claims of misunderstanding by those whose interpretations are labeled "incorrect." And it is this kind of question that gives rise to the feeling that on any issue there are only two kinds of philosophies—one's own and incorrect ones.) In short, this kind of question amounts to: *Which of the many different interpretations or conceptualizations of James's political writings achieves complete "theoretic conquest"?*

Before rushing to respond to—or reframe—this question, it is important to critically examine two key presuppositions that give rise to it. Both of these presuppositions or presumptions are very much at odds with both the letter and the spirit of James's own philosophy—very much at odds with both pragmatism and pluralism.

In the first place, it is important not to presume that verbal differences in name all constitute practical differences in fact. It is important to be pragmatic. Faced with so many different names or labels for James's political philosophy—anarchist, anti-imperialist, communitarian, democratic, participatory democratic, fascist, individualist, liberal, mugwump, pacifist, pluralist, progressive, racist, reformist, republican, sexist, socialist, Victorian—it is crucial to determine the *pragmatic* meaning of each of these labels—to trace their respective *practical* differences, if any—and not simply to presuppose that all verbal differences constitute practical disagreements.

---

[30] John Patrick Diggins, *The Promise of Pragmatism: Modernism and the Crisis of Knowledge and Authority* (Chicago: University of Chicago Press, 1994), 137.

[31] Barbara Thayer-Bacon, "A Feminist Re/examination of William James as a Qualified Relativist," in *William James and Education*, edited by Jim Garrison, Ron Podeschi, and Eric Bredo (New York: Teachers College Press, 2002), 108.

Indeed, the situation with respect to interpreters of James's political writings is to a large extent similar to the situation of the members of the camping party, described by James in "What Pragmatism Means," who are all arguing with one another about whether or not someone rapidly circling a tree "goes round" a squirrel moving on that tree so as to keep the tree between itself and the person. In this familiar example, James responded that whether or not the person "goes round," the squirrel " 'depends on what is practically meant by 'going round' the squirrel' "— for example, passing from north to east to south to west of the squirrel or instead being in front of the squirrel and then on its left side and then behind it and then on its right side. James concluded that the pragmatic method interprets a notion or label or concept "by tracing its respective practical consequences":

> What difference would it practically make to any one if this notion rather than that notion were true? If no practical difference whatever can be traced, then the alternatives mean practically the same thing, and all dispute is idle. Whenever a dispute is serious, we ought to be able to show some practical difference that must follow from one side or the other being right. . . .It is astonishing to see how many philosophical disputes collapse into insignificance the moment you subject them to this simple test of tracing a concrete consequence. (P, 28, 30)

In this light, is James, for example, an individualist *or* a democratic theorist? As noted above, Bush claimed that James's politics was one of "democratic individuality"—both democratic *and* individualist, two labels here not at odds with each other. Further, in light of James's claim that "the practical consequence of [pluralism] is the well-known democratic respect for the sacredness of individuality" (TT, 4)—that the flip side of pluralism is individualism—Bush added, "The flip side of individuality is pluralism."[32] If this is correct, as I think it is, then James's political writings are democratic, individualist, *and* pluralist, and these three verbally different labels are not practically at odds with one another. And surely it would be odd to label James's anti-dualist philosophy with merely one side of a supposed individual/social dualism. As James Abrecht has noted, "any stark opposition"

---

[32] Bush, *William James on Democratic Individuality*, 2.

between "individual versus collective approaches to reform" is explicitly rejected by pragmatist thinkers.[33]

Or, instead, is James a participatory democrat, as Joshua I. Miller has argued in his thoughtful *Democratic Temperament: The Legacy of William James*? Miller noted that "in this book, I translate James's thinking into the language of democratic politics" and then observed that although he was attempting "to articulate a coherent democratic theory in James's writings," "the individual was perhaps his [James's] central value" even as James also "insisted that people had strong obligations to serve the community."[34] And just as Miller saw James as both democratic *and* individualist, Bush, who focused on individualism, saw James as both individualist *and* democratic. He stated: "I endorse the way Miller relates James to radical democratic theory. I too think that James's views of action and mutual respect have important implications for participatory democracy."[35] In these interpretations, James is labeled both individualist *and* democratic.

Is James's political thought properly labeled anarchist? Virtually everyone recognizes that James is an anti-imperialist, but is he also, as a final example, an anarchist rather than, say, a democrat? James's pragmatic method teaches us to answer this question by first specifying the practical meaning of "anarchy." Deborah Coon has labeled James's political thought, following U.S. military action against the Philippines, as anarchist (specifically, "pacifist, communitarian anarchism")—an anarchism that means "individualism combined with spontaneous and flexible organization," formed freely and operating in a non-coercive manner.[36] Given this meaning, the label "anarchism" is not at odds with "individualism" or "communitarianism" but, instead, contains and is constituted by those other labels. Moreover, to define "anarchism" in this way (rather than as commitment to the abolition of all government) is to make it compatible with participatory democracy—at least as long as that democracy is free and non-coercive in its formation, maintenance, and operation. Accordingly, in this light, James's political thought may be labeled, without contradiction, as anarchist, communitarian, democratic, individualist, *and* pluralist. And if James's "anarchism" is understood as Alexander Livingston characterized it—"an intellectual repudiation of

---

[33] James Albrecht, *Reconstructing Individualism: A Pragmatic Tradition from Emerson to Ellison* (New York: Fordham University Press, 2012), 129.

[34] Joshua I. Miller, *Democratic Temperament: The Legacy of William James* (Lawrence: University of Kansas Press, 1997), 3, 7.

[35] Bush, *William James on Democratic Individuality*, 31.

[36] Coon, "'One Moment in the World's Salvation,'" 86, 81.

necessity, dogmatism, and rationalism" and "an intervention into the very craving for authority at the core of empire as a way of life"[37]—then surely there is no contradiction in labeling James an anarchist *and* an individualist *and* a democrat *and* a pluralist *and* so on. To some significant extent, many (admittedly not all) of the labels often applied to James's political writings are verbal differences that make only a small practical difference. A little pragmatic method goes a long way here.

However, some of the different ways of labeling, naming, and classifying James's politics are not merely, or even primarily, verbal differences that make little or no difference in practice. Instead, they are genuine conceptual and theoretical differences—different ways of carving out or cutting up, different mappings, different ways of discriminating and comparing James's writings. *Accordingly, in the second place, it is important not to presuppose or pretend that conceptual differences reflect or mirror some supposedly antecedent reality independent of particular selective attentions and interests. It is important to be pluralistic.* As James explained in *The Principles of Psychology*, different concepts, and the different perceptions they fund, originate in and reflect the selective attention and interests of their thinkers—the differently selective attentions and interests of different thinkers. Just as James wrote that we *choose* the sort of universe we appear to ourselves to inhabit by the ways we selectively attend to things, so too we choose an interpretation of James's writings by the ways (conscious or unconscious) we selectively attend to, and are interested in, that philosophy.

Moreover, if philosophy as a whole, as James urged, must recognize many realms of mutually interpenetrating reality—a pluralistic universe—so too we must recognize many realms of overlapping realities in James's work, a pluralistic philosophy (and not simply a monistic philosophy about pluralism). Because the whole function of conceiving, theorizing, interpreting, and abstracting, as James pointed out, has no significance apart from the partial purposes, particular perspectives and preperceptions, and private ends of specific conceivers, it can never be complete or full. It is always partial; no single conception or interpretation ever can be final. To seek a full and final "theoretic conquest" or complete conceptual decomposition is to affirm, whether wittingly or unwittingly, the intellectual creed and vicious intellectualism that James so strongly opposed. What James wrote about reality in

[37] Livingston, *Damn Great Empires!*, 11.

his conclusion to *A Pluralistic Universe* applies equally to accounts of James's writing:

> Everything you can think of, however vast or inclusive, has on the plu-
> ralistic view a genuinely "external" environment of some sort or amount.
> Things are "with" one another in many ways, but nothing includes every-
> thing or dominates over everything. The word "and" trails along after every
> sentence. Something always escapes. "Ever not quite" has to be said of the
> best attempts made anywhere in the universe at attaining all-inclusiveness.
> The pluralistic word is thus more like a federal republic than like an empire
> or a kingdom. (APU, 145)

To approach James both pluralistically and pragmatically is to set aside the question "Which interpretation of James's political philosophy is the sole right one, the impersonally true one, the full and final and correct one?" and, instead, to take up two very different questions.

The first question is rooted in James's pluralism and is genealogical in its orientation: *What and whose partial interests, what selective attention, and what habit of preperception give rise to a particular conceptualization and interpretation of James's work?* To what and why has some particular person paid attention and shown interest? (Why, for example, did Bush selectively attend to the notion of individuality, Miller to democracy, Ferguson to pluralism, Coon to radicalism, Whitehead to the feminine, Kloppenberg to a particular kind of theory, and Alexander to anti-authoritarianism?) What labels have been stamped into a particular interpreter's mind, and what labels does that person in turn stamp into our minds? What has that person ignored?

The second question is rooted in James's pragmatism and is instrumental and consequential in its orientation: *Does some conceptualization or interpretation of James's writings work and satisfy, does it help us get into satisfactory relation with other parts of our experience, is it an idea upon which we can ride, does it marry old beliefs and new experience, and does it help us successfully harness our perceptions?* This is not a matter that can be settled by lectures, journal articles, and book chapters. It is a question that can be answered, always tentatively, only in experience, in life, and not in theory alone. And it is a question that returns us to a radically empirical and relational pluralism: "We say that a theory solves [a problem] more satisfactorily than that other theory; but that means more satisfactorily to ourselves, and individuals will emphasize their points of satisfaction differently" (P, 35). Someone else's interpretation of James, like someone else's sense of "the total character of the universe," may always seem "out of plumb and out of key and out of 'whack' " (P, 25). Ever not quite!

And . . .

3. A Radically Empirical, Pragmatic, and Pluralistic Political Philosophy

The fundamental contribution of William James to any morphological analysis of the human condition is that he thickens the discussion. . . . The philosophy of James calls for a never-ending series of descriptions and diagnoses, each from a specific vantage point but no one of them burdened with having to account for everything.[38]

Now, in *Pragmatism*, after explaining pragmatism as a method, a theory of truth, and a temperament or attitude, James moved to "Some Metaphysical Problems Pragmatically Considered" in order to illustrate the pragmatic method's application to particular problems. In that chapter he examined, in turn, what he called the problem of substance, the question of design in nature, and the free-will problem. In the next chapter, "The One and the Many," he took up this "ancient problem," which he considered "the most central of all philosophic problems" (P, 64). And he returned in a later full chapter to "pragmatism's conception of truth" (P, 95–113). Here and in many other writings, James applied his pragmatic method to central notions in metaphysics and epistemology in order to clarify their practical meaning so that the truth or falsity of beliefs containing these concepts could be tested and determined in and by experience.

Neither *Pragmatism* nor any of James's other books contains a chapter titled "Some Political Problems Pragmatically Considered." James nowhere explained or illustrated the pragmatic meaning of concepts central to much political theory: justice, liberty, law, democracy, equality, cosmopolitanism,

---

[38] John J. McDermott, "The Cultural Immortality of Philosophy as Human Drama," in *Streams of Experience: Reflections on the History and Philosophy of American Culture* (Amherst: University of Massachusetts Press, 1986), 26. See also James Gouinlock's analysis of "thin" simplifying systems of ethics and politics—of which he took John Rawls to be the exemplar of "this reductive and prejudicial mode of thought." *Rediscovering the Moral Life* (Buffalo, NY: Prometheus Books, 1993), 267.

liberalism, authoritarianism, individualism (old or new), rights, representation, revolution, slavery, sovereignty, power, property, the public, or the state.
Moreover, James produced no counterpart to his influential *The Varieties
of Religious Experience*, nothing that could have been titled *The Varieties of
Political Experience*. There exists no volume titled *The Meaning of Justice* to
pair with James's *The Meaning of Truth*. And there is no companion volume
to *Essays in Radical Experience* that might have been a collection titled *Essays
in Radical Democracy*. This cluster of facts constitutes a bit of prima facie
evidence, if only a little bit, for the view that James simply had no political
theory—depending, of course, on how one pragmatically understands what
counts as having a "theory."

Nonetheless, James's philosophy, in my view, is *unquestionably and pervasively political*.

Quoting James, biographer Linda Simon got this right:

> There was no doubt in James's mind about the necessity for deep social and
> political reform. America's policy of aggression and imperialism convinced
> James that the country had embraced a sad new identity. America, he said,
> "has deliberately pushed itself into the circle of international hatreds, and
> joined the common pack of wolves . . . We are objects of fear to other lands.
> This makes of the old liberalism and the new liberalism of our country
> two discontinuous things. The older liberalism is in office, the new is in
> the opposition." As part of the opposition, he took his place among other
> intellectuals, in America and in Europe, who formed a "great international
> and cosmopolitan liberal party, the party of intelligence . . . carrying on the
> war against the powers of darkness here."[39]

So too historian George Cotkin, whose work wonderfully contextualizes
and situates James in his time and place. Cotkin claimed that James "fully, if
unevenly" addressed the public issues of his day:

> In this engagement, James accepted and exemplified the role of "public phi-
> losopher"; his philosophical doctrines were public statements, or "social
> expressions," of interest and concern to an audience broader that that of
> professional philosophers. . . . Philosophy as a vehicle for self-examination

---

[39] Linda Simon, *Genuine Reality: A Life of William James* (Chicago: University of Chicago Press,
1999), 313.

and social reflection became a central tenet of James's public philosophy. Public philosophy interrogated social problems and proposed solutions to cultural difficulties.[40]

And historian James Kloppenberg stressed not only that James did address public political issues but that he did this with immense influence and impact:

Through his radical empiricism and pragmatism he helped to nurture the seeds of a new political sensibility, which reached fruition in the writings of John Dewey and other like-minded American radicals between 1890–1920, by insisting that knowledge begins in the uncertainty of immediate experience and that all ideas must remain subject to continuous testing in social practice.[41]

This view has been echoed by José Medina: "James's discussions of truth constitute a reconstruction of the ways in which truth functions as a value in our practices." He continued:

James's radical pluralism yields a very specific conception of solidarity in which bonds and shared commitments are established on the basis of (rather than at the expense of) an irreducible diversity of experiential and agential perspectives, and with an eye to fostering and strengthening this diversity.[42]

Finally, Frank Lentricchia makes this point in this illuminating way:

[40] George Cotkin, *William James: Public Philosopher* (Urbana: University of Illinois Press, 1994), 11. See also Cotkin's staged politics-focused conversation between James and Richard Rorty in his "James and Rorty: Context and Conversation," in *Pragmatism: From Progressivism to Postmodernism*, edited by Robert Hollinger and David Depew (Westport, CT: Praeger, 1995), 38–55. Similarly, biographer Gay Wilson Allen wrote that following the 1898 blowing up of the US battleship *Maine* in Havana, Cuba, and the ensuing American declaration of war, "much of James's precious energies for the next several years would go into resisting this 'barbaric patriotism,' for which he would be attacked and vilified by many people." *William James: A Biography* (New York: Viking, 1967), 389.

[41] James T. Kloppenberg, "William James," in *A Companion to American Thought*, edited by Richard Wightman Fox and James T. Kloppenberg (Cambridge, MA: Blackwell, 1995), 348.

[42] José Medina, "James on Truth and Solidarity: The Epistemology of Diversity and the Politics of Specificity," in *100 Years of Pragmatism: William James's Revolutionary Philosophy*, edited by John J. Stuhr (Bloomington: Indiana University Press, 2010), 127, 137.

James in effect accepts the most famous of Marx's theses on Feuerbach—
that philosophy should be trying to change, not interpret, the world—but
James out-Marxes Marx by saying that all interpretive efforts of philosophy are always simultaneously efforts to work upon and work over things
as they are. All intellectuals play social roles, whether they like it or not,
James believed, because interpretation is always a form of intervention, a
factor in social change or in social conservation. . . . Jamesian pragmatism
is nothing less than the strategy for taking away rationalist theory's theoretical ambition, for encouraging us, in our impulses to theory, to recognize
that we must live with differences, provisional utility, and the necessities of
revision.[43]

This view was echoed by Joan Richardson, who wrote that James under-
took "a recuperative conceptual revolution to complete the political revolution that had established the republic" in the United States.[44] And as Michael
Magee noted, "it is not simply an aside when James ends 'What Pragmatism
Means' by saying of the pragmatic method, 'you can see how democratic she
is.'"[45]

My claim that James's philosophy was pervasively political requires three
points of clarification. First, James's whole philosophy rejected familiar neat
divisions and tidy subclassifications of philosophy into separate areas—
classifications such as metaphysics, philosophy of religion, epistemology,
ethics, and social and political philosophy. Anyone who insists on holding
on to these little categories will miss James's whole personal vision (James
called this the "great fact" about any person), his expression of his own intimate character (James wrote that this is what a philosophy is), and the universe he craved and preferred, and in which he felt at home (APU, 14, 10).
This view of philosophy is relational or "relativistic" in the sense that it is
"expressionist"—it holds that all philosophies are expressions of personal vision, character, temperament, worldview. It is important to understand that

---

[43] Frank Lentricchia, *Ariel and the Police: Michel Foucault, William James, Wallace Stevens*
(Madison: University of Wisconsin Press, 1988), 105–106, 125.

[44] Joan Richardson, *Pragmatism and American Experience: An Introduction* (New York: Cambridge
University Press, 2014), 34. In *New England: Indian Summer 1865–1915* (New York: E. P. Dutton,
1940), Van Wyck Brooks observed that in the 1890s "the old New England was slipping away," and
James's philosophy was an intellectual expression and cause of this fact (412).

[45] Michael Magee, *Emancipating Pragmatism: Emerson, Jazz and Experimental Writing*
(Tuscaloosa: University of Alabama Press, 2004), 17. See also the extended discussion of James and
the political consequences and impact of pragmatism in C. Wright Mills, *Sociology and Pragmatism*,
edited by I. L. Horowitz (New York: Paine-Whitman, 1964).

this view does not entail the claim that all philosophies are perniciously rela-tivistic in the sense of "subjectivism"—that no view is or can be shown more true than any other and that, therefore, any view is just as good as any other. That sort of pernicious, subjectivist relativism is entirely incompatible with James's whole pragmatism—his view that the truth or falsity of any belief or theory has to be demonstrated in and by its consequences.[46] James did not have a political philosophy that was self-contained and separate from the rest of his philosophy. Instead, his whole philosophy is political. His pragmatic method and theory of truth, his temporal and radically relational account of experience, and his "distributive" multiverse and pluralistic account of all acts of attention and conceptualization—all of this is political.[47]

This should surprise no one who recalls that James wrote that all per-ception is pervaded by partial interests and that all attention is selective, a choosing of the sort of universe we seem to ourselves to inhabit. It should surprise no one who recalls that James claimed it is through our concepts that we value and revalue life. It should surprise no one who recalls that James denied there can be a wholly private conception or a wholly private perception (just as Wittgenstein later would deny there can be wholly private language) and that a self's experience, thought, and language are irreducibly historical and social—"discoveries of exceedingly remote ancestors" (P, 83). It should surprise no one who recalls that James asserted that truth is made, not found, and that the true is simply the good with respect to belief. For James, in short, all perception, all conception, all experience is constituted by and irreducibly pervaded by particular interests—and thus is never wholly in "a condition of streamy disinterestedness," complete disinterestedness.[48]

---

[46] This point is discussed in detail in chapter 5.

[47] Joshua I. Miller observed that "much of James's writing is implicitly related to politics" and that any depoliticization of this work "reflects an overly narrow definition of politics rather than its true place in James's thought." *Democratic Temperament*, 1, 2. I think this point is right on the mark, but if we do reject an "overly narrow definition of politics," then it seems to me that James's writing is not merely *implicitly* related to politics but that it, like all philosophy—understood as Jamesian vision—is *centrally* political. In addition, if we do accept this point, then Miller's characterization of his book's undertaking on the next page—"In this book, I translate James's thinking into the language of demo-cratic politics"—might be seen as one that misses what James is up to by attending principally to how to translate it into a significantly different language more familiar to particular political theorists. This translation project may be very valuable, but it also may be very different from a project of reading James, untranslated James, in the original. In this same context, Alexander Livingston noted the "displacement" of James's anti-imperialist writings that this sort of translation project effects. James "politicized philosophy as a response to the problems of empire he faced at the turn of the twentieth century," Livingston added. *Damn Great Empires!*, 6, 15.

[48] Mark Bauerlein, *The Pragmatic Mind: Explorations in the Psychology of Belief* (Durham, NC: Duke University Press, 1997), 49.

These interests, in turn, are the source of values and supply the meaning of values. Values (and their selves), in turn, are intrinsically social and political.

The second point of clarification: James also rejected familiar, habitual dualisms, either/or categories, and one/many problems within political thought—dualisms such as individual/community, personal fulfillment/social reform, and autonomy/authority. Anyone who insists on trying to apply these distinctions or categories to James's philosophy will miss the ways in which his philosophy undermined the very assumptions that have given rise to these distinctions and their uses by much traditional political thought. For example, to differentiate politics as a matter of "ethical practice, a way of life" from politics as a matter of "institutional crafting," as Colin Koopman has done (concluding that James was "unequivocally in favor of the latter"),[49] or in a parallel manner to set forth an "ethics of fulfillment" as separate from "an ethics of reform," as James Campbell observed (concluding that for James social reform was relatively unimportant),[50] is to appear to assume that for James a commitment to an ethical life is wholly or largely unconnected to action to reconstruct social practices and institutions. And it is seemingly to assume that these social practices and institutions do not really impact the quality and morality of people's efforts to live moral and significant lives. James held the opposite view. As Kennan Ferguson observed, for example, "To pluralize is to insist on the irreducibility of connections . . . , to rescue selves from individuals."[51] In a similar spirit, Joshua Miller noted that "there is no reason to restrict James's reflections on action to private life since he made clear that he did not sharply distinguish between public and private action."[52]

In "What Makes a Life Significant," for example, James explained that life takes on significance only as one has ideals that pass to, are recognized by, and are at least in part taken up in the lives of others—so that personal fulfillment includes and is inseparable from the fulfillment of others. And, he added, life is significant only as one labors strenuously to realize those ideals—so that one's own self-practices are also social reform (TT, 163ff.). Again similarly,

[49] Colin Koopman, "William James's Politics of Personal Freedom," *Journal of Speculative Philosophy* 19, no. 2 (2005): 175–186.

[50] Campbell, *Experiencing William James*, 228. Campbell sounds this view also in his "Habits in a World of Change," in *Pragmatism Applied: William James and the Challenges of Contemporary Life*, edited by Clifford Stagoll and Michael P. Levine (Albany: State University of New York Press, 2019), 237–253.

[51] Kennan Ferguson, *William James: Politics in the Pluriverse* (Lanham, MD: Rowman & Littlefield, 2007), xxv.

[52] Miller, *Democratic Temperament*, 2.

in *Pragmatism* he noted that the world changes and grows "piecemeal by the contributions of its several parts." The world, he wrote, "is a real adventure, with real danger, yet it may win through. It is a social scheme of co-operative work genuinely to be done. Will you trust yourself and trust the other agents enough to face the risk?" (P, 139). And James's pragmatic theory of truth similarly takes truth itself to be a social scheme, the work of many contributors who, in the phrase of Stephen S. Bush, have not a sole but rather a "collective responsibility for truth."[53] For James, any "ethics of fulfillment" is a social undertaking; any "ethics of social reform" is a struggle for individual trust and ethical practice. "The community stagnates," James wrote, "without the impulse of the individual. The impulse dies away without the support of the community" (WB, 174).

This point has pressing importance for practice and not just for interpretations of one philosopher by other philosophers. As a matter of fact, there now exists a huge separation between supposedly non-political individual ethical practice, personal fulfillment, and self-care and, on the other side, political institutional reform, community initiatives, and social justice. The assumption is that it is possible to lead a moral life unconnected to and independent of the realities of the social and natural world in and through which that life takes place. As a result, there are mountains of self-help books aimed at individuals who want to lead the good life: rules of life, laws of power, paths to satisfaction, workbooks for self-love, strategies for personal wealth, secrets of successful careers, recipes for greater spirituality, maps to your "true self"—and, in case all this gets to be too much, a "generation-defining self-help guide," *The Subtle Art of Not Giving a F*ck: A Counterintuitive Approach to Living a Good Life*.[54] The problem here is not the desire to provide help. It is the atrophied notion of the self to which that help is directed. Selves— you, me, everyone else—simply are not independent of the social and natural world in which they live. And so a moral self is not independent of its political environment.

Similarly, to contrast a "'personal' conception of justice" with an "institutional" conception of justice, as for example David Rondel has done, and to claim that "James insisted on a bifurcation of the individual from its social

---

[53] Bush, *William James on Democratic Individuality*, 50–62.
[54] Mark Manson, *The Subtle Art of Not Giving a F*ck* (New York: Harper, 2016). I note that in early 2022 Amazon.com lists over 80,000 self-help books.

and economic reality" is to treat individuality not as something *personal* but as something wholly *private*, inaccessible always, everywhere, and in principle.[55] It is to turn James's claim in "On a Certain Blindness in Human Beings" that "the inner significance of other lives *exceeds* all our power of sympathy and insight" (ERM 101; italics added)—that, in other words, we all have blind spots when it comes to others—into the very different (and non-Jamesian) belief that the entire and complete significance that others attach to their own lives is wholly beyond our grasp; put differently, that we are absolutely and forever entirely blind when it comes to others.

This is a claim that the personal is entirely private, and it is one that James explicitly rejected many times. His story about hiking in the North Carolina mountains is perhaps the most familiar: A short conversation with a man who had cleared his rural land allowed James to grasp at least in part the clearing's inner significance for this other person and to reduce his blindness to it:

> Because to me the clearings spoke of naught but denudation, I thought that to those whose sturdy arms and obedient axes had made them they could tell no other story. But, when *they* looked on the hideous stumps, what they thought of was personal victory. The chips, the girdled rees, and the vile split rails spoke of honest sweat, persistent toil and final reward. The cabin was a warrant of safety for self and wife and babes. . . . I had been as blind to the peculiar ideality of their conditions as they certainly would have also been to the ideality of mine, had they had a peep at my strange indoor academic ways of life in Cambridge. (TT, 134)

After even just a little communication, a short conversation, James was no longer *as* blind to the inner significance of the lives of these other people, no longer *as* wholly confined to his earlier preperceptions and preconceptions, and a little more able to see in ways that were unhabitual for him.

James did stress that the inner lives of other persons always exceed our insights. It is surprising here that James did not also and equally focus on the ways in which all persons are partially blind to their own inner lives— not just to other persons but to themselves as well. Given the partiality of our interests and the selectivity of our attention explained in *The Principles*

[55] David Rondel, "William James on Justice and the Sacredness of Individuality," in *Pragmatism and Justice*, edited by Susan Dielman, David Rondel, and Christopher J. Voparil (New York: Oxford University Press, 2017), 310, 319.

of Psychology, it follows that we all always are partially opaque to ourselves, often misperceived or merely preperceived by ourselves, and always in part self-uninterested, self-ignored, and self-unnoticed. Given the multiplicity that is each self, it follows that we all always are creatures different from even ourselves. And so, I think, James's certain "blindness with which we all are afflicted in regard to the feelings of creatures and people different from ourselves" (ERM, 132) extends to ourselves as well. Indeed, it is only because this is so that the Socratic imperative to "know thyself" has both bearing and bite.

Equally, James stressed the fact that it is possible to reduce—not eliminate entirely but reduce—one's blindness to the meanings and values, cares and vision, and day-to-day feel of the lives of others. The upshot, for James, was that individual fulfillment and personal justice are intrinsically bound up with social reform, shared understandings, and institutional justice. Here Rondel surely was right to recognize that James's claim that "no one has insight into all the ideals" implies an "imperative of tolerance" and, as Jim Garrison put it, "epistemological practice of reaching out to others"[56] that constitutes a positive obligation of self-education and self-expansion and not merely a negative injunction to refrain from harming others.[57] All this should surprise no one who recalls James's parallel emphases on:

- The fact that not only our conceptions but also our very perceptions are mediated by social processes, practices, and relations—such that the personal is never only the personal or the in-principle private
- The need for philosophy to give up "metaphysics and deduction for criticism and induction" to "offer mediation between different believers, and help to bring about a consensus of opinion" rather than arrive at a single truth to be imposed on everyone (VRE, 359)
- The ways in which the significance and value of any individual's life are matters of social relations—"Where would any of us be, were there no one willing to know us as we really are or ready to repay us for our insight by making recognizant return?" (TT, 151)
- The obstruction, corruption, or prevention of self-fulfillment effected by anti-individualistic institutions, "all big organizations" (CJR, 5:846) and all anti-pluralistic practices and imperial powers that work against

---

[56] Jim Garrison, "James's Metaphysical Pluralism," in *William James and Education*, edited by Jim Garrison, Ron Podescki, and Eric Bredo (New York: Teachers College Press, 2002), 33–36.
[57] David Rondel, "William James on Justice and the Sacredness of Individuality," 312–313.

self-fulfillment and, as a result, are anything but unconnected to imperialist wars, racial lynching, massively unequal distribution of wealth, universities in the grip of the "Ph.D. octopus" and "officialism"—to use just some of James's own examples

- The moral life as socially inclusive and aimed not merely at the satisfaction of an individual's own or isolated demands but also, as explained in "The Moral Philosopher and the Moral Life," oriented to the satisfaction of the most demand, the best whole, combined with the invention of new ways to realize previously conflicting demands

This leads to a third point of clarification for the thesis that James's philosophy is unquestionably political: Just exactly as James asserted that "we must conclude that no philosophy of ethics is possible in the old-fashioned absolute sense of the term" (WB, 158), so too no philosophy of politics is possible in the old-fashioned absolute sense of the term. James set forth no old-fashioned, absolute, or final political philosophy. Anyone looking for that in James will not find it.

So, what does this mean? What follows from this account of James's philosophy as centrally political? In the first place, it means that notions like justice, rights, political legitimacy and good government, the proper scope of freedom, terrorism, and crimes against humanity—normative political concepts—are *relational and radically experiential.* They exist not absolutely but only in relation to the demands and interests of particular persons, and it is only these demands that provide any basis for them. "Their only habitat," as James put this point with respect to moral philosophy, is "a mind which feels them" (WB, 145). To claim that a policy is just, for example, is to claim that the policy meets some specific demands of some specific people in some specific way. Claims to justice require this kind of specificity and self-knowledge.

In the second place, then, this means that political values are *always perspectival, partial, and pluralistic.* This means that James recognized that he too philosophized and acted from just one particular perspective—and so James frequently stated his vision, as, for example, in this now dated-sounding declaration from "The Will to Believe": "Here in this room, we all believe in molecules and the conservation of energy, in democracy and necessary progress, in Protestant Christianity and the duty of fighting for the doctrine of the immortal Monroe, all for no reasons worthy of the name" (WB, 18).[58]

---

[58] Bruce Kuklick, citing this same passage, remarked that James held his views to be "universalizable if not universal." *The Rise of American Philosophy*, 72.

Indeed, the self that holds political values is plural, a multiplicity: "a *man has as many social selves as there are individuals who recognize him* and carry an image of him in their mind" (PP, 281–282; PBC, 162).

And not simply "a man": As Deborah Whitehead has observed, James's pragmatism sets forth a new, fluid, and unstable notion of "the gendered self that is neither traditionally masculine nor feminine but encompasses a range of possibilities between these extremes."[59] This parallels the line of thought that James Livingston presented in "Hamlet, James, and the Woman Question." Referring to James's interpretation of Mill's *The Subjection of Women*, Livingston argued that "James does not simply recount and accredit Mr. Mill's beliefs" but instead shows they are susceptible to criticism because they grow from a sentimental kernel:

> The kernel, according to James, is the belief that all differences between men and women are unnatural, or artificial, and can—indeed must— be eradicated by education; the "best kind of equality" *between* men and women, or man and wife, thus appears as an "identity of opinions and purposes," not an equal relation of individuals with different opinions and purposes.... Notice that James is not insisting on separate spheres ... He is instead resisting the reduction of female to male which Mill's logic seems to promote. It is a strikingly modern locution because it does not treat "man" as the standard of subjectivity as such, and because it postpones the either/ or choice between difference and equality which Mill offers his readers.[60]

James rejected all monistic, static accounts of identity—whether in terms of sex and gender, race and ethnicity, class, age or ability, nationality or religion, or anything else. Accordingly, his views on race ran along lines similar to his views on gender. He rejected all reductionist and insufficiently pluralistic notions of race understood as biological hierarchy or ranking of nature. As Harvey Cormier explained, for James "there is no such thing" as race understood in that way:

---

[59] Whitehead, *William James, Pragmatism, and American Culture*, 98. From a different perspective, Charlene Haddock Seigfried has claimed that it is "inescapable" that "biased gender distinctions structured his [James's] way of ordering the world" and that his "devaluation of women" runs throughout his work and leaves unchallenged sexist stereotypes. "The Feminine-Mystical Threat to Masculine-Scientific Order," in *Feminist Interpretations of William James*, edited by Erin C. Tarver and Shannon Sullivan (University Park: Penn State University Press, 2015), 15, 16, 51. In this context, in the same volume see also Erin McKenna's "Women and William James."

[60] James Livingston, *Pragmatism, Feminism, and Democracy: Rethinking the Politics of American History* (New York: Routledge, 2001), 133.

There are different groups of people in different physical and social circumstances, they look different from one another, some have societies that are more materially successful than others, and there may even be discoverable differences among these groups as the molecular level that determines heredity. These groups can be seen and understood scientifically, and we can even call them "races" if we like. Nevertheless, there is no scientific truth to the Enlightenment-era belief that nature makes some of these groups as "great" or successful as they are.[61]

Consistent with the line of thought evident in these assessments by Whitehead, Livingston, and Cormier, Richard J. Bernstein contended that "many of the recent discussions of multiculturalism and the politics of identity still have a great deal to learn from the spirit and letter of James's pragmatic pluralism":

James was especially insightful about the dangers of reification—the dangers of thinking that groups have fixed identities. He was acutely aware of how identities change, develop, and mutate in the curse of history. He was never sentimental about blindly celebrating differences. He was just as concerned with searching for commonalities that can bind us together. He consistently championed those pluralistic perspectives that foster individuality. And in the best pragmatic sense, James insisted that changing historical conditions present new challenges for rethinking a pragmatic pluralistic vision.[62]

A pluralistic politics must view itself—itself too—pluralistically.

This important point noted, it is also crucial not to detach James's view of philosophies as personal visions from James himself—from his temperament, his culture, and his particular embodiment of tensions and habits of his time and place. Despite his thoroughgoing pluralism, his openness and desire for new possibilities, his rejection of a supposedly forced choice between political difference and political equality, and his habit of rooting for the underdog and typically excluded, silenced voices, James sometimes expressed less inclusive views in less progressive language. As Paul J. Croce

[61] Harvey Cormier, "William James on Nation and Race," in *Pragmatism, Nation, and Race*, edited by Chad Kautzer and Eduardo Mendieta (Bloomington: Indiana University Press, 2009), 158.
[62] Richard J. Bernstein, "Ethical Consequences of William James's Pragmatic Pluralism," in *The Pragmatic Turn* (Malden, MA: Polity, 2010), 69.

has noted, James held many "mainstream" assumptions about race and gender and class:

> James at once lived the prejudices of his time and announced theories that promote equity. . . . His supporters provide, in effect, a James upgraded for contemporary culture, a cultural theory James, a James 2.0. The use of his thought and life as resources for healing assumptions of racial and gender hierarchy carries forward his own ambivalence from tension between his contexts and his eagerness for change. James's readiness to see both sides and his ambivalence show that his relational thinking, when applied to social issues, prompted him not only to pay attention to contrasting views but also to see the shortcomings of each—and so, ultimately, their need for each other. This shows the depths of his readiness to live without guarantee, and it also indicates that his uncertainties, enlisted as resources for working toward future improvements, could include a wide swath of perspectives, even while steering him away from quick fixes.[63]

A pluralistic philosophy must view itself—itself too—as partial and incomplete, as "ever not quite," as a rest stop for a little while, perhaps, but never a final destination.

Different political demands create genuinely different political values; conflicting political demands create genuinely conflicting political values; and incommensurable political demands create incommensurable political values. This guarantees that all political decisions will "butcher" some of these values and that political life, accordingly and in the absence of an independent, objective, antecedent political order, has a tragic dimension—"the struggle and the squeeze" of life (WB, 157), the pinch between the ideal and the actual (P, 153).[64] Paralleling James's judgment about ethics, there is no abstract political order that is true in itself.

In the third place, this means that political decisions should be as *inclusive and democratic as possible*—that they should satisfy as much demand as possible and that they should seek out new and effective (and thus evidence-based) ways to harmonize demands now in conflict. And given that anyone's

---

[63] Paul J. Croce, *Young William James* (Baltimore: Johns Hopkins University Press, 2018), 17–19.

[64] Among others, Colin Koopman rightly noted this point in contrasting the political thought of James and John Dewey. "Contesting Injustice: Why Pragmatist Political Thought Needs DuBois," in *Pragmatism and Justice*, edited by Susan Dielman, David Rondel, and Christopher J. Voparil (New York: Oxford University Press, 2017), 181.

effort—even a well-meaning one—to do just this will be marked by a certain blindness to the lives of others, the "civic genius" of the other people impacted by a decision must be involved in its making. This is why James claimed that good government must seek connection with the governed, who, in turn, must both have demands and ideals and act on them. It is why he asserted that hatred of alien rulers is an enduring force. It is why he opposed "bigness" in social life. It is why he called "every great institution" "a means of corruption" (CJR, 2:100). And it is why he demanded that the United States must forgo imperialism and become, more and more, an ethical republic.

In the fourth place, commitment to the impossibility of old-fashioned political philosophy means that political thought must be *experiential, experimental, oriented to changing consequences, and pragmatic*. It is only actual social experiment, not abstract theory or pronouncements from preconceived premises, that can determine which institutions, polices, and practice produce the most just social arrangements. James asserted:

> These experiments are to be judged, not a priori, but by actually finding, after the fact of their making, how much more outcry or how much appeasement comes about. What closet-solutions can possibly anticipate the results of trials made on such a scale? Or what can any superficial theorist's judgment be worth, in a world where every one of hundreds of ideals has its special champion[?] . . . The pure philosopher can only follow the windings of the spectacle, confident that the line of least resistance will always be towards the richer and the more inclusive arrangement, and that by one tack after another some approach to the kingdom of heaven is incessantly made. (WB, 157)

Like the moral philosopher, the political philosopher must wait on the facts and be ready to revise conclusions. A democratic political philosophy is a kind of vote for a morally richer universe. It is a personal vote, a tentative hypothesis, a partly blind expression of preferences, and a proposal that invites. It proposes: Let's live these ways rather than those ways. It asks: What if we live this way? It invites: How does this seem to you?

If we do invoke any so-called political philosophy, our choice and use of that conceptual map also are but revelations of our personal (not private) preferences, selective attention, and aptitude or incapacity for some form of political life. Political philosophy, like philosophy more generally, is ultimately an expression of habits of personal passions, preferences, and temperament rather than it a matter of abstract political doctrine.

And . . .

4. A Variety of Political Theory

James's political philosophy was an expression of his own temperament, and one's temperament, he recognized, is any philosophy's "potentest" premise (P, 11). From *The Principles of Psychology* and his other early writings, his temperament or preferred working attitude (APU, 10) was pluralistic, and thus individualistic and democratic; radically empirical and relational, and thus attuned to parts and their many changing conjunctions and disjunctions; pragmatic, and thus empirical, experimental, and oriented toward consequences rather than origins. He demanded a world of genuine possibilities rather than a finished universe, a world in which melioristic human action could both realize and expand its possibilities, an uncertain ethical adventure with real losses and without guarantee of real gains, an adventure best served by unhabitual perceptions that lead to novel ideals and real, strenuous struggles to realize those ideals. This is a world that James felt was consonant with, and supportive of, finite human experience, finite human powers, and desires to feel at home, to feel intimacy.

Here it is crucial to add that not everyone has the same power, the same homes at which to feel at home, or the same material and semiotic resources for intimacy. For James the pluralist, concrete and finite human experience is always concrete and finite human experiences—experiences plural and different. Megan Craig has raised a case in point: In language that has "a potentially dangerous and conservative undercurrent,"

> James seems poised to articulate something in 1895 that would not fully come into focus for a long time—namely, that the dominant features of American life disproportionately subject women to physical/psychological distress and exile them from normative structures of meaning."[65]

---

[65] Megan Craig, "Habit, Relaxation, and the Open Mind," in *Feminist Interpretations of William James*, edited by Erin C. Tarver and Shannon Sullivan (University Park: Penn State University Press, 2015), 174, 173.

In its largest import, James's political philosophy—like every bit of his philosophy—is understood best in terms of sentiment, temperament, and vision rather than overarching doctrine or abstract principle or general policy.[66] These latter matters always wait on facts, always must be revised as those facts change, and always are as partial as the selective attention, preperception, and selective inattention or blindness for which they are facts.

I have called or classified James's temperament as radically empirical, pragmatic, and pluralist. I realize that some of these labels are not traditional, old-fashioned, or commonplace within political philosophy and political theory. So much the worse for tradition! And I realize that there are other labels that fruitfully can be pinned on James (or James pinned on these other labels) in order to enlist his work in the service of different interests and attunements.[67] As James put it, the more we think, the more we see.

My identification of James as political pluralist, political radical empiricist, political pragmatist, political meliorist, and political humanist is admittedly partial and selective. It could not be otherwise. It is motivated by two major concerns, one more theoretical and one more immediately practical. Theoretically, this stresses the links, continuities, and coherence between James's political thought and the rest of his philosophy. His philosophical psychology was pluralistic, radically empirical, and pragmatic. His study of the varieties of religious experience is pluralistic, radically empirical, and pragmatic. His metaphysical and epistemological visions were pluralistic, radically empirical, and pragmatic. His moral philosophy was pluralistic, radically empirical, and pragmatic. So too his political thought was pluralistic (and, thus, individualistic), radically empirical (and thus relational, temporal, situated in his culture and time, and this-worldly), and pragmatic (and thus looked experimentally to consequences and last things). In turn,

---

[66] I take it that this is what Rondel pointed at in his claim that James did not present a theory of justice so much as an "ethos" about justice. "William James on Justice and the Sacredness of Individuality," 315. Similarly, Alexander Livingston called attention to the fact that James held that sentiments and temperament "are the ultimate grounds of men's convictions." *Damn Great Empires!*, 66.

[67] Here I most certainly include Stephen S. Bush's focus in *William James on Democratic Individuality* on James's understanding of individualism and his explication of this commitment in terms of responsibility and action, sensitivity to others in light of the limits of our perceptions of them, meliorism (which I touch on here), and religiousness (which I explored in chapter 3 in the context of James's ethics and his "The Moral Philosopher and the Moral Life"). Alexander Livingston's characterization of pragmatism "not as doctrine, but as an anti-intellectual attitude of orientation" resonates here, and it is a claim that I think applies to James's pluralism and radical empiricism as well as his pragmatism. As noted above, Livingston called this pragmatic shift in attitude from first things to last things "anarchism." *Damn Great Empires!*, 10–11.

THE POLITICAL PHILOSOPHER   143

this means equally that his pluralism and its multiverse are anti-imperial and anti-totalitarian, oriented not to policing the freedom of others so much as to creating and expanding new fields of possibilities beyond what has been previously imagined.[68] It means that his "mosaic" radical empiricism ("pluralism, somewhat rhapsodically expressed") holds together by its own relations, rejects all "alien rule" by "extraneous trans-empirical support" (ECR, 179; MT, 7), and so inclines toward anti-authoritarianism, pacifism, respect, and tolerance while criticizing bigness in all its forms. Moreover, it means that his pragmatism, a temperament that allows no philosophy to "speak up in the universe's name" (P, 25) if it does not reflect the feelings and the worldview of each person, is democratic and demands that government connect with the ideals and the wills of the governed. It is thus as much the case that democracy is pragmatic, that anti-authoritarianism is radically empirical, and that individualism is pluralistic as it is the case that pragmatism is democratic, radical empiricism is anti-authoritarian, and pluralism is individualistic. To think of pragmatism, radical empiricism, and pluralism as independent and stripped of their intrinsic political valence is simply and habitually to preperceive metaphysics and epistemology as politics-free zones. This selective inattention misses "millions of items of the outward order" of James's writings.[69] And it misses the fact that, as Deborah Whitehead put it, "in James we see a move to democratize the philosophical enterprise itself."[70]

There is a second, more immediately practical reason for viewing James as political radical empiricist, political pragmatist, and political pluralist. In a time of nearly endless wars, genocides, ethnic cleansings, rampant xenophobia and nationalistic indoctrination, online and in-person hate communities, terrorism, militarized tribalism, rising authoritarianism, and worldwide climate change and the destruction of non-human animals, James's thought provides the outlines of a democratic political culture and sustainable environment, a culture of multiple attachments.[71] It is a vision

[68] I owe to Vincent Colapietro this idea of James's politics as the creating of expanding possibilities for individuals.

[69] I note here that Kennan Ferguson has stressed the political centrality of James's pluralism: "Pluralism, even more than pragmatism, comprises his [James's] most important legacy." *William James: Politics in the Pluriverse*, xxi. While I agree that James's pluralism is crucial, I think it is a distinctively *pragmatic* pluralism and do not think that James's pluralism and pragmatism can be separated from each other.

[70] Whitehead, *William James, Pragmatism, and American Culture*, 142.

[71] Perry, *The Thought and Character of William James*, 2:315. James Albrecht directly explored resources in the writings of Aldo Leopold and in James's work for hopefully and strenuously (and not merely intellectually) addressing environmental crises in "Do We Love the Creatures of the Future Enough?," in *The Jamesian Mind*, edited by Sarin Marchetti (New York: Routledge, 2021), 529–544.

that rejects imperialism and colonialism (whether at home or abroad) as well as violence and war. In doing this, James becomes, according to Lentricchia, "the first in a hidden history of oddly connected American refusers of imperialism."[72] It celebrates individuality and the many forms of flourishing human lives. And it humbly recognizes the blindness, limits, partiality, and incompleteness in even our own views and our own exercises of power.[73] Horace Kallen captured well the spirit of Jamesian democracy—a spirit that he took to be "a synonym" for James's humanism, which rejects authority, dogma, rationalization, and obedience:

> Institutions and governments are at their best when their oneness is thought of and treated not as organism but as organization; when they express not unity but union; when they consist not in integration but orchestration; they then are modes of the free association of the different—organizations of liberty whose just powers are the hearts and the heads of all the human beings whose organizations they are. . . . [W]hen humanism is taken thus humanly, democracy is humanism, humanism is democracy.[74]

This is a form of democracy that today is very much needed. In a time of expanding totalitarianism (that extends to increasingly illiberal democracies), technologies of normalization and surveillance, massive concentration of economic wealth and power, greedy and selfish materialism, climate destruction, and both old and new forms of control of bodies and minds— Big Pharma, Big Fossil Fuel Energy, Big Agribusiness, Big Weapons Sellers, and Big Tech—commitment to individuality and the social conditions that nurture it, wide tolerance and humility and respect, and attunement to the corrupting enticements and effects of big institutions in James's *radical empiricism* are at a premium. And in a time of absolutism, old prejudices, new conspiracy theories, climate change denial, and so many other instances of

---

[72] Lentricchia, *Ariel and the Police*, 112.

[73] Cleo Cherryholmes concluded her "James's Story of the Squirrel" with the observation that pragmatism is "necessarily political and entwined with the effects and exercise of power." In *William James and Education*, edited by Jim Garrison, Ron Podescki, and Eric Bredo (New York: Teachers College Press, 2002), 96. In "Jamesian Feminism in a Time of Polarization," Erin Tarver constructively stressed the practical political value, when informed by the insights of feminist and anti-racist thought, of James's commitments to habits of meliorism, evidence-based problem solving, both moral and epistemic humility, and the creation of conditions that allow and sustain non-polarizing interaction. In *The Jamesian Mind*, edited by Sarin Marchetti (New York, Routledge, 2021), 508–518.

[74] Horace M. Kallen, "Of Humanistic Sources of Democracy," in *American Philosophers at Work: The Philosophic Scene in the United States*, edited by Sidney Hook (New York: Criterion Books, 1956), 395, 396.

anti-science, anti-fact, and anti-truth ways of thinking, the experimental, consequence-based, fact-loving method of ameliorating problems in James's pragmatism is in as critical demand as it is in short supply.

Finally, because these problems are large, to say the least, they readily give rise to some version of baseless optimism (it's all good, let's just keep doing what we are doing, business as usual), supernaturalism (our fate is not in our own hands), nihilism (life is without meaning or value), and resignation (there is nothing we can do, there are no possibilities, there is no basis for hope, humanity and the world are doomed by waves of pandemics, rising oceans, social disfunction, too few seats available on the last private space launch to Mars, and much more). In this context, James's political *meliorism* and *humanism* have far-reaching practical import.[75] We live, James held, in an unfinished universe with genuine possibilities. These possibilities include ways in which our actions might contribute to and change that universe for what we take (and make) to be the better. We are not wholly stuck, and James's philosophy can help "unstiffen" our politics as well as our theories. We need this. A yoga mat, a 401(k) account, a big silo of social media "friends," and a bunker on high ground are not enough. There is no guarantee (and even the social conditions and resources to sustain this meliorism are threatened). There are real dangers. There will be real losses. Given a Jamesian political vision, however, the possibility is enough to call forth imagination and creative ideas with strenuous action on behalf of their realization.

Practically, this is a political philosophy that points us toward questions of social action and institutional reform: What institutions, organizations, associations, practices, and policies create and nurture individuals—genuinely different individuals—committed to more inclusive forms of social life? Which ones produce habits and preperceptions of violence and abuse, insignificance and inferiority, entitlement and authority, fear and hatred, and, yes, desire for final theoretic conquest? Which ones nurture individuals with the necessary imagination to frame novel ideals of greater harmony and respect, the skills to cooperate with others to realize these ideals, and the energies and will to overcome "moral flabbiness" (CJR, 11:267) and take up the strenuous action demanded if we are to realize them all around us day to day? Avoiding "moral flabbiness" and the resignation of a mere spectator, this strenuous

---

[75] Stephen Bush discussed meliorism as James's political or "social commitment" in *William James on Democratic Individuality*, 156–161. So too does Joshua I. Miller in *Democratic Temperament*, chap. 1.

action must also avoid moral idiocy. Writing about the U.S. war and occupation in the Philippines, James noted: "We think that the violent imposition of our own entirely desperate ideals will be an act of charity? Oh the big idiots we are!" (CJR, 9:207) And what political arrangements in a given society best nurture individuals more capable of hearing "the cries of the wounded" (WB, 158; TT, 138) that will sound when this commitment to greater inclusivity and less imposition at least in part misses the mark—and so must be redirected, always redirected? I note here that James's attention to what acts of oppression and policies of imperialism say about the oppressors and imperialists led Cornel West to judge that "James's anti-imperialism is based on a concern with what imperialism reveals about his own class and white fellow citizens."[76]

"The solving word," James wrote, "for the learned and the unlearned man alike, lies in the last resort in the dumb willingness and unwillingness of their interior characters, and nowhere else" (WB, 162). Interior character, for James, is not fixed from the start. It is a site of possibilities; it is educative. The realization of some of these more inclusive possibilities is the never-concluded experimental work of Jamesian politics, a politics more attuned to tentative and suggestive narratives than to any supposed final proofs or complete theory. "No people learns to live except by trying" (ECR, 179), James wrote; and no people learn to live differently except by trying anew and again. Pluralistic ends require pluralistic means.

"Ever not quite!" As lives go on and change, James taught wariness of any political philosophy, any philosophy, that offers up fixed foundations and certain conclusions about that which has not yet concluded: our very selves, our lives, and our associations with one another. By its own lights, James's thought, in contrast, is a proposal that awaits the test of being taken up and taken up again—always on trial. This is what pluralistic, radically empirical, pragmatic political philosophy and life look like.

---

[76] West, *The American Evasion of Philosophy*, 63.

5

The Temperament of Pragmatism

> Pretend what we may, the whole man [person] within us is at work when we form our philosophical opinions. Intellect, will, taste, and passion co-operate just as they do, in practical affairs; and lucky it is if the passion be not something as petty as a love of personal conquest over the philosopher across the way. (WB, 77)

> No abstract concept can be a valid substitute for a concrete reality except with reference to a particular interest in the conceiver. (WB, 62).

In "What Pragmatism Means," William James told his audience, and later his readers, that his pragmatism would be a "conquering destiny" (P, 30). In 1907, the year *Pragmatism* was published, he told his brother, Henry, that he would not be surprised if a decade later his pragmatic philosophy appeared "epoch-making" and something "quite like the protestant reformation," explaining that he had no doubt at all about the "definitive triumph" of its "general way of thinking" (CJR, 3:339). He even spelled out the stages by which he expected this would happen: Pragmatism first would be considered absurd and crazy, then it would be admitted to be true but trivial, and finally it would be declared an insightful invention created earlier by others and commonly known all along (P, 95).

More than a century later, has it turned out that James was right?

And does it matter? If so, how? And for whom?

1. The Meaning of Pragmatism: Method, Theory of Truth, and Temperament

It is not possible to determine whether James was right, or whether this matters at all, unless we know what he meant. This is one of the lessons taught by Peirce, James, Dewey, and other pragmatists (and other philosophers

No Professor's Lectures Can Save Us. John J. Stuhr, Oxford University Press. © Oxford University Press 2023.
DOI: 10.1093/oso/9780197664629.003.0006

too): The truth of a claim cannot be determined if the meaning of that claim and its ideas are not clear. So, what does James mean by "pragmatism"? Moreover, what does it mean for any philosophy's general way of thinking to be a "definitive triumph," to be a "conquering destiny" (P, 30), or to be "epoch-making"?

So, what exactly is pragmatism? James characterized it in three related but distinct ways that are worth distinguishing.[1] First, it is, he said, a new name for a way or method of thinking that makes it possible to settle otherwise interminable metaphysical disputes by tracing the practical meaning of beliefs—thereby determining what practical difference, if any, it would make if one belief rather than others were true (P, 28). Pragmatism is a method.

Now, when pragmatism is understood as a method, it is important to recognize that James did not claim it is a method for settling *all* disputes—every single dispute. James wrote that it was a method for settling metaphysical disputes only. The settling or successful resolution of other kinds of disputes—experiential or practical disputes both trivial and important—requires practical inquiry and its results. It requires investigation and evidence. It requires experimental method rather than pragmatic method.

Examples can illustrate and clarify this point. Consider the following questions. How many scholarly books are in my office? Does a particular hiker one afternoon walk continuously in a circling pattern from the north to the east to the south and then to the west of a squirrel in a tree near camp? Does drinking coffee regularly cause elevated blood pressure? What colors were dinosaurs? Would increasing the federal tax on petroleum products stimulate greater conservation and/or development of alternative energy sources and technologies? Is social media the main source in the United States of misinformation about politics and public health? Is it the main source in Belarus? If you finish reading this chapter and carefully think about it, will you understand James's pragmatism much, much better than if you do not? These are not the kinds of questions any philosophical method effectively answers. Pragmatism, as James well knew, does not all by itself provide answers to questions like these. It is not an armchair philosophy. It provides no offhand, speculative account of the number of books in my office. It holds

---

[1] H. S. Thayer, noting that James understood pragmatism to be both a method and a theory of truth, called James's vision "bifocal." But since James also, indeed perhaps primarily, took pragmatism to be a temperament or attitude, it might be useful to think of his vision as "trifocal." See H. S. Thayer, *Meaning and Action: A Critical History of Pragmatism* (Indianapolis, IN: Hackett, 1981 [1968]), 135.

that this kind of question or dispute cannot be settled without experience, practical consequences, active investigation, experimentation, and inquiry.

James's pragmatism, as he carefully explained, is a method for settling only "metaphysical" disputes. What are "metaphysical" disputes? James provided no concise definition, but his examples make clear that metaphysical disputes are disputes about the meaning of some particular, given notion. For example, what does it mean for a book to be a "scholarly" book? What does it mean for a hiker to "go around" a squirrel on a tree? What does it mean to drink coffee "regularly"? What does it mean to say an action is "good"? What does it mean for "God" to "exist"? What does it mean to "carefully think about" a chapter or a book or a philosophy? In settling "metaphysical" disputes by making clear the practical, experiential meaning of the notions involved, James's pragmatism makes it possible, subsequently, to engage in practical, experiential inquiry. Also note that in "The Moral Philosopher and the Moral Life," James explicitly labeled as "metaphysical" all questions about "the very *meaning*" of value words such as "good," "ill," and "obligation" (WB, 142, 145). So, until the practical meaning—the "cash-value"—of an idea is clear, no amount of practical inquiry can determine the truth or falsity of beliefs that include and make use of this idea. As Peirce recognized, making our ideas clear does not by itself fix or determine belief and remove doubt, but the former is a necessary precondition of the latter. As James put it, with his pragmatic method, "science and metaphysics would come much nearer together, would in fact work absolutely hand in hand" (P, 31). In this way, pragmatism, as a method, is "a program for more work" and "an indication of the ways in which existing realities may be *changed*": "Pragmatism unstiffens all our theories, limbers them up and sets each one at work" (P, 32). As a method, then, James's pragmatism does not pretend to settle all disputes. Instead, it simply provides a means to clarify the meaning of beliefs so that they become instruments, so that their results can be determined, and so that they can be put to a practical, test, the test of experience—that is, our plural experiences.[2] In so doing, James's pragmatism connects theory to practice and breathes life into the very meaning of ideas and beliefs. Pragmatism is

---

[2] F. Thomas Burke combined what I, following James in *Pragmatism*, separate as pragmatism understood as a method and pragmatism understood as an attitude or temperament. He wrote that pragmatism "as a philosophical method or attitude" consists of "a conception of *belief*" formed in response to doubt and "individuated in terms of rules of action," along with "a corollary conception of *meaning*" as operational and inferential—as stressing tangible and implied consequences of action under specific conditions. *What Pragmatism Was* (Bloomington: Indiana University Press, 2013), 143.

not a method for establishing the truth or falsity of beliefs. Instead, it is a method for determining meanings (and meanings are clear or not clear rather than true or false).

What is it about the pragmatic method that allows it to settle metaphysical disputes? In these kinds of disagreements, the meaning of belief and its practical consequences have been separated. Pragmatism connects them by insisting that questions of meaning are questions about practical differences, differences in practice. It thereby turns metaphysical beliefs into hypotheses that are open to experiential testing (and it is this testing, again, that determines the truth or falsity of beliefs). In this context, Ellen Kappy Suckiel observed that the notion of the *pragmatic* meaning of a belief is not intended as *cognitive* meaning *if* cognitive meaning "is taken to be constituted by abstract conceptual relations" while, at the same time, pragmatic meaning points to the use and value of beliefs only in terms of their meaning or import in cognition. Pragmatic meaning, she summarized, bridges the gap between thought and action and, as such, is "intended to replace" alternative accounts of meaning.[3] Similarly, Sandra Rosenthal captured James's anti-dualism this way: "We do not have purely abstract categories of understanding on the one hand, and a brute sensory manifold on the other. Rather, pragmatic meaning, as the inseparable mingling of the sensuous and the relational, is the vehicle by which we think about and recognize objects in the world."[4] Absent pragmatic method, a belief has no abductive structure—it is not a hypothesis that can be tested in experience by inquiry.

Second, James wrote that pragmatism is not only a method but that it is also a theory of truth.[5] What is this theory of truth? In "The Function of Cognition," first published in 1885 and reprinted with only slight revisions in 1909 as the first chapter in *The Meaning of Truth*, James set forth an experientialist account of thought, belief, knowledge, justification, and truth wholly in terms of plural, finite, non-Absolute minds led to finite self-transcendent reality

[3] Ellen Kappy Suckiel, *The Pragmatic Philosophy of William James* (Notre Dame, IN: University of Notre Dame Press, 1982), 44; more generally, see 30–44.

[4] Sandra B. Rosenthal, *Speculative Pragmatism* (Amherst: University of Massachusetts Press, 1986), 28.

[5] In his "Introduction" to *Pragmatism*, H. S. Thayer made the important point that James's "theory of truth" is not, and was not intended as, a "theory" in the sense in which philosophers often use this term: "The purpose of his theory is not to provide a general definition of 'truth,' but to develop an explanation of the particular characteristics of ideas (or beliefs and assertions) and the circumstances in which they occur that endows them with truth" (P, xxx). In effect, this is, I think, the pragmatic meaning of "theory."

through the pointing or leading function of cognition (MT, 15).[6] Here the truth of a belief is instrumental. It is a function of where the belief guides, leads, and terminates, a function of being put into acquainted and bodily "working touch" with reality so as to "handle" it better (MT, 18). For James, Richard Rorty observed, true beliefs do not "decode" reality but are useful in it.[7] In the "Preface" to *The Meaning of Truth*, James explained it this way:

> *True ideas are those we can assimilate, validate, corroborate and verify. False ideas are those we cannot.* That is the practical difference it makes to us to have true ideas; that, therefore is the meaning of truth, for it is all that truth is known-as. The truth of an idea is not a stagnant property inherent in it. Truth *happens* to an idea. It *becomes* truth, is *made* true by events. Its verity is in fact an event, a process: the process namely of verifying itself, its *verification*. Its validity is the process of its valid-*ation*. (MT, 3–4)

And he asked: "Unless, then, my critic can prove that my feeling does not 'point to' those realities which it acts upon, how can he continue to doubt that he and I are alike cognizant of one and the same world" (MT, 23)? Put differently: The process in which beliefs become true involves both making (production) and also finding (discovery). Not one or the other, but both.[8]

Cognitive experience points—through action—to reality. Action is a sign of cognition of reality; common or shared action is a sign of cognition of a common or shared reality. James state his thesis this way: "*A percept knows whatever reality it directly or indirectly operates on and resembles; a conceptual feeling, or thought, knows a reality, whenever it actually or potentially terminates in a percept that operates on or resembles that reality, or is otherwise connected with it or with its context*" (MT, 27–28). Stressing the practical force of this view, he added that cognition that resembles reality without operating

---

[6] Ellen Kappy Suckiel observed in this context that James's account of truth renders truth "describable exclusively by reference to what human beings can experience." *The Pragmatic Philosophy of William James*, 105. Gerald E. Myers emphasized the way in which the notion of function links James's psychology and his pragmatism. *William James: His Life and Thought* (New Haven, CT: Yale University Press, 1986), 291–306. And in his "Introduction" to *The Meaning of Truth*, H. S. Thayer explained how Josiah Royce's and then F. H. Bradley's arguments for idealism and its absolute mind provided James the initial challenge to which his pragmatic theory of truth is a response (MT, xxii).

[7] Richard Rorty, *Consequences of Pragmatism* (Minneapolis: University of Minnesota Press, 1982), 153.

[8] John E. Smith faulted James for not distinguishing between truth-making and truth-discovering. I think James's whole point is that truth-making involves both—both engagement with the world as it is and activity in that world that transforms it, even if only a little. See "The Theory of Truth: Basic Conceptions," in *America's Philosophical Vision* (Chicago: University of Chicago Press, 1992).

on it is a "dream," and cognition that operates on reality without resembling it is an "error" (MT, 26).

This theory of truth is not only instrumental but also processive. For James, truth *becomes*. Elizabeth Flower and Murray G. Murphey put this in context by stressing how in the nineteenth century what had earlier been considered eternal laws of logic and nature "came to be looked upon as approximations rather than as eternal verities":

> The notion of an absolute truth, at least an available absolute truth, had to
> fall before the constant replacements and discoveries in physical theory,
> physiology, biology, geology, and sociology. . . . Pragmatism, then, followed
> these cues. It needed to examine the particular cases where truth is decided,
> to be responsive to this newer and more adequate notion of truth derived
> from science and to generalize the criteria.[9]

This pragmatic theory of truth holds that beliefs are true insofar as "*they help us get into satisfactory relation with other parts of our experience*," insofar as "we can ride" on them and be led or carried "prosperously from any one part of our experience to any other part," insofar as they are "a smoother-over of transitions" and successfully marry "old opinion to new fact" (P, 35). When a belief works this way in practice, James explained, it "makes itself true, gets itself classed as true" (P, 36), and becomes true.[10] The practical difference between true and false ideas, James insisted, is that true ideas can be assimilated, validated, and corroborated. They can be verified, and their verity, thus, is this process of verification, of truth-making (P, 97). Moreover, this truth-making process is never absolutely or in principle complete. John J. McDermott linked this fact to American culture more broadly: "James's pluralistic approach to inquiry is distinctively American in that it allows everyone to have his or her say before the inquiry is put to rest, and even a reopening of the discussion awaits the slightest hint of new information, data, or perspective."[11]

[9] Elizabeth Flower and Murray G. Murphey, *A History of Philosophy in America* (New York: Capricorn Books, 1977), 2:673–674.

[10] In this context, Joseph Blau pointed out that for James, truth thus "has social reference" but also individual reference "as long as an idea has agreeable consequences in the particular experience of some individual, somewhere." *Men and Movements in American Philosophy* (Englewood Cliffs, NJ: Prentice-Hall, 1952), 256.

[11] John J. McDermott, "William James: Introduction," in *Pragmatism and Classical American Philosophy: Essential Readings and Interpretive Texts*, edited by John J. Stuhr (New York: Oxford University Press, 2000), 147.

This is the pragmatic meaning of truth, the practical consequence of holding a true belief, as opposed to holding a false one. It is the result of unstiffening traditional theories of truth: "Purely objective truth, truth in whose establishment the function of giving human satisfaction in marrying previous parts of experience with newer parts played no role whatever, is nowhere to be found" (P, 37). This account of truth is the result of breathing life into the truth of beliefs: "Truth independent; truth that we *find* merely; truth no longer malleable to human need; truth incorrigible, in a word . . . means only the dead heart of the living tree, and its being," "means only that truth also has its paleontology and its 'prescription,' and may grow stiff with years of veteran service and petrified in men's regard by sheer antiquity" (P, 37). Pragmatism is a theory of truth.

It is imperative to address a misunderstanding here—not simply a possible misunderstanding but an actual and widespread one voiced not only by some introductory or careless beginners but also by otherwise-accomplished philosophers ranging from G. E. Moore and Bertrand Russell to Max Horkheimer and Theodor Adorno onward to contemporary thinkers.[12] Because James characterized true beliefs as beliefs that work, have cash value, help us get into satisfactory relations with other parts of experience, and because he denies the existence of purely objective, experience-independent truths, it is often wrongly claimed that his view of truth is subjective and that

[12] See John E. Smith's "The Pragmatic Theory of Truth: The Typical Objection," in *America's Philosophical Vision* (Chicago: University of Chicago Press, 1992), 37–52. See also Nancy Frankenberry's "Pragmatism, Truth, and Subjectivity," in *Pragmatism and Religion: Classical Sources and Original Essays*, edited by Stuart Rosenbaum (Urbana: University of Illinois Press, 2003), 245–248. Hilary Putnam addressed this issue by examining and rejecting the critical misunderstandings of James's view set forth by Russell, Morton White, and Martin Gardner. See Putnam's *Pragmatism: An Open Question* (Cambridge, MA: Blackwell, 1995), 8–12. White set forth his views in his chapter "Creative Intelligence" in his *Social Thought in America: The Revolt Against Formalism* (New York: Oxford University Press, 1976 [1947]). And Joseph Margolis discussed this kind of misguided subjectivism in the context of the views of Richard Rorty in his *Reinventing Pragmatism: American Philosophy at the End of the Twentieth Century* (Ithaca, NY: Cornell University Press, 2002), 24–30. In his *Pragmatism, Democracy, and the Necessity of Rhetoric* (Columbia: University of South Carolina Press, 2007), Robert Danisch observed that James was an orator-philosopher who "performed a rhetoric that abandoned the technical jargon of professional academics and instead used metaphors that adapted his ideas to broad audiences." But then he immediately added, "Such an approach meant that his philosophy did not seek to express and transmit truth but to create an instrument and useful set of ideas applicable to a wide array of problems—a pragmatic method" (18). But it is, I think, just this separation of truth from use and effective application that James's theory of truth wholly undercuts. Michael Bacon has repeated this charge and sided with those who make it in his *Pragmatism: An Introduction* (Malden, MA: Polity Press, 2012), 35. James T. Kloppenberg provided a particularly helpful overview of the ways in which James and Dewey effectively responded to this misguided objection in his "Pragmatism: An Old Name for Some New Ways of Thinking?," in *The Revival of Pragmatism: New Essays on Social Thought, Law, and Culture*, edited by Morris Dickstein (Durham, NC: Duke University Press, 1998), 86–87.

any belief that a person finds happiness-producing or satisfying to hold is, therefore, true. This is a silly view of truth—Perry called it the truth-as-license view[13]—and it is not a view that James or any other pragmatist has voiced or endorsed. Ever.

So, what accounts for the persistence in some quarters of this misunderstanding and off-base criticism? Two factors loom large. First, because James explicitly rejected the view that truths are objective and independent of human experience, inveterate dualists conclude that he must view truth as subjective. They reason that if truth is either objective or subjective, then anyone who denies that truth is objective must believe that truth is subjective. This way of thinking simply misses the radical, relational character of James's pragmatic theory of truth: He did not simply give up one side of a dualism—objectivity—for the other side—subjectivity; rather, he rejected the dualism entirely. For James, truth is not objective and it is not subjective. It is relational. A truth may be about me or you—about some subject—but that does not make the truth subjective. Similarly, I might hold a belief that is true, but that does not make the belief essentially or in principle or privately "my truth." True beliefs, for James, assert existential relations and, unlike false beliefs, these relations are assimilated, corroborated, validated, verified. It is a last thing, a never-final thing, not a first thing or antecedent condition.

There is a second factor at work when the pragmatic theory of truth is mistakenly held to be subjective in the sense that any view an individual finds satisfying to believe is, according to pragmatists, therefore true. When James claimed that true beliefs in practice satisfy and work, he did not assert that true beliefs are ones that make those who hold them feel warm and fuzzy, happy and satisfied. He did not claim, for example, that if it would make you feel elated if you were the smartest, deepest, and most nuanced reader of philosophy books, then on this basis, therefore, it is true (for you) that you are the world's best reader of philosophy books. To take a more far-reaching example, he did not claim that if it would make me feel secure and in harmony with those around me, confident, content, clever, and satisfied to believe that the COVID-19 pandemic has always been a hoax and that vaccines and mask recommendations are part of a nefarious plot by pedophilic deep-state agents, then on this basis, therefore, it is true that this pandemic was always a hoax and true that vaccines and masks are pushed by a shadowy immoral

---

[13] Ralph Barton Perry, *The Thought and Character of William James* (Westport, CT: Greenwood Press, 1974 [1935]), 1:248.

cabal. He did not proclaim that just because it would make me happy to be the world's greatest basketball player, that therefore—presto—my belief that I am the very best basketball player is a true belief. Instead, James claimed that true beliefs are those that put us in satisfactory relation with other, subsequent experiences. If I really am the world's greatest basketball player, then I should beat everyone else I play most of the time. If this is not what we experience—if I lose game after game to professional players, to college players, to high school players, to local pickup game players—then my belief that I am the best is not in satisfactory relation to what actually happens. I may have thought I was the best player, I may have felt strongly that I was the best player, I may have desperately wanted to be the best player, but experience showed us all—me included—that I am not (even if that makes me unhappy). Actual experience did not corroborate or verify my belief. If my belief had been true, particular consequences would have occurred, but, it turned out, they did not. My belief, despite my feelings—even my strong feelings—was found to be false. It could not assimilate or satisfy actual experience.

This is also the case for the public health example. It may be the case that someone believes strongly that vaccines and masks do not work against a particular virus. This belief might produce feelings of happiness and contentment. It might be an article of deep faith. It might cohere with one's other beliefs and feelings such as distrust of government or the scientific community or drug manufacturers or most of mainstream media. Moreover, these beliefs and feelings might be shared by family, neighbors, a favored news outlet, or often-visited social media sites. The roots of these beliefs and feelings might run deep; their origins might be multiple and real, conscious and unconscious. All this may be the case. For James, however, the truth or falsity of a belief is a function of its *consequences* rather than its *origins*. If public health agency data shows that a virus is present and circulating widely, if clinical trials demonstrate that vaccines prevent infection or reduce illness and death, if experimental studies strongly indicate that masks reduce viral transmission, then these beliefs are validated, verified, found to be true. Even if one wanted a pandemic to be a hoax and even if one felt strongly that a particular vaccine does not work, truth is a function of the evidence that inquiry yields. Verity is the product of verification processes. It is a consequence.

And this is the case for any other examples of belief. Of course, it might be nice to live in a world—a kind of fairy-tale world—in which any belief that one wanted to be true really became true just because this was wanted. But, as experience teaches, that subjectivist utopia is not the actual world we inhabit, and it definitely is not the pragmatic view of truth.[14] Throughout, James maintained a kind of complete democracy and pluralism about the equal *reality* of any and all experience and an insistence that only some experiences give rise to true beliefs while others produce false beliefs (no matter what one wishes). Hallucination is real, but the belief it creates turns out to be false. This is not in any way anti-pluralist. It is anti-subjectivist. If someone believes that drinking bleach provides protection or cure from COVID-19 viral infection, that is false, and explaining that it is false is not anti-pluralist or elitist.

James's rejection of the either/or dualism that truth is objective or truth is subjective is paralleled by his rejection of the either/or dualism of realism/anti-realism, the dualism of materialism/idealism.[15] James's radical empiricism is neither realist nor anti-realist. It is this point that marks a major difference between James and Charles Peirce, labeled the founder of pragmatism by James. Peirce, claiming that James had "kidnapped" his pragmatism, held that truth is independent of the effort to know it and belief or non-belief in it. In contrast, James held that things may be experienced as independent of the effort to know them, but that truths about those things—since *it is only beliefs that are true or false*—cannot be independent of the effort to know them and the resulting belief in them. Truth is a property of belief. Without or independent of belief, there is no truth and no falsity.

Now, when James's pragmatism is understood as a theory of truth, it is important to recognize that this pragmatic theory of truth is just a small part of a larger pragmatic epistemology that, in turn, is itself just one branch of a much larger pragmatic account of values.[16] Pragmatic epistemology, as

---

[14] Of course, "we" may find that we do not inhabit a fully shared or common world. This points the pragmatist in three directions. First, when there is disagreement in belief that results from lack of shared meaning—recall James's story about the camping party and the squirrel and tree—the pragmatic method is a solution. Second, when there is disagreement about the truth of a belief but agreement about how to settle that disagreement, more experimental inquiry is the needed solution. Third, in difficult cases where there is disagreement about the truth of a belief and also disagreement about how to settle that disagreement—for example, by the methods Charles Peirce called tenacity, agreeableness to reason, authority, or science—then the task for pragmatists is educational and political in the largest sense. The task is the spread of a pragmatic temperament and the creation of community habits of belief based on the result of experienced consequences—whether those consequences prove shared or different in the lives of different persons.

[15] Sandra Rosenthal provided an extended discussion of precisely this point in "Meaning and the Structure of Verification," in *Speculative Pragmatism*, 43–60. She wrote, for example, that the pragmatist position "can be captured neither by the traditional epistemic alternatives of realism or idealism, nor by the more recent alternatives of realism or antirealism or of foundationalism or antifoundationalism" (59).

[16] Trygve Throntveit—rightly, I think—referred to this as "the ethical origins of James's pragmatism." *William James and the Quest for an Ethical Republic* (New York: Palgrave Macmillan, 2014), chap. 1.

John J. McDermott noted in his "Foreword" to Charlene Haddock Seigfried's *Chaos and Context: A Study in William James*, is an important part of James's thought, but "it does not occupy the center of his vision.[17]" To fail to recognize this point is to fail almost entirely to understand James's philosophy. And it is probably to find strange or mistaken or absurd that, insofar as a belief is "profitable to our lives" and thus has cash value, James, for this reason, calls the belief true (P, 42). Nonetheless, James set forth his view very clearly and directly, writing: "Truth is *one species of good*." Contrary to long-petrified divisions within philosophy, truth is not "a category distinct from good, and co-ordinate with it." Instead, truth is a subset or subcategory of good; epistemology is a subset of ethics. There are lots of goods; some of them are truths. James continued: "*The true is the name for whatever proves itself to be good in the way of belief*" (P, 42). It is "*only the expedient in the way of our thinking, just as 'the right' is only the expedient in the way of our behaving*" (P, 106). Paul Anderson and Max Fisch put this particularly nicely: For James, "beliefs be[came] true by making good."[18]

If truth is a species of good and if epistemology is a subset of ethics, as James held, what is the good? Contrary to the image of James as happy individualist, his pragmatic ethics is a thoroughgoing social and political philosophy fully attuned to struggles for solidarity and to the tragic dimension of human life. Noting that goods have "no absolute natures, independent of personal support" but instead "are objects of feeling and desire, which have no foothold or anchorage in Being, apart from the existence of actually living minds" (WB, 150), James explained that values are pluralistic in two important respects. First, there are many different sentient beings and cultures with (not only shared but also) different feelings and desires and standpoints and experiences. There are equally real, plural goods, and there is, for James, no "abstract moral order in which the objective truth resides" in some goods rather than others (WB, 148). Because "*the essence of good is simply to satisfy demand*" (WB, 153), and because there are many different demands, there are many different goods. Accordingly, we live not in a moral universe but, instead, a social pluriverse of

---

[17] Charlene Haddock Seigfried, *Chaos and Context: A Study in William James* (Athens: Ohio University Press, 1978), ix. In her later book on James, Seigfried identified the center of James's vision this way: "the establishment of a secure foundation in experience which would overcome both the nihilistic paralysis of action and the skeptical dissolution of certain knowledge brought on by the challenge of scientific positivism." *William James's Radical Reconstruction of Philosophy* (Albany: State University of New York Press, 1990), 2.

[18] Paul Russell Anderson and Max Harold Fisch, "William James," in *Philosophy in America: From the Puritans to James* (New York: D. Appleton-Century, 1939), 523.

values. No individual consciousness enjoys the prerogative of obliging others to conform to its rule, no single moralist rightly rules (WB, 147, 155). By understanding goods as relations and by noting that "the elementary forces in ethics are probably as plural as those of physics are" (WB, 153), James developed what amounts to relativity theory in philosophy—his pragmatism, radical empiricism, and pluralism—more or less at the same time as Albert Einstein, the William James of physics, developed relativity theory in physics.

Second, values are pluralistic in another sense. Each individual has multiple, crisscrossing, conflicting feelings and desires and experiences. Each individual self is a plurality. The fulfillment or actualization of any one is at once the loss or destruction of other possible goods, other objects of other desires. James wrote that this is always a "tragic situation": "There is always a *pinch* between the ideal and the actual which can only be got through by leaving part of the ideal behind. . . . Some part of the ideal must be butchered. . . . It is a tragic situation" (WB, 153, 54). This is not a view of tragedy as incidental to the lives of some, an occasional occurrence in a few unlucky lives and places. Instead, it is a view of tragedy as central, intrinsic, and irreducible to human life—even to the realization of any good by anyone at any time.

For James, life is triply tragic. First, at times our deepest values are unfulfilled, our most cherished hopes are crushed, and evils defeat goods—this is tragic, genuine loss.[19] Second, at other times we succeed and reach our goals and realize our values but we do so only by forever sacrificing or "butchering" other, competing, mutually exclusive goals—this too is tragic, unrecoverable. Third, and finally, our lives are finite and no matter how we strive or how much we succeed for a relatively short time, we all die—and this is tragic, a tragedy common to us all. William Gavin captured this particularly well:

> If the fact of "no" does "stand at the very core of life," then, on an individual personal level, we are all, in a sense, "dregs." . . .The self can be incorporated into a larger picture; consequently, death can be "accepted." But to the extent that the personal is emphasized and the uniqueness, that is, nonreplacability of the specific individual in question is stressed, to that extent, death remains inexplicable, even "tragic."[20]

---

[19] Cornel West noted James's deep attunement "to the depths of evil in the world." Cornel West, *The American Evasion of Philosophy: A Genealogy of Pragmatism* (Madison: University of Wisconsin Press, 1989), 57.

[20] William J. Gavin, *William James in Focus: Willing to Believe* (Bloomington: Indiana University Press, 2013), 88. Gavin presented his ideas earlier in "Pragmatism and Death: Method vs. Metaphor,

This tragic, social account of the moral life is, finally, pragmatic. It counsels action and turns from theory to practice. As Alexander Livingston noted, a philosophy "can be tragic without being pessimistic and inspiring without being optimistic."[21] Rather than pretending to justify in theory one set of values—including the set of values that are truths—above or against all others, James advised that we "*invent some manner* of realizing our own ideals which will also satisfy the alien demands—that and that only is the path of peace" (WB, 155). Rather than claiming the prerogative to oblige others to think as one wants (WB, 147) or seeking to theorize into submission all views different from one's own, this philosophy directs us to struggle to change the conditions that sustain current conflict and dispute, to try to create new conditions that can support something better and turn out to be more inclusive for all. James asked: "What closet-solutions can possibly anticipate the results of trials made on such a scale" (WB, 157)? The question is rhetorical, for the answer, of course, is none—despite the fact that many lecturing and book-writing professors and lots of higher-priced public speakers continue to pretend otherwise. James here recommended what surely is a strenuous path: hard work on behalf of ideals that cannot be realized in full and might not even be realized in part. And then we die.

Third, this highly strenuous character of pragmatism—that is, the strenuous character of living pragmatically as distinct from the not-very-strenuous character of theorizing about or merely studying pragmatism—points to another main way James described pragmatism. Pragmatism, like all philosophies, James claimed, is a particular "attitude" (P, 31), a "temperament" (P, 11ff.), a "dumb willingness and unwillingness" of interior character (WB, 162), a "vision" and "expression" of "intimate character" (APU, 14), trust in and "loyalty" to one's own experience and world (APU, 10), a personal "feeling" of the whole universe and "total push and pressure of the cosmos" (P, 24, 9), "our more or less dumb sense of what life honestly and deeply means" (P, 9). Different philosophies, for James, are just different "modes of feeling the whole push, and seeing the whole drift of life, forced on one by one's total

Tragedy vs. the Will to Believe" in *100 Years of Pragmatism: William James's Revolutionary Philosophy*, edited by John J. Stuhr (Bloomington: Indiana University Press, 2010). See also Sidney Hook, *Pragmatism and the Tragic Sense of Life* (New York: Basic Books, 1974), and Eddie Glaude, "Tragedy and Moral Experience: John Dewey and Toni Morrison," in *Pragmatism and the Problem of Race*, edited by Bill E. Lawson and Donald F. Koch (Bloomington: Indiana University Press, 2004), 93. This essay reappears in Glaude's *In a Shade of Blue: Pragmatism and the Politics of Black America* (Chicago: University of Chicago Press, 2007), 17–46.

[21] Alexander Livingston, *Damn Great Empires! William James and the Politics of Pragmatism* (New York: Oxford University Press, 2016), 129.

character and experience, and on the whole *preferred*— there is no other truthful word—as one's best working attitude" (APU, 14–15). In talking about vision, temperament, attitude, feeling of the universe, and the whole drift of one's life, James is not pointing to something wholly transitory and fleeting. He is not describing, for example, feeling alert after a good sleep, stymied by a tough problem, saddened by a string of gray and rainy days, expectant as a vacation or holiday nears, or thrilled by unexpected praise or promotion. Instead, he is pointing to one's character, how one feels the whole of life and with what attitude one responds. He is pointing to the worldview that each of us enacts (relatively consciously or relatively unconsciously) in the way we live every day, day after day. Philosophies, then, are not first or fundamentally matters of doctrine, reason, proof, and theory; they are matters of habit, mood, lived experience, and practice. Pragmatism is a temperament.

What, then, is the temperament of pragmatism? James answered: "*The attitude of looking away from first things, principles, 'categories,' supposed necessity; and of looking towards last things, fruits, consequences, facts*" (P, 32). From the standpoint of the dualisms of traditional philosophy, pragmatism may usefully appear as attunement to the temporal rather than the eternal, the future rather than the past, the particular rather than the universal, the fallible rather than the infallible, the vague rather than the certain, differences rather than identity, relations rather than absolutes, the many rather than the one, experience rather than reason, the concrete rather than the abstract, action rather than speculation, feeling rather than logic, and this actual world rather than some other one postulated or logically possible. And although James often made use of these contrasts—very frequently railing against the absolute, the rational, the monistic, the intellectual, and the already complete, for example—his pragmatic attitude of looking to experience, as earlier noted, does not engage or take up these dualisms, at least on traditional terms. Rather, in the pragmatic attitude, traditional dualisms are undercut wholesale and wholly bypassed. In the hands of James, supposed metaphysical dualisms are cashed out as functional distinctions with practical meanings within experience; they become not real or unreal but, rather, useful or useless for particular purposes of particular persons. Because pragmatism itself is a theory, the pragmatic attitude or temperament is not simply an anti-theory attitude. Instead, it is an attitude that, in looking to last things and concrete experiences, produces and is produced by theory reconstructed by pragmatic method. The pragmatic attitude is not an attunement, feeling, or preference that can be mapped onto traditional dualisms so differently attuned.

This orientation to *last* things is, at once, an orientation to traditionally "low" things. In *Pragmatism*, James wrote:

> See, I say, how pragmatism shifts the emphasis and looks forward into facts themselves. . . . The centre of gravity of philosophy must therefore alter its place. The earth of things, long thrown into shadow by the glories of the upper ether, must resume its rights. To shift the emphasis in this way means that philosophic questions will fall to be treated by minds of a less abstrac-tionist type than heretofore, minds more scientific and individualistic in their tone yet not irreligious either. It will be an alteration in "the seat of authority" that reminds one almost of the protestant reformation. (P, 62)

This passage clearly echoes, I think, Ralph Waldo Emerson's words in "The American Scholar":

> This time, like all times, is a very good one, if we but know what to do with it. . . . One of these signs is the fact that the same movement which effected the elevation of what was called the lowest class in the state, assumed in literature a very marked and as benign an aspect. Instead of the sublime and beautiful, the near, the low, the common, was explored and poetized. That which had been negligently trodden under foot by those who were harnessing and provisioning themselves for long journeys into far coun-tries, is suddenly found to be richer than all foreign parts. The literature of the poor, the feelings of the child, the philosophy of the street, the meaning of household life, are the topics of the time. It is a great stride. . . . I ask not for the great, the remote, the romantic. . . . I embrace the common. I explore and sit at the feet of the familiar, the low. Give me insight into to-day and you may have the antique and future worlds.[22]

This focus on insight into day-to-day living is a rejection of what James later would call abstract and vicious intellectualism.

To look, as pragmatism demands, toward last things is messy and always incomplete. First, it is messy because experience—both the looking and the thing looked at, the how and the what of experience—is incomplete,

---

[22] Ralph Waldo Emerson, "The American Scholar," in *Pragmatism and Classical American Philosophy: Essential Readings and Interpretive Texts*, edited by John J. Stuhr (New York: Oxford University Press, 2000), 25.

always unfinished, always under way, always renewing (for better and/or worse). Second, it is messy because experience is always plural. Just as James claimed that "truth" is just "a class-name for all sorts of definite working-values in experience" (P, 38), experience is a class name for all sorts of particular experiences—plural experiences—of particular beings with particular perspectives and standpoints at particular times and places. "Looking toward last things" is a class name for lots of different lookings and lots of different things looked at, none of which has the prerogative to be definitive or final. For this "pluralistic pragmatism," James wrote, "truth grows up inside of all the finite experiences": "Nothing outside of the flux secures the issue of it. It can hope salvation only from its own intrinsic promises and potencies" (P, 125). In just this way, as discussed in chapter 4, James held that democracy depends not on something outside or external to it but, rather, on the ongoing civic genius of its own people.

Third and finally, looking toward last things is messy also because it is not primarily or wholly a matter of language or knowledge. For James, life as lived is different from life reflected, represented, and communicated. For James, individuality outruns all classification (APU, 7), but knowledge is classification. Living is concrete, but its representation is abstraction. Percepts conceptualized are transformed, not mirrored. Accordingly, to be attuned to last things, fruits, consequences, and facts is to be attuned, by means of language and knowledge, to experience that is irreducibly in part other than or excessive to language and knowledge. Pragmatism, for James, is a philosophy of experience, and not a philosophy of language or vocabularies. The pragmatic attitude is a mode of feeling and not *merely* or *only* a mode of knowing, discourse, or communication. Pointing to this, and focusing always on experiences rather than vocabularies, James observed: "There is no complete generalization, no total point of view, no all-pervasive unity, but everywhere some residual resistance to verbalization, formulation, and discursification, some genius of reality that escapes from the pressure of the logical finger, that says 'hands off,' and claims its privacy, and means to be left to its own life" (EP, 189–190).

2. Pragmatism as Naturalization of Mysticism

James held that all experience, in its immediacy, outstrips language, in its mediacy. This means that experience is undertaken and undergone, had and lived, rather than merely or fully represented and known. It means that experience—as it occurs—is immediate and ineffable. Experience is, in James's phrase, much-at-onceness and superabundant, whereas words and concepts are what we might call one-at-a-timeness. Bruce Wilshire captured the spirit of this:

> James wants us to become aware of the ever-present More-ness of the world that constantly pummels, pokes, provokes, pricks, and feeds us from all directions. . . The superabundant, fecund, ever-creating world won't hold still to be measured, defined, and classified once and for all by us.[23]

It is this point, more than any other, that most separates the pragmatism of James and Dewey (and others) from the neo-pragmatism or pragmatism-resonant philosophies of Davidson and Rorty (and others). This is a difference between a pragmatism that takes an experiential turn and one that takes a linguistic turn. The practical difference between these two views is often unclear and frequently lost behind favored terminology and pet allegiances to figures. As a result, the two sides often seem like latter-day camping parties arguing about whether the squirrel goes round the tree. Those who take the linguistic turn—with James, I view this as an error—often point out that it is not possible for pragmatists like James and Dewey to describe (in language) the nature of the aspects or dimensions of experience that are claimed to outstrip language. That much is obvious, and obviously true and agreed to by both parties. To attempt to put into language that which is claimed to be outside or beyond or other than language would be, at the very least, a performative contradiction. The enthusiasts of the linguistic turn then conclude that if experience cannot be described, it cannot play any explanatory role in an account of the supposed inability of concepts to capture adequately the fullness of reality. Again, this is obvious and true by definition: Anything that cannot be fully described by language surely cannot function in any linguistic explanation—it cannot be an item in our discursified knowledge.

None of this, however, addresses or locates James's view that the particularity and flux of reality cannot be captured by language and concepts that render them general and static. If called upon to describe *this* particular meal with friends, for example, the linguistic turn thinker cannot fully

---

[23] Bruce Wilshire, *The Much-at-Once: Music, Science, Ecstasy, the Body* (New York: Fordham University Press, 2016), 1. James, Wilshire explains, is striving to give voice—to help us hear—the "more," the "much-at-once."

do so. Language does not capture its particularity and flow, its superabundant more-ness. In effect, pragmatists committed to an experiential turn challenge the linguistic turn theorists: Please describe *this* particular experienced flux, which is *just what it is and nothing else*, and so please use language that refers to and captures only it *and nothing else*. Unable to meet this challenge, at this point the linguistic turn thinker simply doubles down on language and denies that anything else or anything other can exist because it cannot be conceptualized or said. No matter how adamantly stated, this straitjacket claim is merely asserted or stipulated, never demonstrated or supported by the least bit of evidence. Now, James did not claim that there is a *known* reality that cannot be described. Rather, he claimed that (1) there are dimensions of reality that cannot be known conceptually or discursively; (2) conceptual, linguistic knowing is not the only kind of knowing; and (3) experiencing consists of more than conceptualizing and "linguistifying." Failure to recognize this point results in what James called "intellectualism."[24]

The claim that experience is immediate and ineffable does not mean that experience is *only* immediate and ineffable. Two facts are crucial here. First, experience—as it immediately occurs—is a product of *past mediation*. From *The Principles of Psychology* onward, James was careful to point out that after a baby's initial "blooming, buzzing confusion," all our sensations and all our perceptions are permeated by signs and concepts, all our sensations and perceptions are "presentations" and "preperceptions" irreducibly constituted by and through language and thought. As John Dewey later and frequently pointed out, there is nothing contradictory in holding that experienced immediacy is itself mediated. Second, experience—again, as it immediately occurs—may become the material of *future mediation*. To claim that experience is ineffable is not to claim that experience cannot be "effed"—described, said, or thought. We all do these things all the time; you are doing it now. Rather, it is to claim that *experience described* is *experience transformed*; it is to claim that the activity or work of language and thought do not leave their subject matters unchanged and merely "mirrored." This is another philosophical dualism that pragmatism rejects: Experience is not *either* immediate (as "tender-minded" thinkers have tended to believe) *or* mediated (as "thought-minded" philosophers mostly have claimed). *If* mysticism is understood simply as belief in the immediacy of experience and in

---

[24] This issue is examined in detail in chapters 6 and 7.

the unknowability of this immediacy, then pragmatism may be understood in part as committed to mysticism—not simply as compatible with mysticism but as committed to it. And understood this way, a commitment to the ineffable immediacy of experience is simply another way to express a Jamesian commitment to "the insuperability of sensation thesis" (SPP, 45). As a result, understanding mysticism in this precise and limited way, James may be understood not simply as a pragmatic mystic but as a radically empirical mystic.

The notions of "mysticism" and "mystical experience," of course, have many meanings, and lots of people have big emotional investments in one or more of them. Very often characterizations of mysticism and mystical experience involve much more than a philosophical vision of the ineffability of experience in its immediacy and of the reality of this immediacy. It is for this reason that, in an effort to be precise and clear, James specified the marks or characteristics of mystical experience as he understood it. In *The Varieties of Religious Experience*, he thus proposed that mystical experiences are those experiences that have two particular central features and usually have third and fourth additional ones (which he identified as *transiency*, or relatively short duration, and *passivity*, or an absence of will and the feeling of being held by a superior power). In the first place, as noted above, for James mystical experiences are ineffable:

> The subject of it immediately says that it defies expression, that no adequate reports of its contents can be given in words. It follows from this that its quality must be directly experienced; it cannot be imparted or transferred to others.

Mystical experiences, James added, are more like "states of feeling" than "states of intellect" (VRE, 302). From the standpoint of pragmatism understood as method, theory of truth, and temperament, so far so good. In the second place, James further classified mystical experience as having a "noetic quality," as "states of knowledge" and not only "states of feeling." He explained:

> They are states of insight into depths of truth unplumbed by the discursive intellect. They are illuminations, revelations, full of significance and importance, all inarticulate though they remain; and as a rule they carry with them a curious sense of authority for after-time. (VRE, 302).

In other words, mystical experiences, if we combine these first and second marks, are experiences of *ineffable* and *immediate knowledge*.

Now, after providing many, many examples or "varieties" of both sporadic and cultivated mystical experiences—or, more precisely, reports of mystical experiences—James returned over and over to the issue of mystical experiences as experiences of truth and immediate knowledge:

> No account of the universe in its totality can be final which leaves these other forms of consciousness quite disregarded. How to regard them is the question—for they are so discontinuous with ordinary consciousness. . . . So we stand once more before that problem of truth . . . Do mystical states establish the truth[?] . . . Does it furnish any warrant for the truth of the twice-bornness and supernaturality which it favors? (VRE, 308, 329, 335)

Before critically examining James's reply to this question, it is crucial that this reply first be expressed in his own words. It is a three-part reply:

(1) Mystical states, when well developed, usually are, and have the right to be, absolutely authoritative over the individuals to whom they come.
(2) No authority emanates from them which should make it a duty for those who stand outside of them to accept their revelations uncritically.
(3) They break down the authority of the non-mystical or rationalistic consciousness, based upon the understanding and the senses alone. They show it to be only one kind of consciousness. They open out the possibility of other orders of truth, in which, so far as anything in us vitally responds to them, we may freely continue to have faith. (VRE, 335)

Is this reply, in part or in whole, consistent with a pragmatic temperament?

In some ways it is, but in other ways, I think, it definitely is not—indeed, it dangerously is not.[25] First, there are elements in each of the three parts of James's reply that surely do fit with and flow from his pragmatism. Reply (1) begins by asserting that mystical states of consciousness or mystical experiences usually are authoritative over those persons who have them. This is a wholly naturalistic psychological claim that follows at once from James's

---

[25] For an entirely different assessment, see Robert J. Roth, *Radical Pragmatism: An Alternative* (New York: Fordham University Press, 1998). Roth claimed, "It is my contention that *Pragmatism*, especially in the last two chapters, fulfills James's promise made in the *Varieties* to validate

definition of mystical experiences as noetic.[26] It is simply the claim that particular types of experiences occur, or are reported to occur, and that those who have these experiences regard them in a particular way. Similarly—and even more so—reply (2) is wholly consistent with a fact-loving, consequence-oriented, tough-minded pragmatism. It is simply the claim that the mere fact that someone reports having a particular experience does not by itself establish the truth or falsity of any belief that is formed in or by that experience. Verity, for the Jamesian pragmatist, is never immediate; it is the result of a process of verification. No experience, for pragmatists, comes prepackaged with knowledge of its own cause or the truth of claims that follow at once from it. Truth, for pragmatists, is always established after the fact, never immediately. And a part of reply (3) is also fully pragmatic: Pragmatism treats the question "How many forms of consciousness are there?" as an empirical, experiential question. Perhaps there is only one. Perhaps there are more. If there is experience of plural forms of consciousness—even forms of consciousness foreign to oneself—pragmatists hold no theoretical commitments that would deny this reality. Pragmatism is a philosophy of experience, and if experience includes plural forms of consciousness, then all these forms exist and none is more real than others.

However, there are also key elements in James's reply that are at odds with pragmatism understood as a method, theory of truth, and temperament. As Richard Rorty put it, *The Varieties of Religious Experience* does not offer a coherent position because it is "riddled with inconsistencies" that "stem from James's inability to make up his mind between arguing that supernaturalism might be true because it might be good for you and arguing that it is in fact true because there is ample experiential evidence for it." Rorty expanded this same claim in his "Pragmatism Without Method":

William James sometimes comes on as tough-minded, empirical, in love with hard facts and concrete details. But at other times, notably in "The Will

philosophically the drive of religious experience to a belief in God" (87). James does "validate" the existence and natural function of this drive in many people but does not, I argue, validate that the resulting beliefs are true or constitute knowledge.

[26] In this spirit, Hunter Brown observed that "if one locates James's philosophy of religion within the terms of immediate experience, it is readily apparent that he defended live theism because it is experienced by actual individuals and communities as *reasonable*." Again, taken as a report on experience, this is a psychological fact. This fact, however, does not establish the truth or falsity of any belief that may arise afterward—as, sadly, a short course of experience shows us that often beliefs that seem reasonable at first turn out not to be true. Hunter Brown, *William James on Radical Empiricism and Religion* (Toronto: University of Toronto Press, 2000).

to Believe," it becomes clear that his principal motive is to place his father's belief in Society as the Redeemed Form of Man on a par with the theories of the "hard" sciences.[27]

Similarly, James biographer Linda Simon stated:

James could not be anything other than contradictory. He lived, alternately, in two different universes—one, unified and monistic, inherited from his father; the other, pluralistic and changeable, imagined by Darwin: James wanted the best of both.[28]

In his reply (1), James claimed not only that those who have mystical experiences report that they have an absolutely authoritative character—this is a psychological, empirical, naturalistic description—but that these persons "have the right" to take these experiences as absolutely authoritative warrants for truth. Obviously resonant with "The Will to Believe" and "Is Life Worth Living," the claim that the sheer occurrence of an experience is absolutely authoritative warrant for the truth of some belief is very, very much at odds with James's pragmatism.[29] This opposition is the result of an equivocation: James is right that mystical experiences have absolute *psychological authority* for those who experience them—this is their defining phenomenological or experiential quality—but this is a fact entirely separate from whether or not they have any *epistemic warrant* for those who experience them, much less an absolute one. This same equivocation is evident in reply (3) as James moved from endorsing a pluralism of kinds of consciousness and kinds of experiences, or a multiplicity of psychological states, to endorsing "the possibility of other orders of truth," or a multiplicity of truth warrants. (James seemed to

[27] Richard Rorty, *Objectivity, Relativism, and Truth: Philosophical Papers, Volume 1* (New York: Cambridge University Press, 1991), 63. In his *Philosophical Ideas in the United* States (New York: Octagon Books, 1968 [1934]), Harvey Gates Townsend judged that "the most influential school that James ever attended was the school of his own home" in both matters of philosophical content and style—"the father's unconventional and racy speech was communicated to the children and, in William's case became the core of a particularly plastic, colloquial style which marks him as the great stylist of American philosophy" (135, 136).

[28] Linda Simon, *Genuine Reality: A Life of William James* (Chicago: University of Chicago Press, 1999), xvi. And in her "William James: A Sketch," Simon observed that James knew that each individual is "intensely odd" and "oddness, for James, implied diverse perceptions, angles of vision, and experiences. All of his works stand as testimony to this diversity" (16). In *The Jamesian Mind*, edited by Sarin Marchetti (New York: Routledge, 2021).

[29] In "A Pragmatist's Progress," Philip Kitcher observed that "*Varieties* is set within the epistemological framework of 'The Will to Believe.'" In *William James and a Science of Religious Experience*, edited by Wayne Proudfoot (New York: Columbia University Press, 2004), 115.

acknowledge this equivocation in his "Conclusions": Religion, he wrote there, exerts "a permanent function, whether she be with or without intellectual content, and whether, if she have any, it be true or false" (VRE, 399). In contrast to James's three-part reply in *The Varieties of Religious Experience*, pragmatism is a vision in which (a) there is *no* absolutely authoritative warrant for *any* belief because all beliefs are fallible, partial, personal, perspectival, more or less, and open to possible revision in light of future experience, including our engagements with others;[30] and (b) truth is a matter of the temporal process of valid-ation, a making and becoming, a matter of consequences and last things rather than first things or immediacies. As James himself explained many times, the whole pragmatic temperament looks ahead to consequences and outcomes and cumulative-over-time results, not to origins and insular immediate instants. Truth may live on the credit system, but that credit may be called in at any time. For pragmatism, the very notion of "immediate knowledge" stands in opposition to its method of tracing practical consequences, its theory of truth as the result of processes of validation, and its temperament of looking toward last things. This is a point that James himself recognized in *The Principles of Psychology*: "*Introspection is difficult and fallible*" and so "the only safeguard is in the final *consensus* of our farther knowledge about the thing in question, later views correcting earlier ones, until at last the harmony of a consistent system is reached.... Such a system we ourselves must strive, as far as may be, to attain" (PP, 191).

My point here is not simply yet another contribution to an academic dispute or theoretic disagreement. In the spirit of pragmatism itself, there is an *immense practical difference* between James's stated position that mystical experiences (for those who have them) *rightly* are absolutely authoritative warrants of truth and my view that any self-consistent pragmatism must deny that any experience has absolute authoritative warrant of truth for anyone. What is at stake here? After James provided his general characterization of mystical experience—it is ineffable, noetic, usually transitory, and usually passive—he sought to give a fuller picture by means of "some typical examples" (VRE, 303). He then proceeded to cite Luther, Walt Whitman and a handful of other writers and poets, Indian Vedantists, Buddhists, Muslim theologians, Saint Ignatius, and Saint Teresa. And along the way, he both mentioned how

---

[30] Richard J. Bernstein termed this—and recommended—"engaged fallibilistic pluralism." *The New Constellation: The Ethical-Political Horizons of Modernity/Postmodernity* (Cambridge, MA: MIT Press, 1991), 336.

alcohol and nitrous oxide intoxication can stimulate mystical consciousness (VRE, 307) and, commenting on his own examples, noted in honesty that "in a recital like this there is something suggestive of pathology" (VRE, 307–308). Perhaps so, but James's examples are not very suggestive of pathology in large part because he cherry-picks examples of aesthetic, ascetic, religious, and broadly humanitarian lives and traditions. There is a certain blindness here. A very different list of believers in the noetic character of their own individual experience might include mass murderers, suicide bombers and other terrorists, dictators and cult leaders, school shooters, folks who see dead people or ghosts, and those who report hearing God reveal to them the purpose of their lives or that God is on their side in all things. James wrote that "the mystic is, in short, *invulnerable* [to rationality and evidence] and must be left, whether we relish it or not, in undisturbed enjoyment of his creed" (VRE, 336). Again, here James equivocated—moving from psychological invulnerability (impossibility of change by others) to epistemic invulnerability (infallibility). To the extent the mystic really is invulnerable, everybody else—society as a whole—is far too vulnerable to the mystic's creed and, even more, to the actions that may issue from that creed. A democratic, inclusive, pluralistic society needs pragmatists aware of their own fallibility and open to the experiences of others and the results of future inquiry—not absolutists who are invulnerable to reason and evidence because they have mistaken the psychological depth of a personal experience for the shared truth and epistemic warrant of beliefs that arise from it. From a pragmatic perspective, *noetic* mysticism is a socially dangerous and sometimes genocidal blindness in human beings.

3. Philosophies as Triumphs

Now, what does it mean for a philosophy, whether James's pragmatism or some other philosophy, to be a "definitive triumph," a "conquering destiny," or "epoch-making"? What does it mean for a philosophy, a whole philosophy, simply to be true, even if it is not "epoch-making"? In order to determine whether or not James's account of method, truth, and temperament really is a triumph—whether or not more, than a century after *Pragmatism*, we now live in an epoch of pragmatism—these notions of a philosophy's era-defining "triumph" or "destiny" must be made clear.

However, to the extent that different philosophies understand differently what it would mean for a philosophy to "triumph," it is difficult, perhaps impossible, to provide this clarity in a non-question-begging manner. For example, does "triumph" in, and by, a philosophy mean that this philosophy identifies and expresses universal, eternal, objective truths? Or does it mean instead that such a philosophy produces what James called "the sentiment of rationality" among those who hold it (WB, 57ff.)? Or does it mean that a philosophy is a key factor in bringing about some cultural upheaval or maintaining some status quo? Or does it mean that the philosophy provides proof, valid argument, justification, or overwhelming evidence for all of the major claims it makes? Or does the triumph of a philosophy mean that this philosophy reaffirms some faith or banishes some doubt? Or does it mean that lots and lots of people believe it (for the duration of its triumph and epoch)—or that they poll each other and produce a ranking that puts this philosophy at the top? Or might a philosophy be triumphant if only a se-lect few believe it? Does it mean that people who believe it report their lives happier, healthier, wealthier, more loving, otherwise more satisfied, or more meaningful that those who do not hold this philosophy? Or does it mean that belief in a philosophy delivers to its believers knowledge of eternal life? Or does the triumph of a philosophy mean that it successfully nurtures a stren-uous mood and the willingness to endure immediate hardships in pursuit of a distant ideal or a more-inclusive justice? Or does it mean something else?[31]

If the meaning of a philosophy's "triumph" is relative to, and a function of, some particular philosophy and its temperament, what then is the pragmatic meaning of a philosophy's "triumph"? What does, or would, it mean for prag-matism to "triumph" on its own terms?

It means this. First, if pragmatism is understood as a method for settling metaphysical disputes, it would be "triumphant" to the extent that it works—that is, to the extent that it actually settles, or makes possible the settlement of, metaphysical disputes. Does James's pragmatic method allow us to settle traditional, otherwise interminable metaphysical disputes? A method for doing X is successful on its own terms to the extent that it makes possible achievement of X.

Second, if pragmatism is understood as a theory of truth, it is "triumphant" to the extent that this theory is true—that is, to the extent that this theory, consistent with itself, is verified, corroborated, marries old opinion and new

---

[31] Nicholas Rescher has claimed that pragmatism has been highly successful—a "pragmatic suc-cess"—in several distinct ways and in relation to several distinct purposes. He concluded that "what this panoramic display of pragmatism makes clear is the deeply constructive nature of pragmatism." *Epistemic Issues in Pragmatic Perspective* (Lanham, MD: Lexington Books, 2018), 211–213.

fact, puts us in satisfactory relation with other parts of our experiences, and works. The pragmatic test for the truth of the pragmatic theory of truth is the same test as that for the truth of any belief. To triumph, this theory must pass its own test.

Third, if pragmatism is understood as a temperament or attitude or intimate mood, pragmatism is "triumphant" when it illuminates the universe in a manner that suits this pragmatic temperament (P, 11), a manner that is not "out of plumb and out of key and out of 'whack'" (P, 25) but rather impressive to this temperament, a manner in which this temperament feels at home (APU, 10), a manner that produces feelings of "ease, peace, rest" (WB, 57), all-pervading fluency, and "intimacy," and that defines "the future *congruously with our spontaneous powers*" (WB, 57, 75, 70).

4. Evaluating Pragmatism

"Philosophy," James observed,

> amplifies and defines our faith, and dignifies it and lends it words and plausibility. It hardly ever engenders it; it cannot now secure it. . . . Philosophy lives in words, but truth and fact well up into our lives in ways that exceed verbal formulation. (VRE, 345, 360)

So, in the more than one hundred years and in the much-changed world since *Pragmatism* was published, has James's pragmatism been made "secure"? Has it proven itself triumphant and epoch-making? Has the pragmatic method shown itself to work and, as a result, been widely employed? Has the pragmatic theory of truth proven itself true and, as a result, been widely adopted? And has the pragmatic temperament found itself increasingly at home in the world articulated by *Pragmatism*, and found itself increasingly the temperament of the epoch, both funding and funded by the times in which we live?

Like most things in life, the verdict appears mixed and messy, and different people will emphasize differently. Metaphysical disputes surely did not come to an end in 1907—despite theorists since that time who have proclaimed an end to metaphysics or taken up "post-metaphysical" thinking in fields from philosophy to architecture, ecology, and political theory. Debates about the nature of God, reality, knowledge, goodness, and beauty continue—in the academy, on the street, and even in some camping parties in the mountains. Moreover, pragmatism seems not to have brought metaphysical sides or opponents together. Instead, pragmatism frequently seems to be just an additional side—and so more "divider" than "uniter." If there were Platonists and Aristotelians and Cartesians and Kantians and Hegelians before James published *Pragmatism*, it seems there still are all those and, in addition, now some Jamesians. Of course, this does not in any way demonstrate that the pragmatic method does not work. It merely indicates that the pragmatic method often is not employed. Nonetheless, on the surface, at least, the evidence does not seem entirely to support the view that pragmatism has become something quite like the Protestant Reformation. (To be fair, it is worth noting that long after the Reformation, there are lots and lots of people who are not Protestants—and so a notion of universal conversion is probably not a useful measure of the impact of a philosophy or school of thought). And, so far at least, there are no hotel rooms furnished with nightstands stocked with a copy of *Pragmatism* in the top drawer.

The verdict appears much the same concerning the pragmatic theory of truth. The "Ph.D. octopus" (ECR, 67ff.) that James diagnosed early now has a near death grip on much of education (including professional philosophy) and much of life, and it produces confident and clever scholars (some following in the footsteps of Moore or Russell, some following Horkheimer or Adorno, and some following Santayana or Royce) armed with tidy arguments (typically with inconspicuous premises) against the pragmatic theory of truth. Of course, the presence of these critics, here again, does not in any way demonstrate that the pragmatic theory of truth is not true. It only shows that even if the oldest truths are plastic (P, 37), as James claimed, still many persons who keep a tight and traditional grip on these oldest truths are creatures of theoretical habits and not equally plastic. Moreover, supposed alternative accounts of truth that extract and abstract truth from practical interests are alternatives to pragmatism only insofar as they are abstract and have "nothing to do with our experiences": "There never was a more exquisite example of an idea abstracted from the concretes of experience and then used to oppose and negate what it was abstracted from" (P, 108–109). Nonetheless, after more than a century, the pragmatic theory of truth seems to be more at the stage of being considered absurd or the stage of being admitted as correct but trivial than at the stage of being broadly held and broadly viewed as insightful. Conquering destiny and "mission accomplished"? No, not yet at least.

This same mixed verdict and anything but fully positive picture emerges when pragmatism is understood as a temperament or attitude or vision. As James recognized, there are many persons whose vision is not pragmatic, who do not find pragmatism to capture and illuminate their experience and world, who do not feel and prefer pragmatism's pluralistic universe. James's pragmatism is not what life honestly means to them, and it is not their deepest preferred working attitude. Their lives are not attuned to the whole push of pragmatism: that reality is unfinished; that finite sentient beings contribute to the ongoing remaking of it and its ideals (including truth); that the success or failure of this remaking is found in practical consequences in plural, concrete experiences, in last things rather than first principles; and that this is strenuous work with no guarantee of even passing success—success that always carries with it real loss and tragedy. Even cheerleaders for pragmatism must admit that more than a hundred years after *Pragmatism,* this temperament is not the omnipresent or even characteristic temperament of our times. There are pragmatists, to be sure, but there are many, many absolutists, fundamentalists, rationalists, monists, authoritarians, and philosophical flat-earthers. The many decades after James have been marked by at least as many efforts to eliminate, frustrate, ignore, or silence demands other than one's own as by the invention, urged by James, of ways to realize both one's own and alien demands. It has been marked by many points of view claiming to be the one, total point of view and the one requisite path to redemption and salvation.

Does this mixed verdict on the pragmatic method, theory of truth, and temperament show that James was wrong? Friends of James may be inclined to try to make this verdict less mixed. They might point out, for example, that there are persons who in their theories do not endorse pragmatism but who in their lives affirm and make use of it. To be a pragmatist on pragmatism's own terms, they might add, is a matter of practice and not just theory. (Of course, to be fair, this also means that there can be persons who claim in their theories to be pragmatists but who affirm a very different philosophy in practice. This is a special danger, perhaps, for dreary disciples of pragmatism who are inclined to say, in effect, "Oh, William James must have thought it all before" (APU, 13).) Fair enough: There may be persons, practices, and aspects or chunks of culture that are pragmatic before, or without ever, being recognized, theorized, or self-reflected as pragmatic. Friends of James might also stress James's pluralism and his recognition that there is a multiplicity of temperaments—such that his pragmatism is not rendered false just because it does not resonate with persons with different temperaments. Pragmatism is pluralistic about pragmatism itself. It does not announce itself as the one philosophy for everyone. Again, fair enough: A philosophy may be a "conquering destiny" without conquering every mind, and no philosophy ever has taken the mere existence of non-believers as sufficient evidence of its own falsity or failure.

Even granting these points, however, it is not clear that pragmatism has been triumphant to the degree that James, or some of his rhetoric, hopefully projected. There are persons who reject pragmatism in practice as well as theory. And there continue to be many of them. It is tempting, therefore, to conclude that James did not establish the pragmatic method, theory of truth, or pragmatic temperament (and, so, tempting to understand any triumph of pragmatism in terms of the establishment and broad endorsement of its truth).

That conclusion would be a mistake and a thorough misunderstanding of James's philosophy and its importance.

This is the key point: James's pragmatism, as he repeatedly recognized, is not something that can be established (one way or the other) by, and in, theory or abstraction alone. *Pragmatism,* the lectures and book, is not an attempt (whether triumph or failure) to *prove* the truth of pragmatism. James never offered a theoretical proof of pragmatism. He never attempted to do so. His *Pragmatism* is not a successful proof of the truth of pragmatism and it is not a failed proof of the truth of pragmatism. For James, book chapters, journal articles, and lectures do not and cannot ever prove the truth or falsity of a philosophy—pragmatism or any other philosophy. Instead, truth or falsity are located and found in last things, fruits, consequences, facts. They are found in concrete experiences of leading, marrying, cashing out, satisfying, riding on, and corroborating. They live in life, in life's feelings, preferences, attitudes, fluencies and intimacies, attunements.

In *Pragmatism,* James did not provide a theoretical, abstract proof of the truth of pragmatism. Instead, he showed that merely theoretical, abstract arguments and objections do not and cannot constitute proof of the falsity of pragmatism. Indirectly, James suggested as well that this is not what philosophy is about, not what philosophy does. Against these critics, James argued that pragmatism is a live hypothesis for experience and that there is no theoretical case against it. James made this point repeatedly. Here is one particularly clear example:

Pragmatism, pending the final empirical ascertainment of just what the balance of union and disunion among things may be, must obviously range herself upon the pluralistic side. Some day, she admits, even total union, with one knower, one origin, and a universe consolidated in every conceivable way, may turn out to be the most acceptable of all hypotheses. Meanwhile the opposite hypothesis, of a world imperfectly unified still, and perhaps always to remain so, must be sincerely entertained. This latter hypothesis is pluralism's doctrine. Since absolute monism forbids its being even considered seriously, branding it as irrational from the start, it is clear that pragmatism must turn its back on absolute monism, and follow pluralism's more empirical path. (P, 79)

If pragmatism is to be known false, for James, it must be shown false— shown false in, and by, somebody's concrete experience. James's message to his audience is that if his pragmatism fits and works in their experience and is verified, validated, and corroborated in that experience, then they need not worry that there is some valid abstract argument that disproves or outlaws in theory what they find to be so in practice.

James swept aside all the "pretended logic" (P, 142) and the would-be theoretical objections to pragmatism. He established pragmatism as an empirical hypothesis or experiential possibility waiting on last things, waiting on the experiences of his audiences, waiting on you and what you want (P, 17). He did this by recasting philosophical disputes not primarily as disputes of inference and reason (as though some philosophers just need to retake a logic or critical thinking course or enroll in a remedial calculus tutorial) but as differences of temperament and vision (in which different persons have different experiences, none able to legislate for, or against, all others).

This is why James described his objective in *Pragmatism* in language other than the language of "proof" and "argument," the language of "Being," or the language of language itself. James explained his purpose in the language of suggestion and temperament, the language of hypotheses, interests, inspirations, approvals, experienced satisfactions, preferences and feelings, and last things. He did not announce his purpose or objective as demonstration of the truth of pragmatism, but, instead, said this sort of thing:

I stand desirous of interesting you in a philosophy. (P, 10)

I hope I may end by inspiring you with my belief. (P, 30)

I hope that as these lectures go on, the concreteness and closeness to facts of pragmatism . . . may be what approves itself to you as its most satisfactory peculiarity. (P, 39)

I leave it to you to judge. (P, 111)

James concluded *Pragmatism* by simply stating that persons with a pragmatic temperament may find his pragmatism "exactly what you require" (P, 144). And he consistently postponed the justification of his pragmatism (P, 39), making clear that any such justification must wait on the experience that followed from its consideration—on whether pragmatism is or is not exactly what is required by and validated in concrete experiences.

5. Pragmatism 2.0

James thought *Pragmatism*, his book, would be "epoch-making" in part because he thought his era already was pragmatic, increasingly populated by persons with a pragmatic temperament that combines "tender-minded" and "tough-minded" orientations and wants a philosophy that combines both (P, 17). He sought to inspire that temperament, generalize its philosophy, and make it conscious of itself (P, 30). Was James's era pragmatic, with pragmatism triumphant a decade after the publication of *Pragmatism*? Well more than a century after, is the era today pragmatic? Were Anderson and Fisch correct to judge that "there is scarcely a current of thought in twentieth-century America which does not derive part of its vitality from the general invigoration of philosophy and psychology which was perhaps James's chief service to it"? Or, more recently, were Hester and Talisse right to claim that "there is no denying that pragmatist ideas are once again at the center of philosophical discussion and debate"?[32]

These are sweeping questions, and their answers probably depend on what one chooses to stress and on what John Dewey called "selective emphasis." What is clear enough, however, is that just as James offered no theoretical proof for his pragmatism, there is no point in pretending to do so today. James strove to show that there is nothing in theory that constitutes

[32] D. Micah Hester and Robert B. Talisse, *On James* (Belmont, CA: Wadsworth, 2004), 53.

reason to reject pragmatism, or to affirm it. Accordingly, today the task for Jamesian pragmatists—and here I mean to refer to a kind of life rather than an allegiance in the academy—is to create the cultural conditions that in turn produce experiences that validate pragmatism and further attune that experience itself to its reasonableness and its vision. That practical turn—a turn to practice—would be epoch-making. And it would be, for pragmatism, the moral equivalent of abstract, old-fashioned philosophy.

What conditions give rise to a pragmatic temperament, to habits of pragmatism? Three points loom largest. First, a pragmatic temperament is melioristic. Distinct from optimism and pessimism, meliorism holds that the salvation of the world is "neither inevitable nor impossible": "It treats it as a possibility, which becomes more and more of a probability the more numerous the actual conditions of salvation become" (P, 137). It holds that the salvation of the world, this-worldly salvation, and the realization of hope may—just may (not will)—be possible if we work hard toward these ends. It requires hope and hard work. However, when life is without hope, when there is no ability or no incentive to imagine something better than the way things are and the way things have been, when despair dominates and resignation pervades, and when imagination is ground down, then hope will not be experienced as one's best working attitude, will not be felt in the whole push and drift of life, and will not be part of one's intimate character and temperament. Accordingly, anyone concerned to spread the pragmatic temperament, understood as, in part, a melioristic temperament, must be concerned to actively create and spread conditions that foster hope, imagination, and the experience of the existence of unrealized possibilities. And while these conditions may in part depend upon acts of individual will to engage in hope, they depend more basically and broadly on the attunements of cultural conditions—including political institutions, economic arrangements, social relations, systems of meaning, and ecological realities. Hope requires not only the will to hope but also the social material conditions of hope. Pragmatism and its temperament depend on both.

Meliorism demands more than hope. It also demands hard work. However, when life evidences unbridgeable chasms between one's reach and one's grasp, between means and end, between one's effort and its results, between struggle and achievement, then hard work will not be one's best working attitude, will find no home in one's character, and will not fit one's life. If one's own experience is that one is impotent to make a difference, then striving to make a difference—even or especially when advised by a privileged Harvard philosopher to strive to make a difference—looks like a game only for suckers, a game to be won only by the more fortunate and the more powerful. Actions that never seem to pay off have no cash value, and any philosophy addressed to lives filled principally with such actions will seem bankrupt and out of whack. And, of course, there is nothing particularly pragmatic about linking theory and practice in theory but doing nothing to join them in practice. Accordingly, anyone concerned to make triumphant the pragmatic temperament must be concerned to enlarge conditions that forge experienced connections between effort and achievement, thus empowering otherwise relatively powerless persons. Like the conditions of hope, these conditions are cultural, institutional, and political, not merely individual. They are matters of social change and cultural revolution, and not merely personal transformation or individual self-help makeover.

Second, a pragmatic temperament is pluralistic, irreducibly pluralistic. Distinct from absolutism and nihilism, pluralism holds that values (including truth) are relations made in experience, and that this experience is always perspectival, always personal, and always partial. James noted: "We say this theory solves it on the whole more satisfactorily than that theory; but that means more satisfactorily to ourselves, and individuals will emphasize their points of satisfaction differently" (P, 35). Though many philosophers continue to be eager to show that some one point of view (typically their own) is the Real, True, Good, or Beautiful point of view, no consciousness enjoys the prerogative of obliging others to conform to its rule and point of view, and no person's theory trumps someone else's experience, feelings, and faith in that experience. Pragmatism, then, requires humility. However, when life is marked not only by blindness to the values of the differences of others but also by blindness to this very blindness, when God is experienced as on one side only, and when one's beliefs fully feel absolute, certain, infallible, or final, then pluralistic humility will have little or no resonance, little or no fluency and intimacy, and little or no satisfaction. The result will be a tribalism of increasingly authoritarian tribes.

Accordingly, anyone committed to the growth of the pragmatic temperament must commit to extending the conditions that foster humility and felt opportunity in the face of what is different and even unfamiliar, the determination to invent ways to realize multiple demands, and the realization that this invention must be a process that includes effectively from the start the perspectives of those who make these multiple demands. While there is a role in all this for inspiration and exhortation to live with less self-certainty

and less self-centeredness, here too the transformation demanded by pragmatism is fundamentally change in wide-ranging social conditions and the
cultural moods, habits, and character they educate and produce. Humility
does not require quietism or self-effacement. It requires selves committed
in action to living without false pride. It requires selves committed to partic-
ipating not in varieties of colonization but, rather, in work to produce what
James called "an ethical republic here below" (WB, 150).

Third, this melioristic, pluralistic, pragmatic temperament is irreducibly
a matter of faith—wholly this-worldly faith, but faith nonetheless. Why?
James's pragmatism, as discussed in chapter 1, simultaneously holds both
of the following: first, that justification of belief is located in last things, that
it is a function of consequences and results and outcome; and second, that
action is always undertaken in advance of its consequences and results and
outcome. No belief about our lives, therefore, can be fully or finally justified in advance of action undertaken on its behalf. And until there can be
no further such action, no justification on behalf of action to date can be
full or final. As Robert D. Richardson nicely put it, for James "beliefs look
very much like conclusions tumbled out in advance of evidence." And this
is faith, faith in action, pragmatic faith. "When you get right down to it,"
Richardson added, it is "a way of facing final things, pragmatism's escha-
tology."[33] James recognized that his own pragmatism, just like any other
philosophy, cannot be a final philosophy, a philosophy made up in advance
of last things.

Accordingly, anyone interested in fostering a pragmatic temperament must
work to create conditions that stimulate and sustain before-the-fact melioristic
and pluralistic commitments in advance of their after-the-fact consequences.
To do this is to encourage what James called "the strenuous mood," to call forth
action on behalf of ideals for which there is no guarantee of realization. There
is no crystal ball—no advance guarantee for pessimism, such as the belief that
climate change now under way surely will destroy human life on earth, and no
advance guarantee for optimism, such as the belief that there will be a "technological fix" to climate change and destruction. Neither of these outcomes is
guaranteed; both are possible. Instead of this kind of speculation, the pragmatic
temperament is a call to action on the part of those who hold the belief "we
might" with equal commitment and energy as those who believe "we can" or

[33] Robert D. Richardson, *William James in the Maelstrom of American Modernism* (New York:
Houghton Mifflin, 2006), 445, 488.

"we will." The tone of this action cannot be that of "conquering destiny," a phrase that easily appears doubly problematic and even antithetical to pragmatism—a philosophy that (a) denies fate and predeterminism and so understands destinies not at all as predestinations but only as eventual outcomes and how things turn out to be for a while, and (b) focuses not on conquest and prerogative but rather on multiplicity, difference, and invention of ways to satisfy otherwise competing demands. In this context, pragmatism, understood as a philosophy, cannot be a conquering destiny. It can be only a hypothesis awaiting verification in experiences of persons temperamentally inclined or disinclined by cultural conditions as much as individual will to experience, or not experience, that verification, leading, working, satisfying, preferring.

Pragmatism, understood as James's book, may be seen as a conquering destiny to the extent that it successfully rendered obsolete and remote merely theoretical arguments against the possibility of its truth, and so helped stimulate the making of cultural conditions that give rise to broadly pragmatic temperaments. More than a century later (and despite the still-present nostalgia and traditionalism of philosophical reality-resisters who yearn for something they take to be more real or at least something they want to be more authentic), this appears to be not the Copernican Revolution but, rather, a theoretical quantum leap forward.

The pragmatic task is only a little theoretical. It is an unfinished task, and even centuries from now it will remain so. As James pointed out, there can be no final conclusion until everything finally has concluded (EP, 190). Pragmatism's cash value is not based in, or backed by, any metaphysical, epistemological, or moral gold standard or other permanent deposits. It is based on, and in, exchange systems marked by credit, gains and losses, and ineliminable risk. What is that risk? It is life in a world without eternity, permanence, certainty, or absolutes—or the confidence they enable. It is life in which today's seeming certainties are eroded tomorrow—and so not certainties at all—and one in which today's meanings are questioned, contested, destabilized, and resignified endlessly and without any illusion of finality.[34] It is a world that we cannot ultimately represent to ourselves, a world that

---

[34] Focusing on the intellectual and cultural context in which James's views developed, Paul Croce has termed this "the erosion of certainty," "the elusive certainty of science," and "the culture of uncertainty." *Science and Religion in the Era of William James: Eclipse of Certainty, 1820–1880* (Chapel Hill: University of North Carolina Press, 1995). Croce insightfully captured James's development in his concluding sentence: "While he had come to understand the problems of uncertainty, it would be years before he could comprehend the possibilities for reconstructing belief despite uncertainty" (231).

is not the best of all possible worlds but is, instead, often less than decent and always tragic. It is a world still, always, in the making, unmaking, and remaking by cooperative activity. This is not a world in which one's fate can be surmounted by scorn, as Camus said of Sisyphus. It is a world without fate, determinism, or complete maturity, without gods or final Enlightenment, a world in which experiences *might* be changed by hopes, actions, and faiths.

In *Pragmatism,* James strove to show that *there is no theoretical reason to reject this worldview.* For those who think—who feel, who experience—that he is right, there is little reason to repeat this task. Instead of showing itself possible in theory, the task for pragmatism in its second century and beyond is making itself actual in practice. To produce the conditions upon which a pragmatic temperament, habit, or attunement depends is an immense and complex task. In a world marked by intolerance, arrogance, self-righteousness, self-certainty, violence, custom, hatred, closed-mindedness, fatalism, imperialism, fundamentalism, and absolutism, what James described—looking toward last things, plural last things—may seem so out of touch as to be out of reach. Maybe so. This really might be so. The last hundred-plus years have not been a hundred years of pragmatism. It does not now seem likely that the next hundred will be so. But James's *Pragmatism* points in the direction of the work that alone has provided, and can provide now, a basis for hope that the next hundred years might be increasingly, bit by bit, more pragmatic.

For pragmatists, that is all there is, and that is enough. For persons unsure whether this is enough, the pragmatic meaning of *Pragmatism* is this: Give it a try, make the effort, put it to the test in practice, look ahead, see what's possible.

James's vision, his temperament, the whole fashion and force of his worldview—all are melioristic. Pragmatism is simply the expression of that temperament in matters of meaning and truth.

6

Everything Here Is Plastic

Radical Empiricism and Worlds of Relations

> The history of philosophy is to a great extent that of a certain clash
> of human temperaments. . . . There is no reason to suppose that this
> strong temperamental vision is from now onward to count no longer
> in the history of man's beliefs. (P, 11, 12)

> In short, it is almost certain that personal temperament will here
> make itself felt, and that although all men will insist on being spoken
> to by the universe in some way, few will insist on being spoken to in
> just the same way. (WB, 75)

The real world is a world of relations, dynamic relations.

This is the revolutionary thesis of radical empiricism understood as a vision of the world or a way in which the universe speaks to some persons. For radical empiricists, the real world is *not* at base a world of minds (as idealism holds) or bodies (as materialism holds), or even minds and bodies together (as dualism holds). It is *not* a world of spirit or nature or some permutation of them. It is *not* in the broadest sense a world of any static substances or any self-contained things. These notions of reality as substances and things have marked sites of so many endless philosophical disputes—disputes about which things are real or most real or ontologically primary and the building-block bedrock of which everything else consists and to which, therefore, everything else is reducible. For radical empiricists, the world is a world of relations, not a world of things.

When reality is viewed not as a container of things but as irreducibly relational in character, then things have functional or instrumental status. Things are simply class names for clusters of relations in which some persons have particular interests and thus identify and distinguish one cluster of relations from other relations. In this way, radical empiricism turns *dualisms* posited by metaphysics into *distinctions* generated by and at work in practice.

No Professor's Lectures Can Save Us. John J. Stuhr, Oxford University Press. © Oxford University Press 2023.
DOI: 10.1093/oso/9780197664629.003.0007

This, of course, was James's point in his 1904 essay, "Does Consciousness Exist?," later the first chapter of *Essays in Radical Empiricism*. James's answer to his title question is thoroughly pragmatic: Consciousness exists not *as an entity* but, instead, *as a function*. James summarized his thesis:

> Consciousness connotes a kind of external relation, and does not denote a special stuff or way of being. *The peculiarity of our experiences, that they not only are, but are known, which their "conscious" quality is invoked to explain, is better explained by their relations—these relations themselves being experiences—to one another.* (ERE, 14)

1. Radical Empiricism

James frequently referred to his philosophy as "radical empiricism." In his 1897 "Preface" to *The Will to Believe*, he named this his own philosophical temperament:

> Were I obliged to give a short name to the attitude [his "tolerably definite philosophic attitude"], I should call it that of *radical empiricism*, in spite of the fact that such brief nicknames are nowhere more misleading than in philosophy. I say "empiricism," because it is contented to regard its most assured conclusions concerning maters of fact as hypotheses liable to modification in the course of future experience; and I say "radical," because it treats the doctrine of monism itself as an hypothesis.... This is pluralism.... There is no possible point of view from which the world can appear an absolutely single fact. (WB, 5–6)

Similarly, in his 1909 "Preface" to *The Meaning of Truth*, James claimed that pragmatism was a crucial step toward making radical empiricism prevail, explaining radical empiricism in the following terms:

> Radical empiricism consists first of a postulate, next of a statement of fact, and finally of a generalized conclusion.
> The postulate is that the only things that shall be debatable among philosophers shall be things definable in terms drawn from experience. [Things of an unexperienceable nature may exist ad libitum, but they form no part of the material for philosophic debate.]

The statement of fact is that the relations between things, conjunctive as well as disjunctive, are just as much matters of direct particular experience, neither more so nor less so, than the things themselves.

The generalized conclusion is that therefore the parts of experience hold together from next to next by relations that are themselves parts of experience. The directly apprehended universe needs, in short, no extraneous trans-empirical connective support, but possesses in its own right a concatenated or continuous structure. (MT, 6–7)

If pragmatism is a crucial step in making radical empiricism prevail, so too radical empiricism is a crucial step in making pragmatism prevail. As James pointed out in *Pragmatism*, both pragmatists and their intellectualist critics agree that true ideas agree with reality, and "quarrel only after the question is raised as to what may precisely be meant by the term 'agreement' and what by the term 'reality'" (P, 96). Radical empiricism is what pragmatists mean by "reality." It is, moreover, the link between James's pragmatism and his later pluralism. "The 'workableness' which ideas must have, in order to be true"— James's pragmatism—"means particular workings, physical or intellectual, actual or possible, which they may set up from next to next inside of concrete experience" (MT, 7). Radical empiricism is the account of that concrete experience.

James's radical empiricism was already evident in his early writings on psychology. Consider, for example, this important, lengthy passage in "On Some Omissions of Introspective Psychology." Criticizing the views of Herbert Spencer, James set forth his own radically empiricist perspective:

There is not a conjunction or a preposition, and hardly an adverbial phrase, syntactic form, or inflection of voice, in human speech, that does not express some shading or other of relation which we at some moment actually feel to exist between the larger objects of our thought. If we speak objectively, it is the real relations that appear revealed; if we speak subjectively, it is the stream of consciousness that matches each of them by an inward colouring of its own. In either case the relations are numberless, and no existing language is capable of doing justice to all their shades. . . .

We ought to say a feeling of *and*, a feeling of *if*, a feeling of *but*, and a feeling of *by*, quite as readily as we say a feeling of *blue* or a feeling of *cold*. Yet we do not: so inveterate has our habit become of recognizing the existence of the substantive parts alone, that language almost refuses to lend itself to any other use. [The empiricists have said nothing of the error of] supposing that where there is no name no entity can exist. All *dumb* psychic states have, owing to this error, been coolly suppressed; or, if recognized at all, have been named after the substantive perception they led to, as thoughts "about" this object or "about" that, the stolid word about engulphing all their delicate idiosyncrasies in its monotonous sound. Thus the greater and greater accentuation and isolation of the substantive parts have continually gone on.

But the worst consequence of this vicious mode of mangling thought's stream is yet to come. From the continuously flowing thing it is, it is changed into a "manifold," broken into bits, called discrete; and in this condition, approved as its authentic and natural shape by the most opposite schools, it becomes the topic of one of the most tedious and interminable quarrels that philosophy has to show. (EP, 146–147; ERE, xix)

To understand radical empiricism, we must understand, as John J. McDermott noted in his insightful "Introduction" to *Essays in Radical Empiricism*, "that our metaphysics has been overrun by our language" (ERE, xx) and restricts reality to those atomistic, discrete particulars for which we have assigned a name, overrun by mistaking the leap from name to name for the move from thing to thing and the relations that conjoin them (ERE, xx). As James put it in *The Principles of Psychology* (and later quoted himself in *Essays in Radical Empiricsm*):

The thought of the object's recurrent identity is regarded as the identity of its recurrent thought; and the perceptions of multiplicity, of coexistence, of succession, are severally conceived to be brought about only through a multiplicity, a coexistence, a succession of perceptions. The continuous flow of the mental stream is sacrificed, and in its place an atomism, a brickbat plan of construction, is preached, for the existence of which no good introspective grounds can be brought forward, and out of which presently grow all sorts of paradoxes and contradictions, the heritage of woe of students of the mind. (PP, 196; ERE, xx)

This means that the traditional categories and dualisms of Western philosophy—for example, subject and object, knower and known, thought and thing, representer and represented, consciousness and its contents—are distinctions, ways of dividing, chopping up, categorizing, separating, transforming experience for particular purposes and attentions. James thus cautioned:

> We must remember that no dualism of being represented and representing resides in the experience per se. In its pure state or when isolated, there is no self-splitting of it into consciousness and what consciousness is "of." Its subjectivity and objectivity are functional attributes solely, realized only when experience is "taken," i.e., talked-of, twice, considered along with its two differing contexts respectively, by a new retrospective experience, of which that whole past complication now forms the fresh content. (ERE, 13)

This is what James meant when he wrote that *"the separation of* [experience] *into consciousness and content comes, not by way of subtraction, but by way of addition"* (ERE, 6–7). A pragmatist/radical empiricist thus replaces the question "How many fundamental or basic kinds of things are there in reality?" with the question "Given a particular purpose or orientation, into how many kinds of things is it useful to divide some reality?" It is important to understand that James never denied or even underestimated the practical value of making distinctions between consciousness and its contents or between subjects and objects. He merely insisted that any reflection that creates these distinctions not pretend that the distinctions existed prior to, and independent of, its selective operation. In this context, Paul J. Croce observed helpfully that James rejected "both scientific interpretations of experience in material terms and religious interpretations of experience in immaterial terms," instead integrating "objectivity and subjectivity as different expressions of what he would formally label, in 1896, 'pure experience,' with two divergent kinds of context . . . woven . . . into . . . the general course of experience."[1]

So, in response to the question "What is real?," James's response, in a sense, was that reality is real—no philosopher's largest and all-inclusive ontological category can be included fully in terms of some other category—and that we would do better to ask about whose purposes and interests are served by making particular distinctions. By understanding this, we begin to understand the positive side of this first claim that consciousness does not exist, or exists only as a function. It is in this context that James wrote:

---

[1] Paul J. Croce, *Young William James Thinking* (Baltimore: Johns Hopkins University Press, 2018), 5.

[There is] no aboriginal stuff or quality of being, contrasted with that of which material objects are made, out of which our thoughts of them are made. . . . My thesis is that if we start with the supposition that there is only one primal stuff or material in the world, a stuff of which everything is composed, and if we call that stuff "pure experience," then knowing can easily be explained as a particular sort of relation. . . .

Although for fluency's sake I myself spoke early in this article of a stuff of pure experience, I have now to say that there is no general stuff of which experience at large is made. There are as many stuffs as there are "natures" in the things experienced. If you ask what any one bit of pure experience is made of, the answer is always the same: "It is made of that, of just what appears, of space, of intensity, of flatness, knownness, heaviness, or what not." (ERE, 4, 14–15)

Throughout these passages, James consistently identified this radical empiricism in terms of pluralism, possibilities, and the irreducibly partial, perspectival, and pragmatic or constructive nature of thought.[2] John Dewey grasped this point in his 1925 "The Development of American Pragmatism." Noting that "pragmatism thus has a metaphysical implication," Dewey wrote:

The doctrine of the value of consequences leads us to take the future into consideration. And this taking into consideration of the future takes us to the conception of a universe whose evolution is not finished, of a universe which is still, in James' term, "in the making," "in the process of becoming," of a universe up to a certain point still plastic.[3]

In this light, James contrasted radical empiricism with traditional empiricism, positivism, scientific naturalism, materialism, and reductionism—as well as, of course, all forms of monism, idealism, rationalism, subjectivism,

---

[2] David Lamberth stressed the connections between James's radical empiricism and his pragmatism (and especially his distinction between conceptual knowledge and direct acquaintance)—between his metaphysics and his epistemology—in the first two chapters of his *William James and the Metaphysics of Experience* (New York: Cambridge University Press, 1999). And as William J. Gavin succinctly put it: "Pragmatism is not metaphysically neutral. It has metaphysical presuppositions or commitments about the universe itself—viewing it as unfinished, pluralistic, and concatenated, and both inviting and requiring participation by each of us." *William James in Focus: Willing to Believe* (Bloomington: Indiana University Press, 2013), 44.

[3] John Dewey, "The Development of American Pragmatism," in *John Dewey: The Later Works, 1925–1953* (Carbondale: Southern Illinois University Press, 1984 [1925]), 13.

and dualism.[4] Near the start of his 1904 "A World of Pure Experience" (republished in *Essays in Radical Empiricism*),[5] noting that all empiricism "lays the explanatory stress" upon parts rather than wholes, treats relations among parts as external to those parts,[6] and views "the whole as a collection and the universal as an abstraction," James put it in this much-quoted way:

> I give the name of "radical empiricism" to my *Weltanschauung*. . . . It is essentially a mosaic philosophy, a philosophy of plural facts, like that of Hume and his descendants, who refer these facts neither to Substances in which they inhere nor to an Absolute Mind that creates them as its objects. But it differs from the Humean type of empiricism in one particular which makes me add the epithet radical. To be radical, an empiricism must neither admit into its constructions any element that is not directly experienced, nor exclude from them any element that is directly experienced. *For such a philosophy, the relations that connect experiences must themselves be experienced relations, and any kind of relation experienced must be accounted as "real" as anything else in the system.* (ERE, 22)

Ordinary, non-radical empiricism, James continued, has been atomistic and focused on disjunctions, thus doing away with conjunctive relations. As a result, he added, non-empirical philosophies have tried to account for these connections "by the addition of transexperiential agents of unification, substances, intellectual categories and powers, or Selves." James thus observed:

> *Radical empiricism*, as I understand it, *does full justice* to conjunctive relations, without however treating them as rationalism always tends to treat

---

[4] In "James's Holism: The Human Continuum," Alan Malachowski wrote about "finding James's rightful place in the history of philosophy": "And in doing so, we allude to a possible upgrading that makes him a key figure in the empiricist tradition," perhaps having "parity with, or even some priority over, other figures that eclipsed him in the past (that might include Russell and Ayer, for example)." The view I develop here places James almost entirely outside the tradition of Russell and Ayer. In *The Cambridge Companion to Pragmatism*, edited by Alan Malachowski (New York: Cambridge University Press, 2013), 48–49.

[5] *Essays in Radical Empiricism* was published in 1912, and was assembled by Ralph Barton Perry following comments James wrote in 1907 on the outside of a manila folder (but with additions and deletions because of James's earlier publication of some of the essays intended for the book—some of which date back almost thirty years earlier).

[6] This view stands in marked opposition to Hilary Putnam's onetime judgment that James's pragmatism "is at its least successful when it tries to find the 'external relations' which make reference and truth possible." Hilary Putnam, "James's Theory of Truth," in *The Cambridge Companion to William James*, edited by Ruth Anna Putnam (New York: Cambridge University Press, 1997), 183.

them, as being true in some supernal way, as if the unity of things and their variety belonged to different orders of truth and vitality altogether. (ERE, 23)

In this way, James's radical empiricism adds to the universe of traditional empiricism—and locates those additions all within experience itself. James made this addition evident in this account of experience: "A conscious field *plus* its object as felt or thought of *plus* an attitude towards the object *plus* the sense of self to whom the attitude belongs . . . It is a *full* fact" (VRE, 447).

There are three central points here. First, for James radical empiricism is a *process philosophy of relations*. Things are not metaphysical substances or blocks. The names of things—for example, the too-expensive green philosophy book, the very scary and surprising horror film, and the negatively charged atomic particle—are simply the names of groups of relations. Accordingly, it is not simply that things *have* relations—for example, the white papers are *on* the podium—but, rather, that things *are* relations. For example, radical empiricism holds that the sheet of paper is not white *in itself*, but, rather, white under—*in relation to*—certain lighting conditions for beings with certain kinds of vision and systems of meanings. James's world of pure experience is a world of relations, a world of experienced relations conjoining and disjoining. Robert D. Richardson captured this well: "It is the relations that matter, not the objects. Indeed, objects are bundles of relations."[7] And, as James explained in "The Moral Philosopher and the Moral Life," his radically empirical ethics, some of these experienced relations are moral ones. Values are relations. They are existential relations between the demands of sentient beings and the objects of those demands. There are no more values-in-themselves than there are things-in-themselves.[8] And this holds too for our very selves—for you and for me. John Dewey claimed that

---

[7] Robert D. Richardson, *William James in the Maelstrom of American Modernism* (New York: Houghton Mifflin, 2006), 449.

[8] Ellen Kappy Suckiel identified the centrally relational character of James's philosophy by noting that for James "it makes no pragmatic sense to speak of 'absolute realities,' or realities independent of the subject's constructive act. If what is real is to be understood at all, it must be understood as what is real-for-the-individual." *The Pragmatic Philosophy of William James* (Notre Dame, IN: University of Notre Dame Press, 1982), 129. As a result, I think John E. Smith was mistaken to judge that radical empiricism "is inadequate because the stream of experience does not contain all of the concepts and relations by which it is to be understood" and thus leads to "a world of pure nonsense, at least to one of unreason." Indeed, it is precisely James's move from the "stream of consciousness" of *The Principles of Psychology* to the notion of "pure experience" in his radical empiricism that overcomes this supposed problem. See John E. Smith, *Themes in American Philosophy: Purpose, Experience and Community* (New York: Harper and Row, 1970), 40–41. Smith reprised this same concern in "The Reconception

the self does not *have* a history; rather it *is* a history. And as John J. McDermott aptly put it in his "Possibility or Else!": "We have no fixed self. We are selving, richly or by impoverishment."[9] Elizabeth Flower and Murray G. Murphey also put it succinctly: "Radical empiricism extends the model of the stream of consciousness to metaphysics."[10]

It is this idea of radical empiricism that John Dewey later cited in the first chapter of his *Experience and Nature*:

> We begin by noting that "experience" is what James called a double-barreled word. Like its congeners, life and history, it includes *what* men do and suffer, *what* they strive for, love, believe and endure, and also *how* men act and are acted upon, the ways in which they do and suffer, desire and enjoy, see, believe, imagine—in short processes of *experiencing*. "Experience" denotes the planted field, the sowed seeds, the reaped harvests, the changes of night and day, spring and autumn, wet and dry, heat and cold, that are observed, feared, longed for; it also denotes the one who plants and reaps, who works and rejoices, hopes, fears, plans, invokes magic or chemistry to aid him, who is downcast or triumphant. It is "double-barreled" in that it recognizes in its primary integrity no division between act and material, subject and object, but contains them both in an unanalyzed totality.[11]

Second, this radically empirical world is a world *only of relations in process and in time*. As Bertrand Helm put it, "For James, reality is essentially temporal."[12] As James explained in *The Principles of Psychology*, it is a dynamic world,[13] a world *in flux*, an irreducible flux. James affirmed this view in *Some Problems of Philosophy*, calling it his "insuperability of sensation" thesis (SPP, 45). Reality is always in transition. It *is* transitioning. It is not backed by

of Experience in Peirce, James and Dewey" in *America's Philosophical Vision* (Chicago: University of Chicago Press, 1992), 28.

[9] John J. McDermott, *The Drama of Possibility: Experience as Philosophy of Culture* (New York: Fordham University Press, 2007), 136.
[10] Elizabeth Flower and Murray G. Murphey. *A History of Philosophy in America* (New York: Capricorn Books, 1977), 2:662.
[11] John Dewey, *Experience and Nature*, in *John Dewey: The Later Works, 1925–1953* (Carbondale: Southern Illinois University Press, 1988 [1925]), 1:18.
[12] Bertrand Helm, *Time and Reality in American Philosophy* (Amherst: University of Massachusetts Press, 1985), 42.
[13] The centrality of dynamism is detailed by James Pawelski in his *The Dynamic Individualism of William James* (Albany: State University of New York Press, 2007).

any permanence—some Substance, Form, God, Spirit, Absolute, or super-experiential being. James explicitly addressed this[14] by returning to his characterization of his radical empiricism as a "mosaic philosophy." He wrote:

> In actual mosaics the pieces are held together by their bedding, for which bedding the Substances, transcendental Egos, or Absolutes of other philosophies may be taken to stand. In radical empiricism there is no bedding; it is as if the pieces clung together by their edges, the transitions experienced between them forming their cement. Of course, such a metaphor is misleading, for in actual experience, the more substantive and the more transitive parts run into each other continuously, there is in general no separateness needing to be overcome by an external cement; and whatever separateness is actually experienced is not overcome, it stays and counts as separateness to the end. But the metaphor serves to symbolize the fact that Experience itself, taken at large, can grow by its edges. That one moment of it proliferates into the next by transitions which, whether conjunctive or disjunctive, continue the experiential tissue. . . . Life is in the transitions. (ERE, 42)

James's radical empiricism is a rejection of all trans-experientialism. He insisted that any notion of transcendence can and must be *experienced* transcendence. Transcendence, for radical empiricists, thus becomes transition, experienced transition, dynamic transition.[15] "Life is in the transitions": This means that life *is* transitioning, that it *is* transitionings—not, of course, that life is some substance that is changing into another substance. As Giles Gunn has pointed out, James here has developed Emerson's observation:

> Everything teaches transition, transference, metamorphosis; therein is human destiny, not in longevity but in removal. We dive & reappear in new places.[16]

---

[14] Stephen C. Rowe noted that James's work is relational not just in its content but in its style or the genre of his writing: "He always speaks to people, with people, from inside a conversation . . . he never strays from the nexus of vital relationship." *The Vision of James* (Rockport, MA: Element, 1996), 34.

[15] Colin Koopman called this notion of transition a "recurring theme" throughout James's work. *Pragmatism as Transition: Historicity and Hope in James, Dewey, and Rorty* (New York: Columbia University Press, 2009), 53.

[16] Emerson, *Journals*, June 1847, quoted in Giles Gunn, "The Pragmatic Turn: Religion and the Enlightenment in Nineteenth- and Twentieth-Century American Letters," in *Thinking Across the American Grain: Ideology, Intellect, and the New Pragmatism* (Chicago: University of Chicago Press, 1992), 141.

One of the many, many ways in which James took this to heart is evidenced by the fact that he never claimed that his own philosophy was the final word, that his own thought was "the end of philosophy," that his irreducibly temporalist worldview was itself timeless. Louis Menand was right, in my view, to note in *The Metaphysical Club* that for James and other pragmatists "the eventual obsolescence of their work would hardly have shocked them."[17]

Third, this radically empirical world is a world of *plural, multiple kinds of relations in process and in time.* This means that reality is constituted by disconnections as much as connections, external relations as much as internal ones, disjunctions as much as conjunctions, divorce as much as marriage, unravelings as well as knittings together, and departures as well as arrivals. We can say offhandedly that reality is a world of relations, but experience is always a matter of specific concrete relations—some rather than others. The point here is concrete rather than abstract. John McDermott made this viscerally clear in his descriptive account of the dangers of the making and unmaking of relations, dangers he called "relation starvation," "relation amputation," "relation saturation," "relation seduction," and "relation repression." He concluded that the world is "active, energizing, and potentially creative" but also "enervating, treacherous, and self-deceiving": "For those of us who wish to become persons, the world does not come ready-made." It is a question of "the set of relations which we ourselves fashion, knead, and impose."[18] And this, in part, is a question of the individual and societal habits we establish.

To his novelist brother, Henry, William James wrote that he considered his radical empiricism to be a metaphysics that was waiting on a new physics. Assessing James's importance as the equal of Plato's, Aristotle's, and Leibniz's, Alfred North Whitehead judged that James achieved this goal, observing that James developed relativity theory in philosophy before its articulation in physics—a judgment later shared by physicist Niels Bohr.[19]

[17] Louis Menand, *The Metaphysical Club: A Story of Ideas in America* (New York: Farrar, Straus and Giroux, 2001), 439.

[18] John J. McDermott, "Experience Grows by Its Edges: A Phenomenology of Relations in an American Philosophical Vein," in *The Drama of Possibility: Experience as Philosophy of Culture* (New York: Fordham University Press, 2007), 384–388, 389. See also McDermott's account of the negative results of particular sorts of relations or the absence of other kinds of relations in his "The Promethean Self and Community in the Philosophy of William James," in *Streams of Experience: Reflections on the History and Philosophy of American Culture* (Amherst: University of Massachusetts Press, 1986), 52.

[19] See Michael Epperson, *Quantum Mechanics and the Philosophy of Alfred North Whitehead* (New York: Fordham University Press, 2012), 36–37. See also my "It's All Relative: Beyond Absolutism and Nihilism," *Pragmatic Fashions: Pluralism, Democracy, Relativism, and the Absurd* (Bloomington: Indiana University Press, 2016), 98–115.

2. Radical Empiricism and Transcendental Empiricism: The "Insuperability of Sensation" and the Movement from Language to Sense

Throughout his writings, James was mainly and repeatedly concerned to articulate and defend his radical empiricism against monistic and absolutist rationalism, against idealists such as Hegel and Royce whose influence loomed large at that time. James argued that their attempts to mount theoretical, abstract, logical proofs against radical empiricism, pragmatism, and pluralism all failed and that, accordingly, his views were plausible, reasonable hypotheses that had to be tested in and by experience and could not be ruled out by abstract conceptual rearrangements. In addition, of course, he was intent on showing how his radical empiricism was superior to what he took to be the traditional, atomistic, non-relational, non-radical English- language empiricism of the seventeenth, eighteenth, and nineteenth centuries.

James was less engaged in drawing distinctions between his own views and those of other thinkers who *shared* at least many of his largest philosophical commitments. This gives rise to a question: What are the main similarities and differences and what are the main strengths and weaknesses between radical empiricism and other philosophies that share its pluralism and its commitments to different but still broadly empirical, parts-rather-than-wholes, scientific worldviews (and also share its rejection of monism, absolutism, and idealism)? More specifically: Are there reasons to prefer James's radical empiricism to the radically empirical worldviews of some other philosophers? And are there reasons to prefer James's radical empiricism to some version of philosophical naturalism and realism?

I address these two questions (in this section and the next) by means of two case studies. Engagement with the radical empiricism of Gilles Deleuze makes clear why James rejected transcendentalism and any non-experiential backing to the mosaic of experience. And contrast with the materialism of George Santayana sharpens James's commitment to empiricism rather than naturalism. Taken together, they highlight both what is "radical" and what is "empirical" in James's radical empiricism, thus providing illuminating perspective on James's philosophical vision and its practical import and value.

James's understanding of his radical empiricism as a new metaphysics waiting on, or in harmony with, a new physics finds resonance in the twentieth-century French thinker Gilles Deleuze's description of himself as an empiricist and "pure metaphysician of modern science." "I have always felt that I am an empiricist" in terms of Whitehead's two defining characteristics of empiricism," Deleuze asserted: "the abstract does not explain, but must itself be explained; and the aim is not to rediscover the eternal or the universal but to find the conditions under which something new is produced (creativeness)."[20] For empiricism, Deleuze wrote, "nothing is ever transcendental."[21] This is a potentially confusing claim given the fact that Deleuze also called his view "transcendental empiricism" as well as "radical empiricism." However, this label is not so odd or perplexing when, with Deleuze, it is understood as concerned with *conditions of actual experience* rather than *supposedly necessary conditions of possible experience*. For Deleuze, like James, the mosaic is immanent and has no backing. Deleuze, interpreting Hume in a manner very different than James, thus observed:

In Hume there is something very strange which completely displaces empiricism, giving it a new power, a theory and practice of relations, of the AND, which was to be pursued by Russell and Whitehead, but which remains underground or marginal in relation to the great classifications, even when they inspire a new conception of logic. (D, 15)

Deleuze's point here is pragmatic—and recalls his claim that "philosophy must constitute itself as the theory of what we are doing, not as a theory of what there is" (ES, 133). Opposed to an image of thought that Deleuze claimed "effectively stops people from thinking" (D, 13), radical empiricism is not a paint-by-numbers philosophy (stay within the lines), not a philosophy of thought as re-presentative, but a philosophy of concept construction, of creativity, of genuine novelty, of process and becoming.

This view of radical empiricism is central in Deleuze's account of Hume's focus on the subject as transcending the given:

We can now see the special ground of empiricism: nothing in the mind transcends human nature, because it is human nature that, in its principles, transcends the mind; nothing is ever transcendental. (ES, 24)

[20] Gilles Deleuze and Claire Parnet, *Dialogues*, trans. Hugh Tomlinson (New York: Columbia University Press, 1987 [1977]),vii. Further references to this book are included in the text and abbreviated D, followed by the page number(s).
[21] Gilles Deleuze, *Empiricism and Subjectivity*, Empiricism and Subjectivity: An Essay on Hume's Theory of Human Nature, trans. Constantin V. Boundas (New York: Columbia University Press, 1981 [1953]), 24. Further references to this book are included in the text and abbreviated ES, followed by the page number(s).

For Deleuze, the idea of subjectivity is only the idea of the production of tendencies, of habits, the affective creation (which James famously called "the sentiment of rationality") of the idea of subjectivity, the determination of practice (ES, 30, 33). Here, Deleuze explained transcendence as invention and integration (ES, 35–36, 86). He observed: "In this formulation of the problem, we discover the absolute essence of empiricism" (ES, 86–87).

For Deleuze, three focal points stand out. First, the subject develops immanently—by and in the construction of the given. This invites a question that Deleuze immediately addressed: "What is the given?" Deleuze named empiricism's anti-representational, anti-phenomenological, and anti-dialectical response to this question "the principle of difference"—that the given is a sensible flux in which everything separable is distinguishable and everything distinguishable is different (ES, 87). What does the mind do after becoming subject? asked Deleuze, and he answered that it "advises" some ideas rather than others. "To transcend means exactly this," he added (ES, 127). The subject is both the product of principles or functions of the mind and also, as such, the mind's transcendence of itself—that is, the mind's advising itself (ES, 132).

Second, for Deleuze as for James, relations are external to their terms—and so all transcendence is immanent. All transcendence is inside life. Transcendence is a variety or form of immanence; transcendence is lived or experienced.

Third, as a consequence, subjectivity is practical rather than theoretical. There "is only a practical subject":

> Its definitive unity—that is, the unity of relations and circumstances—will be revealed in the relations between motive and action, means and end. . . . The fact that there is no theoretical subjectivity, and that there cannot be one, becomes the fundamental claim of empiricism. . . . [T]here is only a practical subject. (ES, 104)

This description of the self resonates strongly with the account of James's view that both John Wild and Bruce Wilshire provided in their landmark studies of James and phenomenology. For example, Wilshire wrote:

> For him [James] there is no substantial self that the person can carry around with him like a diamond sewn into his pocket. The self is whatever is cared about, judged to be one's own—and the body here takes preeminence. The

maintenance of self-identity is a continuous achievement, one marked by peril. . . . This is so because he denies that thoughts are contents of one's subjectivity, which refer immediately only to one's self. Thoughts are "out there" with the things cognized, and the self is something "out there" along with all the rest of things.[22]

And so Deleuze's radical empiricism is a philosophy of the imagination (ES, 120), a philosophy in which the passions are primary because they are the instruments of action.

Indeed, Deleuze's Hume comes across as downright Jamesian. Deleuze wrote:

[Hume] created the first great logic of relations, showing in it that all rela-tions . . . are external to their terms. As a result, he constituted a multifar-ious world of experience. . . . We start with atomic parts, but these atomic parts have transitions, passages, "tendencies," which circulate from one to another. These tendencies give rise to habits. Isn't this the answer to the question "what are we?" We are habits, nothing but habits—the habit of saying "I." Perhaps there is no more striking answer to the problem of the Self. (ES, x)

Now, in his essay "Pure Immanence," Deleuze proclaimed, "We will speak of a transcendental empiricism in contrast to everything that makes up the world of subject and object" (PI, 25), and he noted in his book on Bergson—an account of difference without negation—that "the concrete will never be attained by combining the inadequacy of one concept with the inadequacy of its opposite."[23] Here the parallels between Deleuze's use of Bergson and the ways in which William James earlier deployed Bergson are striking once

[22] Bruce Wilshire, *William James and Phenomenology: A Study of The Principles of Psychology* (Bloomington: Indiana University Press, 1968), 139. A year later, in *The Radical Empiricism of William James*, Wild offered this judgment: "I hope that my work may more solidly confirm a histor-ical fact that others have suspected, namely that around the turn of the century, a native American philosopher began to think in an existential manner, and made important contributions to the phe-nomenological movement, in that broader sense which we are beginning to recognize is required to understand it as a whole." *The Radical Empiricism of William James* (Garden City, NY: Doubleday, 1969), ix. See also Wilshire's "The Breathtaking Intimacy of the Material World: William James's Last Thoughts," in *The Cambridge Companion to William James*, edited by Ruth Anna Putnam (New York: Cambridge University Press, 1997), 103–124.

[23] Gilles Deleuze, Pure Immanence: Essays On a Life, trans. Anne Boyman (New York: Zone Books, 2005 [2001]), 25. Gilles Deleuze, Bergsonism, trans. Hugh Tomlinson and Barbara Habberjam (New York: Zone Books, 1988 [1966]), 44.

again. James had identified the heart of Bergson's philosophy as the seeking of a "living understanding of the movement of reality" and not an idle playing with the negations and contradictions among concepts abstracted from it. Bergson's target, James held, was intellectualism that substitutes a logic of concepts for sense:

> The times directly *felt* in the experience of living subjects have originally no common measure. . . . All *felt* times coexist and overlap or compenetrate each other thus vaguely; but the artifice of plotting them on a common scale helps us to reduce their aboriginal confusion. . . . But do we not also escape from sense-reality altogether? . . . Intellectualism here does what I said it does—it makes experience less instead of more intelligible. . . . Bergson denies that mere conceptual logic can tell us what is impossible or possible in the world of fact. . . . What really exists is not things made but things in the making. Once made, they are dead, and an infinite number of alternative conceptual decompositions can be used in defining them. (APU, 101–124)

If a philosophy were to aim at lived realities in the making, if it were to aim at duration rather than some pet conceptual decomposition, how would or could it proceed? For Deleuze, if we attempt to aim our language at duration (or, with Lewis Carroll, hunt a snark), then we find that it has vanished and we find ourselves through the looking glass. We find "sense as a fourth dimension of the proposition." We find ourselves with a condition of truth that would be defined not as signification or conceptual possibility "but rather as sense" (LS, 19). In his "Preface: From Lewis Carroll to the Stoics" in *The Logic of Sense*, Deleuze wrote:

> We present here a series of paradoxes which form the theory of sense. It is easy to explain why this theory is inseparable from paradoxes: sense is a nonexisting entity, and, in fact, maintains very special relations with nonsense.[24]

What is this theory (or logic) of sense? Is it compatible with James's "insuperability of sensation" thesis? What is this "nonexisting" entity Deleuze

---

[24] Gilles Deleuze, *The Logic of Sense*, ed. Constantin V. Boundas (New York: Columbia University Press, 1990 [1969]), xiii. Abbreviated hereafter in the text as LS followed by page number.

called "sense"? Is it really "pure" and, if so, is this idea of "pure events" much like the notion that James invoked with his "pure experience," his "world of pure experience"? And is this nonexistent entity, we might also crucially ask in a Jamesian spirit, experienced rather than a mosaic's supposed or experience-transcendent backing?

For Deleuze, sense is "pure events," "a becoming whose characteristic is to elude the present" and reflection on it. Paradoxically (LS, 1), it "receives the action of the Idea" "and eludes this action"; it "subsists and occurs on the other side of the order that Ideas impose and things receive" (LS, 2). Sense is verbs (LS, 5), not nouns, not things, not substances. Pure events inhere or subsist (LS, 5) in language, in the dramatization by means of signs that "transcends" its own limits, the limits or surface effects of language (LS, 3).

Pure events are "expressed" in relations between propositions; they are expressed in language (LS, 8). Deleuze wrote that it is the task of language both to set limits *and to go beyond these limits*—something that James held language cannot do (except in an idealist sense of language and thought *acknowledging* their own inability to say or think flux). Deleuze wrote:

> Therefore language includes terms which do not cease to displace their extension and which make possible a reversal of the connection in a given series (thus too much and not enough, few and many). The event is coextensive with becoming, and becoming is itself coextensive with language. (LS, 8)

(Recalling Deleuze's *Difference and Repetition*, perhaps we might say that language is a necessary illusion of pure events, that being is a necessary illusion of becoming.) There is nothing *beneath* language, no mosaic backing; there is no *depth or height*; there is only event and language at the *surface*. And so, like the snark, sense must be hunted both with "thimble" and "fork" and also with "hope" and "care" (LS, 26). Thus: "Sense is that which is expressed" (LS, 20) by the proposition.

This is a highly important point because it allows Deleuze to identify sense not simply as an external condition of the proposition but as a relation *within* it, not just as an external, transcending condition of it but as a characteristic internal to it. Sense is always presupposed as soon as one begins to speak (LS, 28).

In the important "Third Series of the Proposition," Deleuze identified three—and then a total of four—"relations within a proposition" (LS, 12–16). They are:

1. *Denotation (or indication)*, the relation of a proposition to a state of affairs external to it—e.g., the relation between the proposition "that is a cup of tea" and the state of affairs of something being a cup of tea is a relation of denotation or indication.
2. *Manifestation*, the relation of a proposition to the person who employs the proposition—e.g., the relation between the proposition "that is a cup of tea" and the "I" who puts forth the proposition (and in so doing is manifest as an "I" who denotes and thus is presupposed by every denotation).
3. *Signification*, the relation of words in a specific proposition to general concepts and their implications (that in principle are not limited or restricted to any specific proposition)—e.g., the relation between the word "cup" in the proposition "that is a cup of tea" and the general or universal concept "cup" is a relation of signification.[25]

So, is there a fourth relation or dimension within the proposition, within conceptualization and language? Deleuze wrote that this is "an economic or strategic question" (LS, 17). What does this mean? Deleuze did not think that we experience or know a posteriori (LS, 17) a fourth dimension or relation within propositions. If this is the case, then why did he invoke some sort of a priori dimension or relation within propositions—a dimension "we can only infer indirectly on the basis of the circle where the ordinary dimensions of the proposition lead us," a dimension that "transcends the experiential dimensions of the visible without falling into Ideas" (LS, 20)? If there is such a dimension—at this point I stress "if" and assume it is clear that this

---

[25] Deleuze went on (LS, 15–16) to consider whether signification is primary or logically prior or presupposed by manifestation (which he has explained is presupposed by denotation). He claims that from the "domain of speech" manifestation is primary—the act of signifying presupposes an agent, an "I" who is doing the signifying. From the "domain of language," a domain defined as one in which significations are "developed for themselves," however, Deleuze claims that signification is primary—any would-be agent could engage in the act of signification if and only if there were signs to be used. In his earlier book *Proust and Signs* (1964), Deleuze had demonstrated some awareness of the tripartite semiotic theory of Charles Peirce, who argued at length that speech is one form of language and that all language (thus speech included) involves irreducibly and equally relations among sign users, signs (subdivided into icons, indexes, and symbols), and things signified. This, in turn, led Peirce to a tripartite phenomenology that—as Deleuze would approve—is not subjective.

language of "transcending experience" would raise hesitancy and suspicion among Jamesian radical empiricists, if not rejection—Deleuze argued that this fourth relation is not reducible to, or contained in, any of the other three relations. He argued the point this way: The "localization [of sense] seems impossible within denotation" (LS, 17); it is impossible within manifestation (which depends on signification) (LS, 18); and the localization of sense is impossible within signification, which "presupposes an irreducible denotation" (LS, 18). But this does not address the central question here: Why think there is—or must be—such a fourth dimension or relation, a seemingly experience-transcending dimension, at all? Why move from radical empiricism to transcendental empiricism?

If Deleuze cannot satisfactorily respond to this question, then there is no "sense," no theory or "logic of sense," and thus no *transcendental* empiricism. *The Logic of Sense* would be a work of fiction—perhaps a "psychological novel" but not very much a "logical" one (LS, xiv). To address just this issue, Deleuze presented a short, difficult, very compressed case for a fourth dimension of the proposition. This passage deserves close attention and interrogation. Here are its steps, and following each is a Jamesian response.

1. Deleuze claimed: "Signification can never exercise its role of last foundation since it presupposes an irreducible denotation." He called this a "circularity between ground and grounded" and referred to it as the failure of signification or signification alone (LS, 18).

A radically empirical follow-up question in response: Why think that it is the role of signification to be a *foundation* of relations within propositions? Why—on the basis of what presuppositions—think there must be any *ground* at all? Why even desire such a *ground*?

2. Deleuze continued: "When we define signification as the condition of truth, we give it a characteristic which it shares with sense, and which is already a characteristic of sense. But how does signification assume this characteristic?" (LS, 18).

A radically empirical follow-up question in response: Why identify signification as *the one condition* of truth? Why think that any one of the three relations within propositions is *the sole condition of truth*? More important still, does it not beg the question to assume that sense is the condition of truth? So far Deleuze has provided no argument for the existence of sense. To assume that something has a particular characteristic is not to prove that it exists or is real.

3. Deleuze next added: "In discussing the conditions of truth, we raise ourselves above the true and false, since a false proposition also has a sense or signification" (LS, 18).

A radically empirical follow-up question in response: Why still think that signification is *the* condition of truth rather than a condition of truth, just one of the conditions of truth? Why think there is a height above the true and false to which one rises when one considers conditions of truth, rather than thinking that to consider the conditions of truth is to be very much within, or at the surface of, truth and falsity? Why think that supposed meta-truths or transcendent truths are not just other truths, more truths, different truths? Moreover, the fact that a false proposition is not thereby meaning-less (without signification) does not establish that the condition of its truth is other than signification in general, but only that it is other than some partic-ular significations.

4. Deleuze continued: "We define this superior condition solely as the possibility for the proposition to be true. This possibility is nothing other than the form of possibility of the proposition itself. . . . [I]t involves rising from the conditioned to the condition, in order to think of the condition as the simple possibility of the conditioned. Here one rises to a foundation, but that which is founded remains what it was, independently of the operation which founded it and unaffected by it" (LS, 18).

A radically empirical follow-up question in response: First, isn't there a kind of bait-and-switch at work here? Deleuze began by asserting that "many authors agree in recognizing three distinct relations *within* the proposi-tion" (LS, 12; emphasis added). His argument for the reality of sense just a few pages later seems at first (see below) to be that sense is the condition or form of possibility for the proposition—a condition *of* the proposition, not a condition or relation *within* it. Why not think that the conditions of any given proposition are themselves propositional? That is, if we do ask about the *condition* of the proposition—the condition of the conditioned proposition—why not simply take other propositions to be, collectively, the condition of a given proposition? Why not locate the form of possibility of a proposition *within* other, just still more, propositions? Why think that denotation, manifestation, and signification are "external to the order which conditions" (LS, 19) any particular denotation, manifestation, or signification? Why jump to embrace an extra-propositional, extra-experiential, transcendental entity or mosaic backing—sense?

5. Deleuze explained: "One is perpetually referred from the conditioned to the condition, and also from the condition to the conditioned. For the condition of truth to avoid this defect, it ought to have an element of its own, distinct from the form of the conditioned. It ought to have something unconditioned capable of assuring a real genesis of denotation and of the other dimensions of the proposition. Thus the condition of truth would be defined no longer as the form of conceptual possibility... but rather as sense." (LS, 19)

A radically empirical follow-up question in response: Why see the relation between some particular conditioned truth and some particular condition as one of *transcendental ontological difference* in kind between the actual and the virtual rather than one of *actual experienced difference* in time (within the actual)—such that what is the condition in one context is the conditioned in another in complex, changing, overlapping ways and transitions? Well, Deleuze here noted that his own view is "inspired in its entirety by empiricism" (LS, 20), but to many empiricists it is only a weak or frail (and perhaps humorous) empiricism that identifies the conditions of actual experience in something transcendental or other than additional actual experience.

Setting aside momentarily an assessment of this case for the existence of sense, Deleuze noted—surely correctly—that "if there is" sense, then it is "irreducible to individual states of affairs, particular images, personal beliefs, and universal or general concepts": "Better yet, perhaps sense would be 'neutral'" (LS, 19). This label, of course, is reminiscent of another label by which James identified his own philosophy: "neutral monism." Deleuze's sense is the "expressed" of the proposition—not what is stated in or by the proposition: "Sense is that which is expressed" (LS, 20) by the proposition. This is a highly important, even crucial point because it allowed Deleuze to identify sense *not simply as an external condition* of the proposition but as *a relation within it*, to identify sense not just as an external condition of propositions and conceptualizations and theories and languages but as a characteristic within or internal to them. Deleuze put it this way near the start of "The Fifth Series of Sense":

> Sense is like the sphere in which I am already established in order to enact possible denotations, and even to think their conditions. Sense is always presupposed as soon as I begin to speak. (LS, 28)

Similarly, in a key passage reminiscent of James's claim that accounts of the world must not be overrun by language, Deleuze claimed that sense "does not exist outside the proposition which expresses it"; he claimed that "what is expressed does not exist outside its expression":

> That is why we cannot say that sense exists, but rather that it inheres or subsists. On the other hand, it does not merge at all with the proposition, for it has an objective (*objectité*) which is quite distinct. What is expressed has no resemblance whatsoever to the expression. Sense is indeed attributed, but it is not at all the attribute of the proposition—it is rather the attribute of the thing or state of affairs. (LS, 21)

Sense, Deleuze concluded, "is the boundary between propositions and things" (LS, 22). Thus a pure event or becoming does not *have* sense; the event *is* sense.

Deleuze described this boundary between propositions and things as "the cutting edge, or articulation of the difference" between propositions and things (LS, 28). It is for this reason that persons can never state the sense of what they are saying—the sense that inheres in what they are saying. In turn, it is why the effort to do so necessarily constitutes an infinite regression (LS, 28–31) and impenetrable (or "dry") reiteration (LS, 31–32),[26] unaffected by objects of propositions (whether possible or impossible things) (LS, 35).

This is the cutting edge or difference between propositions and things—an edge for Deleuze between two things that James views *both* as fully run together and mixed-up *in experience* and as always and "ever-not-quite" *different* because concepts presuppose sensations and percepts but can never capture, say, or think them except by making them abstractions. For James,

---

[26] In the poem Deleuze cites, Carroll writes, "Where life becomes a Spasm, / And History a Whiz: / If that is not Sensation, / I don't know what is."

however, there is nothing transcendental here: Sense is the condition of propositions and concepts, of language and thought, but it is a wholly experienced condition—all mosaic and no backing. Of course, if we understand the "transcendental" in terms of conditions of actual experience that themselves are experienced (rather than necessary), then there is no pragmatic difference between what Deleuze called "transcendental empiricism" and what James (often joined by Deleuze) named "radical empiricism."

For Deleuze, this difference between signification and sense (presupposed by signification) points to another difference between sense and nonsense (presupposed by sense, an effect of non-sense). Deleuze claimed that sense is an effect, like an optical or aural or surface or position or language effect (LS, 70). Nonsense's perpetual displacement through structure produces (or "donates" or effects) sense—in fact, for Deleuze, sometimes too much sense (LS, 71)—just as in *What Is Philosophy*? Deleuze and Guattari observed that there is too much rather than too little communication today.

Deleuze identified the production of sense and, for this work, new machines of sense production as "today's task."[27] For Deleuze, this gives rise to an anti-fascist ethic: to be worthy of living in a new world. And for philosophers specifically: to be creators, producers, machines of, concepts of, for, and in such a new world. And this is how we might view James—as a creator of a world of flux and possibility, a world of real losses and real gains, a world congruous to human powers, a pluralistic universe that we might work to make more inclusive.

3. Radical Empiricism and Naturalism: Experience and the Pragmatic Meaning of "Nature"

The brilliant Spanish American philosopher George Santayana is definitely not part of the current philosophical canon, not a member of its A-list. Given the quality of his thought, not to mention the beauty of his writing, that is unfortunate all the way around. It is also ironic in light of Santayana's one familiar aphorism, from his 1905 *The Life of Reason*: "Those who cannot remember the past are condemned to repeat it."

---

[27] I have expanded on this point and its political consequences in "From the Art of Surfaces to Control Societies and Beyond: Stoicism, Postmodernism, and Pan-Machinism," in *Pragmatism, Postmodernism, and the Future of Philosophy* (New York: Routledge, 2003), 93–114.

One of Santayana's few extended discussions of James's thought—he was a sharp critic of his Harvard colleague's philosophical commitments, just as he later was a sharp and sharp-tongued critic of John Dewey's *Experience and Nature*—appears in his "The Genteel Tradition in American Philosophy." This essay was originally delivered as an address in California in 1911 shortly after James's death and published two years later in *Winds of Doctrine: Studies in Contemporary Opinion*. In this essay Santayana called "America a young country with an old mentality" and claimed that the broadly Calvinist philosophy it inherited from Europe no longer inspires or expresses the life of its people. In contrast, Santayana viewed James's philosophy, like the writings of Emerson and Whitman, as actually rooted in the individualistic and revolutionary character of American life. He called James's radical empiricism and "radical romanticism" "a new philosophical vista" and "a conception never before presented." He did not, however, judge James's worldview to be true— "who shall know that?"—but only that it was new and that it spoke to a new time and place:

> The force of William James's new theology, or romantic cosmology, lies only in this: that it has broken the spell of the genteel tradition and enticed faith in a new direction, which on second thought, may prove no less alluring than the old. . . . Henceforth there can hardly be the same peace in and the same pleasure in hugging the old proprieties. Hegel will be to the next generation what Sir William Hamilton was to the last. Nothing will have been disproved, but everything will have been abandoned. An honest man has spoken, and the cant of the genteel tradition has become hard for young lips to repeat.[28]

The outlines of Santayana's own materialism or naturalism are evident, at least a little, in his instruction to his audience near the close of his address:

> When you transform nature to your uses, when you experiment with her forces, and reduce them to industrial agents, you cannot feel that nature was made by you or for you, for then these adjustments would have been pre-established. Much less can you feel it when she destroys your labour of

---

[28] George Santayana, "The Genteel Tradition in American Philosophy," in *Winds of Doctrine* (Gloucester, MA: Peter Smith, 1971 [1913]), 211–212.

years in a momentary spasm. You must feel, rather, that you are an offshoot of her life; one brave little force among her immense forces.[29]

For Santayana, a philosophy must above all else avoid egoism, anthropocentrism, and "the conceited notion that man, or human reason, or the human distinction between good and evil, is the centre and pivot of the universe."[30] James, in contrast, had observed that human experience is the center and pivot—not of nature but, rather, of truth:

> The trail of the human serpent is thus over everything. Truth independent; truth that we *find* merely; truth no longer malleable to human need; truth incorrigible, in a word; such truth exists indeed superabundantly—or is supposed to exist by rationalistically minded thinkers; but then it means only the dead heart of the living tree, and its being there means only that truth also has its paleontology and its "prescription," and may grow stiff with years of veteran service and petrified in men's regard by sheer antiquity. But how plastic even the oldest truths nevertheless really are has been vividly shown in our day by the transformation of logical and mathematical ideas, a transformation which seems even to be invading physics. The ancient formulas are reinterpreted as special expressions of much wider principles, principles that our ancestors never got a glimpse of in their present shape and formulation. (P, 37)

"All rationalism"—again, Santayana was not a rationalist but he also definitely did not hold a "plastic" naturalism—has risen against this, James asserted. He continued:

> I should not mention this, but for the fact that it throws so much sidelight upon that rationalistic temper to which I have opposed the temper of pragmatism. Pragmatism is uncomfortable away from facts. Rationalism is comfortable only in the presence of abstractions. This pragmatist talk about truths in the plural, about their utility and satisfactoriness, about the success with which they "work," etc., suggests to the typical intellectualist mind a sort of coarse lame second-rate makeshift article of truth. Such truths are not real truth. Such tests are merely subjective. As against this, objective

---

[29] Santayana, "The Genteel Tradition in American Philosophy," 213.
[30] Santayana, "The Genteel Tradition in American Philosophy," 214.

truth must be something non-utilitarian, haughty, refined, remote, august, exalted. It must be an absolute correspondence of our thoughts with an equally absolute reality. It must be what we *ought* to think, unconditionally. The conditioned ways in which we *do* think are so much irrelevance and matter for psychology. Down with psychology, up with logic, in all this question! (P, 37–38)

So, is nature or Being or existence independent of human experience? James's radical empiricism answers no while Santayana's materialism replies yes. This is a metaphysical dispute.[31] What is the practical difference between these two views? Can James's pragmatic method resolve it by tracing the respective practical differences of each view? James definitely thought so, but he also recognized how personal temperament colors what someone counts as a "resolution" of a problem. He observed:

It is astonishing to see how many philosophical disputes collapse into insignificance the moment you subject them to this simple test of tracing a concrete consequence. . . . We say that this theory solves it [the problem of marrying old opinion and new fact] on the whole more satisfactorily than that theory; but that means more satisfactorily to ourselves, and individuals will emphasize their points of satisfaction differently. To a certain degree, therefore, everything here is plastic. (P, 30)

Santayana surely did emphasize his points of satisfaction differently from James, and he did this in a way that throws light on a naturalistic temperament. At times Santayana's temperament appears very close to James's. For example, just as James argued for the "reinstatement of the vague and inarticulate,"[32] Santayana urged philosophers to use language loosely. He wrote:

---

[31] The important issues here are often muddied by the many meanings philosophers have given to the terms "nature" and "experience." It is the multiplicity of meanings of "naturalism" that made James ambivalent about it—sometimes affirming and advancing it, sometimes rejecting it. Vincent Colapietro presented a nuanced treatment of these issues in his "Introduction: Present at the End? Who Will Be There When the Last Stone Is Thrown?" in the volume of selected essays by Peter Hare, *Pragmatism with Purpose: Selected Writings*, edited by Joseph Palencik, Douglas R. Anderson, and Steven A. Miller (New York: Fordham University Press, 2015), 1–18. See also Matthew Bagger's "Introduction," in *Pragmatism and Naturalism: Scientific and Social Inquiry After Representationalism*, edited by Matthew Bagger (New York: Columbia University Press, 2018).

[32] James urged: "It is, the reader will see, the reinstatement of the vague and inarticulate to its proper place in our mental life which I am so anxious to press on the attention. Mr. Galton and Prof. Huxley have, as we shall see in the chapter on Imagination, made one step in advance in exploding the ridiculous theory of Hume and Berkeley that we can have no images but of perfectly definite things. Another is made if we overthrow the equally ridiculous notion that, whilst simple objective qualities

In practice the ambiguities of language are neutralized by looseness and good sense in the interpretation of it, but a philosopher leads himself into foolish difficulties and more foolish dogmas if he assumes that words have fixed meanings to which single facts in nature must correspond. He ought, therefore, to use language more freely than the public rather than more strictly, since he professes to have a clearer view of things.[33]

As another example, just as James argued that philosophies should be understood as hypotheses to be tested in and by practice, so too Santayana believed that issues about the nature of reality cannot be settled by theoretical arguments or other mere wordplay. It is in this context that Santayana declared his own worldview, his own philosophy, *not metaphysical* at all, not any kind of metaphysics. Santayana explained: "Metaphysics, in the proper sense of the word, is dialectical physics, or an attempt to determine matters of fact by means of logical or moral or rhetorical constructions."[34] Santayana, like James, took all such attempts to be failures. Describing James's pragmatism in this context, Charlene Haddock Seigfried has claimed that "pragmatism denies the legitimacy of metaphysics so far as its principles of reality are not derived from experience and not subject to its veto, but allows metaphysical claims understood as hypotheses subject to later verification—what works best in concrete and collective experience."[35]

As a third and final example, just as James viewed concepts in pragmatic terms and claimed that the whole function of conceiving is tied to one's purposes and interests, Santayana understood his own central, basic concepts—essence, matter, truth, and spirit, his four realms of being—as concepts or categories that he found useful or instrumental or practically valuable to employ in his thinking. He claimed that the realms of being that

---

are revealed to our knowledge in 'states of consciousness,' relations are not. But these reforms are not half sweeping and radical enough. What must be admitted is that the definite images of traditional psychology form but the very smallest part of our minds as they actually live" (PBC, 150).

[33] George Santayana, "Some Meanings of the Word 'Is,'" in *Obiter Scripta: Lectures, Essays and Reviews* (New York: Charles Scribner's Sons, 1936), 212. Further references to this work are included in the text and abbreviated SMWI followed by the page number(s). Compare John Dewey's similar claim: "I am not equipped with capacities which fit one for the office of a lexicographical autocrat." John Dewey, "'Half-Hearted Naturalism,'" in *John Dewey: The Later Works, 1925–1953* (Carbondale: Southern Illinois University Press, 1984 [1927]), 3:73.

[34] George Santayana, *Scepticism and Animal Faith: An Introduction to a System of Philosophy* (New York: Charles Scribner's Sons, 1923), vii.

[35] Charlene Haddock Seigfried, *William James's Radical Reconstruction of Philosophy* (Albany: State University of New York Press, 1990), 244–245; see also her discussion of radical empiricism as a metaphysics, 324–327.

he identified and named are not "parts of a cosmos, nor one great cosmos together," but only "kinds or categories of things which I find conspicuously different and worth distinguishing." He added:

> Logic, like language, is partly a free construction and partly a means of sym-
> bolizing and harnessing in expression the existing diversity of things; and
> whilst some languages, given a man's constitution and habits, may seem
> more beautiful and convenient to him than others, it is a foolish heat in a
> patriot to insist that only his native language is intelligible or right. . . . I do
> not ask any one to think in my terms if he prefers others.[36]

Now, there is an important link between this point that worldviews are *not systems* of the cosmos and the prior point that philosophers and other thinkers *cannot defend* claims about the facts of the cosmos, cannot deduce or determine facts about the cosmos simply by the logical, moral, rhetorical, or speculative manipulation of concepts. If worldviews are not systems demanding thought universally in their terms, then there is no need to mount a defense of any such demand. Recognition of this point and realization of its consequences would amount to nothing less than a revolution in philosophy, as Santayana's harsh judgment indicates:

> Professional philosophers are usually only apologists: that is, they are ab-
> sorbed in defending some vested illusion or some eloquent idea. Like
> lawyers or detectives, they study the case for which they are retained, to
> see how much evidence or semblance of evidence they can gather for the
> defence, and how much prejudice they can raise against the witnesses for
> the prosecution; for they know they are defending prisoners suspected by
> the world, and perhaps their own good sense, of falsification. What they
> defend is some system, that is, some view about the totality of things, of
> which men are actually ignorant. . . . What produces systems is the interest
> in maintaining against all comers that some favourite or inherited idea of
> ours is sufficient and right.[37]

---

[36] Santayana, *Scepticism and Animal Faith*, vi. The American novelist John Barth termed this "the tragic view of categories"—the view that categories, "though indispensable[,] are more or less arbitrary" and reflect the particular ways that particular people, understand, talk about, and register "what's going on around us." "The American New Novel," in *The Friday Book: Essays and Other Nonfiction* (New York: G. P. Putnam's Sons, 1984), 257.

[37] George Santayana, "The Genteel Tradition in American Thought," in *Winds of Doctrine* (New York: Charles Scribner's Sons, 1913 [1911]), 44–45.

Santayana added: "For good or ill, I am an ignorant man, almost a poet, and I can only spread a feast of what everybody knows."[38] Here I would add that "what everybody knows" frequently turns out to be *what someone thinks everybody knows* (or what someone thinks everybody should know or what someone wants everyone to know).[39] The ignorant man, I think, does not know "what everybody knows." I picture the ignorant man, "almost a poet," as a pluralist, not simply about categories and languages and habits but also about worlds and realities, a pluralist about worlds and realities even when the "favorite or inherited idea"—the "vested illusion" and "eloquent idea" that there is a single, same world or same nature or "same sky" independent of our experience of it—offers up a hefty retainer and asks for evidence, for defense, for prejudice, and for apology.

In this light, what would make an account of nature *metaphysical*? What is a specifically and distinctively *metaphysical* account of nature? Is radical empiricism metaphysical? Is naturalism? We could take Santayana's lead here and understand *metaphysical* accounts of nature as *unnatural* accounts of nature. We could, that is, understand a metaphysics of nature as a failed, always failed, dialectical attempt to derive an account of matters of fact from clever moral and speculative constructions and playful conceptual and rhetorical manipulations. This has considerable resonance, of course, with most of the meanings of "metaphysical" in the *Oxford English Dictionary*. For example, the *OED* defines the "metaphysical" as that which is "not empirically verifiable," as "immaterial, incorporeal, supersensible, supernatural," and as "based on a priori principles." Another definition of "metaphysical" is this: concerning "the branch of philosophy that deals with first principles of things, including such concepts as being, substance, essence, time, space, cause, and identity; theoretical philosophy as the ultimate science of being and knowing"—similar to the earlier definition especially if "ultimate science" is understood as something other than a science of matters of fact. And another definition of the "metaphysical" is that which is "fanciful, imaginary"—the metaphysician as tale spinner, storyteller, and narrative artist. This may be an attractive image of the metaphysician for anyone inclined to view, say, Hegel as failed novelist and Whitman and Baldwin as successful metaphysicians.

---

[38] Santayana, *Scepticism and Animal Faith*, ix.
[39] Here see Gilles Deleuze's rejection of the "dogmatic image of thought" and its commitment and reliance on "everybody knows" *Difference and Repetition*, translated by Paul Patton (New York: Columbia University Press, 1995 [1968]).

Of course, the word "metaphysical" has a great many and loose meanings, and one of these other meanings was employed consistently by William James. As explained in earlier chapters, throughout his lectures, essays, and books, across all his writings on religious experience, truth, and morality, James understood "metaphysical" questions to be questions about the *meaning* of terms. For a Jamesian pragmatist, *metaphysical* questions are questions about the practical *meaning* of ideas and terms. If we understand the metaphysical not as the realm of the fanciful or the immaterial, then we may understand the metaphysical question about nature to be the question about the meaning of "nature." Here, like James encountering a camping party in the woods, we find a "ferocious metaphysical dispute." The situation seems more complex and worse than the well-known one James described in his account of two groups arguing about a man walking around a squirrel that moves on a tree so that the man who walks from north to east to south to west and back north of the squirrel never walks from its front to side to back to other side. Ahhh: *Does the man go round the squirrel or not?* A metaphysical question indeed, if ever there was one.

In contrast, the dispute about the meaning of "nature" is at least three-sided, the sides having much in common but nonetheless being marked by supposedly basic—as well as seemingly unresolvable—differences: realistic and non-reductive naturalism (understood as a metaphysics of being—a metaphysics that takes both an ontological and an emergentist turn); radical empiricism (understood as a metaphysics of experience—a metaphysics that takes an experiential or phenomenological turn); and anti-realist textualism (understood as concerned with vocabularies of "nature" and committed to the impossibility of getting behind or beneath language of "nature" to nature itself, understood as a would-be post-metaphysical philosophy that takes a linguistic or semantic turn). In the light of this campfire, it is clear that each group has many members, but Santayana can serve well as an exemplar of non-reductive naturalism (and I take this group to include, among others, Randall, McDowell, Chalmers, Hornsby, Johnson, Gallagher, Damasio, Cahoone, and Wahman). James serves well as an exemplar of radical empiricism (and I include in this group Dewey, Mead, Putnam, McDermott, Smith, Margolis, Bernstein, Colapietro, and myself). Finally, though not my focus here, Richard Rorty could serve as the lead representative and exemplar of textualism (a group whose membership includes Brandom, Davidson, Goodman, Price, Voparil, and Frankenberry). Ahhh: *Is nature existence, experience, or text*? Even without a squirrel, another metaphysical question, if ever there was one.

Of course, this question can be put the other way around: Does nature outstrip experience and language? Or is an experience that outstrips language always implicated in nature, always bound up in nature, always an emergent bit of nature? Or is nature, like experience, language, interpretation, and text?

"In the unlimited leisure of the wilderness, discussion had been worn threadbare. Everyone had taken sides and was obstinate" (P, 271). What is nature, really? Which party is right, I now propose pragmatically, depends on what is meant by "nature."

If the answer to the question "What is nature?" depends in part on the meaning of the word "nature," so too it surely depends on the meaning of the word "is." In his "Some Meanings of the Word 'Is,'" Santayana provided careful analysis and great clarity. What is nature? If we understand "is" in Santayana's first sense as identity (or the principle of essence), then metaphysics simply becomes a registering of the obvious and the self-identical: I see what I see, it is what it is, A = A, and so on. In this sense of "is," nothing more can be said about nature and nothing more needs to be said: What is nature? Nature is nature, period; time to head to a bar. Heading to a bar is, of course, a practical matter, and thus Santayana added that "is" in the sense of identity might seem a "vain assertion" to practical minds that "are not interested in anything except for the sake of something else" and for whom the obvious is not enough. Practical minds "are camp-followers or heralds of the flux of nature, without self-possession. Yet if that which is actual and obvious at the moment never had a satisfying character, no satisfaction would ever be possible, and life would be what romantic philosophy would make it—a wild goose chase" (SMWI, 191).

If nature is claimed to be anything else at all, whether by wild-goose chasers or pet-goose owners, then the claim is not one of identity. In all such cases, one is asserting that nature is . . . well, *not* nature but something else, something that is not self-identical to nature. In this way, all "is" claims that are not identity claims are metaphorical, perhaps even poetic. And so different kinds of "is" claims are so many different metaphors, metaphors presumably employed by different narrative artists.

Now, Santayana distinguished six additional meanings of the word "is." I will focus on the last three. He calls them "existence," "actuality," and "derivation." And I will draw two conclusions that emerge from this analysis.

First, non-reductive naturalists who, contra radical empiricism, claim that there "is" an experience-independent nature or mind-independent existence are claiming that nature *is*—is real—*in the sense of existence and the sense of derivation*. Santayana called this view an *assumption* but stresses that it is an assumption forced on us by our animal faith, by our actions and expectations and the intuitions to which they give rise. He wrote that whenever one assumes that there is—that there exists—a mind-independent substance, one is using the word "is" in the sense of an assertion of existence, and he added:

> This assertion of existence is imposed on me antecedently by the actions or expectations in the midst of which intuition arises, and without which it would never arise; and to this underlying faith is due the habit of predication, and the function of giving names . . . . The vague light, without outline or colour, which may first come to me from the church window is certainly not the composition which I afterwards discover there, yet I call them perceptions of the same thing because I am convinced a priori, by the persevering attitude of my body and other converging circumstances, that a common source existed for both images, namely a single material window fixed in its place, designed by its particular architect and built by his particular masons and glaziers. If no such natural object existed, that vague light and the precise composition would have nothing to do with each other. (SMWI, 203)

The naturalist claims that multiple perceptions and actions presuppose a priori the antecedent existence of things available to perception and action. As Santayana put it, "I am compelled to believe in the butt of my action" (SMWI, 203). In other words, the experience of objects and action involving them presupposes a nature that exists independently of that experience and action and, in turn, an experience-independent nature that sustains this working faith. The non-reductive naturalist here stands with Santayana: Nature is independent of mind and nature; nature is—here understanding "is" in the sense of existence.

This belief in the existence of nature leads, Santayana explained, to another meaning of the word "is" that he labeled "derivation." For example, I perceive a point of light, say to myself "there is a spark," and so take this perception "as the sign of some existence." Santayana wrote: "But in the world of nature, to which I am now addressed, a spark is no isolated fact; it has some origin" and so "I may say to myself, 'This spark is a firefly and not a star.'" Santayana summed this up:

> I have thus travelled in search of explanation very far indeed from my datum. Instead of saying, "A point is a point," I first said, "A spark exists": and then I said, "This spark is an insect." The word "I" has become a synonym of "*comes from*"; it attributes to an alleged fact a source in another fact, asserting that the two are continuous genetically, however different they may be in character. (SMWI, 210)

Such claims that nature "is" in the sense of derivation, Santayana stressed, must be taken "loosely": It is not that a spark *is* "nothing but" a firefly; instead, the claim that there *is* (in the sense of derivation) a firefly merely indicates a claimed partial origin of a particular fact or idea (SMWI, 211). Here, Santayana—as much as James, interestingly—was at pains to avoid what James called "the intellectualist fallacy," the fallacy of taking an object to be only that which a definition of it includes, only what it *is* in the sense of derivation.

Now, in sharp contrast to the non-reductive naturalist who understands derivation as an inference of one existence (say, a firefly) from another existence (a spark), radical empiricists view derivation as an inference from one experience to another. In his famous early essay "The Postulate of Immediate Empiricism"—not a postulate of naturalism—John Dewey employed a different meaning of the word "is." He wrote:

> I start and am flustered by a noise heard. Empirically that noise *is* fearsome; it *really* is, not merely phenomenally or subjectively so. That is *what* it is experienced as being. But when I experience the noise as a *known* thing, I find it to be innocent of harm. It is the tapping of a shade against the window, owing to movements of the wind. The experience has changed; that is, the thing experienced has changed—not that some reality has given place to a reality, nor that some transcendental (unexperienced) Reality has changed, not that truth has changed, but just and only the concrete reality experienced has changed.[40]

---

[40] John Dewey, "The Postulate of Immediate Empiricism," in *John Dewey: The Middle Works, 1899–1924* (Carbondale: Southern Illinois University Press, 1977 [1905]), 160.

Here we have the being or "is-ness" of nature in the sense in which "is" means derivation as understood by a radical empiricist: To say the spark is a firefly, for example, is to say that one experience (say, perceiving a spark some distance away) does or would lead to some subsequent other experience (say, perceiving a firefly as one walks with steady gaze nearer to the blinking spark). Seemingly slightly agitated by philosophers he labels "rationalists," "absolutists," "dia-lectical thinkers," and "transcendentalists"—those who posit existences that are not directly experienced—James thus asked rhetorically: "Have we not explained that conceptual knowledge is made such wholly by the existence of things that fall outside of the knowing experience itself—by intermediary experiences and by a terminus that fulfills?"[41] Here the work of derivation is accomplished not by inferring that there is nature in the sense of "is" as experience-independent existence. Instead, derivation is made possible by and is a function of the *continuity of experience*—of nature in the sense of "actu-ality." Indeed, this is just how James expressed the thesis of radical empiricism:

> *The relations that connect experiences must themselves be experienced rela-tions, and any kind of relation experienced must be accounted as real as any-thing else.* (APU, 22)

> *Tho*[ugh] *one part of our experience may lean upon another part to make it what it is in any one of several aspects in which it may be considered, experi-ence as a whole is self-containing and leans on nothing.* (ERE, 99)[42]

My second conclusion: To say that there is a fearsome noise or that there is a shade heard tapping is to use the word "is" in the sense that Santayana la-beled "actuality." Radical empiricists who deny that there "is" an experience-independent nature or mind-independent existence are claiming that nature *is*—is real—*in the sense of actuality.* It is in this sense of "is" that one claims "That sound is scary," "My childhood memories are happy," "The sixth chapter of this book is brilliant, not unorganized," or "Today is gray and rainy." Santayana called each such actuality a "phase of animal life," "a very vivid and notable event, an existence possessing such unity, scope, and concentration

---

[41] William James, "A World of Pure Experience," in *Essays in Radical Empiricism* (Cambridge, MA: Harvard University Press, 1976 [1912]), 33.

[42] Peter Jones claimed "continuity, diversity, vagueness: these are three essential features of experi-ence which James wishes to underline." Peter Jones, "William James," in *American Philosophy*, edited by Marcus G. Singer (New York: Cambridge University Press, 1985), 49.

as no other existence possesses." He concluded that although actualities—
"intrinsic incandescences" that "create the world of appearances"—are not
existences "in the same sense as natural things" or events,

> yet we must say . . . that they exist and arise, unless we are willing to banish
> spirit from nature altogether and to forget, when we do so, that spirit in us
> is then engaged in discovering nature and in banishing spirit. Why should
> philosophers wish to impoverish the world in order to describe it more
> curtly? . . . This spiritual hypostasis of life into intuition is therefore less
> and more than natural existence and deserves a different name. I will call
> it actuality. *Is*, applied to spirit or to any of its modes, accordingly means is
> actual. (SMWI, 208–209)

Here, of course, the radical empiricist poses a different question about
actuality than Santayana did. The radical empiricist does not ask why
philosophers should wish to impoverish the world in order to describe it,
but, instead, why naturalists should wish to impoverish experience in order
to transcend it. As James put it, "When we talk of reality 'independent' of
human thinking, then, it seems a thing very hard to find." "You can't weed
out the human contribution," he added, noting that any assertion of a reality or nature independent of mind, any existence independent of experience, "has already been *faked*" by being an assertion of independence only in,
and for, experience. From the standpoint of tough-minded thinking, James
called this "a piece of perverse abstraction worship" (P, 119–120, 128). James
observed:

> Not *being* reality, but only our belief *about* reality, it [any claim to truth]
> will contain human elements. . . . What shall we call a thing anyhow? . . . We
> break the flux of sensible reality into things, then, at our will. We create
> the subject of our true as well as of our false propositions. We create the
> predicates too. . . . Our nouns and adjectives are all humanized heirlooms.
> (P, 120, 122)

A radical empiricist here stands with James: Nature is not independent of
mind and nature; nature is—understanding "is" in the sense of actuality.
   Finally, while I will not develop this point here, I note that when textualists
like Rorty make claims about what is or is not the case, they are using
the word "is" in the three senses of that term that Santayana identified as

"equivalence" (different words that signify the same thing), "definition" (Santayana characterizes this as "perfectly useless for natural knowledge" but "a fountain of deductions which are unimpeachable in themselves"), and "predication" (the attribution of qualities to substances, which are never exhausted by such attribution) (SMWI, 195–202). In these senses of the word "is," everything *is* a sign. And so Santayana observed: "Animal faith, with the intent which expresses it intellectually, may use any or all essences as predicates of a substance posited beyond them; but these predicates are poetic epithets for that substance, not constituents of it. They vary with the senses and genius of the observer" (SMWI, 202). So: "Geist" *is* "spirit"; man *is* a rational animal; the wine *is* red; cruelty *is* immoral; Mother Nature *is* on the run; Santayana *is* right. The insight here is both real and small: Certainly it is not possible to offer a *description* of nature (what nature is) that is wholly *independent of description*. If taken as a basis for an account or knowledge of reality, the textualist's "poetic epithets" appear, to coin a phrase, to both the naturalist and the empiricist as a kind of *vicious semioticism*, taking a reality to exclude everything that a sign for it does not include. This textualism—nature as vocabulary, nature as "nature"—ends in subjectivism. As Steven Levine has shown in *Pragmatism, Objectivity, and Experience*, a pragmatic philosophy that avoids subjectivism cannot proceed merely by "communicative-theoretic" terms but, instead, requires "experiential-theoretic" commitments—for example, radical empiricism.[43] Moreover, this textualism amounts to concluding invalidly that there is no secondness simply because there is thirdness (in Peircean terms); that there is nothing qualitatively immediate because there are mediating relations (in Deweyan terms); that there is no flux because there are things (in Jamesian terms); and that poor and almost poetic speaking, writing, and thinking about nature prove that nature was merely what was spoken, written, and thought (in Santayana's terms).

Well . . . in the words of William James, "you see how differently people take things" (P, 126). However, thanks to Santayana's careful account of multiple meanings of the word "is," any disagreement here will not be metaphysical disagreement in the sense of "metaphysical" employed by James: It will not be disagreement about the *meaning* of terms; it will not be disagreement

---

[43] Steven Levine, *Pragmatism, Objectivity, and Experience* (New York: Cambridge University Press, 2019), 1–15, 123–192.

because different thinkers, like the squirrel-observing camping party that James described, are using the same word but with different meanings.

In light of Santayana's clarifications and distinctions, it follows, then, that the disagreement between non-reductive naturalist and radical empiricist is *not a metaphysical disagreement*—not a disagreement about meaning. Well, is it a metaphysical disagreement in some other, non-Jamesian sense of the "metaphysical"? To return to the dictionary, is it a disagreement about the fanciful and imaginary? Is it, in the end, a matter of different stories, just two different narratives—perhaps narratives of the incorporeal and super-sensible? That would be exciting: Actuality Kid vs. Existence Monster. Almost everyone these days seems to love superheroes and supervillains and their struggles—and, to further enliven the plot, surely it does not seem a stretch to think of metaphysical views as the zombies of the theory world, killed and buried so many times but still apparently undead (The Return of the Scholastic Realists! Dawn of the Eliminative Materialists! Idealist Apocalypse! Materialists: The Next Generation!).

Are the narrative differences between non-reductive naturalism and radical empiricism generated by different a priori principles or by *different inferences*?

Yes.

The naturalist and the radical empiricist agree about what is in the sense of "is" as actuality. Given different experiences of the same thing, Santayana inferred a prior, experience-independent "common source" of these different experiences. The first blurry, blinded perception of the church window as one steps into darkness from outdoor light is a perception of the *same* church window that one perceives as clearer, sharper, more brilliant, and more mul-ticolored after one has become accustomed to relative indoor darkness. The blurry perception and the vivid one are both perceptions of the same church window only if there is a church window prior to and independent of those perceptions. That this church window is real in the sense of "is" as existence is not verified in or by our experience—which, as actuality, can never warrant either belief or doubt in existence. This is why Santayana fairly called it an assumption: Given our actual experience, given our animal life, it must be assumed. It is the necessary product of animal faith. Without it, Santayana reasoned, two different perceptions could never be perceptions of the same thing.

Here, I think, is the root of every difference between naturalist and rad-ical empiricist. The radical empiricist makes a different—yes, radically different—inference. Given different experiences of the same thing, James inferred only additional experience (actual or possible). We conclude that we saw the same object because of definite experienced continuities between the two experiences. These experienced continuities are, for radical empiricists, the "butt" of all action. And this kind of conclusion about our past perceptions establishes habits of perception that fund subsequent perceptions. In short, it is the same church window because it is experienced as the same church window.

The disagreement may appear interminable unless its meanings are cashed out in practice. The radical empiricist cannot prove that there is nothing independent of experience merely by claiming that experience provides no evidence of any such existence; that would be dialectical physics. (The radical empiricist can, of course, point out that the characterization of reality as independent of human experience can itself be only a categorization within that experience in an effort to render that experience more intelligible.)[44] There is an actuality/existence gap here: No number of claims about what there is when "is" is understood in the sense of actuality entail anything at all about the impossibility of the being of anything else when "is" is understood in the sense of existence. Attempted inferences of this sort all fail because all logically beg the question. However, in parallel fashion, the non-reductive naturalist also cannot prove that there is something independent of experience merely by claiming that experience is explained on this assumption (rather than radical empiricism), explained if one makes this naturalist leap of (animal) faith; that would be more, different dialectical physics. There is a logic/fact gap here: No claim that something could be the case entails that it actually is the case. Attempted inference of this sort all fails because, as Santayana himself pointed out in his criticism of metaphysics, the attempt to determine matters of fact by logical (or moral or rhetorical) constructions—"dialectical physics"—is always invalid (unless one imports question-begging premises). Both radical empiricism and non-reductive naturalism are hypotheses equally logically possible (because not internally inconsistent) and equally empirically unfalsified (because both hold the same view about what is in the sense of "is" as actuality). Which of these languages should we speak? Which philosophical fashion should we don? Which is more beautiful? Santayana's pluralistic counsel bears repetition:

[44] Sandra Rosenthal effectively made this point in "From Pragmatic Meaning to Process Metaphysics," in *Speculative Pragmatism* (Amherst: University of Massachusetts Press, 1986), 96.

It is a foolish heat in a patriot to insist that only his native language is intelligible or right. . . . I do not ask any one to think in my terms if he prefers
others. Let him clean better, if he can, the windows of his soul, that the variety and beauty of the prospect may spread more brightly before him.[45]

4. Temperamental Relations: Meliorism, Hope, and Action

Two final observations are in order. First, as James observed, "it is impossible not to see a temperamental difference at work in the choice of sides" (P,
124). If this is right—I strongly think it is—then it follows that any characterization *of* this temperamental difference will be work *by* some particular
temperament (and not by others), whether James's temperament, Deleuze's
temperament, Santayana's temperament, my temperament, or your temperament. This can be a recipe for one-sidedness and special pleading. I've tried
to avoid this, but I am sure only partial success ever is possible.

From the standpoint of a radical empiricism—both a Jamesian radical
empiricism of pure experience and relations and also a Deleuzian transcendental empiricism of sense as an experienced condition of the proposition
(and the transcendental as a form of the immanent, the virtual as a feature of
the actual, and the "boundary" between propositions and things as a mixed-
together continuity rather than a divide), naturalism, even "non-reductive"
naturalism, easily can appear reductionistic and readily seems to reflect an
essentially *theological* and *conservative* temperament—a desire for an universe in which the individual is assured that there is a greater and more permanent reality. I have called this preference "the adoration of matter," a reality
that endures even as human lives begin and end, come and go, satisfy and
suffer for a little while in a world of sport and striving that so easily can seem
all-important such that we would do well instead to adopt the role of cosmic
spectator rather than self-important actor.[46] This holds also for a transcendental empiricism for which sense is wholly external to the proposition, an
unexperienceable condition of the proposition, the adoration of nonsense.
I suspect, however, that the radical empiricist who makes an effort to grasp

---

[45] Santayana, *Scepticism and Animal Faith*, vi–vii.
[46] John J. Stuhr, "Experience and the Adoration of Matter: Santayana's Unnatural Naturalism,"
in *Genealogical Pragmatism: Philosophy, Experience, and Community* (Albany: State University of
New York Press, 1997), chap. 7.

this temperament on its own terms would do well to see it as *humility*—not in the sense of having little prestige or engaging in self-abasement or taking a low view of oneself but in the sense of having an *honest* view of oneself and *reverence* for the world. It is a temperament at odds with narcissism, hubris, conceit, and pride. It is just this sort of conceit, I believe, that Santayana found in radical empiricism, a philosophy in which, in his view, experience, the mere foreground of nature, is taken to be reality in full—human beings not simply as the measure of all things but all things as measured by human beings.

I find some truth in this view—I hear the universe speak, or at least whisper in this way in rare moments—but I find it mostly misses the mark. The radical empiricist is committed to striving in an always unfinished and reconstructed world, a world always in the remaking by its actors (even when that action takes the form of inaction or mere spectatorship). This temperament is not egoism. It is *meliorism* and the strenuous *responsibility* that meliorism confers in an *unfinished* universe. Experience leans on nothing else. There is nothing else on which to lean. There is only further experience. There are no guarantees and there is nothing fixed or certain. The world is precarious and full of possibility. Human action on behalf of human ends may help realize them a little more fully. The worldview that sustains such action is the pragmatically preferable.

The second final observation: Individuals do—I think James was right—emphasize their points of satisfaction differently, and so everything here is plastic. Everything here is plastic. Everything here is plastic. Yes . . . maybe . . . wait, what do you mean by "is"? Everything is plastic if "is" is understood in the sense of actuality. But everything surely is not plastic if "is" is understood in the very different sense of existence.

On all matters of reality (or nature or being) *understood as actuality*, non-reductive naturalists and radical empiricists (for whom sensations, perceptions, and conceptions all continuously run together, leaving no unbridgeable cutting edge between sense and word) agree. They agree and they emphasize their points of satisfaction in like manner. On all matters of reality (or nature or being) *understood as existence*, these two kinds of theorists disagree. They disagree and they find and take satisfaction very differently. It is here that a pragmatically inclined radical empiricist will point out that theories that do not have different concrete consequences are practically the same—that is, the same in matters of practice. From the standpoint of radical empiricism, so-called experience-independent existence (whether called "matter," "nature," or "sense wholly external to propositions") simply amounts in practice to—turns out in human life to be—the *relational continuity* of experience. From the standpoint of non-reductive naturalism, of course, this practical equivalence is no *real* equivalence at all.

John Dewey recognized this in his response to Santayana's critical review of *Experience and Nature*. Santayana had called Dewey's radically empirical naturalism "half-hearted," to which Dewey, in reply, concluded:

> I find two movements and two positions in Santayana which are juxtaposed, but which never touch. In his concrete treatments of any special topic when a matter of controversy to which traditional school labels are° attached is in abeyance, he seems genuinely naturalistic; the things of experience are treated not as specious and conventional, but as genuine, even though one-sided and perverse, extensions of the nature of which physics and chemistry and biology are scientific statements. . . . When he lets himself go in any body of subject-matter, free from the influence of traditional and professorial labels, I not only learn much from him, but I flatter myself that I am for the most part in agreement with him. But when he deals with a system of thought and finds it necessary to differentiate his own system from it, his naturalism reduces itself to a vague gesture of adoring faith in some all-comprehensive unknowable in contrast with which all human life—barring this one gesture—is specious and illusory. Only in this way can I explain the fact that while I find myself in so much agreement with him he is in such profound disagreement with me. The case seems to resemble that of the Irishman who said the two men looked very much alike, especially one of them. Barring that feature of Mr. Santayana's thought to which exception has been taken, I am happy to be that one.[47]

Santayana was right that radical empiricists from James to Dewey and beyond "cannot feel that nature was made by you or for you." But the radical empiricist can and should feel that we are part of nature, that some of it has been made—remade, added to, reconstructed—by us, and that nature contains possibilities and novelties yet to come and, in part, yet to be made by us. With creative intelligence, will, and action, some of these possibilities may be realized so as to allow more fulfilling and flourishing lives and more inclusive and just societies. Radical empiricism's world, a world of relations,

---

[47] Dewey, " 'Half-Hearted Naturalism,' " 81.

is a world of possibilities and connections, unfinished but also congruous at least in part with our powers.

This is the pragmatic, practical meaning of a world of pure experience: meliorism, hope and action.

And if this, as James observed in "What Pragmatism Means," disappoints and angers all parties to what had been assumed to be a genuine disagreement, the disagreement is still genuine—now practical rather than only theoretical.

Everything is plastic.

7

Pluralism Unconcluded

It is already evident from the letters I am getting about the *Pluralistic Universe* that the book will be 1st, *read*; 2nd, be *rejected* almost unanimously at first, and for very diverse reasons; but, 3rd, will continue to be bought and referred to, and will end by strongly influencing English philosophy. (CJR, 12:271)

1. The Pragmatic Meaning of Pluralism

"Pluralism," the term, fittingly has plural meanings in plural contexts—from anthropological and sociological pluralism, epistemological pluralism, moral or values pluralism, legal pluralism, political pluralism, cultural pluralism and multiculturalism, and religious pluralism to cosmic pluralism. At base, these claims and theories are commitments to irreducible multiplicity—that there is such multiplicity, that there should be this multiplicity, or that there both is and should be this multiplicity. Accordingly, ontological pluralism in all its forms is belief that reality is irreducibly many. This pluralism is a class name for views that affirm there are multiple instances and kinds of things or relations or events or characteristics or quantifiers. Ontological pluralists, unlike monists or dualists, hold that the modes of being are various and multiple, many rather than one or even two.

This is easy enough to write or to say—"there are multiple realities, the universe is pluralistic"—but what is the pragmatic meaning of this claim? What does it mean in practice? And does anything hang on how one answers this question? Does it make any difference, and is there any importance to it? For busy people, is this question just a "How many angels can dance on the head of a pin?" time-wasting and speculation-filled puzzle?

William James, a pluralist in his ethics, politics, and epistemology (a pluralist about goods, rights, and truths) was also a thoroughgoing ontological pluralist (a pluralist about the universe or reality). Moreover, he assigned

No Professor's Lectures Can Save Us. John J. Stuhr, Oxford University Press. © Oxford University Press 2023.
DOI: 10.1093/oso/9780197664629.003.0008

very top significance to the ancient philosophical problem of "the one and the many"—even as he usually called it the problem of "the many and the one," thereby signaling his pluralism. In a chapter in *Pragmatism* devoted to this issue, he announced:

> I wish to illustrate the pragmatic method by one more application. I wish to turn its light upon the ancient problem of "the one and the many." I suspect that in but few of you has this problem occasioned sleepless nights, and I should not be astonished if some of you told me it had never vexed you. I myself have come, by long brooding over it, to consider it the most central of all philosophic problems, central because so pregnant. I mean by this that if you know whether a man is a decided monist or a decided pluralist, you perhaps know more about the rest of his opinions than if you give him any other name ending in *ist.* To believe in the one or in the many, that is the classification with the maximum number of consequences. (P, 64)

James definitely was a "decided pluralist" in temperament and text. Throughout all his writings from beginning to end, he consistently and passionately expressed belief in the many rather than only the one—the parts rather than simply a whole—even as he struggled to overcome the many/one dualism that is presupposed in the traditional, old-fashioned way of posing this whole issue. His pluralism was thorough and far-reaching. He believed that the universe contained many, many parts, all irreducible to one another and all "ever not quite" capable of being amalgamated, integrated, unified, or totalized. Further, he believed that the universe was a pluriverse; he believed not merely that reality has multiple parts but that there are plural realities.

James did clearly recognize that pluralism goes against the grain of much philosophy when philosophy is taken to be a quest for unification of the world's manifold variety. But why should philosophy seek unity but not multiplicity? He wondered:

> But how about the *variety* in things? Is that such an irrelevant matter? If instead of using the term philosophy, we talk in general of our intellect and its needs, we quickly see that unity is only one of these. . . . What our intellect really aims at is neither variety nor unity taken singly, but totality. In this, acquaintance with reality's diversities is as important as understanding their connexion. The human passion of curiosity runs on all fours with the systematizing passion. (P, 64)

Because of this fact of human psychology, even pluralists are monists in the abstract:

> Of *course* the world is one, we say. How else could it be a world at all? Empiricists as a rule, are as stout monists of this abstract kind as rationalists are.
>
> The difference is that the empiricists are less dazzled. Unity doesn't blind them to everything else. (P, 65)

James continued with the humorous observation that monists engage in a kind of "number-worship" of Oneness:

> "Three" and "seven" have, it is true, been reckoned sacred numbers; but, abstractly taken, why is "one" more excellent than "forty-three," or than "two million and ten"? In this first vague conviction of the world's unity, there is so little to take hold of that we hardly know what we mean by it. (P, 65)

Unsurprisingly, in this context James proposed:

> The only way to get forward with our notion is to treat it pragmatically. Granting the oneness to exist, what facts will be different in consequence? What will the unity be known-as? The world is one—yes, but *how* one? What is the practical value of the oneness for *us*? (P, 65–66)

The *practical* value of oneness, when such value exists, is a function of a practical interest in connection, interdependence, system, and unity, just as the practical value of manyness, when it exists, is a function of some practical interest in separation, disjunction, dynamic novelty, and difference. Because we have *both* these interests it is sheer dogmatism to recognize only one of them. James observed, "The great point is to notice that the oneness and the manyness are absolutely co-ordinate here":

> Neither is primordial or more essential or excellent than the other. . . . [S]ometimes one function and sometimes the other is what comes home to us most, so, in our general dealings with the world of influences, we now need conductors and now need non-conductors, and wisdom lies in knowing which is which at the appropriate moment. (P, 68)

None of this is a logical proof of pluralism. It was not intended to be. Instead, it is a reconstruction of the problem of the one and the many from a metaphysical question to a psychological and empirical one, from a matter of "dialectical physics" to one of experiential inquiry. Do we, for example, *experience* an "All-Knower" such that the parts of the universe are conjoined in "a single stroke" or absolutely? Or do we *experience* many separate knowers in an imperfectly rational world such that "everything gets known by *some* knower along with something else; but the knowers may in the end be irreducibly many" and knowledge is strung along and overlapped" (P, 72)?

The experiences of manyness uncollected, whether in James's day or the present, are likely to disappoint persons who feel a strong longing or need for "One Life, One Truth, one Love, one Principle, One Good, One God" (a phrase James quoted from a Christian Science leaflet) or those who feel misery in the prospect of cosmic and moral separations in the absence of some primordial unity (P, 74–75). Of course, simply wanting this to be so does not make it so. And so James summarized:

> The world is one just so far as its parts hang together by any definite connexion. It is many just so far as any definite connexion fails to obtain. And finally it is growing more and more unified by those systems of connexion at least which human energy keeps framing as time goes on. . . . Pragmatism, pending the final empirical ascertainment of just what the balance of union and disunion among things may be, must obviously range herself upon the pluralistic side. Some day, she admits, even total union, with one knower, one origin, and a universe consolidated in every conceivable way, may turn out to be the most acceptable of all hypotheses. Meanwhile the opposite hypothesis, of a world imperfectly unified still, and perhaps always to remain so, must be sincerely entertained. This latter hypothesis is pluralism's doctrine. (P, 76, 79)

For James, then, the universe of the pluralist is never fully unified, never fully complete, never fully known, and never fully captured in thought, language, or logic. It is a universe—a pluriverse—of parts and vagueness, partial doings and local undergoings, temporal beginnings and endings, real fulfillments and forever losses, multiple manys and multiple ones, and all kinds of purposes and activities. Its outcomes and fortunes are still in part to be made—or lost. It has possibilities and genuine novelties, none of which come prepackaged with any guarantees of realization.

This is, I think, *the practical, pragmatic meaning of pluralism*: Each of us is responsible for our small but real part in striving to actualize some of the existing worlds of possibilities and in failing to contribute to actualizing other worlds and other possibilities. For a pluralist, none of us can wholly outsource this agency or escape the responsibility of how we do or do not use it. We cannot transfer or unload this responsibility and opportunity to some single absolute knower, an eternal god, an all-encompassing spirit, a permanent principle, a universal truth, or divine forgiveness or grace. Our salvation, to the extent this notion can be repurposed for finite lives, is in *our own hands*—not entirely, but each of us as our variable powers allow; in Santayana's phrase, each of us is "one brave little force."[1]

2. A Philosophy of Lived Experiences, Not Abstract Proof

It would be odd—a performance contradiction if not a logical one—if pluralists were to insist that everyone be a pluralist. Is there some other way to understand James's endorsement of pluralism?

To begin, it is obvious that different persons hold different philosophies. Why is that? Are some just really bad at inference and proof? James rejected this view and instead took these differences to be matters of psychology rather than logic: Different people have different experiences, feel the whole drift and push of life in different ways, and "find their minds more at home in very different fragments of the world" and find different best working attitudes (APU, 10, 14–15).

As a result, James's objection to monism is not a practical one; if monism really proved itself to be verified (and thus preferred) in someone's experience, in the whole push and pull and drift of that person's life, James would have no objection to such a person's affirmation of monism. (James thought this would be unlikely once the pragmatic meaning of monism is made clear, but he recognized it is a possibility in experience.) Instead, James's objection to monism is a metaphysical one: He argued that monism's efforts to disprove pluralism by reason, logic, dialectics, conceptual analysis, or thought alone all fail. For James, there can be no philosophical argument or proof against pluralism—or for it; it is an empirical hypothesis.

---

[1] George Santayana, "The Genteel Tradition in American Thought," in *Character and Opinion in the United States* (New York: W. W. Norton, 1967 [1920]), 213. See also chapter 6.

James repeatedly made this point through a focus on the monistic ide-alism of Bradley, Royce, and especially Hegel.[2] In his 1882 "On Some Hegelianisms," James granted that "there is no doubt that, as a movement of reaction against the traditional British empiricism, the Hegelian influence represents expansion and freedom, and is doing service of a certain kind." But he quickly added: "Such service ought not to make us blindly indulgent. Hegel's philosophy mingles mountain-loads of corruption with its scanty merits" and must stand ready to defend itself (WB, 196). James viewed his essay as a kind of preliminary raid on Hegelianism, a raid designed not to convince disciples of Hegel but merely to articulate a viable alternative for those who might be interested, "a skirmisher's shot, which may, I hope, soon be followed by somebody else's heavier musketry."

What is "Hegelianism"? At first, James characterized it as the philosophic effort to show that "the real is identical with the ideal" and that the ideal is one rather than many, a unity rather than "a republican banquet" (WB, 201). He described Hegel's universe in these sarcastic, even dismissive, terms:

> But, hark! What wondrous strain is this that steals upon his ear? Incoherence itself, may it not be the very sort of coherence I require? Muddle! Is it any-thing but a peculiar transparency? Is not jolt passage? Is friction other than a kind of lubrication? Is not a chasm a filling?—a queer kind of filling, but a filling still. Why seek for glue to hold things together when their very falling apart is the only glue you need? Let all that negation which seemed to disin-tegrate the universe be the mortar that combines it, and the problem stands solved. The paradoxical character of the notion could not fail to please a mind monstrous even in its native Germany, where the mental excess is endemic. . . . In the exceedingness of the facts of life over the formulas lies a standing temptation at certain times to give up trying to say anything ad-equate about them, and to take refuge in wild and whirling words which but confess our impotence before their ineffability. . . . Hegel's originality lies in his making their mood permanent and sacramental, and authorized to supersede all others—not as a mystical bath and refuge for feeling when tired reason sickens of her intellectual responsibilities (thank Heaven! That

---

[2] Joel D. Rasmussen discussed James's criticism of absolute idealism in the context of more re-cent Anglo-American philosophy in "William James, *A Pluralistic Universe*, and the Ancient Quarrel Between Philosophy and Poetry," in Martin Halliwell and Joel D. S. Rasmussen, *William James and the Transatlantic Conversation: Pragmatism, Pluralism, and the Philosophy of Religion* (New York: Oxford University Press, 2014).

bath is always ready), but as the very form of intellectual responsibility it-self. (WB, 203, 204)

Sarcasm and impatience aside, in this early essay James mounted two dif-ferent raids on the monistic idealism that he here called "Hegelianism." The first engagement is focused on temperament and the sentiment of rationality. The second raid is focused on inference and reasoning. The first case James makes against Hegelian monism itself has three parts. The parts are interre-lated and draw on one another, but I believe that they nonetheless may be clearly and usefully distinguished. First, when James focused on tempera-ment and the personal aspects of philosophies, he argued that his radical plu-ralism better supplies the intimacy sought by the monist and pluralist *alike*. Here he made no effort to change temperaments or convert personalities—as if a few words from a professor were likely to override established habits rooted in experiences and ways of life. He simply sought to show that his view delivers more of what those who hold to monistic idealism *already* want by their own lights. The logical structure of this three-step argument is simple and clear enough:

1. A philosophy should be held only if it produces the "intimacy" or senti-ment of rationality that expresses one's preferred working attitude.
2. Monistic idealism does not produce this intimacy or express this attitude.
3. Therefore, monistic idealism should not be held.

This argument is valid. Is it sound? Are its two premises true?

The first claim is a claim about the criterion of adequacy of any philos-ophy. James claimed over and over that any such criterion must be more than merely formal, that any number of philosophies are logically possible, and that a successful or satisfactory philosophy must be made true and not be out of whack in experience—my experience, your experience, someone's experience.

The second claim is, in effect, a statement of fact. Why accept it—especially if one supposes that monistic idealism must have *some* appeal to and satisfactions for those who hold it? It is at this point that James mounted a second sort of argument or subargument, a case intended to establish this claim about monistic idealism. This subargument, in turn, has two parts or moments. In the first place, James argued that the intimacy that monistic idealism would otherwise provide is destroyed when "pluralism breaks out" in it—when it turns out that the many, qua many, are not one and, so, that we, invincibly parts, are not intimate with the whole and are not at home with the one. But, in the second place, having analyzed the ways in which pluralism breaks out and reinscribes itself within monism, James came face-to-face with the way in which monistic idealism attempts to contain this "breakout" or to render this breakout its own. For example, he wrote:

> Contradiction, shown to lurk in the very heart of coherence and continuity, cannot after that be held to defeat them, and must be taken as the universal solvent—or, rather, there is no longer any need of a solvent. To "dissolve" things in identity was the dream of earlier cruder schools. Hegel will show that their very difference is their identity, and that in the act of detachment the detachment is undone, and they fall into each other's arms. (WB, 205)

Accordingly, James claimed that this monist strategy of "dynamic self-contradiction" fails on its own terms. He thus identified and named his point of attack: "The principle of contradictoriness of identity and the identity of contradictories is the essence of the hegelian system" (WB, 205).

Why is the monist's attempt to establish this principle a failure—if indeed it is a failure? Here James's focus changed from matters of temperament to matters of rational inference. Is the Hegelian, monist, rationalist, idealist, absolutist argument for this principle sound? From the standpoint of every bit of James's entire pragmatism, it is *not* sound. Why not? Pragmatists, I think, claim that *all* arguments of this kind are not sound—not just this one but all such arguments. So, what kind of argument is it? It is a transcendental argument—by which I mean simply that it is an argument that begins with some beliefs rooted in and drawn from experience in, and of, the world and then, on the basis of these beliefs taken as premises and on that basis alone, concludes that some other belief about the world also *must* be true. *Must* be true? The force of "must" here is understood by its proponents to be logical (an inference of entailment) rather than experimental (an inference from results of inquiry).

This kind of argument can have many steps but in skeleton or basic form it has only three:

1. Experience (or kind of experience) X is the case.
2. If experience X is the case, then Y must be the case.

3. Therefore, Y is (and must be) the case.

The transcendental argument, no matter what the specifics, always has this form: Because such-and-such is true about the universe (for example, that experience is full of varieties and disjunctions as well as unities and conjunctions), *therefore* this other claim is and must be true about the universe (for example, that there is an All-Knower, a Cosmic Spirit, a God, Universal Truth and Goodness, or the Unity of all humankind or all living beings). For James and pragmatists more generally, all instances of this transcendental argument form are invalid (because the inference in the second premise is invalid): Nothing *(logically) must* be the case simply because something else *is* the case. To employ this transcendental form of reasoning is to engage in what Santayana memorably called "dialectical physics." It is what pragmatists (and other non-transcendental philosophers) reject and replace with evidence-based experimental inquiry. In this experimental inquiry, we well may learn that because one thing is the case that something else indeed is the case, but this inference, to be valid, always is based on evidence, consequences, things working out or not working out in subsequent experience, and last things—not definitions and mere definitional reasoning,[3] wordplay, concept massage, flights of imagination, strong wishes, or antecedent posits played like trump cards in the face of actual experience. This is bad news for armchair philosophers; it means that even with a patron or tenure one cannot by mere speculation or deduction determine what actually is the case.

So, transcendental arguments for the anti-pluralistic "principle of contradictoriness of identity and the identity of contradictories" are invalid. Even so, is this principle itself false? (Or could the principle could be true and simply in need of stronger, valid argumentation?) Is the principle itself false? The pragmatic response: maybe. James argued that the only way to assess this principle is in practical, experiential terms. If the monist genuinely finds in experience—in the fullness of experience and not simply in conception— no plurality, no parts, no disjunctions, no external relations, then insofar the anti-pluralist "principle of contradictoriness of identity and the identity of contradictories" is verified. James did not rule out a monistic vision so long

---

[3] Harvey Cormier used this fact about James's pragmatism to explain how and why it is not a "subjectivist" philosophy. *The Truth Is What Works: Willliam James, Pragmatism, and the Seed of Death* (Lanham, MD: Rowman & Littlefield, 2001), 129.

as (and if and only if) the beliefs that give rise to and result from it are verified in concrete experience rather than dialectical logic—in the actual experience of some people in some place at some time. To grasp James's pluralism, to move toward the center of his pluralistic worldview, it is crucial to understand why and how this is so.

3. The Many *and* the One: "God Help Thee, Old Man"

In his 1905 "The Thing and Its Relations," an essay later collected in *Essays in Radical Empiricism*, James addressed Francis Herbert Bradley (1846–1924), arguably then the dominant philosopher in the United Kingdom.[4] James let many criticisms of his own work pass without comment, so it is worth considering what it is about Bradley's view—and what James took to be Bradley's misunderstanding of radical empiricism—that merited detailed response.

In their correspondence—they never met in person—James and Bradley certainly recognized in each other different temperaments. In response to a letter from James in which James called Bradley *"you,* the bogey and bugbear of most of my beliefs," Bradley responded in a telling defense of monism—and one that identified James, against his intent and self-understanding, as a monist rather than pluralist. This is an important expression of how a pluralist looks to a monist:

> [James's] finite selves seem to be constituted by the presence at certain parts of the great flow (of the One Experience) of other elements. The identity of the contents of the Universal Stream plus the addition of floating superimposed diversities (bubbles or eddies) *makes* the finite selves, while they really and veritably arise and perish utterly.
>
> This you *cannot* mean, but this is what arises in my mind as I read you. Of course we have here no Pluralism but an extreme Monism—only the Absolute here is a Stream or Flux....
>
> If however he can say "As I already *am* the others' world as well as my own, I have not to transcend my contents in order to know the Universe"—he is

---

[4] T. L. S. Sprigge presented a highly detailed, voluminous study—a particularly Bradley-friendly study—of the philosophical and personal connections between James and Bradley. See his *James and Bradley: American Truth and British Reality* (Chicago: Open Court, 1993). See also his essay "James, Aboutness, and His British Critics," in *The Cambridge Companion to William James*, edited by Ruth Anna Putnam (New York: Cambridge University Press, 1997), 125–144.

in a very different position. The interesting thing is that he, so far, exactly is in the position of the "Absolutist." For he (though you will not have it so) is not leaving his own actual experience to seek the Absolute (the real World). He has the Absolute there in experience from the first, and the only question with him is as to how far the first experience he has is merely a first experience to be replaced by a fuller one. As to going outside or looking outside—that believe me or not believe me—is to him out of the question. It is one of his condemned heresies. . . .

Have we one great immediate experience containing all things and selves? If so, how does the one self among others know the whole?[5]

James and Bradley agreed that concepts and language cannot fully capture or do full justice to the immediate and qualitative concreteness and flux of experience. This led James to pluralism—the stream of experience is, as experienced, a stream of plural experiences. It led Bradley to monism—the stream of experience, in its fullness, is an Absolute and logically must come to recognize itself as such, as having always and already been such.

James viewed Bradley's monism, his Absolutism, to be the result of a dialectical trick, an intellectual sleight of hand in which existential relations of experience are replaced by logical relations of thought. The trick, James thought, is accomplished by abstraction. In "The Thing and Its Relations," James hoped to reveal the trick as a trick, and thus to negate its magic. At the outset, James directed his readers to see through this trick: The difficulties of experience "are disappointments and uncertainties. They are not intellectual contradictions" (ERE, 45). James reminded his readers that experience in its immediacy and fluency flows as the experience of conjunctions and disjunctions. As such, it is lived or had rather than reflected or known. It is not, in its immediacy, a matter of equivalences and contradictions, for these are logical relations; it is a matter of differences and connections, for these are existential relations. In a crucial sentence, James wrote: "When the reflective intellect gets at work, however, it discovers incomprehensibilities in the flowing process" (ERE, 45). James's point here was not that the flow of experience *is not comprehended* by reflection—as though reflection needs to roll up its sleeves and work harder. Rather, it is that the flow of experience *cannot be comprehended* by reflection, that the flow of experience in its

---

[5] Quoted in Ralph Barton Perry, *The Thought and Character of William James* (Westport, CT: Greenwood Press, 1974 [1935]), 1: 445–46.

immediate concreteness cannot be made by reflection an object of knowledge, that the flux of life, as flux, is literally "incomprehensible." As a result,
no philosophy—no language, thought, critical reflection—can recover "in-
nocence," the immediacy of experience as it occurs. At most, a philosophy
can dispense "redemption," a negation of its own negations, a negation of its
own destructions of immediacy. Accordingly, "The Thing and Its Relations"
is, in this sense, an effort at and an account of redemption.

For James, the redemption of immediate experience by philosophy does
not require abstinence from philosophy. James was not advocating that we
just generally stop thinking or strive to live reflection-free lives. Instead,
he explained that life itself teaches the lesson of the practical importance
of intellectualizing, reasoning, abstracting, thinking. In making this point,
James at first called himself not a radical empiricist or a pragmatist, but a
"naturalist" (perhaps in part because this term stands in sharper contrast to
the idealism of Bradley, which James sought to expose and reject). On the
"naturalist account," James explained:

> Whenever we intellectualize a relatively pure experience, we ought to do so
> for the sake of redescending to the purer or more concrete level again; and
> that if an intellect stays aloft among its abstract terms and generalized rela-
> tions, and does not reinsert itself with its conclusions into some particular
> point of the immediate stream of life, it fails to finish out its function and
> leaves its normal race unrun. (ERE, 47)

In this way, rationalism converts something useful into something supposedly valuable independent of that use: The intellect "originated as a practical means of serving life; but it has developed incidentally the function of
understanding absolute truth; and life itself now seems to be given chiefly as
a means by which that function may be prosecuted" (ERE, 48).

This is why James called Bradley an "ultra-rationalist." From James's
perspective, Bradley began by breaking up, chopping up, separating, distinguishing immediate experience into separate parts, subjects and object, thoughts and things. In this form, as James put it, "intellectualized, it
is all distinction without oneness" (ERE, 48). Bradley's "ultra-rationalism"
emerged first in his demand that these distinctions, this manyness, *must*
be distinctions or components of some unity, some oneness, and then in
his claim that finite experiences cannot unify these "diversities" or "conge-
ries in the lump" and therefore must be unified by reason in and through a

conception of absolute (and not merely experienced) being. From this point onward, James explained, rationalism walks a different path or takes a different road than naturalism, pragmatism, and radical empiricism.

These paths diverge, James thought, at the issue of the nature and status of relations. This is the question: Are a thing's relations internal or external to it? This question separates and illustrates dramatically the different ways of thinking—perhaps the different temperaments—of rationalistic monists and radically empirical pluralists. Consider any given thing—say, a bottle of water. Bradley recognized, of course, that the thing has relations. The water bottle, for example, is spatially located on the table at this moment, looks relatively transparent and clear to most human observers under the glare of institutional lighting, and is not alarming or menacing under usual circumstances. (In the language of some philosophical traditions, the thing has relations that can be stated as primary, secondary, and tertiary or affective qualities.) If it were not on the table, Bradley reasoned, it would not be the particular water bottle that it is; it would not be *this* water bottle. Being on the table is part of what it is to be this water bottle; this relation is internal to this thing—part of its being what it is. But the water bottle, for example, was also purchased by Sammy at the grocery store. If it had not been purchased by Sammy at that grocery store, it would not be *this* bottle. Being, or having been, purchased by Sammy at that store is part of what it is to be precisely *this* bottle; this relation also is internal to this thing—part of its being what it is. But the notion of *water bottle on the table*, on the one hand, and the notion of *water bottle bought by Sammy at the grocery store*, on the other hand, are two different notions, two distinct conceptions with two distinct meanings. Given that these conceptions are different (and easily distinguished), how can the water bottle on the table be the *same* bottle as the water bottle bought by Sammy at the store? Or, to change the example, how can a water bottle you see be the *same* water bottle I see? Or, how can a water bottle you see now be the *same* water bottle as the one you saw a moment ago? Logically, these are all distinct notions; they are different concepts. How can reason overcome these differences and synthesize or unite them? Does it turn out that commonsense belief in the sameness of the bottle requires, or logically presupposes, belief in a not-so-commonsensical uniting Absolute?

Bradley's position, as James saw it, was that all relations of all things are *internal* to those things. Each thing has just the relations it has, and it would not be that particular thing if it did not have those relations: If this is not the water bottle that Sammy bought at the grocery store, then it is a different bottle. But to even talk about things as having internal relations is to presuppose a perspective from which that thing's internal relations are external—a perspective from which the water bottle on the table, the water bottle bought by Sammy, the water bottle seen as transparent and clear by you, and the water bottle that is not in the least menacing or scary is in reality one water bottle, the same identical water bottle. This is the *function* of Bradley's Absolute: As an object of reflection (rather than experience), it constitutes a perspective from which a thing's relations are external to that thing—and thus a perspective from which a thing may be known as a thing, a perspective from which it may be a thing, one thing, the same thing.

In response, James observed in effect that the philosophical emperor that is monism, idealism, rationalism, absolutism has no clothes. He wrote:

> But the starting-point of the reasoning here seems to be the fact of the two phrases [e.g., the water bottle's relation to a table and a water bottle's relation to a purchaser and place of purchase]; and this suggests the argument may be merely verbal. Can it be that the whole dialectic achievement consists in attributing to the experience talked-about a constitution similar to that of the language in which we describe it?

"Must we assert the objective doubleness," James continued, "merely because we have to name it twice over when we name its two relations?" He added: "Candidly, I can think of no other reason than this for the dialectic conclusion! For, if we think, not of our words, but of any simple concrete matter which they may be held to signify, the experience itself belies the paradox asserted" (ERE, 50–51).

For pluralistic radical empiricism, everything Bradley claimed is reversed. We do not begin with manyness and diversity and distinction, having then to reason abstractly to oneness. Instead, we begin with oneness—the neutral monism of pure, immediate experience—and then, to advance our concrete practical purposes, we may create manyness and diversity and distinction and thus separate the flux into many different things. Bradley's error (and the error of idealism and rationalism in all of its forms more generally), for James, is to treat all the relations of a thing as internal relations. Why is this an error? It is an error because any *thing* is already the *product* or consequence of reflection, of a selective chopping up the fluent immediacy and flow of experience. When I pick out any thing as that thing, I do so precisely by treating some of its relations as *external* to it or on the fringes of it.[6]

To return to the example: At the grocery store and eager to quench his thirst, Sammy spots this bottle of water and buys it—with no regard at all for, say the size of its label or the height of the shelf that held it or whether the worker who stocked it on that shelf was or was not female or . . . These relations are all external to this bottle of water. External to and independent of Sammy's purposes and selective attention, by contrast, all these (and all other) relations are internal to the stream of experience, the immediate flux. The thing, this water bottle, named and disjoined from this flowing process, has relations that are external to itself, as selective interests and purposes determine. In this example, it is the same water bottle whether or not Sammy places it on the table or in a briefcase. These relations are external.

For radical empiricism, experience as such is neutrally monistic, and this means that experienced relations are internal to the experiences that they constitute (rather than name or represent). The work of reflection transforms parts of this experience into thoughts and things, and in so doing creates or makes external relations (externalizes or ejects relations from particular conceptions of given things). James concluded that "Mr. Bradley's understanding shows the most extraordinary power of perceiving separations and the most extraordinary impotence in comprehending conjunctions." James continued:

> When a common man analyzes certain *whats* from out the stream of experience, he understands their distinctness *as thus isolated*. But this does not prevent him from equally well understanding their combination with each other *as originally experienced in the concrete*, or their confluence with new sensible experiences in which they recur as "the same." (ERE, 57)

Bradley treated separate things, objects of reflection, as though they were separate *independent* of reflection, and then sought to unify them in further reflection that posits an Absolute by which differences constituted by distinguished internal relations can be unified independent of external relations. In contrast, James treated separate things as distinctions

---

[6] M. Gail Hamner has nicely linked James's commitment in his radical empiricism and pluralism to the existence of external relations with his notion in his psychology of experience's "fringes" that lie outside experience but push its boundaries. *American Pragmatism: A Religious Genealogy* (New York: Oxford University Press, 2003), 138–141.

(with external relations) made in reflection for various purposes; he then asked whether or not these distinctions prove useful (and for what purpose, and for whom) in the flow of experience to which we (different, plural "subjects") return them.

Now, James was confident that his account of a thing's external relations refuted the view of Bradley and all rationalistic monists. But there were other criticisms of his view that left him less confident about his pluralistic radical empiricism, criticisms that he struggled with for years, criticisms that in the end brought on a major shift in his understanding of pluralism.

In the preface to his first book of philosophy, *The Will to Believe* (1896), James explained that the addresses collected there illustrated the radically empiricist attitude but did not constitute *argument* for it. He expressed the hope that he "may be spared" to do this "technical" work at a later date. He seems to have turned to this work in 1903 after the publication of *The Varieties of Religious Experience*. At times with optimism and at other times with deep pessimism, he regarded this endeavor—its working title was "The Many and the One"—as his future magnum opus. Nonetheless, James never completed it, never returned to it, and never published it as such—whether for personal, professional, or philosophical reasons. Nevertheless, it profoundly shaped and radically reframed James's subsequent views and writing.

James worked on "The Many and the One" from mid-1903 until mid-1904, abandoning the project in part due to the press of public lecturing (which he always found difficult to turn down); in part due to the steady deadlines of shorter writing projects, often aimed at broad (rather than merely professional) audiences; and perhaps (as many have speculated) in part due to his impatient personality and his distaste for systems of thought. Whatever the causes, this was to be James's only effort to write a systematic and comprehensive statement of his philosophy for a professional audience. James thought his project would constitute a "new rallying-point of opinion in philosophy" and added, in a letter to British pragmatist F. C. S. Schiller, that "the times are fairly crying aloud for it."[7] However, as Ignas Skrupskelis and others have observed, that very year Bertrand Russell published *The Principles of Mathematics* and much English-speaking philosophy rallied around Russell, a severe (if clumsy) critic of James, and, so, around an approach to philosophy very different from pragmatism, humanism, fallibilism, meliorism, radical empiricism, and pluralism.

---

[7] Perry, *The Thought and Character of William James*, 2:376.

As his prospects for completing "The Many and the One" lessened, James quoted a passage from *Moby Dick* and called it "motto for my book":

"God help thee, old man, thy thoughts have created a creature in thee; and he whose intense thinking thus makes him a Prometheus; a vulture feeds upon that heart for ever; that vulture the very creature he creates." (MEN, xix, 10)

What is the creature, the self-devouring vulture, that James created? Is it his notion of experience, of pure or immediate experience, and the dynamic pluralism that it involves? Is it his effort to paint a picture of, to represent, that which cannot be represented? Is it his determination to paint many pictures, pictures that include the struggling of the painter? Is it his desire for an intellect that is reconstructive, not "destructive," an intellect engendered by life but not in turn preying on it (MEN, 11)? These questions in mind, it is clear that James began with his long-standing commitment to the irreducibly personal character of philosophy and, at least in his case, to a philosophy of a world that is unfinished and in which we really struggle. In his "Introduction: Philosophies Paint Pictures," he thus wrote:

It makes no difference what pretensions the philosopher may parade as to the coercive nature of his arguments. Whatever principles he may reason from, and whatever logic he may follow, he is at bottom an advocate pleading to a brief handed over to his intellect by the peculiarities of his nature and the influences in his history that have moulded his imagination. The reasons that have seemed so coercive to a man with one hypothesis have in point of fact usually seemed fallacies or irrelevancies to men with different hypotheses. (MEN, 4)

I do not believe, picturing the whole as I do, that even if a supreme soul exists, it embraces all the details of the universe in a single absolute act either of thought or of will. In other words, I disbelieve in the omniscience of the Deity, and in his omnipotence as well. The facts of struggle seem too deeply characteristic of the whole frame of things for me not to suspect that hindrance & experiment go all the way through. (*MEN*, 5)

Of course, these facts of struggle do not establish by themselves that the world really is not one rather than many. Instead, they led James, armed with his pragmatic method for settling metaphysical disputes, to note that there are plural senses of "oneness"—each being a different sense of "connexion" between things, such that "the Many and the One are both likely to obtain their rights" (MEN, 15). Stated in the language of the many and the one, this is the point that James would make in the writings collected after his death in *Essays in Radical Empiricism* about the irreducibly reciprocal relationship between conjunctive and disjunctive relations (and so here James addressed the many *and* the one rather than the many *or* the one). And, stated in the language of subject and object, this is another point that James would make in *Essays in Radical Empiricism* about the non-dualistic nature of experience and the status of subject (consciousness) and object (content) as functions rather than substances. James made this point in "The Many and the One" at some length in his account of the concept of pure experience. He wrote, for example:

> A suspicion therefore steals upon us that this whole method of analysis may be vicious, that experiences may have no inner duplicity, that their object and subject character, instead of being reachable by subtraction, is conferred upon them by addition, the addition namely of other experiences which make them *function* differently. (MEN, 19)

> Our philosophy assumes the whole bipolar [or "double-barreled"] conception as its constructive unit. . . . The whole world is of one tissue. As to be is to be experienced, so to be connected is to be experienced as connected. . . . But as painted fishes can live in a painted sea, and a storied palace hold a storied king and court, even so experienced connexions are sufficient fasteners together of experienced terms, and transitions realized by us are the only relations possible between such things as our experiences grasp. This refusal to go beyond concrete experience, and this insistence that conjunctive and disjunctive relations are, when experienced, equally real, is what I mean by giving the name of radical empiricism to the philosophy of this book. (MEN, 21, 22, 23)

> There is no such entity as consciousness, as thought-stuff, and there is no such entity as thing-stuff, either separable or inseparably combined. There is only one original Stuff, and that is the undivided stuff of what I shall call "pure" experience. (MEN, 24–25)

"No object without a subject, no subject without an object," is the watch word of this kind of thought, for which the minimum fact that can be has therefore a definitely duplex sort of nature. When I say "pure-experience," the reader may very likely think that I also mean to suggest world-units of this bipolar sort of inner constitution. But such is far from being my intention. . . . I mean to denote a form of being which is as yet neutral or ambiguous, and prior to the object and subject distinction. (MEN, 26–27)

[E]xperiences in their totality are reported to one another. The present experience is the only witness we need to suppose of the past one, the future experience the only witness we need to suppose of the present one. . . . An experience is not intrinsically conscious; but another experience beyond it is conscious of it, in the sense of growing out of it and keeping retrospective hold of it. (MEN, 29)

These sorts of passages, familiar in upshot to readers of *Essays in Radical Empiricism*, evidence an account of radical empiricism and its concept of pure experience that is ontological rather than (merely) methodological. In his short characterization of radical empiricism in *The Meaning of Truth*, for example, James had offered up a postulate, a statement of fact, and a generalized conclusion. He termed the postulate "methodological," explaining that "the only things that shall be debatable among philosophers shall be things definable in terms drawn from experience" and noting that things of an unexperienceable nature may exist *ad libitum*, though forming no part of philosophic debate (MT, 6–7). This postulate is "methodological" because it merely specifies how and about what philosophers may speak. Ontologically, it is non-committal. By contrast, James's claims that the whole world is of one tissue, his rejection of any world beyond or independent of that of concrete experience, and his insistence that the only witness to experience is other experience are, assuredly, not ontologically non-committal. This is not simply discourse about experience but an ontology of experience. And because James took "experience" to be a class name for multiple, plural, different experiences, it is an ontology of plural experiences, an ontology of a pluralistic universe.

One of the most important topics that James introduced in "The Many and the One" is the notion of *virtual* experience (as distinct from actual experience). James introduced this notion in order to make clear the differences between his position and that of idealism (and also that version of idealism often labeled "panpsychism"). Having noted that to be connected is to be *experienced* as connected, James then added:

> We have laid down the idealistic principle, and agreed to abide by it, that *esse is experiri*, and that a thing must be actually "realized" in order to be real. But there are hosts of things which were never realized as we experience them and as they figure in our philosophies, and hosts of relations between things which were never noticed or named as we name them until we came upon the scene. . . . It might accordingly be charged that we ought in pursuance of our pure experience principle, to deny that the stars of the great bear formed a group at all before men's advent. . . . But this violates our instinct of truth, for we feel that in all such cases the facts which we experience and name have pre-existed to our act of naming them. We feel ourselves to be finders of truth, not Creators of it for the first time. But if we hold by this instinct, and also by the idealistic principle that facts exist only for someone, we seem committed to the doctrine of absolute Mind cognizant throughout a previous eternity, of all that our finite minds may successively come to learn. (MEN, 37)

The notion of virtual experience is the vehicle by which James struggled to avoid idealism and, most important, its universe, which is finished and struggle-free. As Bruce Kuklick put it, "James often saw that the issue between him and Royce hinged on their doctrines of possible experience" and the reality of possibility.[8] Consider: "There are hosts of *things which were never realized as we experience them* and as they figure in our philosophies" (MEN, 37; italics added). What are we to make of this? Well, yes and no. Yes: For James the ontological and not merely methodological radical empiricist, things simply are *as* we experience them or *as* we realize them. As experienced, they are. No: For this James, this does not mean that things are, or only are, at the time(s) *when* we experience them or *when* we realize them. We experience the mountains in California or a stained-glass window or a small dim light not as existing *independent in every way* from our experience; this would be self-contradictory and absurd. Rather, we experience them as existing *prior* to our experience and its discoveries. From the standpoint of the present, we experience the stars and the mountains,

---

[8] Bruce Kuklick, *The Rise of American Philosophy: Cambridge, Massachusetts, 1860–1930* (New Haven, CT: Yale University Press, 1977), 283.

the church window and the speck of light, as having come into existence prior to our experience (but not independent of our experience, such that we need to posit an eternal Absolute—whether in the Idealist form of God or the Naturalist's form of matter). From the standpoint of the prehuman past, we may say that the stars and mountains would have been humanly experienced long ago if there had been human experience at that time, that they were a possible but not actual content of experience. As James put it with respect to the stars:

> If we say that the great bear's configuration . . .[was] at all events slumberingly, latently, potentially, implicitly, or *virtually* there before they were expressly recognized by man, we admit everything that either party can lay claim to on practical grounds. The absolutist's claim, that they were actually thought-of before man, enables him to point to no particular results which the virtualist could not equally foresee and expect. When a thing is "virtually" known and named, that means that all the objective "conditions" for the act of knowing and naming are present, and only the act itself has yet to be supplied. (MEN, 37–38)

To say that the objective conditions for the act of experiencing were present is, of course, to say that these conditions are actually experienced now as having been present then. This is a point about experience, and not a claim about something independent of experience.

Near the end of this discussion, James threw out a familiar-sounding line (at least to persons who recall the squirrel story that opens *Pragmatism*): "The dispute between absolutism and pluralism seems thus to have no pragmatic importance at all" (MEN, 38). This, however, cannot be literally correct. James meant that both absolutist and pluralist agree on the (experienced) facts: We experience the stars and mountains as having existed prior to our experiencing them. To note this, though, is not to establish that there is no pragmatic difference between the views. The absolutist and the pluralist explain this fact differently—one makes experience "lean" on a God or Absolute or Spirit or Matter or One, while the other makes individual experiences lean only on other experiences—and this explanation is connected to, and enters into, the facts themselves. For James, the universe of the pluralist is neither complete nor fully known. It is a universe of parts and vagueness, of hindrances and experiments. Its outcomes and fortunes are still to be made, it has possibilities and genuine novelties, and it is a *struggle* with real and final losses as well as gains, a strenuous place that demands our energies and action.

However, this pluralistic universe or world of pure experience appeared to some rationalist critics to be little more in the end than traditional empiricism. It also appeared to some rationalist, realist critics to be dangerously close to traditional idealism. In part this was the result of a failure of imagination by James's critics—idealists who thought any view other than their own must be traditional empiricism, and empiricists who thought any view other than their own must be traditional idealism. But in another part this was the result of the fact that James himself characterized pure experience in more than one way or at least with more than one stress.

In "Does Consciousness Exist?," James's radical empiricism constitutes what amounts to a "duplicity-free experience thesis." James stressed that experience is a unity, an undifferentiated flux, and, as it takes place, has no "inner" duplicity or dualism. Experience is divided and categorized into consciousness and content only in subsequent reflective experience. On this thesis, the difference between consciousness and content (or subject and object) is a functional difference; they are not primordial different kinds of "things" but instead are ways of taking up an experience by some subsequent experience. They constitute a distinction, not a dualism. Experience is conjoined and disjoined in plural, overlapping ways, and these relations may be chopped up and grouped together to serve particular interests. The point is that "subject" and "object" are functions, not things. As Ralph Barton Perry put it, for James, "functionalism meant keeping constantly in view the total concrete individual, conceived as active and as occupying an environment."[9] Notions of subject and object are the results of reflection on experience rather than antecedent conditions of experience. This characterization of radical empiricism appeared to many of James's idealist critics as dangerously close to the sensationalism they attributed to traditional, run-of-the-mill, un-radical empiricists.

In partial contrast, in "The Thing and Its Relations," James stressed the immediacy of pure experience, what we might call an "immediacy of experience thesis." Here experiences are immediate and different; they are just what they are and not something else. On this view, the pure immediacy and flux of experience—of any experience—cannot be verbalized or classified. As a

---

[9] Ralph Barton Perry, *The Thought and Character of William James* (Westport, CT: Greenwood Press, 1974 [1935]), 2:51.

result, any description of any pure experience is literally impossible. The attempt to describe pure experience must miss its mark; it amounts to transformation, as the experience described is not the experience lived. Given this thesis, pure experience is a class name for a multitude of experiences that simply, immediately, and barely are, whatever and just what they are, and nothing properly may be predicated of them. This characterization of radical empiricism appeared to James's realist critics as dangerously close to the abstract unity of manyness that they attributed to idealism.

The criticism that James's pluralistic radically empiricism is internally or self-inconsistent and that it ends in solipsism was advanced by Dickinson Sergeant Miller and Boyd Henry Bode in published articles and correspondence.[10] James sought to respond to this criticism in the pages of two notebooks begun with entries dating from late 1905 until early 1908. Unlike "The Many and the One," James did not view his notes as his magnum opus and did not intend them for publication. He did view these notes as his sustained effort to think through and radically overhaul his entire philosophy.

As indicated, James viewed much of the criticism of his work as simple misunderstanding—as the effort to construe his work as one or the other of a pair of positions that he rejected entirely. And he viewed much other criticism as beginning with assumptions that he rejected and then demanding that his philosophy solve some problem consistent with those assumptions—and finally pointing out that it could not do so. By contrast, James took Miller and Bode to have identified a genuine tension or contradiction or difficulty *internal* to James's own way of thinking, to his own philosophy, to his own personal likes and dislikes. James thus referred to his working out a response to the "Miller-Bode Objections" as going "through" an "'inner catastrophe'"

[10] See B. H. Bode's essays: "'Pure Experience' and the External World" (1905), "Some Recent Definitions of Consciousness" (1908), and "'Pure Experience' and the External World" (1908) all in *Journal of Philosophy, Psychology and Scientific Methods* 2 (1908): 128–133. See also Dickinson Miller's "Naïve Realism: What Is It?," Essays Philosophical and Psychological in Honor of William James, by his colleagues at Columbia University (New York: Longmans, 1908), 231–262. James praised Bode's writing as "much the best critical piece of work the humanistic view has received" (ERE, 217, 219). From a very different perspective, this is similar to the criticism that John Wild made about the "defects" in James's radical empiricism, criticisms that in my judgment do not take note of James's rejection of the intellectualist point of view. See *The Radical Empiricism of William James* (Garden City, NY: Doubleday, 1969), 366–371. John McDermott, among others including John Dewey, called this change a "commentator's truism" and identified it in James's views: "James, while writing the *Principles*, had adopted a methodological dualism between self and world only because he would not resolve the question of consciousness at that time. It was not until some fifteen years later that James presents his mature position." "The Promethean Self and Community in the Philosophy of William James," in *Streams of Experience: Reflections on the History and Philosophy of American Culture* (Amherst: University of Massachusetts Press, 1986), 45.

and emerging from "intellectual bankruptcy" on a new, changed philosophical base. James's response in his notebooks to Miller and Bode issued in *A Pluralistic Universe*, James's final statement of his pluralism.

What were the "Miller-Bode Objections," at least according to James? Miller's and Bode's objections to James's radical empiricism consisted of the charge that James himself held simultaneously two *contradictory* views.

What are these two views? Most succinctly, the view that experience is *many*, multiple immediacies each qualitatively different from one another each in its very immediacy, *and* the view that experience is *one*, an undifferentiated, irreducibly unified flux or flow.

James's thesis that pure experience is irreducibly unified and has no inner duplicity is compatible with, indeed continuous with, three key points or analyses set forth in *The Principles of Psychology*. These analyses concern the impossibility of the compounding, or self-compounding, of consciousness or mental states or experience (PP, 160–164); the constant temporal change of all thought, states of mind, consciousness, or experience, such that no experience past or future can be identical to experience now (PP, 224–230), and the "insuperability of sensation thesis," for which knowledge about anything presupposes sensation—a function we must "postulate" whereby "we first become aware of the bare immediate natures by which our several objects are distinguished," something "all but impossible to adults with memories and stores of associations acquired" that collectively "supersede" and "displace" sensations (PP, 653, 657, 673). James's comments in *Principles of Psychology* on the logical impossibility of the compounding of consciousness are especially instructive and worth recalling at some length:

> One of the [most obscure] assumptions is the assumption that our mental states are composite in structure, made up of smaller states conjoined. This hypothesis has outward advantages [like removing the discontinuity in evolution pre- and post-consciousness] which make it almost irresistibly attractive to the intellect, and yet it is inwardly quite unintelligible. . . . We cannot mix feelings as such, though we may mix the objects we feel, and from *their* mixture get new feelings. We cannot even . . . have two feelings in our mind at once. At most we can compare together objects previously presented to us in distinct feelings; but then we find each object stubbornly maintaining its separate identity before consciousness, whatever the verdict of the comparison may be. But there is a still more fatal objection to the theory of mental units "compounding with themselves" or

"integrating." It is logically unintelligible; it leaves out the essential feature of all the "combinations" we actually know. *All the "combinations" we actually know are* EFFECTS, *wrought by the units said to be "combined,"* UPON SOME ENTITY OTHER THAN THEMSELVES. Without this feature of a medium or vehicle, the notion of combination has no sense. . . . In other words, no possible number of entities (call them as you like, whether forces, material particles, or mental elements) can sum themselves together. Each remains, in the sum, what it always was; and the sum itself exists only *for a bystander* who happens to overlook the units and to apprehend the sum as such; or else it exists in the shape of some other *effect* on an entity external to the sum itself. Let it not be objected that H_2 and O combine of themselves into "water," and thenceforward exhibit new properties. They do not. The "water" is just the old atoms in the new position, H-O-H; the "new properties" are just their combined *effects*, when in this position, upon external media, such as our sense-organs and the various reagents on which water may exerts its properties and be known. . . . The private minds do not agglomerate into a higher compound mind. . . . Idea of a, plus idea of b, are *not* identical with idea of (a + b). It is one, they are two; in it, what knows a also knows b; in them, what knows a is expressly posited as not knowing b; etc. In short, the two separate ideas can never by any logic be made to figure as one and the same thing as the "associated" idea. (PP, 148, 152, 160, 161, 163)

James's thesis that pure experience is immediate, just what it is and not anything else, readily raises critical worries about solipsism, the impossibility of two minds knowing one thing, and related epistemological matters. Because pure experience is what it is—and so is not what it is not—it is qualitatively different from everything else. It is qualitatively different from everything earlier or later rather than now, there rather than here, connected these ways rather than those, yours rather than mine, and so on. Accordingly, how can any two acts of consciousness or knowings or mental states or sensations have the *same* object? James recognized that an answer to this question required an account of objective reference—an account of the object of two or more mental states as somehow transcending those mental states or as identical in them. His account of this objective reference was an account of the ways in which different experiences point to the same object in the sense that they have common or "conterminous" or co-terminating experience or possible experience. But how is this possible for James? Given that experience is not a composite, even if two experiences had the same object, the object is not a component part of the two experiences. Each particular, different consciousnesses, each with its own history and relations, would be conscious of different objects, its objects, and not common objects, the same objects.

If consciousness is always changing, always in flux or stream, and if this changing can never include compounding, then—so the Miller-Bode objections would have it—sensation could never be displaced by knowledge and so experience would always be bare and immediate. Bode made the argument this way: Two minds can know one thing only if the one thing is numerically one and, thus, conterminous; but radical empiricism requires that the things of multiple minds always be qualitatively different and insists that they cannot be compounded; and because things that are qualitatively different logically cannot be numerically the same, radical empiricism cannot account for knowledge or for experience as other than bare sensation. Much of James's work in his notebooks here consisted of an effort to state just how this problem should be understood. James came at this issue in multiple ways, but it is clear that he understood the issue not primarily as an epistemological problem about the possibility of knowledge (of other people, or by different people of the same object), but instead as a problem of *the many and the one*: How can experience be many (qualitatively different from every other experience) and at the same time one (shared, common, compounded, objective, transcendent)?

James confronted unhappily what he took to be a choice forced on him by this criticism: the manyness of non-decomposable fields of consciousness or the oneness of common objects of knowledge. He wrote: "How can I rescue the situation? Which doctrine must I stand for?" (MEN, 65). Can two states of mind point to one terminus? James wanted to say yes, of course, but understood that "in a philosophy of pure experience, the terminus must be represented as a possible *terminating experience*":

> As such it must (whatever it may be actually before we get there) potentially and finally be an experience conterminous to us both. Our two several terminal fields must either stop *at* it, or both run *into* it and include it in such a wise that, though it is common to us both, the rest of the fields are cut off from each other. So the psychological difficulty recurs. It was only delayed a bit. *How can our two fields be units, if they contain this common part?* We must overhaul the whole business of connexion, confluence and the like, and do it radically. (MEN, 66)

This issue may be put another way: What is the relation of a fact to experience of that fact? Does the experience of the fact make a difference to the fact, to the very being of the fact? James observed that all of his writing has revolved around this difficulty, as Miller had put it to him (MEN, 75). Of course, if the experience of a fact is independent of the fact's being just the fact it is, then it would be easy to establish that there could be multiple experiences of the *same* fact. Experience, context, would be an "external addition" (MEN, 68)—something very much at odds with a view of experience as having no inner duplicity and, even more, as immediate. Again, James saw that this turn still left him pitted against himself:

> In *every* sensational object alteration occurs, & the doctrine of the psychology is true. . . . When the apperception varies . . . the object varies. . . How then can the pen be the "same" (no difference) if it figures in two minds? "By being transcendent!" ordinary "epistemology" will reply. But what does this word mean pragmatically except that *there shall be no difference* in what the minds mean. An experienced object, it is admitted, *can't* be the same *what*. Call it a transcendent object and it *can* be the same *that* at least. "Transcendency" in an object means (or *shall stand for*) inalterability, permanent identity, a property which it is supposed (or proved) that experiences taken in themselves can't have, and that consequently no object identified with any part or parts of experience can have. Now, rad. Empiricism insists that every object is identical with some part of experience. So if any degree of permanent identity is postulated by reason (as it is assumed by common sense) transcendency must also be postulated as its vehicle. (MEN, 69)

Put differently, James understood that he could not respond to Bode by making qualitative sameness the mark of numerical identity—because there is no qualitative sameness among different experiences (that are different precisely qualitatively). He could not claim that the experience of the pen makes no difference to the pen (MEN, 72). James despaired:

> If there is to be confluence (our hypothesis) there is no *logical* reason why the pen should be *qualitatively different* when confluent and when not confluent. On the contrary, it would then be *another* kind of pen, so it *must* be the same pen qualitatively. Is it then numerically other? That also would seem to violate the hypothesis. So the thought comes up:—Is the hypothesis

(of the same in different relations) absurd anyhow? Ought we never to have fallen for it. Bradley here claps his hands—"I told you so." But how is the absurdity relieved by lugging in the Absolute as its vehicle, and by saying "we don't just mean 'same' and we don't just mean 'relations' when we talk of absolute truth"? (MEN, 80)

Despair deepening, James considered a "scholastic" solu-tion: transcendent subjects or souls and transcendent objects, such that "the world of immediate experience is itself mediatorial between these two transcendencies" (MEN, 85). But, of course, James temperamentally and as a radical empiricist could not take this direction (MEN, 104). In December 1905 he noted he had made no progress and considered having to give up his heroic campaign. Returning six months later, he considered what he termed a "cosmic omnibus of being" for every experience in which "what is true *of* it is realized, while *it* realizes only what it is immediately of" (MEN, 97). This idea, surely far from clear and far from an advance, was quickly abandoned.

A few months later, although he had arrived at no resolution to the problem, his despair seemed to lift, and James observed:

> May not my whole trouble be due to the fact that I am still treating what is really a living and dynamic situation by logical and statical categories?

He continued:

> I ought not to be afraid to postulate activity and all that it involves in my account of all this mental union of the nevertheless distinct. (MEN, 104)

Unable to *resolve* the logical, intellectual problem of the many and the one, James had realized he must *dissolve* it.

4. Against Vicious Intellectualism

By treating living situations in dynamic practical terms—as activity— rather than static theoretical ones, James advanced a new account of pure experience and a new form of pluralism that allowed him to undercut the objections of both his realist and idealist critics.[11] James signaled this basic direction late in *The Principles of Psychology* by claiming that what he himself had identified as the central or elementary subject matter of psychology—states of consciousness—"are not verifiable facts" (or at least facts about which he could "feel sure") (PP, 400). As Gerald Myers noted, *The Principles of Psychology* "can be viewed as a logical step toward a metaphysics that interprets psychology more deeply than common sense can."[12] And so James suggested replacing concern with states of consciousness by a focus on an undifferentiated "sciousness" or pure experience that precedes reflective separations of states of consciousness and their objects (PP, 290–291).

This new account of pure experience and this new pluralism were more fully on display a couple of years after James had given up his notebook attempts to respond to the Miller-Bode objections. In a pair of 1908 articles, for example, Bode again took aim at James's radical empiricism.[13] He charged that radical empiricism, despite its intent, ultimately ends in solipsism because, first, it cannot give an account of objective reference—cannot escape the subjectivity and merely "biographical order" (ERE, 119) of experience—and in turn because, second, it cannot give an account of objective reference because it rejects all notions of transcendence of experience, notions required to explain its own account of the way in which some experiences "point" beyond themselves to others. Bode's argument may be summarized in this way: If no objective reference, then solipsism. If no pointing (of one experience beyond itself to others), then no objective reference. If no transcendence of experience, then no pointing. Radical empiricism denies transcendence of experience. Therefore, radical empiricism entails, or leads to, or is one form of, solipsism. If these problems are to be addressed, James needs to supply more detail, Bode concluded in a constructive tone.

---

[11] An upshot of this, I think, is that James's later radical empiricism and pluralism cannot be fully explained by means of categories drawn only from *The Principles of Psychology*. When this is attempted, James's rejection of both realism and anti-realism is missed—in matters of both ontology and morals. As an example, see Wesley Cooper, *The Unity of William James's Thought* (Nashville: Vanderbilt University Press, 2002), chap. 2. David Leary provided a very clear, very thorough account of precisely this dramatic shift in *The Routledge Guidebook to James's Principles of Psychology* (New York: Routledge, 2018), 214–221.

[12] Gerald E. Myers, *William James: His Life and Thought* (New Haven, CT: Yale University Press, 1986), 55.

[13] Bode, "'Pure Experience' and the External World"; Bode, "Some Recent Discussions of Consciousness," *Psychological Review* 15 (1908): 255–264.

James replied that Bode had misunderstood him. How?[14] James argued that Bode approached radical empiricism with at least three commitments that James had explicitly rejected: a representational view of knowledge, a dualistic view of reality, and an intellectualistic or "rationalistic" view of experience (which reduces experience to knowing and then regards the results of reflection having existed independent of, and antecedent to, reflection). Given this approach, James took Bode to be criticizing his philosophy for failing to account adequately for just what it denies. Thus, in "Is Radical Empiricism Solipsistic," James wrote:

> I suspect that he [Bode] performs on all these conjunctive relations (of which "pointing" is only one) the usual rationalistic act of substitution—he takes them not as they are given in their first intention, as part constitutive of experience's living flow, but only as they appear in retrospect, each fixed as a determinate object of conception, static, therefore, and contained within itself. (ERE, 120)

"Against this rationalistic tendency," James sought to demonstrate, in his reply to Bode, just what Bode claimed to be impossible for radical empiricism. James sought to *point*—to point beyond rationalistic tendencies (to "understand backwards")—to experience as it takes place, flows, transitions, continues:

> Consider, for example, such conjunctions as "and," "with," "near," "*plus*," "towards." While we live in such conjunctions our state is one of *transition* in the most literal sense. We are expectant of "more" to come, and before the more has come, the transition, nevertheless, is directed *towards* it. I fail otherwise to see how, if one kind of more comes, there should be satisfaction and feeling of fulfillment; but disappointment if the more comes in another shape. One more will continue, another more will arrest or deflect the direction, in which our experience is moving even now. We can not, it is true, *name* our different living "ands" or "withs" except

---

[14] Robert J. Roth claimed that James addressed this sort of issue by developing an account of "transcendence and immanence"—with an emphasis here on the "and." In contrast, the view I set forth takes James to have rejected the entire either/or dualism of transcendence/immanence as an abstraction. See Roth's chaps. 4, 5, and 6 in *Radical Pragmatism: An Alternative* (New York: Fordham University Press, 1998).

by naming the different terms towards which they are moving us, but we *live* their specifications and difference before those terms explicitly arrive. (ERE, 120–121)

Bode claimed, at a crucial step in his argument (as James took it), that *pointing* requires the transcendence of experience. In response, James explained—pointed out—that experience itself includes pointing. This is a fact of, and in, experience rather than a mark of the transcendence of experience by, or in, knowing. In other words, the process by which an experience points beyond itself or is "transcended" "occurs within experience" as the mediation of some experience by other experience. "Epistemology," James concluded, takes this pointing or conjoining or transcending to be immediate or super-empirical—the only options open to it given that it has rendered relations into "static objects" (ERE, 121).

It is revealing that James supposed his quarrel with Bode might be "purely verbal." He viewed Bode as a fellow fighter for "the same continuities of experience in different forms of words" (ERE, 121–122). Bode can get the objective reference and commonsense world he wants if he will just give up his representationalism, dualism, and rationalism—if he will move away from what John Dewey later called "the epistemology industry" and move toward a pluralistic radical empiricism. James's supposition strikes a tone very different from his responses to thinkers he identified as monists and absolutists. In these cases, James took the disputes not to be purely verbal or purely logical but, instead, something deeper. He observed:

> It costs nothing, not even a mental effort, to admit that the absolute totality of things may be organized exactly after the pattern of one of these "through-and-through" abstractions. In fact, it is the pleasantest and freest of mental movements. (ERE, 139)

But logic, rational thought, dialectic, conceptual analysis, and so on— intellectualism—cannot, James stressed, show us that any such system that logically *might* be real *actually* is real. James noted:

> Logic may determine what the system must be, *if* it is, [but] something else than Logic must tell us *that* it is. . . . The question "Shall Fact be recognized as an ultimate principle?" is the whole issue between the Rationalists and the Empiricism of vulgar thought. (ERE, 139, 140)

Facts, in a world of pure experience, have an irreducibly affective dimension. James thus construed the dispute between absolutist and pluralist as in large measure a reflection of difference in affective experience. Is rationalism or absolutism or monism, James asked, "anything more than a fantastic dislike" of fact (ERE, 141)? If so, James asked honestly: "But, dislike for dislike, who shall decide? Why is not their dislike at having me 'from' them, entirely on a par with mine at having them 'through' me?" He immediately added: "I feel sure that likes and dislikes must be among the ultimate factors of their philosophy as well as of mine":

> We should both then [if this were admitted] be avowedly making hypotheses, playing with Ideals. Ah! Why is the notion of hypothesis so abhorrent to the Hegelian mind? . . . [W]e might go on and frankly confess to each other the motives for our several faiths. I frankly confess mine—I cannot but think that at bottom they are of an aesthetic and not a logical sort. (ERE, 141, 142)

Then, in a brilliant and appropriately personal passage, he concluded:

> I show my feeling; why *will* they not show theirs? I know they have a personal feeling about the through-and-through universe, which is entirely different from mine, and which I should very likely be much the better for gaining if they would only show me how. Their persistence in telling me that feeling has nothing to do with the question, that it is a pure matter of absolute reason, keeps me forever out of the pale. Still seeing a *that* in things which Logic does not expel, the most I can do is to *aspire* to the expulsion. At present I do not even aspire. Aspiration is a feeling. What can kindle feeling but the example of feeling? And if the Hegelians *will* refuse to set an example, what can they expect the rest of us to do? To speak more seriously, the one *fundamental* quarrel Empiricism has with Absolutism is over this repudiation by Absolutism of the personal and aesthetic factor in the construction of philosophy. That we all have feelings, Empiricism feels quite sure. (ERE, 142–143)

In responding to his critics, both those who were tender-minded idealists and those who were tough-minded realists, James explained over and over that radical empiricism does not suffer from logical contradictions or dialectical flaws or rational inconsistencies. Radical empiricism, for James, is free of invalid inferences and self-contradiction. It is rational. But for James, rationality is a sentiment of personal satisfaction. In this light, a philosophy is an instrument for living. If one combines this view with the belief that, in fact, there are multiple aesthetic factors and personal satisfactions, then one is led from the relations and conjunctions and pluralities within experience to the plurality of experiences and, thus, to a pluralistic universe, a veritable multiverse.

This focus on a philosophy as an instrument for satisfactory living, for the dynamic and experienced sentiment of rationality, lies at the heart of James's pluralism, radical empiricism, and pragmatism:

> A pragmatist turns his back resolutely once and for all upon a lot of invet-
> erate habits dear to professional philosophers. He turns away from abstrac-
> tion and insufficiency, from verbal solutions, from bad a priori reasons,
> from fixed principles, closed systems, and pretended absolutes and origins.
> He turns toward concreteness and adequacy, toward facts, towards action,
> and towards power. That means the empiricist temper regnant, and the ra-
> tionalist temper sincerely given up. It means the open air and possibilities
> of nature, as against dogma, artificiality and the pretence of finality in truth.
> (P, 29)

James's pluralism presupposes and goes hand in hand with his rejection of abstraction, absolutism, any view of reason that disconnects it from the purposes and interests of the reasoner, and intellectualism.

Moreover, James's criticism of intellectualism was not a rejection of the very real and very practical value of theory or the need to develop and employ thought-out methods—what Dewey later called "the method of intelligence." It was, instead, a rejection of the view that human knowledge is wholly derived from reason and that things are only as and what they are conceived to be. James often called this "vicious intellectualism" or "vicious abstractionism"—metaphysics overrun by words and concepts and restricted to the particulars we have named.[15] As F. Thomas Burke put it: "Pragmatism is thus not anti-intellectual. It is anti-intellectualist."[16] Horace Kallen had

---

[15] John J. McDermott provided a useful account of this in the context of James's development of his thought in his "Introduction" to *Essays in Radical Empiricism* (ERE, xx). And in his "Introduction" to *A Pluralistic Universe*, Richard J. Bernstein discussed this in the context of James's view of philosophies as personal visions (APU, xiv).

[16] F. Thomas Burke. *What Pragmatism Was* (Bloomington: Indiana University Press, 2013), 155.

expanded on this point in his 1960 assessment of James, the intellectual, and the modern world. Kallen's way of putting this bears repetition:

> The words "intellect," intellectual," "intelligence," "intelligent," are no longer synonymous. The first two signify the strengths and the skills of the Word; the second the strengths and skills of the Hand and the Word together. As against the ultimate knowledge which is vision only, they set the tentative knowings which are vision and power both. "Intellectual" continues to connote the superiorities of the authoritarian wordman as usual inspecting existence, judging and deprecating and denouncing it as insufficient and unreliable, Taking no part in the unceasing struggle to render it sufficient and reliable.
>
> "Intelligent" now tends to connote the wordman whose vision is a faith which compenetrates his action and lives in his works; his research, on whatever level, is action-research in an open world without foregone conclusions where events, however they come, are appraised by what they lead to and not by "first principles."

James, Kallen claimed, was "the sage who first prized intelligence above intellect without undervaluing intellect."[17]

In "Abstractionism and 'Relativismus,'" James called vicious intellectualism "one of the great original sins of the rationalistic mind" and clearly defined it:

> Let me give the name of "vicious abstractionism" to a way of using concepts which may be thus described: We conceive a concrete situation by singling out some salient or important feature in it, and classing it under that; then, instead of adding to its previous characters all the positive consequences which the new way of conceiving may bring, we proceed to use our concept privately; reducing the originally rich phenomenon to the naked suggestions of that name abstractly taken, treating it as a case of "nothing but" that concept, and acting as if all the other characters from out of which the concept is abstracted were expunged. . . . It mutilates things; it creates difficulties and finds impossibilities; and more than half the trouble that metaphysicians and logicians give themselves over the paradoxes and

---

[17] Horace M. Kallen, "The Modern World, the Intellectual, and William James," *Western Political Quarterly* 13, no. 4 (1960): 869, 870.

dialectic puzzles of the universe may, I am convinced, be traced to this relatively simple source. (MT, 135)

Now, James did not mount—and could not consistently have mounted—an abstract, intellectualist argument against intellectualism. Nowhere in any of James's writings is there a formal, logical proof against intellectualism. James's critics who judged that he failed to provide a successful abstract proof against monism or idealism were right. He did not. Of course, it is difficult to succeed at a task that one is determined not to even take up. Instead, he argued that if his pluralism was to be genuinely pragmatic—if it was to be fact-loving and empirical—he had to give up intellectualism and its fixed conceptions and dialectical physics. He had to give up static logic for dynamic lives. He thus wrote that he found himself "compelled to *give up the logic*, fairly, squarely, and irrevocably" (APU, 96). Why? He replied:

Reality, life, experience, concreteness, immediacy, use what word you will, exceeds our logic, overflows and surrounds it . . . so I prefer bluntly to call reality if not irrational then at least non-rational in its constitution. (APU, 97)

James here replaced a static point of view with a dynamic point of view—his "insuperability of sensation" thesis. Conceptualizing or discursifying experience renders it fixed and static, turns it into an instance of an unchanging whole, category, or class from the perspective of which it is only what it is thought to be. It is for this reason, as William Gavin observed, that "more and more, James became suspicious of language."[18] James claimed the story of intellectualism is an old one. It is a story of "a useful practice first becoming a method, then a habit, and finally a tyranny that defeats the end it was used for." James continued:

Concepts, first employed to make things intelligible, are clung to even when they make them unintelligible. Thus it comes that when you have conceived things as "independent." You must proceed to deny the possibility of any connexion whatever among them, because the notion of connexion is not contained in the definition of independence. . . . The definitions are

---

[18] William Joseph Gavin, *William James and the Reinstatement of the Vague* (Philadelphia: Temple University Press, 1992), 85.

contradictory, so the things defined can in no way be united. You see how unintelligible intellectualism here seems to make the world of our most accomplished philosophers. Neither as they use it nor as we use it does it do anything but make nature look irrational and seem impossible. (APU, 99, 100)

Vicious intellectualism must be cleared away so as to make possible any verification of pluralism. What is at stake here, and how, if at all, is it possible to proceed in a non-question-begging manner? In his 1910 essay for the *Journal of Philosophy, Psychology, and Scientific Methods*, "Bradley or Bergson," James returned to this theme by noting that for both Bergson and Bradley, "sense-perception first develops into conception; and then conception developing its subtler and more contradictory implications, comes to an end of its usefulness for both authors, and runs itself into the ground" (EP, 152). James then contrasted sharply these two thinkers. Discussing Bergson, he wrote:

Bergson *drops* conception—which apparently has done us all the good it can do; and turning back towards perception with its transparent multiplicity-in-union, he takes its data integrally up into philosophy, as a kind of material which nothing else can replace. The fault of our perceptual data, he tells us, is not of nature, but only of extent; and the way to know reality intimately is, according to this philosopher, to sink into those data and *get our sympathetic imagination to enlarge their bounds. Deep* knowledge is not of the conceptually mediated, but of the immediate type. Bergson thus allies himself with old-fashioned empiricism, on the one hand, and with mysticism, on the other. His breach with rationalism could not possibly be more thorough than it is. (EP, 152)

Moving next to Bradley, the idealist philosopher, James aimed to pinpoint Bradley's principal difference from Bergson. Primarily quoting Bradley at some length to allow him to speak in his own words, James claimed that Bradley understood that "concepts are an organ of misunderstanding rather than of understanding, that they 'turn the "reality" which we "encounter" into an "appearance" which we "think."'" Bradley thus came face-to-face with "anti-rationalist *matter*[s]" but, James judged, held to "anti-empirical *manner*[s] to the end." James explained this view and also what he took to be its crucial limits:

Crude unmediated feelings shall never form a part of "truth." "Judgment, on our view," he writes, "transcends and must transcend that immediate unity of feeling upon which it cannot cease to depend. Judgment has to qualify the Real ideally. . . . This is the fundamental inconsistency of judgment. . . . For ideas cannot qualify reality as reality is qualified immediately in feeling. . . . The reality as conditioned in feeling has been in principle abandoned, while other conditions have not been found." Abandoned in "principle," Mr. Bradley says; and, in sooth, nothing but a sort of religious principle against admitting "untransformed" feeling into philosophy would seem to explain his procedure from here onwards. "At the entrance of philosophy," he says, "there appears to be a point where the roads divide. By the one way you set out to seek truth in ideas . . . if you choose to take this way . . . no possible appeal to designation [i.e., to feeling] in the end is possible. . . . This I take to be the way of philosophy. . . . It is not the way of life or of common knowledge . . . [which] rests on dependence on feeling. . . . Outside of philosophy there is no consistent course but to accept the unintelligible. . . . For worse or for better the man who stands on particular feeling must remain outside of philosophy. . . . I recognize that in life and in ordinary knowledge one can never wholly cease to rest on this ground. But how to take over into ultimate theory and to use there this certainty of feeling, *while still leaving that untransformed*, I myself do not know how. I admit that philosophy, as I conceive it, is onesided. I understand the dislike of it and the despair of it while this its defect is not remedied. But to remedy the defect by importing bodily into philosophy the 'this' and 'mine,' as they are felt, to my mind brings destruction on the spot." (EP, 153)

James just shook his head at all this. Instead of dropping the view that truth is an improvement on reality, Bradley sided with supposedly transexperiential truth. James called this a religious loyalty, and suggested that thinkers who note that their philosophy parts company with life are thereby not recommending their philosophy. James added: "Not to enter life is *a higher vocation* than to enter it, on this view" (EP, 154). By contrast, Bergson and empirical pluralists, in James's rhapsodic phrase, "tumble to life's call, and turn into the valley where the green pastures and the clear waters always were":

When the alternative lies between knowing life in its full thickness and activity, as one acquainted with its *me's* and *thee's* and *now's* and *here's*, on the one hand, and knowing a transconceptual evaporation like the absolute, on the other, it seems to me that to choose the latter knowledge merely because it has been named "philosophy" is to be superstitiously loyal to a name. But if names are to be used eulogistically, rather let us give that of philosophy to the fuller kind of knowledge, the kind in which perception and conception mix their lights. (EP, 155)[19]

If Bradley's religion is not that of Bergson or that of James, is it problematic for being "religious" in some manner that Bergson's or James's own strongest commitments are not problematic? How should a thoroughgoing pluralist respond to this question? Or, as James parted company with Bradley's religious intellectualism here, did he also part company with Bergson's religious mysticism? Moreover, if Bradley did hold his rationalism and intellectualism on grounds that he acknowledged in the end are not rational or intellectual (but instead a matter of choice and will), is his James-labeled rationalism or intellectualism actually less rational or intellectual, or less viciously so, than otherwise would be the case? Is this principally a matter of temperament, of personality, of working attitude, of preference, of vision, of finding one's home in different bits of the universe (and all the other sorts of things that James notes in "The Types of Philosophic Thinking" at the opening of *A Pluralistic Universe*)?

Second, James pointed out the sharp distinction that Bradley drew between the way of philosophy, as Bradley understood it, and the way of common life; between reality and appearance; and between the rational absolute one and feeling multiplicities. And he then quickly pointed out that to draw a distinction between two things is not, thereby, to provide any reason at all for preferring one over the other. Granting James this logical— even intellectualist—point, does it not apply also to the contrast that James draws between the full thickness of life and the trans-conceptual evaporation of the absolute; the distinction he draws between radical empiricism and absolutism; and the distinction he draws between feeling multiplicities and rational absolute? Just as Bradley's statement of alternatives provides, by itself, no argument for choosing one or the other of them, according

[19] In this context Paul K. Conkin judged James "less a Puritan than any other American pragmatist" in part because he was "too swayed by diverse, often European influences." *Puritans and Pragmatists: Eight Eminent American Thinkers* (Waco, TX: Baylor University Press, 2005 [1976]), 344. See also H. S. Thayer, "Pragmatism in Europe: Alliances and Misalliances," part III of his *Meaning and Action: A Critical History of Pragmatism* (Indianapolis, IN: Hackett, 1981 [1968]), 270–347.

to James, does not James's own statement of alternatives of pluralism and monism also, by itself, provide no argument for choosing one or the other of them? James's contrast of Bradley and Bergson was not intended as an argument for either; it was intended as a tracing out of the respective practical consequences of each view. James was not providing an intellectualist proof; he was providing practical clarification, employing the pragmatic method.

Third, suppose this choice pressed upon us anyway: Bradley or Bergson, monism or pluralism, idealism or radical empiricism, intellectualism or pragmatism. If one were choosing on the basis merely of this articulation of alternatives, would doing so not be mere superstitious loyalty to a name, one name or the other? Once more, recall how James began *A Pluralistic Universe*: "Everyone is nevertheless prone to claim that his conclusions are the only logical ones, that they are necessities of universal reason, they being all the while, at bottom, accidents more or less of personal vision which had far better be avowed as such" (APU, 10). And James added this intellectualist-sounding note: "What distinguishes a philosopher's truth is that it is reasoned. Argument, not supposition, must have put it in his possession" (APU, 11).

What, then, was Bergson's (and James's) *argument*, his critique, against intellectualism? James took Bergson not to have solved a problem (common to idealists and traditional empiricists) but, rather, to have found a way around it:

Monistic idealists after Kant have invariably sought relief from the supposed contradictions of our world of sense by looking forward towards an *ens rationis* conceived as its integration or logical completion. . . . Pluralistic empiricists, on the other hand, have remained in the world of sense, either naively or because they overlooked the intellectualistic contradictions, or because, not able to ignore them, they thought they could refute them by a superior use of the same intellectualistic logic. . . . The important point to notice here is the relation of both sides to the intellectualist logic. Both treat it as authoritative, but they do so capriciously: the absolutists smashing the world of sense by its means, the empiricists smashing the absolute—for the absolute, they say, is the quintessence of all logical contradictions. Neither side attains consistency. . . . Each party uses it or drops it to suit the vision it has faith in, but neither impugns in principle its general theoretic authority. Bergson alone challenges its theoretic authority in principle. He alone denies that mere conceptual logic can tell us what is impossible or possible in the world of being or fact. (APU, 108–109)

Bergson, as James read him (and as James read many other writers), is a pragmatist who, like all genuine pragmatists, holds that "the conceptual method is a transformation which the flux of life undergoes at our hands in the interests of practice primarily, and only subordinately in the interests of theory" (APU, 109). Here is a crucial point: Conceptualization and its logic become "vicious intellectualism" *only* when this fact of transformation is not acknowledged. When this transformation is not acknowledged, reality appears to be thin and ready-made (indeed, already-made), thinking appears to be only computation and calculation, and life appears to be without struggle in an open future. James wrote:

> To understand life by concepts is to arrest its movement, cutting it up into bits as if with scissors, and immobilizing these in our logical herbarium where, comparing them as dried specimens, we can ascertain which of them statically includes or excludes which other. This treatment supposes life to have already accomplished itself, for the concepts, being so many views taken after the fact, are retrospective and post mortem. (APU, 109)

And so philosophy, for James, must avoid being a tidy, neat, and clear post mortem for experiences and lives. The Bergsonian alternative, as James put it, is to "dive back into the flux itself"; "turn your face toward sensation, that flesh-bound thing which rationalism has always loaded with abuse"; attend to the "continuously changing character" of life which can no more be caught by concepts than water can be caught by nets; recognize that "static cuts" made in experienced duration are instruments for navigating that duration rather than more real or higher-order substitutes for it; and not confuse a "conceptual decomposition" of life for life itself (APU, 112–114). These instructions all are of a piece with James's earlier account of his project in *The Principles of Psychology*: "It is, in short, the re-instatement of the vague to its proper place in our mental life which I am so anxious to press on the attention" (PP, 246).[20]

---

[20] For a thorough account of the notion of vagueness across James's writings, see *Gavin, William James and the Reinstatement of the Vague*. See also Gavin's "William James, 1842–1910," in *The Blackwell Guide to American Philosophy*, edited by Armen T. Marsoobian and John Ryder (Malden, MA: Blackwell, 2004), 101–116.

Sometimes James described this contrast as a contrast between "two ways of knowing" that are "best summed up in the intellectualist doctrine that 'the same cannot exist in many relations,'" the thesis of the identity of contra-dictories (APU, 116). I suspect this is an overly intellectualist and reason-centered way of stating the contrast, and one ultimately at odds with James's own view. More often he described the contrast as one between experience and knowledge, between the ongoing reconstruction of reality that is living and the fixed decompositions that are concepts of reality:

> When you have broken the reality into concepts you never can reconstruct it in its wholeness. Out of no amount of discreteness can you manufacture the concrete. . . . So it is with every concrete thing, however complicated. Our intellectual handling of it is a retrospective patchwork, a post-mortem dissection, and can follow any order we find most expedient. . . . But place yourself at the point of view of the thing's interior doing, and all these back-looking and conflicting conceptions lie harmoniously in your hand. Get at the expanding centre of a human character, the *élan vital*, of a man, as Bergson calls it, by living sympathy, and at a stroke you see how it makes those who see it from without interpret it in such diverse ways. (APU, 117).

This passage echoes James's account of plural ways of knowing and his famous distinction between conceptual "knowing that" and embodied "knowing how." This recognition of multiple, different ways of knowing, I think, does not require us (or James) to believe that a thing has an "inte-rior doing" at the point of which we can place ourselves. In fact, this whole notion of "interiority" readily appears to be a kind of intellectualist hang-over. For a pluralist, pragmatist, radical empiricist, isn't it enough to claim that realities are different and plural, none more intimate, more sympathetic, more really real independent of particular purposes? Might not pragmatism be able to live, as Deleuze described in *The Logic of Sense*, wholly at the sur-face, in a pluriverse of surfaces without depths? If, as James wrote, "we know the inner movements of our spirit only perceptually," then can't we hold that these movements too "lie along the world of space" and practical adaptation (APU, 111)? This would make possible an account of life's meanings and illuminations and its nonsense and opacities that has nothing in common with either Bradley's "religious" commitments or Bergson's "mysticism." And it would be an understanding of intimacy not as some kind of pantheism but a kind of "pan-surfacism."

Bergson or Bradley, pragmatism or intellectualism, pluralism or monism: James recommended the Bergsonian alternative, and closed by telling his audience to become again "as foolish little children in the eyes of reason" (APU, 121). Such children, I suspect, do not engage in "critique" any more than in dialectics or the games of Plato, Spinoza, Kant, Fichte, Hegel, Marx, or Adorno. Does James present any argument for this? Once again, no, I think not—at least not in any normal sense of the word "critique," at least not in any way that goes beyond articulating a revolution and permitting himself to hope that his audience may share his desire for it and help to bring it about (APU, 122). Santayana's observation is spot-on here:

> I think it is important to remember, if we are not to misunderstand William James, that his radical empiricism and pragmatism were in his own mind only methods; his doctrine, if he may be said to have had one, was agnosticism. . . . All faiths were what they were experienced as being in their capacity as faiths; these faiths, not their objects, were the hard facts we must respect.[21]

As a result, the intellectualist is bound to be disappointed at this performance. That disappointment, in turn, only sharpens the contrast between the way in which James philosophized and the way in which, for example, Bradley, Royce, and Hegel philosophized. It is tempting here to turn toward the discrete rather than the concrete, to pick out James's concepts, propositions, arguments. Indeed, James himself suggested an alternative, an alternative that we might apply to James himself and that we might ask James to apply not only to the Bergsons of the world but also to its Bradleys, Royces, and Hegels. James suggested:

> Place yourself similarly at the centre of a man's philosophic vision and you understand at once all the different things it makes him write or say. But keep outside, use your post-mortem method, try to build the philosophy up out of the single phrases, taking first one and then another and seeking to make them fit "logically," and of course you fail. You crawl over the thing like a myopic ant over a building, tumbling into every microscopic crack

---

[21] George Santayana, "William James," in *Character and Opinion in the United States* (New York: W. W. Norton, 1967 [1920]), 75–76. Vincent Colapietro has provided an insightful analysis of Santayana and James and the art of one philosopher painting the philosophy of another in his "Philosophical Portraiture: George Santayana's 'William James,'" *Limbo* 40 (2020): 43–61.

or fissure, finding nothing but inconsistencies, and never suspecting that a centre exists. I hope that some of the philosophers in this audience may occasionally have had something different from this type of criticism applied to their own works! (APU, 117)

The point is to *not* conceptually decompose James—or anyone or anything else—and then pretend the result was real prior to and independent of the purposes and acts of decomposition. If James's philosophy—or anyone's philosophy or, more important still, any experience—is merely broken into concepts and doctrines, its vision, its wholeness, can never be reconstructed.

5. Multiplicity and Non-Abstract Differences

If one approaches James "from the outside," his pluralism may appear to be an answer to the traditional, old-fashioned question about how many things there are in the universe. Is there one kind of thing, or two or three or seven, or forty-three, or two million and ten, or indefinitely many? James, who called his own view both "pluralism" and "neutral monism," did not answer this question. He rejected the question and urged everyone else to do the same. Or, put differently, he reconstructed the theoretical, ontological issue (how many kinds of things are there in the world?) into a practical, functional issue (how many kinds of things is it useful to distinguish for a given purpose?). As noted above, James thought that the number of things we distinguish or the number of categories we employ depends entirely on our purpose and interest: "Neither [oneness or manyness] is primordial or more essential or excellent than the other.... [S]ometimes one function and sometimes the other is what comes home to us most" (P, 68). It is not a question of the one *or* the many; it is a question of the one *and* the many, a question of sometimes the one and sometimes the many, *depending on the given interest and purposes.* Accordingly, James's pluralism, radical empiricism, and pragmatism are not better answers to old problems; they are engagements with new problems of practical relations.

This is a point that French philosopher Jean Wahl stressed in *The Pluralist Philosophies of England and America,* a book mostly about William James. Recognizing insightfully that James turned ontological issues into functional ones, Wahl called James a "teleological pluralist" and observed:

To his [James's] mind, a philosophy is . . . an expression of temperament. . . . We must insist on the fact that love of detail in James is always accompanied with respect for the concrete whole. . . . This does not set up the dilemma between absolute unity and absolute diversity, and they are not incompatible, but rather complementary. . . . Pluralism, realism, the pragmatist theory of knowledge, the theory of possibility, the theory of time, all these different conceptions of William James are aspects of this affirmation of the externality of relations. . . . [I]n *A Pluralistic Universe* there is a change in one very important point. Whereas previously James sometimes opposed monism almost as an intellectualist, and with rationalistic weapons, in *A Pluralistic Universe*, he uses those given to him by anti-intellectualism and seems even to be an opponent of monism, not so much because it is a doctrine of unity as because it then appears to him a doctrine of the intellect. . . . Gradually James gives away the idea that the real is conformable to principles. . . . The anti-intellectualism of James is one aspect of his empiricism . . . that closely approaches the theories of Bergson.[22]

This line of thought has been developed and extended by one of Wahl's well-known students, Gilles Deleuze. Deleuze remarked that at the center of Bergson's philosophic vision, "the notion of multiplicity saves us from thinking in terms of 'One and Multiple.' " He explained:

There are many theories in philosophy that combine the one and the multiple. They share the characteristic of claiming to reconstruct the real with general ideas. We are told that the Self is one (thesis) and it is multiple (antithesis), then it is the unity of the multiple (synthesis). Or else we are told that One is already multiple, that Being passes into nonbeing and produces becoming. The passages where Bergson condemns this movement of abstracts are among the finest in his oeuvre. To Bergson, it seems that in this type of dialectical method, one begins with concepts that, like baggy clothes, are much too big. The One in general, the multiple in general, nonbeing in general . . . In such cases the real is recomposed with abstracts; but of what use is a dialectic that believes itself to be reunited with the real when it compensates for the inadequacy of a concept that is too broad or

---

[22] Jean Wahl, *Pluralist Philosophies of England and America*, translated by Fred Rothwell (London: Open Court, 1925), 117, 118, 139, 144, 148, 156, 158. See also H. S. Thayer's account of James's view of mind as teleological, *Meaning and Action: A Critical History of Pragmatism* (Indianapolis, IN: Hackett, 1981 [1968]), 141–145.

too general by invoking the opposite concept, which is no less broad and general? The concrete will never be attained by combining the inadequacy of one concept with the inadequacy of its opposite. The singular will never be attained by correcting a generality with another generality.[23]

At this point, the philosophical resonance between Deleuze and James is very large indeed.[24] The above passage strongly echoed James's warning that "when you have broken the reality into concepts you never can reconstruct it in its wholeness. Out of no amount of discreteness can you manufacture the concrete" (APU, 116)

Deleuze's self-professed radical empiricism is equally in evidence in his analysis of pluralism in terms of difference rather than negation. He wrote:

Two forms of the negative are often distinguished: The negative of simply limitation and the negative of opposition. We are assured that the substitution of the second form for the first by Kant and the post-Kantians was a revolution in philosophy. It is all the more remarkable that Bergson, in his critique of the negative, condemns both forms. Both seem to him to involve and to demonstrate the same inadequacy. For if we consider negative notions like *disorder or nonbeing*, their very conception . . . amounts to the same thing as our conceiving of them in opposition to being and order; as forces that exercise power and combine with their opposites to produce (synthetically) all things. Bergson's critique is thus a double one insofar as it condemns, in both forms of the negative, the same ignorance of *differences in kind*, which are sometimes treated as "deteriorations," sometimes as oppositions. The heart of Bergson's project is to think differences in kind independently of all forms of negation. (B, 46)

I take this to be, or at least to parallel in an important way, the Jamesian project of thinking manyness independently of the form of not-oneness. James's pluralistic universe is, I think, a universe of differences in kind, a universe of multiplicities rather than a universe of one *or* many or even one *and* many. It is a reality or world of different and dynamic relations.

---

[23] Gilles Deleuze, *Bergsonism*, translated by Hugh Tomlinson and Barbara Habberjam (New York: Zone Books, 1988 [1966]), 44. Further references to this book are in text and abbreviated B followed by page number(s).

[24] Kennan Ferguson charted some of the lines of historical influence and philosophical similarities between James and Bergson, and then James and Deleuze, in "La Philosophie Américaine" in his *William James: Politics in the Pluriverse* (Lanham, MD: Rowman and Littlefield, 2007), 51–71.

In this context of Bergson, Deleuze asked, "What has happened?" He answered: "Undoubtedly the confrontation with the theory of Relativity" (B, 79). However, in books like *Time and Free Will*, Bergson repeatedly cited James (rather than Einstein)—even as James returned the favor in his own writing. No one, no many. No rationalism, no empiricism. No object except as for some subject, no subject except directed at some object. No consciousness, no things. No mere conjunction or mere disjunction. These are all intellectual abstractions, intellectualist products of failing to recognize that abstractions are the results of abstracting activities, not realities antecedent to and independent of those activities. James's "relativity theory," his radically plural theory of relations, the dynamic continuity and discontinuity of experience, of things—different things, things in the making rather than things made—is the consequence of recognition of this fact. As such, it is a recommendation that still largely awaits adoption in philosophy.

6. Pluralism After Intellectualism

Here is how James put this recommendation in the penultimate chapter, "The Continuity of Experience," in *A Pluralistic Universe*:

> On the principle of going behind the conceptual function altogether, however, and looking to the more primitive flux of the sensational life for reality's true shape, a way is open to us . . . Not only the absolute is its own other, but the simplest bits of immediate experience are their own others, if that hegelian phrase be once for all allowed. The concrete pulses of experience appear pent in by no such definite limits as our conceptual substitutes for them are confined by. They run into one another continuously and seem to interpenetrate. What to them is relation and what is matter related is hard to discern. . . . There is no datum so small as not to show this mystery, if mystery it be. The tiniest feeling that we can possibly have comes with an earlier and a later part and with a sense of their continuous procession. . . . Here, then, inside of the minimal pulses of experience, is realized that very inner complexity which the transcendentalists say only the absolute can genuinely possess. . . . You cannot separate the same from its other, except by abandoning the real altogether and taking to the conceptual system. (APU, 127–128)

However, if anytime one takes "to the conceptual system"—if anytime one thinks, reasons, theorizes, interprets, deliberates, discursifies, distinguishes, names, or categorizes—how is it possible to "go behind" this system? If this cannot be done by, and in, thought and reason, how can it be done? How is it possible to engage in some sort of "looking for the more primitive flux of the sensational life for reality's true shape" and "inner complexity" and "wider self" (APU, 127)? "Every bit of us," James wrote, "at every moment is part and parcel of a wider self." And then, returning to the line of thought he introduced via Fechner, James added: "And just as we are co-conscious with our own momentary margin, may not we ourselves form the margin of some more really central self in things which is co-conscious with the whole of us? May not you and I be confluent in a higher consciousness, and confluently active there, though we now know it not" (APU, 131)? I think that James's desire that a "higher consciousness" exists—or at least his desire that this be a live possibility—is at work in his introduction of this idea of a pure flux of sensation, in which this higher consciousness remains permanently a possibility even though it is unknown to us now as we lead lives of our narrower selves. James's point here, against both intellectualistic rationalists and intellectualistic empiricists, was that there is nothing self-contradictory or logically impossible about this hypothesis and that it, therefore, awaits testing (somehow) in experience for verification or not. What sort of experience would this be? Is this really possible, or is it just an unfulfillable dream of some would-be mystics?

These are important questions for any worldview, but they are very difficult, even odd, questions for pragmatists because they appear to presuppose two related but different commitments that pragmatists strongly reject. First, pluralistic and radically empirical pragmatism is at odds with the very notions of "the more primitive flux of sensational life," its "true shape," and the "inner complexity" of reality. The idea that some experience (call it "sensational life") is *more real* or more basic or more "primitive" than other experience (call it "intellectual life") runs counter to the democratic nature of radical empiricism. Radical empiricism treats *all* experience as equally real and rejects the metaphysical *Animal Farm* view that all experiences are real but some are more real than the others. For radical empiricism, accounting, studying medical lab reports, and thinking hard while reading a philosophy book are no less real, no less part of "reality's true shape," than looking at a lake, perceiving a superior (arctic) mirage, seeing a burning bush, or "being appeared to redly."[25] And looking at a lake is no less real than feeling happy, sensing danger, or suffering trauma. As James put it in "A World of Pure Experience" (and as discussed in chapter 6), "any kind of relation experienced must be accounted as 'real' as anything else" (ERE, 22). Of course, only some experiences give rise to beliefs instrumental for particular purposes. And of course, some do not. But for the radically empirical pragmatist, no experience is *more real* than another; none is "reality's true shape." Radical empiricism's task and orientation are descriptive, not reductionist.

There is a second commitment of pragmatism at odds with any search for any supposed primitive flux of pure sensational life supposed to lie at the heart of being. This commitment concerns the pragmatic view of conceptions, perceptions, and sensations. On this issue, James wrote (as noted in chapter 4) that the intellectual life of human beings consists almost wholly in the substitution of a conceptual order for the perceptual order in which experience originally comes (SPP, 32, 33). Does this mean that we lead dual different lives—an intellectual life in and through conceptualization, and a separate non-conceptual life in and through "primitive" perception? No, not at all. For James, perceptions, at least after the newborn's initial "blooming buzzing confusion," irreducibly intermingle with conceptions and are shot through with them. There is no such thing as a concept-free perception; there is no such thing as concept-free knowledge by acquaintance. What James called "knowledge by acquaintance" and "this dumb way of acquaintance" in *The Principles of Psychology* is experiential rather than propositional "knowledge about," but precisely because this knowledge is experiential it is therefore shot through with the results of previous conceptualization. Knowledge by acquaintance is not conceptual knowledge, but it also is not knowledge entirely independent of, or void of, conceptualization. To know immediately is not to know independent of mediation of that immediacy. Knowledge by acquaintance is "pre-conceptual" only in the sense that it pre-exists or is prior to *possible later* reflection on it; it does not pre-exist and is not prior to *all* reflection.[26] As James put it in *Some Problems of Philosophy*, asserting that percepts and concepts are "made of the same kind

[25] This is Rodrick Chisholm's phrase, famous among many philosophers of a particular persuasion, in, for example, *A Realistic Theory of Categories: An Essay on Ontology* (Cambridge, UK: Cambridge University Press, 1996).

[26] Ellen Kappy Suckiel contrasted experiential and propositional knowledge by calling the former "pre-conceptual" but without noting this temporal distinction between possible conceptualization after the fact of an experience and actual conceptualization prior to an experience and embedded in that experience. For James, I think, experience is not an either/or matter of conceptualization or

of stuff": "No one can tell, of the things he now holds in his hand and reads, how much comes in through his eyes and fingers, and how much, from his apperceiving intellect, unites with that and make of it this particular 'book'" (SPP, 58). Similarly, for James there is no such thing as a percept-free sensation. And as he put it in *The Principles of Psychology*: Perception always involves sensation and sensation always involves perception, such that "a pure sensation is an abstraction" (PP, 652–654). So, for pragmatists, not only is it impossible for humans beings to "go behind the conceptual function" but, even if that were possible, instead of discovering a "more primitive flux of the sensational life" we would find instead sensational life always and already permeated by concepts. We would go behind some particular conceptual function only to find and only by means of some other conceptual function. "Sensational life"—or anti-intellectual life—is not "primitive"; it is from the start preconceived, just as conceptual or "intellectual life" is permeated by sensations and perceptions.

James did recognize that he could provide no concepts or words or arguments as description or evidence of the "primitive flux of sensational life." The immediate, as immediate, is beyond or other than all mediation. He thus confessed to his audience:

> I am tiring myself and you, I know, by vainly seeking to describe by concepts and words what I say at the same time exceeds either conceptualization or verbalization. As long as one continues *talking*, intellectualism remains in undisturbed possession of the field. The return to life can't come about by

experience but, rather, a matter of the concrete relations between particular acts of conceptualization before and after a particular experience. See *Heaven's Champion: William James's Philosophy of Religion* (Notre Dame, IN: University of Notre Dame Press, 1996), 39–59. This applies also to the discussion of perceptual knowledge that Eugene Taylor and Robert H. Wozniak provided in their "Introduction" to *Pure Experience: The Response to William James* (Bristol, UK: Thoemmes Press, 1996), xvii. And this same problem, I think, is evident in John Wild's discussion of knowledge by acquaintance as an "empirical *a priori*" rather than an experience prior to later conceptualization but after earlier conceptualization. The idea of a pure acquaintance is as much a myth as the idea of a pure sensation. See *The Radical Empiricism of William James* (Garden City, NY: Doubleday, 1969), 44–53. Finally, while I entirely share Nancy Frankenberry's desire to avoid any notion of "prereflective experience" (at least beyond James's "blooming buzzing confusion" stage), this is not a problem from which radical empiricism needs to be saved. It is only a problem if one holds a percept/concept dualism and claims that experienced immediacy is incompatible with prior mediation and preparation. See her "The Fate of Radical Empiricism and the Future of Pragmatic Naturalism," in *Pragmatism and Naturalism: Scientific and Social Inquiry After Representationalism*, edited by Matthew Bagger (New York: Columbia University Press, 2018), 224. In contrast to these writers, James Pawelski argued that James adopted an "integrated" view of perception and conception in which conception of some perception is simply *temporally* secondary to perception. *The Dynamic Individualism of William James* (Albany: State University of New York Press, 2007), 119–124.

talking. It is an *act*; to make you return to life, I must set an example for your imitation, I must deafen you to talk . . . Or I must *point*, point to the mere that of life . . . I saw that philosophy had been on a false scent ever since the days of Socrates and Plato, that an intellectual answer to the intellectualist's difficulties will never come, and that the real way out of them, far from consisting in the discovery of such an answer, consists simply in closing one's ears to the question. (APU, 131)

Just as life lived is different from life conceptualized, reflected on, and known, so too life is lived just as it is lived in part though the activity of transformative conceptualization.

This is a consistent and omnipresent refrain in James's writings. It is at this point, however, that James, toward the end of his lectures on pluralism, slips in a startling announcement mid-paragraph:

The absolute is not the impossible being I once thought it. . . . It is only the extravagant claims of coercive necessity on the absolute's part that have to be denied. (APU, 132)

Has James endorsed the One, the Absolute, the Whole? Stop the presses: pragmatism as Absolutism? No, not exactly, but this is a highly revealing claim that sheds the following four rays of light on James's pluralism.

First, when the "problem of the one and the many" is construed in intellectualist terms, James strongly embraced pluralism. He argued that inside every form of monism, despite its proponents' best efforts, pluralism breaks out. Parts as parts prove not to be parts of a whole. In response to the traditional, ever-since-Socrates ontological issue, James was a pluralist. And in passage after passage he was unsparing in his criticism of monism and its One or Absolute. Here is a final example (and one that makes clear why Wahl and Deleuze were right to stress radical empiricism's commitment to external relations):

For what have they invoked the absolute except as a being the peculiar inner form of which shall enable it to overcome the contradictions with which intellectualism has found the finite many as such to be infected? The man-in-one character that, as we have seen, every smallest tract of finite experience offers, is considered by intellectualism to be fatal to the reality of finite experience. What can be distinguished, it tells us, is separate; and what is separate is unrelated, for a relation, being a "between," would bring only a twofold separation. Hegel, Royce, Bradley, and the Oxford absolutists in general seem to agree about this logical absurdity of manyness-in-oneness in the only places where it is empirically found. But see the curious tactics! Is the absurdity *reduced* in the absolute being whom they call in to relieve it? Quite otherwise, for that being shows it on an infinitely greater scale, and flaunts it in its very definition. The fact of its not being related to any outward environment, the fact that all relations are inside of itself, doesn't save it, for Mr. Bradley's great argument against the finite is that in any given bit of it (a bit of sugar, for instance) the presence of a plurality of characters (whiteness and sweetness, for example) is self-contradictory. (APU, 134)

"If the relative experience was inwardly absurd," James immediately added, "the absolute experience is infinitely more so."

Second, by construing the "problem of the one and the many" in anti-intellectualist terms, James dissolved it. If there are no parts and no whole, if there is no many and no one, if there is no identity and no contradiction—except as these are intellectualism's concepts—then there is no (intellectualist) problem of the one and the many. James simply replaced the notions of the many and the one and the many-in-one and the one-in-many with the anti-intellectualist lived *sense* of the *continuity* of experience—not a sense of sameness or oneness, not a sense of difference or manyness, but a sense of *continuity*.

Third, keeping this context in mind, when James claimed that "the absolute is not the impossible being I once thought it," he meant that he had thought of the absolute only in the terms of intellectualism and its problems. He had thought of the absolute only as a supposedly logically necessary first principle, the necessary condition of experience, or the difference-eliminating, parts-transcending identity of all being. However, he had come to think about the absolute in the terms of anti-intellectualism—as a possible compounding of consciousness, as an ineffable eventuality, as a possible outcome or last thing. He had come to think of the absolute not as a trans-experiential unity or a logically necessary first principle or the necessary condition of the possibility of experience but a last thing, an eventuality, a strung-out by-and-by development, a consequence, a possibility created.

Now James claimed that there was inductive and analogical evidence for the existence of an absolute understood as compounded, superhuman consciousness—or, at least, that there is such evidence for persons who are open to it. That evidence included what James called paranormal, "patholog-ical," "psychic," "abnormal," "supernormal" facts of experience. But he called those facts "perhaps too spook-haunted" for his academic audience and so he based his case for a compounded, superhuman consciousness on what he called "ordinary religious experience":

> I think it may be asserted that there *are* religious experiences of a specific nature, not deducible by analogy or psychological reasoning from our other sorts of experiences. I think that they point with reasonable proba-bility to the continuity of our consciousness with a wider spiritual environ-ment from which the ordinary prudential man (who is the only man that scientific psychology, so called, takes cognizance of) is shut off. (APU, 135)

James characterized this religious experience as "experiences of an unex-pected life succeeding upon death." However, James immediately explained that by "death" he did *not* mean the death of the body and by "life" he did *not* mean immortality. Rather, he meant "the deathlike termination of cer-tain mental processes within the individual's experience, processes that run to failure, and in some individuals, at least, eventuate in despair" (APU, 137). He wrote movingly that in this experience "there is a light in which all the naturally founded and currently accepted distinctions, excellences, and safeguards of our characters appear as utter childishness. Sincerely to give up one's conceit or hope of being good in one's own right is the only door to the universe's deeper reaches." He continued (in language reminiscent of what he had earlier criticized in Whitman):

> Here is a world in which all is well, in *spite* of certain forms of death, indeed *because* of certain forms of death—death of hope, death of strength, death of responsibility, of fear and worry, competency and desert, death of eve-rything that paganism, naturalism, and legalism pin their faith on and tie their trust to ... In a word, the believer is continuous, to his own conscious-ness, at any rate, with a wider self from which saving experiences flow in. (APU, 138)

Fourth, what is relevant here need not be the evidence—if there be any evidence—that James assembled for belief in a superhuman consciousness. And what is relevant is not whether or not this evidence is sufficient to val-idly infer and justify belief in the existence of some such compounded or higher consciousness. James thought it is sufficient, but I think it is not. Here I note only that description of an experience, even description of it as "superhuman," is something very different from inquiry-produced evidence about the origin of that experience. Experiences do not come prepackaged with knowledge of their own causes. This aside, the relevant key point is that exactly as James affirmed pluralism in response to the intellectualist problem of the one and the many, so too he strongly affirmed pluralism in response to the anti-intellectualist question about the nature of the continuity of experience and the existence of any compounded consciousness. James argued that any compounded, superhuman consciousness—if any—should be understood pluralistically and radically empirically. He explained:

> Only one thing is certain, and that is the result of our criticism of the absolute: the only escape from the paradoxes and perplexities that a consistently thought-out monistic universe suffers from as from a species of autointoxication—the mystery of the "fall" namely, of reality lapsing into appearance, truth into error, perfection into imperfection; of evil, in short; the mystery of universal determinism, of the block-universe eternal and without a history, etc.—the only way of escape, I say, from all this is to be frankly pluralistic and assume that the superhuman consciousness, however vast it may be, has itself an external environment and consequently is finite. . . . The line of least resistance, then, as it seems to me, both in theology and philosophy, is to accept, along with the superhuman consciousness, the notion that it is not all-embracing, the notion, in other words, that there is a God, but he is finite, either in power or in knowledge, or in both at once.[27] (APU, 140)

Each consciousness—the human, the non-human, any superhuman—is finite. Each has external relations, an outside. Each is one of plural parts. Each is dynamic. Each has possibilities. Each is part of a wider self and is taken up into the universe of which it is a part—a part that reshapes that universe, a *brave* force even if, as Santayana put it, only a "brave *little* force" (italics added). It is this pluralism and radical empiricism that Santayana claimed constituted "a rude" shock to the genteel tradition:

[27] For an extended analysis of this notion of a finite God, see David C. Lamberth's "Interpreting the Universe After a Social Analogy: Intimacy, Panpsychism, and a Finite God in a Pluralistic Universe," in *The Cambridge Companion to William James*, edited by Ruth Anna Putnam (New York: Cambridge University Press, 1997), 237–259.

What! The world a gradual improvisation? Creation unpremeditated? God a sort of young poet or struggling artist? . . . [H]e is a neighbouring being, whom we can act upon and rely upon for specific aids, as upon a personal friend or physician, or an insurance company. How disconcerting! Is not this new theology a little like superstition? And yet, how interesting, how exciting, if it should happen to be true.[28]

James called this radically empirical and pluralistic vision of the world "the philosophy of humanism in the widest sense" (APU, 140). This label makes clear, I think, both the psychological and ethical import—its practical or pragmatic import—of James's pluralism. For this humanism, "our philosophies swell the current of being" and thus change and add to that being, theory and action working "in the same circle indefinitely" (APU, 143). In a pluralistic universe, of course, different experiences give rise to different philosophies, and different philosophies transform the world in different ways and must be reckoned with as parts of a new universe, giving rise to yet different experiences, and so on. In this pluralistic universe, some of the philosophies, at least initially (as James realized well), may not be pluralistic. If they turn from bare and thin logical considerations to the thick experiences and the faiths and visions that call forth and are confirmed by these experiences, James suggested, they will come to see themselves as parts of the mosaic of being, and so must become pluralistic visions. When this happens—if it were to happen—the existence of different philosophies would not be seen as the mark of a logical problem still awaiting solution and even colonization. Instead, they would be seen as the mark of multiple experiences, histories, and hopes—as expressions of different forms of life, different streams of thought, different fashions of living.

For James, it is the *result* of this that matters: By means of pluralism, "thus does foreignness get banished from our world" (APU, 143).

This is an idea at the very heart of James's philosophical temperament or vision, itself a far-reaching view of connected parts: His pluralism begins in his pragmatism and its rejection of vicious intellectualism in any of its many forms; this pragmatism, in turn, focuses on practical consequences in a radically empirical world, a world of changing relations of partial connections and partial separations; and in this radically empirical world of relations, the

---

[28] George Santayana, *Character and Opinion in the United States* (New York: W. W. Norton, 1967 [1920]), 210.

experienced reality of parts is a world in which there are relations external to one another, a genuinely pluralistic universe. This worldview's demand to banish foreignness and live in intimacy with the world runs throughout James's writings, clearly evident in his judgments in "The Sentiment of Rationality" that a successful philosophy is one that can make good on expectancy and "banish uncertainty from the future" (WB, 67) and *define the future congruously with our spontaneous powers*" (WB, 70); his argument for the rationality of religious faith given certain conditions in "The Will to Believe"; in "The Moral Philosopher and the Moral Life" both his analysis of religious belief as the most effective means to call forth the ethically strenuous mood and his concluding claim that it is only with a divine thinker that a fully moral universe is possible to his defense; and his case for understanding the continuity of experience and the compounding of consciousness in fully pluralistic terms such that God is not the absolute or first thing but just another part and a possible last thing, a development, functioning similarly to us—"having an environment, being in time, and working out a history just like ourselves, he escapes from foreignness from all that is human, of the static timeless perfect absolute" (APU, 144). In short, for James, "the notion of the 'one' breeds foreignness and that of the 'many' intimacy" (APU, 145).

The centrality of this concern is evidenced by how frequently it crops up. For pluralism, "the intimate and human must surround and underlie the brutal" (APU, 16). With pluralism, for James, there exists the permanent possibility of living against a background of both intimacy and unfinished openness in which we struggle—and, so, of transforming that background and making reality different (APU, 19, 143). The reality of pluralism is one in which "your relations with it [the universe], intellectual, emotional, and active, remain fluent and congruous with your own nature's chief demands" (APU, 144). For pluralism, the world is a genuine mix of irreducible individuality and intimacy—a sense that the individual in a strung-out union can make a difference and that this difference matters (APU, 147).

This pluralism is a hypothesis. James did not assert that it is or must be true for everyone or for every temperament. Instead, he asked his audience members to investigate whether it expresses, reflects, and illuminates their own experience.

This notion of intimacy—of experienced intimacy as the test of the relative success or failure of a philosophy—has not only a psychological dimension but also moral and political implications. Consider again, a chorus to many of James's verses:

Everything you can think of, however, vast or inclusive, has on the pluralistic view a genuinely "external" environment of some sort or amount.
Things are "with" one another in many ways, but nothing includes everything, or dominates over everything. The word "and" trails along after every
sentence. Something always escapes. "Ever not quite" has to be said of the
best attempts made anywhere in the universe at attaining all-inclusiveness.
The pluralistic world is thus more like a federal republic than an empire or
a kingdom. (AU, 145)

The pluralistic universe is morally and politically pluralist. It is a culture in
which we all are *with* one another—and our own selves—in many dynamic
ways but not in relations, by practices, and through institutions of domina-
tion and the destruction of intimacies.

This philosophy is at once an expression of a vision and an effort to clear
away old habits of thought and action that block its further consideration
and expansion. As such, it must aim to change the material and cultural
conditions and resources that sustain those old habits. It must recognize
that the most pressing and dangerous threats to pluralism are not logical but
social: the multiple actual and possible regimes, associations, and cultural
conditions that enforce and call forth growth-inhibiting standardization and
uniformity, blocked inquiry and withering dogmatism, and obedience to
commands (some of which have been internalized as habits and thus function uncritically). The demand to purge plurality from being slides into the
demand to purge plurality from conception and reason, which in turn slides
into the demand to purge plurality from action and life. In this context, pluralism for a Jamesian pragmatist is a cause for action as much as a reality for
reflection.

To do this is to think and philosophize "from the particulars of life" (APU,
149)—James's last advice in *A Pluralistic Universe*. And trailing even this sentence, as every sentence, is the word "and." In philosophy—at least in pragmatic, radically empirical, pluralistic philosophy—there is no conclusion.

Works Cited

From the vast literature that engages the writings of William James, I have cited the following books, as well as many articles, essays, chapters, and editor introductions in the volumes of *The Works of William James*. I have learned a great deal from these books (although, I suppose, this fact might not be evident to every one of their authors or readers). Philosophers these days often reference other thinkers principally to criticize and then to dismiss them. I refer to the authors listed here primarily to expand the vision of this book and to express appreciation for their work.

Albrecht, James. *Reconstructing Individualism: A Pragmatic Tradition from Emerson to Ellison* (New York: Fordham University Press, 2012).

Alcoff, Linda. *Visible Identities: Race, Gender, and the Self* (New York: Oxford University Press, 2006).

Allen, Gay Wilson. *William James: A Biography* (New York: Viking Press, 1967).

Al-Saji, Alia. "The Racialization of Muslim Veils: A Philosophical Analysis." *Philosophy and Social Criticism* 36, no. 8 (2010): 875–902.

Anderson, Paul Russell, and Max Harold Fisch. *Philosophy in America: From the Puritans to James* (New York: D. Appleton-Century, 1939).

Bacon, Michael. *Pragmatism: An Introduction* (Malden, MA: Polity Press, 2012).

Bagger, Matthew, ed. *Pragmatism and Naturalism: Scientific and Social Inquiry After Representationalism* (New York: Columbia University Press, 2018).

Baghramian, Maria, and Sarin Marchetti. *Pragmatism and the European Traditions: Encounters with Analytic Philosophy and Phenomenology Before the Great Divide* (New York: Routledge, 2018).

Barth, John. *The Friday Book: Essays and Other Nonfiction* (New York: G. P. Putnam's Sons, 1984).

Bauerlein, Mark. *The Pragmatic Mind: Explorations in the Psychology of Belief* (Durham, NC: Duke University Press, 1997).

Bernstein, Richard J. *The New Constellation: The Ethical-Political Horizons of Modernity/ Postmodernity* (Cambridge, MA: MIT Press, 1991).

Bernstein, Richard J. *The Pragmatic Turn* (Malden, MA: Polity, 2010).

Blau, Joseph L. *Men and Movements in American Philosophy* (Englewood Cliffs, NJ: Prentice-Hall, 1952).

Brooks, Van Wyck. *New England: Indian Summer 1865–1915* (New York: E. P. Dutton, 1940).

Brown, Hunter. *William James on Radical Empiricism and Religion* (Toronto: University of Toronto Press, 2000).

Burke, F. Thomas. *What Pragmatism Was* (Bloomington: Indiana University Press, 2013).

Bush, Stephen S. *William James and Democratic Individuality* (New York: Cambridge University Press, 2017).

Campbell, James. *Experiencing William James: Belief in a Pluralistic World* (Charlottesville: University of Virginia Press, 2017).

Cooper, Wesley. *The Unity of William James's Thought* (Nashville, TN: Vanderbilt University Press, 2002).

Cormier, Harvey. *The Truth Is What Works: Willliam James, Pragmatism, and the Seed of Death* (Lanham, MD: Rowman & Littlefield, 2001).

Craig, Megan. *Levinas and James: Toward a Pragmatic Phenomenology* (Bloomington: Indiana University Press, 2010).

Conkin, Paul K. *Puritans and Pragmatists: Eight Eminent American Thinkers* (Waco, TX: Baylor University Press, 2005 [1976]).

Cotkin, George. *William James: Public Philosopher* (Urbana: University of Illinois Press, 1994).

Croce, Paul J. *Science and Religion in the Era of William James: Eclipse of Certainty, 1820–1880* (Chapel Hill: University of North Carolina Press, 1995).

Croce, Paul J. *Young William James Thinking* (Baltimore: Johns Hopkins University Press, 2018).

Danisch, Robert. *Pragmatism, Democracy, and the Necessity of Rhetoric* (Columbia: University of South Carolina Press, 2007).

Deleuze, Gilles. *Bergsonism*, trans. Hugh Tomlinson and Barbara Habberjam (New York: Zone Books, 1988 [1966]).

Deleuze, Gilles. *Difference and Repetition*, trans. Paul Patton (New York: Columbia University Press, 1995 [1968]).

Deleuze, Gilles. *Empiricism and Subjectivity: An Essay on Hume's Theory of Human Nature*, trans. Constantin V. Boundas (New York: Columbia University Press, 1981 [1953]).

Deleuze, Gilles. *The Logic of Sense*, ed. Constantin V. Boundas (New York: Columbia University Press, 1990 [1969]).

Deleuze, Gilles. Pure Immanence: Essays On a Life, trans. Anne Boyman (New York: Zone Books, 2005 [2001]).

Deleuze, Gilles, and Claire Parnet. *Dialogues*, trans. Hugh Tomlinson (New York: Columbia University Press, 1987 [1977]).

Dewey, John. *Experience and Nature*, vol. 1 of *John Dewey: The Later Works, 1925–1953* (Carbondale: Southern Illinois University Press, 1988 [1925]).

Dewey, John. *Human Nature and Conduct*, vol. 14 of *John Dewey: The Middle Works, 1899–1924* (Carbondale: Southern Illinois University Press, 1983 [1922]).

Dewey, John. *John Dewey: The Later Works, 1925–1953*, vol. 3 (Carbondale: Southern Illinois University Press, 1984 [1927])

Dewey, John. *John Dewey: The Middle Works, 1899–1924* (Carbondale: Southern Illinois University Press, 1977 [1905]).

Dickstein, Morris, ed. *The Revival of Pragmatism: New Essays on Social Thought, Law, and Culture* (Durham, NC: Duke University Press, 1998).

Dieleman, Susan, David Rondel, and Christopher J. Voparil. *Pragmatism and Justice* (New York: Oxford University Press, 2017).

Diggins, John Patrick. *The Promise of Pragmatism: Modernism and the Crisis of Knowledge and Authority* (Chicago: University of Chicago Press, 1994).

Dooley, Patrick Kiaran. *Pragmatism as Humanism: The Philosophy of William James* (Chicago: Nelson-Hall, 1974).

Ferguson, Kennan. *William James: Politics in the Pluriverse* (Lanham, MD: Rowman and Littlefield, 2007).

Flower, Elizabeth, and Murray G. Murphey. *A History of Philosophy in America*, 2 vols. (New York: Capricorn Books, 1977).

Fox, Richard Wightman, and James T. Kloppenberg. *A Companion to American Thought* (Cambridge, MA: Blackwell, 1995).

Frankenberry, Nancy. *Religion and Radical Empiricism* (Albany: State University of New York Press, 1987).

Garrison, Jim, Ron Podescki, and Eric Bredo, eds. *William James and Education* (New York: Teachers College Press, 2002).

Gavin, William J. *William James and the Reinstatement of the Vague* (Philadelphia: Temple University Press, 1992).

Gavin, William J. *William James in Focus: Willing to Believe* (Bloomington: Indiana University Press, 2013).

Glaude, Eddie. *In a Shade of Blue: Pragmatism and the Politics of Black America* (Chicago: University of Chicago Press, 2007).

Goodman, Russell B. *Wittgenstein and William James* (New York: Cambridge University Press, 2002).

Gouinlock, James. *Rediscovering the Moral Life* (Buffalo, NY: Prometheus Books, 1993).

Gunn, Giles. *Thinking Across the American Grain: Ideology, Intellect, and the New Pragmatism* (Chicago: University of Chicago Press, 1992).

Halliwell, Martin, and Joel D. S. Rasmussen. *William James and the Transatlantic Conversation: Pragmatism, Pluralism, and the Philosophy of Religion* (New York: Oxford University Press, 2014).

Hamner, M. Gail. *American Pragmatism: A Religious Genealogy* (New York: Oxford University Press, 2003).

Hare, Peter. *Pragmatism With Purpose: Selected Writings*, ed. Joseph Palencik, Douglas R. Anderson, and Steven A. Miller (New York: Fordham University Press, 2015).

Helm, Bertrand. *Time and Reality in American Philosophy* (Amherst: University of Massachusetts Press, 1985).

Hester, D. Micah, and Robert B. Talisse. *On James* (Belmont, CA: Wadsworth, 2004).

Hollinger, Robert, and David Depew, eds. *Pragmatism: From Progressivism to Postmodernism* (Westport, CT: Praeger, 1995).

Hook, Sidney, ed. *American Philosophers at Work: The Philosophic Scene in the United States* (New York: Criterion Books, 1956).

Hook, Sidney. *Pragmatism and the Tragic Sense of Life* (New York: Basic Books, 1974).

Kautzer, Chad, and Eduardo Mendieta. *Pragmatism, Nation, and Race: Community in the Age of Empire* (Bloomington: Indiana University Press, 2009).

Kitcher, Philip. *Preludes to Pragmatism: Toward a Reconstruction of Philosophy* (New York: Oxford University Press, 2012).

Kloppenberg, James T. *Uncertain Victory: Social Democracy and Progressivism in European and American Thought, 1870–1920* (New York: Oxford University Press, 1988).

Koopman, Colin. *Pragmatism as Transition: Historicity and Hope in James, Dewey, and Rorty* (New York: Columbia University Press, 2009).

Kuklick, Bruce. *The Rise of American Philosophy: Cambridge, Massachusetts, 1860–1930* (New Haven, CT: Yale University Press, 1977).

Lachs, John. *Freedom and Limits*, ed. Patrick Shade (New York: Fordham University Press, 2014).

Lawson, Bill E., and Donald F. Koch. *Pragmatism and the Problem of Race* (Bloomington: Indiana University Press, 2004).

Lamberth, David C. *William James and the Metaphysics of Experience* (New York: Cambridge University Press, 1999).

Langsdorf, Lenore, and Andrew R. Smith, eds. *Recovering Pragmatism's Voice: The Classical Tradition, Rorty, and the Philosophy of Communication* (Albany: State University of New York Press, 1995).

Leary, David E. *The Routledge Guidebook to James's* Principles of Psychology (New York: Routledge, 2018.

Lentricchia, Frank. *Ariel and the Police: Michel Foucault, William James, Wallace Stevens* (Madison: University of Wisconsin Press, 1988).

Levine, Steven. *Pragmatism, Objectivity, and Experience* (New York: Cambridge University Press, 2019).

Livingston, Alexander. *Damn Great Empires! William James and the Politics of Pragmatism* (New York: Oxford University Press, 2016).

Livingston, James. *Pragmatism, Feminism, and Democracy: Rethinking the Politics of Amerian History* (New York: Routledge, 2001).

Magee, Michael. *Emancipating Pragmatism: Emerson, Jazz and Experimental Writing* (Tuscaloosa: University of Alabama Press, 2004).

Malachowski, Alan, ed. *The Cambridge Companion to Pragmatism* (New York: Cambridge University Press, 2013).

Marchetti, Sarin. *Ethics and Philosophical Critique in William James* (New York: Palgrave Macmillan, 2015).

Marchetti, Sarin. *The Jamesian Mind* (New York: Routledge, 2021).

Margolis, Joseph. *Reinventing Pragmatism: American Philosophy at the End of the Twentieth Century* (Ithaca, NY: Cornell University Press, 2002).

Marsoobian, Armen T., and John Ryder. *The Blackwell Guide to American Philosophy* (Malden, MA: Blackwell, 2004).

McDermott, John J. *The Drama of Possibility: Experience as Philosophy of Culture* (New York: Fordham University Press, 2007).

McDermott, John J. *Streams of Experience: Reflections on the History and Philosophy of American Culture* (Amherst: University of Massachusetts Press, 1986).

Menand, Louis. *The Metaphysical Club: A Story of Ideas in America* (New York: Farrar, Straus and Giroux, 2001).

Miller, Joshua I. *Democratic Temperament: The Legacy of William James* (Lawrence: University Press of Kansas, 1997).

Mills, C. Wright. *Sociology and Pragmatism*, ed. I. L. Horowitz (New York: Paine-Whitman, 1964).

Mullin, Richard P. *The Soul of American Philosophy: The Ethical and Spiritual Insights of William James, Josiah Royce, and Charles Sanders Peirce* (Albany: State University of New York Press, 2007).

Myers, Gerald E. *William James: His Life and Thought* (New Haven, CT: Yale University Press, 1986).

Ngo, Helen. *The Habits of Racism: A Phenomenology of Racism and Racialized Embodiment* (Lanham, MD: Lexington Books, 2017).

Oliver, Phil. *William James's "Springs of Delight": The Return to Life* (Nashville: Vanderbilt University Press, 2001).

Pawelski, James O. *The Dynamic Individualism of William James* (Albany: State University of New York Press, 2007).

Perry, Ralph Barton. *The Thought and Character of William James*, 2 vols. (Westport, CT: Greenwood Press, 1974 [1935]).

Poirier, Richard. *Poetry and Pragmatism* (Cambridge, MA: Harvard University Press, 1992).

Proudfoot, Wayne, ed. *William James and a Science of Religious Experience* (New York: Columbia University Press, 2004).

Putnam, Hilary. *Pragmatism: An Open Question* (Cambridge, MA: Blackwell, 1995).

Putnam, Ruth Anna. *The Cambridge Companion to William James* (New York: Cambridge University Press, 1997).

Rescher, Nicholas. *Epistemic Issues in Pragmatic Perspective* (Lanham, MD: Lexington Books, 2018).

Richardson, Joan. *A Natural History of Pragmatism* (New York: Cambridge University Press, 2007).

Richardson, Joan. *Pragmatism and American Experience: An Introduction* (New York: Cambridge University Press, 2014).

Richardson, Robert D., ed. *The Heart of William James* (Cambridge, MA: Harvard University Press, 2010).

Richardson, Robert D. *William James in the Maelstrom of American Modernism* (New York: Houghton Mifflin, 2006).

Rorty, Richard. *Consequences of Pragmatism* (Minneapolis: University of Minnesota Press, 1982).

Rorty, Richard. *Objectivity, Relativism, and Truth: Philosophical Papers, Volume 1* (New York: Cambridge University Press, 1991).

Rosenbaum, Stuart. *Pragmatism and Religion: Classical Sources and Original Essays* (Urbana: Univeristy of Illinois Press, 2003).

Rosenthal, Sandra B. *Speculative Pragmatism* (Amherst: University of Massachusetts Press, 1986).

Roth, Robert S. *Radical Pragmatism: An Alternative* (New York: Forham University Press, 1998).

Rowe, Stephen C. *The Vision of James* (Rockport, MA: Element, 1996).

Santayana, George. *Character and Opinion in the United States* (New York: W. W. Norton, 1967 [1920]).

Santayana, George. *Obiter Scripta: Lectures, Essays and Reviews* (New York: Charles Scribner's Sons, 1936).

Santayana, George. *Scepticism and Animal Faith: An Introduction to a System of Philosophy* (New York: Charles Scribner's Sons, 1923).

Santayana, Geroge, *Winds of Doctrine* (Gloucester, MA: Peter Smith, 1971 [1913]).

Seigfried, Charlene Haddock. *Chaos and Context: A Study in William James* (Athens: Ohio University Press, 1978).

Seigfried, Charlene Haddock. *Pragmatism and Feminism: Reweaving the Social Fabric* (Chicago: University of Chicago Press, 1996).

Seigfried, Charlene Haddock. *William James's Radical Reconstruction of Philosophy* (Albany: State University of New York Press, 1990).

Shade, Patrick. *Habits of Hope: A Pragmatic Theory* (Nashville, TN: Vanderbilt University Press, 2001).

Shook, John R., and Joseph Margolis, eds. *A Companion to Pragmatism* (Malden, MA: Blackwell, 2006).

Simon, Linda. *Genuine Reality: A Life of William James* (Chicago: University of Chicago Press, 1999).

Singer, Marcus G., ed. *American Philosophy* (New York: Cambridge University Press, 1985).

Smith, John E. *America's Philosophical Vision* (Chicago: University of Chicago Press, 1992).

Smith, John E. *Purpose and Thought: The Meaning of Pragmatism* (New Haven, CT: Yale University Press, 1978).

Smith, John E. *The Spirit of American Philosophy*, rev. ed. (Albany: State University of New York Press, 1983).

Smith, John E. *Themes in American Philosophy: Purpose, Experience and Community* (New York: Harper and Row, 1970).

Sprigge, T. L. S. *James and Bradley: American Truth and British Reality* (Chicago: Open Court, 1993).

Stuhr, John J., ed. *100 Years of Pragmatism: William James's Revolutionary Philosophy* (Bloomington: Indiana University Press, 2010).

Stuhr, John. *Genealogical Pragmatism: Philosophy, Experience, and Community* (Albany: State University of New York Press, 1997).

Stuhr, John J., ed. *Philosophy and Human Flourishing* (New York: Oxford University Press, 2022).

Stuhr, John J. *Pragmatic Fashions: Pluralism, Democracy, Relativism, and the Absurd* (Bloomington: Indiana University Press, 2016).

Stuhr, John J., ed. *Pragmatism and Classical American Philosophy: Essential Readings and Interpretive Texts* (New York: Oxford University Press, 2000).

Stuhr, John J. *Pragmatism, Postmodernism, and the Future of Philosophy* (New York: Routledge, 2002).

Suckiel, Ellen Kappy. *Heaven's Champion: William James's Philosophy of Religion* (Notre Dame, IN: University of Notre Dame Press, 1996).

Suckiel, Ellen Kappy. *The Pragmatic Philosophy of William James* (Notre Dame, IN: University of Notre Dame Press, 1982).

Tarver, Erin C., and Shannon Sullivan, eds. *Feminist Interpretations of William James* (University Park: Penn State University Press, 2015).

Taylor, Eugene, and Robert H. Wozniak, eds. *Pure Experience: The Response to William James* (Bristol, UK: Thoemmes Press, 1996).

Thayer, H. S. *Meaning and Action: A Critical History of Pragmatism* (Indianapolis, IN: Hackett, 1981 [1968]).

Townsend, Harvey Gates. *Philosophical Ideas in the United States* (New York: Octagon Books, 1968 [1934]).

Throntveit, Trygve. *William James and the Quest for an Ethical Republic* (New York: Palgrave Macmillan, 2014).

Van Der Kolk, Bessel. *The Body Keeps the Score: Brain, Mind, and Body in the Healing of Trauma* (New York: Penguin Books, 2014).

Wahl, Jean. *Pluralist Philosophies of England and America*, trans. Fred Rothwell (London: Open Court, 1925).

Weiss, Gail. *Refiguring the Ordinary* (Bloomington: Indiana University Press, 2008).

West, Cornel. *The American Evasion of Philosophy: A Genealogy of Pragmatism* (Madison: University of Wisconsin Press, 1989).

White, Morton. *Science and Sentiment in America: Philosophical Thought from Jonathan Edwards to John Dewey* (New York: Oxford University Press, 1972).

White, Morton. *Social Thought in America: The Revolt Against Formalism* (New York: Oxford University Press, 1976 [1947]).

Whitehead, Deborah. *William James, Pragmatism, and American Culture* (Bloomington: Indiana University Press, 2015).

Whitman, Walt. *Whitman: Poetry and Prose* (New York: Library of America, 1982 [1891–1892]).

Wild, John. *The Radical Empiricism of William James* (Garden City, NY: Doubleday, 1969).

Wilshire, Bruce. *The Much-at-Once: Music, Science, Ecstasy, the Body* (New York: Fordham University Press, 2016).

Wilshire, Bruce. *William James and Phenomenology: A Study of The Principles of Psychology* (Bloomington: Indiana University Press, 1968).

Index